COM PROGRAMMING
WITH MICROSOFT .NET

Julian Templeman
John Paul Mueller

Microsoft®
.net™

PUBLISHED BY
Microsoft Press
A Division of Microsoft Corporation
One Microsoft Way
Redmond, Washington 98052-6399

Copyright © 2003 by Julian Templeman and John Mueller

All rights reserved. No part of the contents of this book may be reproduced or transmitted in any form or by any means without the written permission of the publisher.

Library of Congress Cataloging-in-Publication Data

Templeman, Julian.
 COM Programming with Microsoft .NET / Julian Templeman, John Paul Mueller.
  p. cm.
  Includes index.
  ISBN 0-7356-1875-5
  1. Application software--Development. 2. COM (Computer architecture) 3. Microsoft .NET. I. Mueller, John, 1958- II. Title.

QA76.76.A65T45   2003

2003042025

Printed and bound in the United States of America.

1 2 3 4 5 6 7 8 9   QWE   8 7 6 5 4 3

Distributed in Canada by H.B. Fenn and Company Ltd.

A CIP catalogue record for this book is available from the British Library.

Microsoft Press books are available through booksellers and distributors worldwide. For further information about international editions, contact your local Microsoft Corporation office or contact Microsoft Press International directly at fax (425) 936-7329. Visit our Web site at www.microsoft.com/mspress. Send comments to *mspinput@microsoft.com*.

ActiveX, IntelliSense, Microsoft, Microsoft Press, MS-DOS, MSDN, Visual Basic, Visual C++, Visual C#, Visual Studio, Win32, Windows, and Windows NT are either registered trademarks or trademarks of Microsoft Corporation in the United States and/or other countries. Other product and company names mentioned herein may be the trademarks of their respective owners.

The example companies, organizations, products, domain names, e-mail addresses, logos, people, places, and events depicted herein are fictitious. No association with any real company, organization, product, domain name, e-mail address, logo, person, place, or event is intended or should be inferred.

Acquisitions Editor: Danielle Bird Voeller
Project Editor: Kathleen Atkins
Technical Editor: Brian Johnson

Body Part No. X09-06383

To all the other JATs, with love and appreciation.

Table of Contents

Acknowledgments	xv
Introduction	xvii

Part I The .NET View of COM and COM+

1 COM and .NET — 3

Is COM Dead?	3
How Does COM Work in the .NET World?	5
Differences in the COM and .NET Philosophies	7
Locating Components	7
Component Identification	8
Object Lifetimes	9
Determining Object Capabilities	9
Constructors and Destructors	10
Nondeterministic Finalization	10
Error Handling	13
Type Information	13
Visibility	14
Data Handling	15
Event Handling	19
Using the IDE to Access Components	19
Locating the Component You Need	20
Simple COM Access Examples	21

2 COM+ and .NET — 27

What Is the Place of COM+ in the .NET World?	28
COM+ Problems and Improvements	29
Using the Component Services MMC Snap-In	30
An Overview of the Interface	30
Creating COM+ Applications and Installing Components	34

		Using the .NET Framework Configuration MMC Console	47
		Managing Components and Controls	48
		Remoting Services Configuration	49
		Defining a Runtime Security Policy	50
3	**Using COM Components in .NET Code**		**53**
	COM Interop: Principles and Mechanisms		53
		Interop Assemblies	54
		Primary Interop Assemblies	54
	Generating Runtime Callable Wrappers		55
		Using Visual Studio .NET	56
		Using the TlbImp.exe Tool	57
		Using the *TypeLibConverter* Class	61
		Assemblies and the GAC	67
		Generating and Installing Primary Interop Assemblies	73
	How COM Entities Are Converted		74
		Dealing with Attributes	74
		Importing Libraries	74
		Importing Data Types	75
		Importing Classes	83
		Importing Interfaces	85
		Importing Structures, Unions, and Enumerations	88
		Importing Typedefs	90
		Importing Modules	91
	How to Design COM Components for Use with .NET		91
	Responding to COM Events		94
		Connection Points	95
		Handling Events from a COM Source	96
	Using ActiveX Controls with .NET		99
		Adding an ActiveX Control to the Toolbox	100
		Using the Command Line	102
4	**Using .NET Components in COM Applications**		**103**
	The COM Callable Wrapper		103
		Object Identity	104
		Object Lifetime	104
		Standard COM Interfaces on .NET Components	105
		Custom Interfaces on .NET Components	106

	Generating and Using COM Callable Wrappers	108
	Using COM-Related Attributes	108
	Creating a Type Library	114
	Signing the Assembly	119
	Registering the Component	119
	Using .NET Components from COM Client Code	120
	Exporting Metadata to Type Libraries	125
	Exporting Assemblies	125
	Exporting Namespaces	126
	Exporting Classes	127
	Exporting Interfaces	128
	Exporting Data Types	136
	Exporting Value Types	137
	Exporting Enumerations	138
	How to Design .NET Components for Use with COM	139
	Provide a Default Constructor	139
	Avoid Using Static and Overloaded Methods	139
	Be Aware of Possible Naming Problems	139
	Avoid Altering Interfaces	140
	Define Event Source Interfaces	141
	Use of Attributes	141
	Provide *HRESULT*s	142
	Use Versioning Correctly	142
	Hosting Windows Forms Controls in ActiveX Control Containers	143
	Registry Entries	144
	Example: Hosting a Windows Forms Control in Internet Explorer	145
	Exposing .NET Events in COM	148
	Using Explicit Source Interfaces	149
5	**An Overview of COM+ Coding for .NET**	**155**
	COM+ Begins with COM	156
	A Look at COM+ Interoperability	156
	COM+ Design Goals	163
	Transactions and COM+	164
	Messages and COM+	166
	COM+ Services	169

	Understanding the Role of DCOM in COM+	172
	How Does the Connection Work?	173
	Connection-Oriented Data Flow Optimization	178
	COM+-Specific Issues	179
	Application Types	179
	Error Handling	182
	Security	183

Part II Writing COM Code

6 Attributed Programming — 189

What Are Attributes?	190
How Do Attributes Work?	192
Using Attributes in C++ Code	193
Walkthrough: Creating a Simple COM Component	194
Seeing the Inserted Code	195
Adding COM Objects	196
Adding Methods and Properties	200
Testing the Component	203
Creating the Server by Hand	204
Basic Attributed Programming	207
Creating Modules	207
Creating Interfaces	211
Creating Coclasses	216
Stand-Alone Attributes	219
Handling Aggregation	221
Review of COM Aggregation and Delegation	221
The *aggregatable* and *aggregates* Attributes	223
Handling Errors	224
Events	224
Adding Event Support	225
Handling Events	228
Compiler Options	230
Generating IDL	231
Suppressing IDL Generation	231

7 ATL and ATL Server — 233

- Changes in ATL 7.0 — 233
  - New Module Classes — 234
  - Data Handling and Collections — 234
  - Shared Classes — 243
  - The *CSimpleStringT* Class — 244
  - The *CStringT* Class — 246
  - String Conversion Classes — 250
  - Security Classes — 252
  - Regular Expression Classes — 256
  - Other Changes — 257
  - Breaking Changes Since Visual C++ 6.0 — 258
- Introduction to ATL Server — 259
- ATL Server Architecture — 259
  - ISAPI Extensions — 260
  - Web Application DLLs — 261
  - Server Response Files — 261
- Writing Web Applications Using ATL Server — 266
  - Using Attributes — 266
  - Defining Handler Methods — 268
  - A Sample ATL Server Application — 270
- Writing Web Services Using ATL Server — 277
  - ATL Server Web Service Architecture — 277
  - Example: Creating a Web Service — 281
- Consuming Web Services in C++ — 283

Part III Writing COM+ Code

8 A Simple COM+ Example — 289

- The Importance of Using GUIDs — 289
- A Simple Component Example — 290
  - Creating the Simple Component — 291
  - Registering the Component on the Server — 293
  - Exporting the Application — 295
  - Creating the Client — 296
  - Testing the Application — 298

	A *Component* Class Example	300
	Deriving from the *Component* Class	300
	Performing the *Component* Class Setup	305
	Creating the Client	306
	A *ServicedComponent* Class Example	308
	Deriving from the *ServicedComponent* Class	309
	Performing the *ServicedComponent* Class Setup	310
	Creating the Client	311
9	**Working with Disconnected Applications**	**315**
	Understanding the Role of MSMQ in this Application	316
	Creating a Simple Recorder/Player	320
	Defining the Message Queue	320
	Accessing the Message Queue	322
	Creating the Recorder	323
	Testing the Recorder	324
	Creating the Player	325
	Creating a Simple COM+ Listener/Player	327
	Creating the Listener/Player Component	328
	Defining the MSMQ Rule and Trigger	331
	Testing the Listener/Player Application	334
	Creating the MSMQ Client Application	335
	Designing the Data Encapsulation Component	336
	Designing the Message Queue Component	337
	Installing the Message Queue Component	339
	Designing a Managed Client	341
	Testing the Application	341
10	**Creating Subscriptions**	**345**
	An Overview of the COM+ Catalog	345
	What Are Subscriptions?	347
	Understanding Transient Subscriptions	349
	Understanding Permanent Subscriptions	349
	Understanding the Need for Dynamic Registration	349
	Creating the Event Object	350
	Designing the Component	350
	Installing the Event Object	352

	Creating the Publisher	353
	Creating a Component Subscriber	355
	Designing the Subscriber Component	355
	Installing and Testing the Subscriber Component	357
	Creating a Dialog-Based Subscriber	360
	Creating a Permanent Subscription	363
	Testing the Permanent Subscription	368
	Creating a Transient Subscription	369
	Testing the Transient Subscription	372
11	**Web Application Scenarios**	**373**
	How Do Web-Based Applications Differ?	374
	COM+ 1.5 and SOAP	374
	COM+ 1.5 and Application Dumps	380
	Component Interactions	381
	Scripting Error Handling	382
	Human-Language Support	384
	Accessibility Concerns	385
	ASP and Component Communication	386
	Defining the Database	386
	Creating the Data Access Component	390
	Using ASP to Access the Database	393
	Testing the Application	396

Part IV Interoperability

12	**Interacting with Unmanaged Code**	**401**
	Managed and Unmanaged Code	402
	Manual and Automatic Memory Management	403
	Interoperating Between Managed and Unmanaged Code	403
	Garbage Collection in .NET	404
	Platform Invoke	410
	Using Platform Invoke from Visual Basic .NET	410
	Converting Windows API Parameter Types	416
	Using Platform Invoke from Visual C#	417
	Using Platform Invoke from Managed C++	421

Visual C# Concerns	422
The *unsafe* Keyword	423
The *fixed* Keyword	425
The *stackalloc* Keyword	427
Visual C++ Concerns	428
Marshaling Argument Types	428
Pinning	429
Calling Exported C++ Member Functions	430
IJW (It Just Works)	431
IJW vs. P/Invoke	431

13 Advanced Interaction — 435

The *MarshalAs* Attribute	435
Marshaling Strings	437
String and *StringBuilder*	439
Marshaling Structs	440
The *StructLayout* Attribute	440
Handling Nested Structures	'443
Marshaling Arrays	447
Marshaling Arrays in Platform Invoke	447
Marshaling Arrays in COM Interop	451
Passing Managed Pointers to Unmanaged Code	452
Pinning in Managed C++	455
Using *gcroot* in Managed C++	456
Dynamically Loading Platform Invoke DLLs	458
Choosing the Path to the DLL at Run Time	458
Using Callbacks	461
Introduction to Delegates	463
Using Delegates for Callbacks	464
Garbage Collection Considerations	467
Using the *KeepAlive* Method	467
Using the *HandleRef* Type	468
Performance Considerations	469

14	**Working with Predefined Interfaces**	**471**
	COM Requires Specific Interfaces	471
	Using the OLE/COM Object Viewer	474
	A Quick Overview of Interfaces	475
	Viewing the .NET Category	477
	Viewing an Unmanaged Control	480
	Performing Interface Analysis	481
	Re-creating COM Interfaces Using Managed Code	483
	Creating a Component with Specialized Interfaces Example	487

Index   491

Acknowledgments

As always, many people have been involved in the development of a book such as this.

Many thanks go to the team at Microsoft Press, who have done such a good job of steering this project through the writing and editing process. As commissioning editor, Danielle Bird Voeller was brave enough to believe Julian's assertions that this would be a worthwhile project. Kathleen Atkins provided excellent guidance and support as editor, and made the writing process as smooth as it could be. Thanks must also go to the other reviewers and editors involved in the project, especially Marc Young and Brian Johnson, who provided valuable technical support. Any errors which may remain in the book are, of course, our responsibility and not theirs.

Finally, we'd like to thank our respective families for putting up with the disruption involved in producing a book like this.

Introduction

With the release of .NET, Microsoft has introduced a whole raft of new technologies, and has even invented a new programming language. At the same time, Microsoft has updated many existing technologies and redefined the way in which Microsoft Windows applications are written.

If you read much about .NET, you'd be forgiven for thinking everything you've used for years has been consigned to the trash can—the Windows API, COM, COM+, ActiveX controls...all gone. Nothing could be further from the truth.

The Windows API is still part of current Windows versions, and COM and COM+ are part of the Windows infrastructure. In addition to companies and developers having a huge investment in COM and COM+ code, these technologies are so tied to the way Windows works that they will be around for a long time to come. Microsoft recognizes this and has put a great deal of work into ensuring that COM, COM+, and .NET code can operate together. You can use your existing COM code in .NET projects, write .NET components that will work with COM clients, and even host .NET components in COM+. You don't have to throw away anything you've already produced if you don't want to.

You can also call Windows API functions—or other functions hosted in DLLs—from .NET code, so you don't have to rewrite your existing APIs to use them with a .NET client.

The name of the game is interoperability, and this book will show you how to bridge the gap between unmanaged code and .NET. By the time you've finished reading, you'll have an appreciation of how to transition seamlessly between .NET and the world of traditional Windows code, and you'll be able to move into the new world of .NET while maintaining compatibility with your existing code base.

What's in This Book

The book is divided into four parts. We don't provide an overview of .NET and the .NET Framework because good overviews are available in so many other books that it seems unnecessary to add another one here.

Part I deals with the basics of how COM, COM+, and .NET work together. Chapters 1 and 2 provide an overview of how COM and COM+ fit into the .NET world, and they show how the philosophies of the COM, COM+, and

.NET programming models differ. Chapter 2 also provides you with procedures you'll need to create and install COM+ applications on your server. Chapters 3 and 4 introduce the basics of COM interop, explaining how COM components can be used in .NET code and vice versa. These chapters introduce the wrappers used by .NET to work with COM components, and they show you how to create and use both Runtime Callable and COM Callable Wrappers. Passing data between COM and .NET code is of enormous importance, so these chapters also explain how COM entities are exposed to .NET code and vice versa. Chapter 5 rounds off this part of the book by providing an overview of COM+ coding for .NET. You'll learn about basic interoperability concerns, connectivity issues, and COM+ application types.

Part II focuses on COM programming, and is intended for C++ programmers. New features have been added to C++ to make it much easier to write COM code using ATL. Chapter 6 looks at attributed programming, a new feature that allows developers to write COM code directly in C++, without having to see the ATL source code. This feature will greatly simplify the development of most COM code, and it will no longer be necessary for most programmers to edit IDL and ATL source code.

Chapter 7 is divided into two parts. The first part looks at new features that have been added to version 7.0 of the ATL library. The second part introduces ATL Server, a powerful new library for writing server-side code—including Web applications and Web services—in C++.

Part III is concerned with writing COM+ code. Chapter 8 presents a simple example, showing how to create, install, and use a COM+ component written using COM+. You'll learn several ways to create components and discover the advantages and disadvantages of each component development strategy. The following three chapters deal with specific COM+ technologies, namely using MSMQ, using subscriptions, and using Web applications. Chapter 9 shows how to create disconnected applications—those in which the client and server don't run at the same time. Chapter 10 discusses subscriptions and shows how to create the subscriber, event object, and publisher. Chapter 11 shows you how to use COM+ with Web applications. You'll learn how to create a Simple Object Access Protocol (SOAP) application by making simple modifications to a standard COM+ application.

The final part looks at interoperability between .NET and unmanaged code. Chapter 12 introduces the Platform Invoke mechanism .NET code uses to call unmanaged code in DLLs. Chapter 13 builds on this lesson, discussing how strings, structures, and arrays are marshaled; how to load DLLs dynamically; and how to handle callbacks from unmanaged code by using delegates. Chapter 14 shows you how to work with predefined interfaces, defining equivalents of COM interfaces in managed code so that it appears to COM clients as if a .NET component exposes the COM interface. This is an especially important technique when you're working with container applications such as the Microsoft Management Console (MMC).

Who Is the Audience for This Book?

Because this book describes how to use COM and .NET together, we assume you have some familiarity with COM programming, either in Microsoft Visual Basic or in C++ using ATL. You should be familiar with the basic concepts: what coclasses and interfaces are and how they work, how COM uses the registry, and the lifecycle of a COM object. You can still use the book if you don't have COM experience, but you will benefit more if you have COM experience.

For the COM+ chapters, we assume you're familiar with the basic principles behind COM+. Although these chapters will show some basic procedures, in-depth information isn't provided because we assume you have already worked with COM+ to some extent. Because the development technique and installation of managed components differs slightly from those of unmanaged components, you'll want to pay special attention to the procedures in these chapters and the use of managed component utilities.

On the .NET front, we assume you're familiar with the basics of .NET and have written some code using Microsoft Visual Basic .NET, Microsoft Visual C#, or managed C++. You don't have to be a .NET expert, but you'll get more out of the book if you have some appreciation of how .NET works and some experience with building .NET applications.

Companion Content

You can find a link to the book's companion content installer on the Web at *http://www.microsoft.com/mspress/books/6426.asp*. The installer will place the sample code in the folder My Documents\Microsoft Press\COMinDotNet by default. If you want to make the code available to more than one user on a single machine, we suggest installing to C:\Microsoft Press\COMinDotNet. You can uninstall the samples from Add Or Remove Programs in Control Panel. The Web page for the companion contents includes more details about what gets installed on your machine.

What You Need

Many developers are unaware that Windows XP comes with a newer version of COM+ than Windows 2000 has. Normally, this isn't an issue because the newer version simply contains additional features you can choose to use or not. However, for this book, you'll find that the COM+ 1.5 version supplied with Windows XP is superior when working with managed components—you'll find that COM+ 1.0 works but requires special handling. In addition, COM+ 1.5 is the only version that provides SOAP support. If you plan to create the SOAP example in Chapter 11, you must use Windows XP as your development platform because there is no COM+ 1.5 upgrade for Windows 2000. We'll discuss the advantages of COM+ 1.5 more within the book.

Although the COM+ examples in this book will work just fine with Microsoft Visual Studio .NET 1.0, you'll want to use Visual Studio .NET 2003 whenever possible. Visual Studio .NET 2003 provides features that reduce the time required to create the COM+ components.

Equipment Used

This section details the hardware and software requirements for running the code in this book.

Workstation Setup

To run the COM examples in this book, you will need the following workstation setup:

- A single or dual processor PC. A 600 MHz Pentium III processor is recommended.
- At least 128 MB of RAM; 256 MB of RAM is recommended.
- Windows 2000 or Windows XP Professional
- The .NET Framework version 1.1
- Optionally, Visual Studio .NET 2003
- 3 GB of free disk space if installing Visual Studio .NET

Server Setup

To run the COM+ examples, we strongly recommend you use a separate server machine if possible. You can run the COM+ server and client code on a single machine, but using two machines—especially for the MSMQ examples—provides a far more realistic setup. Here is what we recommend for the server machine:

- A single or dual processor PC. A 600 MHz Pentium III processor is recommended.
- At least 256 MB of RAM; 512 MB of RAM is recommended.
- Windows 2000 Server, or Windows Server 2003 when available
- The .NET Framework version 1.1
- Optionally, Visual Studio .NET 2003
- Internet Information Server, complete installation
- Management and Monitoring Tools
- Microsoft Indexing Service
- Microsoft Queuing Services
- Networking Services
- 3 GB of free disk space if installing Visual Studio .NET

Reader Aids

This book contains several types of Reader Aid paragraphs that help you identify certain types of information. The following paragraphs describe the purpose of some of the Reader Aid items you will see.

> **Note** Notes tell you interesting facts that don't necessarily affect your ability to use the other information in the book. We use notes to give you bits of information we've picked up while creating the programming examples or researching the information in this book.

> **Tip** Tips help you learn new ways of performing tasks you might not have thought about before. They can also provide an alternative way of performing tasks that you might like better than the first approach we provide. In most cases, you'll find newsgroup and Web site URLs in tips as well. These URLs are especially important because they usually lead to products or information that help you perform tasks faster.

> **Caution** Cautions almost always tell you about some kind of system or data damage that'll occur if you perform a certain action (or fail to perform others). The caution icon means watch out! Make sure you understand a caution thoroughly before you follow any instructions that come after it.

Microsoft Press Support

Every effort has been made to ensure the accuracy of the book and its companion content. Microsoft also provides corrections for books through the World Wide Web at the following address:

http://www.microsoft.com/mspress/support/

If you have comments, questions, or ideas regarding the presentation or use of this book or the companion content you can send them to Microsoft using either of the following methods:

Postal Mail:
Microsoft Press
Attn: COM Programming with Microsoft .NET Editor
One Microsoft Way
Redmond, WA 98052-6399

E-mail:

mspinput@microsoft.com

Please note that product support isn't offered through the preceding mail addresses. For support information regarding Microsoft Visual Studio .NET 2003, go to *http://msdn.microsoft.com/vstudio/*. You can also call Standard Support at (425) 635-7011 weekdays between 6 a.m. and 6 p.m. Pacific time, or you can search Microsoft's Support Online at *http://support.microsoft.com/support*.

Part I
The .NET View of COM and COM+

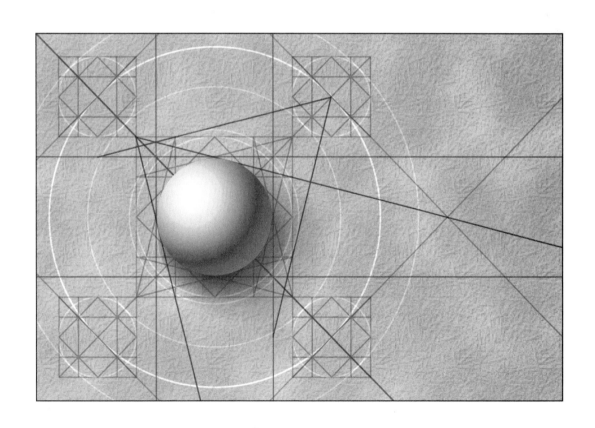

1

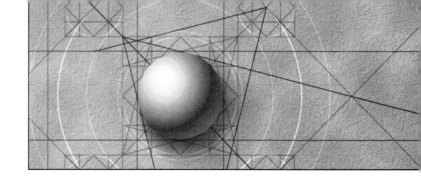

COM and .NET

.NET is the new wave of software development, introducing new technologies and languages. What's happening to the previous wave of technologies, in particular COM? This chapter discusses the place of COM in the new .NET world and presents an overview of the major topics and issues that COM programmers face in the brave new world of .NET. Many of these topics and issues will be covered in more depth in later chapters.

Is COM Dead?

The short answer is "No, not in the foreseeable future."

COM underlies the architecture of the current generation of Windows operating systems, and as such, it is deeply embedded in the operation of just about every facet of Windows programming. Access to many pieces of system functionality, from shell programming through database access to graphics programming using DirectX, is provided by COM interfaces. There are hundreds, if not thousands, of COM components and ActiveX controls in use throughout the world. This situation isn't going to change overnight, so programmers will still need to work with COM.

As if in confirmation of this, Microsoft has provided a new, much simpler way to create COM components using attributed programming, as you'll see in Chapter 6. The fact that Microsoft developers have put a lot of effort into providing a new way to work with COM code shows that COM programming is still regarded by Microsoft as something that needs support in its new generation of programming tools.

But the history of Windows programming is full of examples of technologies evolving to support simpler ways of performing common tasks. Consider

Visual Basic: once everyone had to write Windows programs in C, using the Windows SDK. Such coding required a considerable amount of arcane knowledge, and it was not trivial to write even a simple program. Visual Basic came along and made it possible to produce many types of Windows applications with very little effort, hiding the Windows infrastructure behind a programmer-friendly front end. There were still many obscure or clever programming techniques that forced you to use C, but a large proportion of everyday applications could be produced much more quickly in Visual Basic than in C.

We're seeing the same process at work with .NET and COM. While COM has been successful as a component model, aspects of the development process could be improved. Areas such as manual object lifetime management and cross-language data communication require considerable skill, and in general COM imposes a considerable learning curve on the programmer. The infrastructure required to permit the development of distributed component applications has become complex and hard to master. In addition, the fact that every machine in a distributed COM application needs to understand the DCOM protocol places limits on interoperability, and the lack of security associated with ActiveX controls running in browsers has limited the development of browser-based user interfaces (UIs).

.NET has preserved the many advantages of the COM model, while resolving many of the problems. I'll mention three specific areas here; others will emerge in later chapters.

First, XML Web services provide a way for parts of distributed applications to talk. SOAP (Simple Object Access Protocol) uses XML over HTTP to make method requests to a server. This arrangement has several advantages: HTTP is far more firewall-friendly than the DCOM binary protocol, and the use of XML and HTTP provides compatibility with a wide range of systems.

XML Web services are very useful when parts of applications on different machines are talking across the Internet or intranets, but how useful are they for cross-process communication? .NET Remoting replaces DCOM and can be used for secure, efficient, extendable communication using any .NET language. Unlike DCOM, it supports different transport mechanisms out of the box (HTTP and TCP are currently supported), different encodings (SOAP and binary are standard) and different types of security (Secure Sockets Layer [SSL] and Internet Information Services [IIS] security are standard). And because .NET Remoting is implemented by means of classes and interfaces, you can extend the mechanisms.

Finally, you can now use Windows Forms controls on Web pages. These controls, used mainly with desktop applications, provide the same packaged rich functionality as ActiveX controls, but they are subject to the same versioning and security checking that is applied to all .NET code. This means that using such controls in Web pages will remove the security concerns that currently apply to ActiveX controls.

Future releases of Windows will integrate the .NET common language runtime into the operating system, and system services will be accessible through .NET mechanisms. At that time, most people will be able to do most of what they need to do using .NET mechanisms, and the importance of COM will start to decline for most programmers.

In the future, COM programming will tend to be the preserve of the C++ programmer. To a large extent, C++ programmers have always been the ones doing heavy-duty COM coding, but in the future Visual Basic .NET and Visual C# programmers will find they can do just about all they want and need to do without using COM or ActiveX. However, some COM programming tools, such as the Active Template Library (ATL), remain accessible only through C++. In particular, I'll mention ATL Server, which provides a mechanism for writing compact and efficient ISAPI server extensions in C++. And in the same way that it is still necessary to drop from C or C++ into assembler for performance reasons, sometimes a COM component written in C++ can be far more efficient than a .NET component.

How Does COM Work in the .NET World?

As I've suggested, the many system services and components that use COM will need to be supported for the foreseeable future, so development of COM-based applications will continue during the gradual movement to a .NET-based world.

Technologies provided by Microsoft in the .NET Framework and Visual Studio .NET under the general heading of *COM interop* enable the integration of .NET and COM code in both directions. This will make it possible to move gradually from COM-based applications, which use ActiveX controls and other COM components, toward full .NET applications that use .NET controls.

> **Note** The .NET Framework provides two types of interoperability. The first is used by the Platform Invoke (or P/Invoke) mechanism to call unmanaged functions in Win32 DLLs. The second is COM interop, which is used to interact with unmanaged COM code. Much of the basic functionality is common to both types of interoperability, but COM interop adds another layer of COM compatibility.

COM components cannot be used directly in .NET code. Instead, tools—either within Visual Studio .NET or stand-alone—are used to produce .NET wrapper classes that can be used like any other .NET class. These wrappers are called *Runtime Callable Wrappers* (or RCWs), and they implement all the lifetime management and interface functionality needed to let COM components interact with .NET code, as well as implementing COM interfaces as .NET interfaces.

For example, the RCW code maintains a reference count on the COM object, and when the garbage collector collects the RCW because there are no references to it from .NET clients, the RCW will release the interface pointers being held to the COM object. Note that there is always one RCW per COM object, regardless of the number of clients that might hold references to that object. Figure 1-1 shows how the RCW bridges between managed and unmanaged code, acting as a proxy to the COM object and exposing its interfaces to .NET clients.

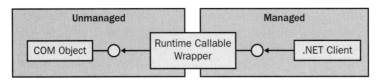

Figure 1-1 The Runtime Callable Wrapper (RCW) bridges managed and unmanaged code.

RCWs are used to wrap COM components, and can also be used to wrap ActiveX controls so that they can be used in the Visual Studio .NET designers. In the majority of cases, RCWs provide transparent access to COM components for the .NET programmer. RCWs are discussed in more detail in Chapter 3.

Although it is less common, you can use .NET components as COM objects. You might want to do this with an ongoing COM-based project if you decide that developing components is much easier using .NET and C# rather than C++ and ATL. Once again, tools enable the creation of a wrapper—this time a *COM Callable Wrapper* (CCW)—which makes a .NET object look and behave like a COM component. There is one CCW per .NET object, no matter how many COM clients are using it.

The CCW has to provide COM interfaces that make the .NET component look like a COM component. This means it has to implement *IUnknown*, and might well implement other standard interfaces, such as *IDispatch* or *ISupportErrorInfo*. The .NET component might not expose functionality via interfaces, in which case the CCW will need to fabricate COM interfaces through which to expose the public members of the component class. Figure 1-2 shows a representation of a CCW.

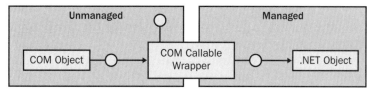

Figure 1-2 The COM Callable Wrapper (CCW) exposes .NET objects to COM clients.

The CCW must also ensure the .NET object stays alive as long as any COM client holds an interface pointer, and since COM client code in C++ deals with raw interface pointers, the CCW must ensure all addresses remain valid if the garbage collector decides to move .NET objects around in memory.

CCWs are discussed in more detail in Chapter 4.

> **Note** Although RCWs let you use ActiveX controls in Windows Forms applications, there is no built-in mechanism currently supplied to let you use a .NET Windows Forms control as an ActiveX control except on Web pages displayed in Internet Explorer.

Differences in the COM and .NET Philosophies

When interoperating between COM and .NET, you need to be aware of the considerable differences between the ways in which COM and .NET implement components. Many of these differences will be of particular interest to C++ programmers, who might be used to implementing COM code using ATL.

Locating Components

COM and .NET take very different approaches to locating COM components. In the COM world, components can be located anywhere, but all the information about where components are located and what they can do is held in a central repository. In the .NET world, components can live in only one of two locations, and all information is bundled with the component code.

COM uses the Windows registry as a repository to hold information about where component code is located. Provided the client knows the component's *GUID* (Globally Unique ID) or *progID* (Programmatic ID), COM can use the registry to find the location of the EXE or DLL that holds the component. The registry also holds details of several other important COM-related entities, such as GUIDs for interfaces (so that it can locate proxy/stub implementations for marshaling) and type libraries.

There are several problems with using the registry to hold component information. I'll highlight just a few here:

1. The registry structure is complex and difficult to work with. Editing entries manually is an error-prone process, and manipulating the registry from code requires learning a whole new API.
2. If anything happens to registry entries, COM components won't work.
3. The information in the registry is separate from the objects it describes. It is possible (and quite common) for information to become out of date.

In .NET, all this information is held along with the component as metadata. The fact that there is no central repository for information means that the runtime has to know where to look for components. .NET allows assemblies to live in one of two places, depending on how they're going to be used.

If an assembly is intended for use by one program only, it is a *private assembly* and can be placed in the same directory as the application, where the common language runtime will look for it at compile time and run time. If you want an assembly to be used by more than one application, it becomes a *shared assembly*. The *Global Assembly Cache* is a series of directories that implement a cache for shared assemblies on a machine; tools are provided to view the cache, and insert and remove assemblies.

So that they can be easily identified, shared assemblies must be digitally signed with a strong name, as explained in the next topic.

Component Identification

COM programmers will be familiar with the GUID, which is used to identify many things in the COM world. GUIDs are 128 bits long and are represented by a structure; it would be nice if they could be integers, but 128-bit integers aren't in general use now, so a struct is used instead. A GUID is really a bit pattern that has been initialized using information specific to the machine it was created on, along with the date and time it was created. There's no information in a GUID to tell you anything about where it comes from.

.NET doesn't use GUIDs to identify components. At its most basic, a type in .NET is identified by its name, and a more fully qualified name will include the namespace in which it resides (if any). For example, the *ArrayList* type is part of the *System.Collections* namespace, so it can be referred to in code by the qualified name *System.Collections.ArrayList*.

Fully qualified names will also include details of the assembly in which the type lives. Assemblies are identified by name, version, and culture information; they can be signed with a digital signature that serves to uniquely identify them. Assemblies must be signed if they are to be used as shared assemblies and installed in the GAC. Since the fully qualified name of an assembly contains version information, you can have more than one version of the same assembly coexisting side-by-side in the GAC, a fact that will make life much easier when you're upgrading applications and components.

Object Lifetimes

When you use COM, clients are responsible for managing the lifetimes of instances by means of the *AddRef* and *Release* methods of the *IUnknown* interface. Care must be taken to ensure calls to *AddRef* and *Release* are made appropriately so that instances are terminated at the correct time. This might require great care in the case of complex object relationships. COM objects will usually destroy themselves when their reference count reaches zero, and COM objects usually release any resources they hold at this point.

In .NET code, the common language runtime manages the lifetime of instances. As long as any client has a reference to an instance, it will be kept alive, and the runtime determines when instance memory and resources are reclaimed. Client code doesn't have to concern itself with lifetime issues, and this has special consequences for C++ programmers, which are detailed in the section titled "Nondeterministic Finalization." This means it usually isn't a good idea for .NET objects to release resources at the point they are destroyed, and it's necessary to implement explicit mechanisms to ensure resources are released at a particular point in the code.

Determining Object Capabilities

All COM types support the *QueryInterface* method defined by *IUnknown*. Clients call *QueryInterface* to discover whether a COM type supports (or will grant access to) a given interface.

.NET assemblies contain metadata that describes the types implemented in the assembly. .NET languages can use *reflection* at run time to discover the properties and methods supported by a type. Part of the task of the RCW is to allow .NET client code to use reflection to query the capabilities of COM objects.

Constructors and Destructors

.NET classes can have constructors and destructors, and Visual Studio .NET will supply a default constructor and destructor for components you create.

COM isn't based on object-oriented (OO) principles: this means that COM objects don't have constructors and destructors, and any initialization must be carried out as a separate step after the object has been created. The lack of constructor support means .NET components that are to be created as COM components must have a default constructor and might need other nonconstructor methods to handle initialization. The use of .NET components as COM objects, along with the restrictions this involves, is discussed in Chapter 4.

> **Note** .NET types that don't have a public default constructor cannot be created by COM (for example, by a call to *CoCreateInstance*), but they can still be used by COM clients if they are created by some other means.

Nondeterministic Finalization

All .NET languages compile down to Microsoft Intermediate Language (known as MSIL or IL, for short). Unlike some other intermediate codes, IL is more than a simple assembly language. It defines many features we take for granted in high-level languages—such as exceptions, interfaces, and events—and defines the single inheritance OO model used by all .NET languages. This definition of high-level constructs in a low-level language makes it easy to interoperate between languages in the .NET world.

One feature provided by the common language runtime is garbage collection. The programmer is responsible for dynamically allocating memory using the *new* operator, but the system takes care of reclaiming memory that can no longer be referenced. At points determined by the common language runtime, the .NET garbage collector will run on a separate thread, compacting memory to reclaim unused blocks.

> **Note** For a full discussion of the .NET memory allocation and garbage collection mechanism, consult Jeffrey Richter's *Applied Microsoft .NET Framework Programming*, Microsoft Press, 2002.

The use of garbage collection has several advantages for the C++ programmer: because you are no longer responsible for freeing memory, you'll no longer see memory leaks in applications and programmer errors will no longer lead to memory being freed while it's still being referenced.

The common language runtime, and not the programmer, decides when an object will be garbage-collected, in a process known as *nondeterministic finalization*. Classes can implement the *Finalize* method that all .NET classes inherit from the *System.Object* base class, and the garbage collector will call this *finalizer* during object collection. The problem for the programmer is that he or she doesn't know when this will happen: the process is nondeterministic.

C++ programmers accustomed to using *delete* to explicitly free dynamically allocated memory need to adapt to a different coding model. Managed C++ and Visual C# both let programmers define destructors for classes. The destructor is mapped onto a call to *Finalize*, which will be called by the garbage collector.

You can use *delete* with managed C++ classes. Using *delete* on a pointer to a managed object will run the code in the destructor. Unmanaged resources will be freed at this point, but managed resources will not be freed until the object is garbage-collected. The managed C++ code in Listing 1-1 demonstrates this behavior. You can find this sample in the Chapter01\ManagedDelete folder in the book's companion content. This content is available on the Web at *http://www.microsoft.com/mspress/books/6426.asp*.

```cpp
#include "stdafx.h"

#using <mscorlib.dll>

using namespace System;

// Unmanaged class
class UnmanagedType
{
public:
   ~UnmanagedType() {
      Console::WriteLine("~UnmanagedType called");
   }
};

// Managed class
__gc class ManagedType
{
```

Listing 1-1 ManagedDelete.cpp

```
public:
   ~ManagedType() {
      Console::WriteLine("~ManagedType called");
   }
};

// Managed container class
__gc class Container
{
   UnmanagedType* pUman;
   ManagedType* pMan;
public:
   Container() {
      pUman = new UnmanagedType();
      pMan = new ManagedType();
   }

   ~Container() {
      delete pUman;
      //delete pMan;
   }
};

void _tmain()
{
   Container* pc = new Container();
   delete pc;
   Console::WriteLine("after delete");
}
```

The *Container* class holds pointers to a managed object and an unmanaged object, both of which are allocated in the constructor. The *Container* class destructor explicitly deletes the unmanaged object, as you'd expect. It does not delete the managed object because that is the job of the garbage collector. You'll see the following output from the program:

```
~UnmanagedType called
after delete
~ManagedType called
```

The *UnmanagedType* destructor is called at the point the managed object is deleted, but the *ManagedType* destructor is not called until the *Container* object is garbage-collected at the end of the program.

Remember that there is no guarantee as to the order in which objects will be finalized, and this can cause problems if you're using COM objects that need to be released in a particular order. For example, suppose COM object A needs to be released before COM object B, and both of them are accessed via RCWs from managed code. The garbage collector might collect the RCWs in either order, so you cannot tell whether A or B will be released first. The *System.Runtime.InteropServices.Marshal* class (discussed in the section "The Marshal Class" later in this chapter) provides a method, *ReleaseComObject*, that enables programmers to explicitly release references on COM objects in managed code. Using this method, you can ensure COM objects are released in a specific order.

Error Handling

There are significant differences in the way that COM and .NET handle error reporting. All COM programmers will be familiar with the way in which COM uses HRESULTs, a simple type that packs error information into a 32-bit integer. All that can be passed in an HRESULT is an indication of whether the HRESULT represents a success or error condition and, in the case of an error condition, an error number and an indication of where the error comes from (for example, a COM interface, RPC, or Windows API call). It is possible to retrieve an error message for system-defined HRESULTs, but whether a message can be obtained for application-defined HRESULTs depends on how the COM component has been implemented.

.NET uses exceptions. Although these exceptions look very similar to C++ exceptions in code, they are significant improvements because they work between .NET languages. This means you can throw an exception in managed C++ code and catch it in Visual Basic .NET. Exceptions are an improvement on HRESULTs in several ways. An exception object contains a lot more information than simply an error code and often includes an error message and stack trace information. Also, inheritance means that a hierarchy of exception types can be defined, which greatly simplifies the design of error-handling code.

Type Information

Type information is provided for COM components via type libraries. A type library consists of binary data that describes COM coclasses and the interfaces they implement. It also provides enough information for consumers to create and use COM components. Type libraries can be implemented as separate files or added into components as resource data.

Type libraries are typically created in one of two ways. IDL files can be written to fully describe coclasses and interfaces, and the MIDL (Microsoft IDL) compiler will compile the text IDL files into binary type libraries. Alternatively, standard methods can be used to directly create type libraries from code; this approach is not usually taken by application programmers.

.NET provides type information through metadata, which is present in every assembly. You can use the standard *reflection* mechanism and the *System.Type* class to inspect the metadata for types to find out what they can do.

Visibility

COM has no notion of member visibility because it is based on interfaces. By definition, members of an interface are public and must be implemented by the coclass code. Implementing languages might use private internal code, but members of interfaces are always public.

As a consequence, when exporting a .NET type for use as a COM component, all methods, properties, fields, and events supported by the type must be public.

By default, generating a COM Callable Wrapper makes all public members visible to COM clients. COM interop provides an attribute, *ComVisibleAttribute*, that can be used to control the visibility of an assembly, a public type, or public members of a public type. The Visual C# code fragment below shows how this attribute can be used to make a class member invisible to COM clients:

```
// Class not visible to COM
[ComVisible(false)]
public class MyClass
{
   // Method not visible to COM
   [ComVisible(false)]
   public long SomeFunction()
   {
   }
}
```

ComVisibleAttribute cannot be used to make an *internal* or *protected* type visible to COM, or to make members of a nonvisible type visible.

In Chapter 4, we'll talk about some pitfalls to be considered when using the *ComVisible* attribute. As a brief example here, you need to be careful when using *ComVisibleAttribute* to control visibility within inheritance hierarchies. If a class is marked as nonvisible, its methods are also nonvisible by default. If, however, that class is used as a base class for a type that is to be exported to COM, its methods will be visible to COM unless they are explicitly marked as nonvisible with *ComVisibleAttribute*. This is a consequence of the fact that exporting a class flattens the class hierarchy so that all inherited base-class members appear as members of the COM-visible derived class.

Before leaving the topic of visibility, note also that when exporting a value type to COM, all fields (both public and private) are exposed in the generated type library. This means that value types might need to be specially designed if you're intending to use them with COM.

Data Handling

COM programmers might be wondering how data is passed between COM and .NET components. Because of the incompatibilities between language data types, COM programmers often devote significant effort to marshaling data in COM method calls. Special data types such as BSTR and SAFEARRAY have been provided so that string and array data can be shared between C/C++ and Visual Basic, but their use often requires code to be written and creates many pitfalls for the unwary.

The .NET interop marshaler marshals data between the common language runtime heap (also known as the managed heap) and the unmanaged heap. COM also marshals data across apartment boundaries, so when calling between .NET code and COM code in different apartments or processes, both the interop and COM marshalers will be involved. Figure 1-3 illustrates the marshaling process.

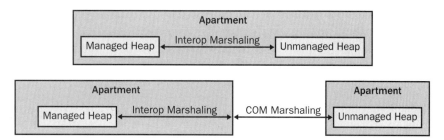

Figure 1-3 Same-apartment and cross-apartment marshaling in COM interop

Using .NET Servers with COM Clients

Exported .NET types will have a registry *ThreadingModel* value of *Both*, indicating that instances can be created in single-threaded apartments (STAs) or multithreaded apartments (MTAs). A consequence of this is that exported .NET classes must be thread safe, since instances may be created in an MTA. Since the .NET component instance will be created in the same apartment as the COM client, the interop marshaler will be the only marshaler used.

Using COM Servers with .NET Clients

Apartments in .NET applications default to an MTA, but this might change depending on the application type. You can use attributes (*STAThreadAttribute* and *MTAThreadAttribute*) and the *Thread.ApartmentState* property to examine or change the apartment type for a thread. The following code fragment shows how you would run the main thread of a console application in an STA:

```
class Class1
{
   [STAThread]
   static void Main(string[] args)
   {
      ...
   }
}
```

Using the *STAThreadAttribute* and *MTAThreadAttribute* attributes doesn't have any effect unless the application uses COM interop, and the attribute doesn't take effect until an interop call is made.

Interop Marshaling

Whether interop marshaling can handle data types automatically depends on whether the types are blittable or nonblittable. Blittable types are those that have a common representation in both managed and unmanaged memory. Examples of blittable types include *System.Byte*, the integer types (*System.Int16*, *System.Int32*, and *System.Int64*), *System.IntPtr*, and their unsigned equivalents. One-dimensional arrays of blittable types and classes that contain only blittable types are also considered blittable.

> **Note** The term *blittable* comes from the computer graphics term *blit*, which originated in Bell Labs and describes the process of copying an array of bits between two memory locations. No one is certain what *blit* actually means.

All other types are nonblittable and have different or ambiguous representations in managed and unmanaged memory. For example, a managed array of type *System.Array* could be marshaled into a C-style array or a *SAFEARRAY*, and a character of type *System.Char* could be marshaled as an ANSI character or a Unicode character.

To marshal nonblittable types, you can let the marshaler pick a default representation or specify how marshaling is to occur by using attributes. For example, *String*s are marshaled to BSTRs by default. If you want to marshal to some other string type, you can use *MarshalAsAttribute* to specify the unmanaged type:

```
public void SomeFunction(
   [MarshalAs(UnmanagedType.LPWStr)]String theString);
```

Marshaling Structures

Before discussing structures, we should quickly review two fundamental divisions of .NET data types: value types and reference types. Value types are declared on the stack, are referenced directly in code, cannot act as base classes, and are not garbage-collected. They are usually small (16 bytes or less) and declared using the *struct* keyword in Visual C#, the *Structure* keyword in Visual Basic .NET, and the __value keyword in managed C++. Value types can be passed by value or reference.

Reference types are declared on the managed heap, are referred to using references (or pointers in managed C++), can be used as base classes, and are garbage-collected. Reference types can be of any size and are declared using the *class* keyword in Visual C# and Visual Basic .NET and the __gc keyword in managed C++. Reference types are always passed by reference and never by value.

Structures can be defined in type libraries for use in COM interface methods, and they will be represented by value types in the RCW code. For example, here is an IDL *struct* plus an interface that uses it:

```
// IDL structure definition
struct Point {
   long x,y;
};

[
   object,
   uuid(E324E9D1-7A1F-4E8C-AC75-6483B9794F92),
   helpstring("IFFF Interface"),
   pointer_default(unique)
]
interface IFFF : IUnknown {
   [helpstring("method UsePoint")] HRESULT UsePoint([in] struct Point p);
};
```

The struct will appear in Visual C# like this:

```
public sealed struct Point
{
   public System.Int32 x;
   public System.Int32 y;
}
```

Value types declared in managed code can also be passed to COM client code, where they will appear as *struct*s in the type library created as part of the CCW. Care might be needed when exporting value types because the structure of .NET value types is richer than that of COM *struct*s, so some features of value types cannot be represented in the type library. For example, even though .NET value types can contain methods as well as fields, only fields are exported to COM.

The Marshal Class

Although the default marshaling supplied by COM Interop will suffice in many cases, you might need to go beyond the basics at times. The *System.Runtime.InteropServices.Marshal* class provides a number of methods that help when interacting with unmanaged code.

The following table lists some of the main methods of the *Marshal* class that will be of interest to COM programmers.

Table 1-1 Methods of the *Marshal* class of Interest to COM Programmers

Method	Description
GetHRForException	Converts a .NET exception to a COM *HRESULT*
GetHRForLastWin32Error	Returns a COM *HRESULT* representing the last error set by Win32 code
GetComInterfaceForObject	Returns a pointer to a specific interface on an object
GetIDispatchForObject	Returns a pointer to the *IDispatch* interface on an object
GetIUnknownForObject	Returns a pointer to the *IUnknown* interface on an object
GetObjectForIUnknown	Returns a reference to a managed object that represents a COM object, given an *IUnknown* pointer
PtrToStringAnsi, PtrToStringAuto, PtrToStringBSTR, PtrToStringUni	Allocates a *String*, and copies part or all of an unmanaged string into it. The *Auto* variant will copy from ANSI or Unicode strings, adjusting the type as necessary.
QueryInterface, AddRef, Release	Allows managed code to interact with *IUnknown* interfaces on COM objects
ReleaseComObject	Decrements the reference count of the RCW wrapping a COM object. Since the RCW typically holds only a single reference, a single call will usually result in the object being freed.

Table 1-1 **Methods of the *Marshal* class of Interest to COM Programmers**

Method	Description
StringToBSTR	Allocates a BSTR, and copies the content of a *String* into it. Use *Marshal.FreeBSTR* to free the allocated memory when the *BSTR* is no longer required.
StringToCoTaskMemAnsi, *StringToCoTaskMemAuto*, *StringToCoTaskMemUni*	Copies the content of a *String* to memory allocated by the unmanaged COM allocator. Such memory must be freed via a call to the *CoTaskMemFree* COM library function when no longer required.
StringToHGlobalAnsi, *StringToHGlobalAuto*, *StringToHGlobalUni*	Copies the content of a *String* into unmanaged memory, using memory allocated from the Windows global heap
ThrowExceptionForHR	Throws an exception representing a given *HRESULT*

Event Handling

COM and .NET use different mechanisms for firing and handling events. COM uses connection points, whereas .NET uses .NET events, which are based on delegates. Both of these are tightly coupled event systems, meaning that the event source and sink objects have to be running at the same time. COM+ also implements a loosely coupled event model, where event sinks can retrieve and handle events after they have been published by an event source.

COM Interop makes it possible to consume COM events in .NET code and vice versa.

Using the IDE to Access Components

Visual Studio .NET provides tools to help you access COM components and integrate them into .NET projects. This section will show you how to locate components and use them in .NET code.

> **Note** C# is used in the sample code in this section, but the same techniques can also be used with Visual Basic .NET and managed C++.

Locating the Component You Need

Although just about every COM component meets the definition of an ActiveX control, Visual Studio .NET treats non-UI components differently from ActiveX controls that have a UI. Non-UI components can be used in both console and Windows Forms applications, but ActiveX controls that have a UI are used in Windows Forms projects and accessed through the Toolbox.

> **Note** I'll use the term *COM component* to mean components without a UI, and *ActiveX control* to mean traditional ActiveX controls, which have a UI.

Locating COM Components

The References folder in a Visual Studio .NET project tree contains details of references to other .NET assemblies used by the project. It is also used to hold references to COM components you want to use in a project.

Right-clicking on the References folder and selecting Add Reference from the context menu will display the Add Reference dialog box, and selecting the COM tab will display details of the COM components currently registered on the machine, as shown in Figure 1-4.

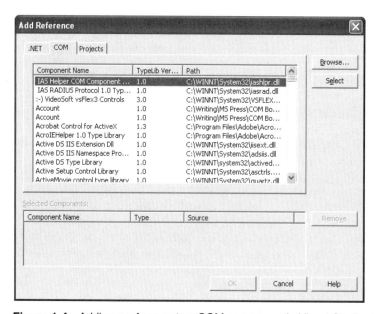

Figure 1-4 Adding a reference to a COM component in Visual Studio .NET

Select the components you want to use from the list, and click Select to add them to the Selected Components list. You can also use the Browse button, which will let you search type libraries for unregistered components. Once you've selected the components, click OK, and the Add Reference wizard will generate the RCW code. The "Simple COM Access Examples" section will show you how to locate and use COM components in code.

Locating UI Components

COM components that have a UI—referred to as "traditional" ActiveX controls—are accessed through the Toolbox of the Visual Studio .NET Windows Forms designer. Display the Toolbox, and make sure the Windows Forms controls are displayed. Right-click anywhere on the Toolbox, and choose Add/Remove Items from the context menu. This will display the Customize Toolbox dialog box, as shown in Figure 1-5.

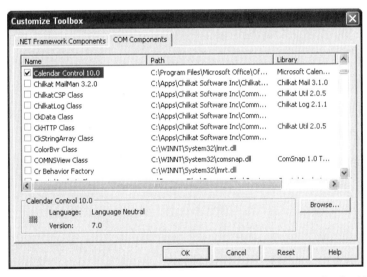

Figure 1-5 Adding a reference to an ActiveX control in Visual Studio .NET

Check the boxes next to the controls you want to add, and then click OK. As with COM components, RCWs are generated for the controls. In addition, an icon for the control is added to the Windows Forms section of the Toolbox, and all properties and methods of the ActiveX control are exposed in exactly the same way as a standard Windows Forms control.

Simple COM Access Examples

To show you how simple it is to use COM components in .NET code, this section will walk you through two examples: using a COM component, and adding an ActiveX control to the Toolbox.

Using a COM Component

I've created a simple in-process ATL component for this example, called Convert, which converts temperatures between Celsius and Fahrenheit. You can find the code in the Chapter01\Convert folder in the book's companion content. Before trying this example, make sure the component is installed and registered.

> **Note** You can open the project in Visual Studio .NET and build it, which will register the control. Alternatively, you can run RegSvr32 from the command line to register Convert.dll from the Convert\Debug directory.

Start by creating a Visual C# Console Application project; I've called my example *ConsoleTest*. Now open Solution Explorer, and right-click the References folder. Select the Add Reference command from the context menu, as shown in Figure 1-6.

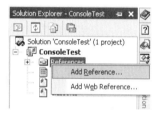

Figure 1-6 Displaying the Add Reference dialog box in Visual Studio .NET

This will display the Add Reference dialog box, which you saw in Figure 1-4. Select the COM tab on the dialog box. If you've installed and registered the Convert component, you should find an entry in the list, as shown in Figure 1-7.

Click Select to add it to the list of selected components, and then press OK to cause the RCW to be generated. After a few seconds, an entry for Convert will be added to the References folder in Solution Explorer. Right-click the new reference, and select Properties; the property display shows the details of which component is wrapped by this reference, including the path to the DLL and the component's CLSID.

You can immediately see the methods and properties exposed by the coclass by bringing up the Object Browser (by pressing Ctrl+Alt+J or selecting Object Browser from the View menu). The browser is shown in Figure 1-8.

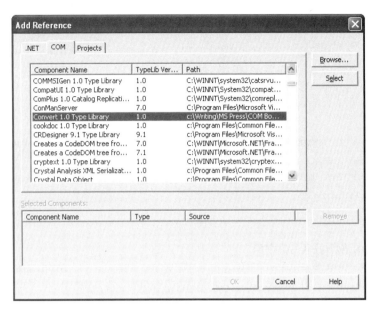

Figure 1-7 An entry for the Convert component appears in the list.

Figure 1-8 The RCW for the Convert component in the Object Browser

The display shows an assembly called interop.convert that contains a *Convert* namespace, which in turn contains the *CConvClass* ATL implementation class.

To use the COM component from code, add the following code to the *Main* method in *ConsoleTest*:

```
try
{
   // Create a wrapper object
   Convert.CConvClass cc = new Convert.CConvClass();
```

```
    // Call a member
    double f = cc.C2F(100.0);
    Console.WriteLine("100C is {0}F", f);
}
catch(Exception e)
{
    Console.WriteLine(e.Message);
}
```

Note how the wrapper object is created and used to call methods on the underlying COM object.

Build and run the application. You should see the following result in the console window:

```
100C is 212F
```

Using an ActiveX Control

The procedure for using an ActiveX control is slightly different, and I'll use the standard Microsoft Calendar control that is installed as part of Microsoft Office to show how it is done.

Create a new Windows Forms application: I've called mine *FormTest*, and I'm using C#. Remember that this example will work in managed C++ and Visual Basic .NET as well. Open the Toolbox, make sure the Windows Forms tab is selected, and then right-click the Toolbox, as shown in Figure 1-9.

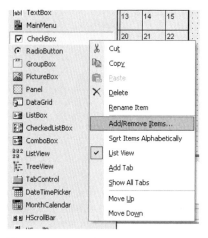

Figure 1-9 Adding an ActiveX control to the Visual Studio .NET Toolbox

Select Add/Remove Items to bring up the Customize Toolbox dialog, which you saw in Figure 1-5. Choose the COM Components tab, and scroll down the list until you come to the Calendar Control 10.0 entry. Select the check box next to the name, and then click OK. You can now scroll to the bottom of the Windows Forms controls in the Toolbox, where you'll see an entry for the Calendar control, as shown in Figure 1-10.

Figure 1-10 The Microsoft Calendar ActiveX control installed in the Visual Studio .NET Toolbox

If you look in the Object Browser, you'll see that two assemblies have been generated to represent this control, called *interop.msacal* and *axinterop.msacal*. The first, *interop.msacal*, is the basic wrapper that allows you to interact with the COM types defined in the ActiveX control; the second, *axinterop.msacal*, adds the functionality to let the control be used as a Windows Forms control.

You can use this control like any other Windows Forms control, placing it on forms and interacting with its methods and properties.

Figure 1-11 shows a Calendar control on a form, together with two Windows Forms button controls that can be used to change the month displayed by the calendar.

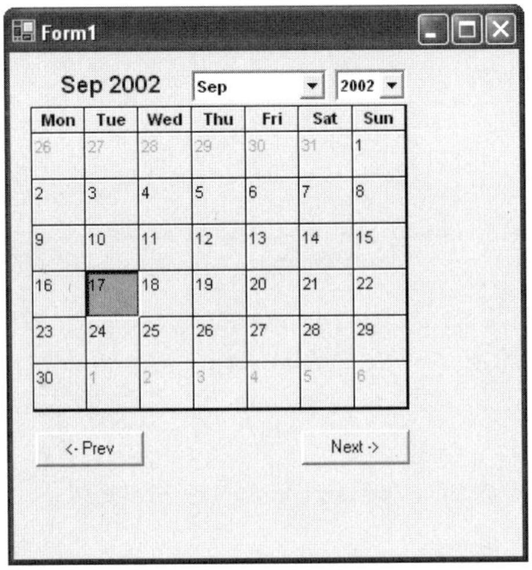

Figure 1-11 A Microsoft Calendar ActiveX control in use in a Windows Forms application

Summary

.NET provides a complete new environment for writing a wide range of application types, from desktop applications and custom controls to Web services and ASP.NET pages. The use of the common language runtime and the Intermediate Language makes it easy to develop mixed languages in distributed or single-process applications, and the provision of .NET Remoting and XML Web services provides an infrastructure for developing distributed applications.

COM-based applications and system services will still be around for some time, and Microsoft has provided the COM Interop technology within the .NET Framework to enable smooth interoperability between COM and .NET components. Runtime Callable Wrappers enable the use of COM components and fully featured ActiveX controls in .NET applications, while COM Callable Wrappers let you use .NET components from COM client code.

There are fundamental differences in the ways in which COM and .NET operate, which means you sometimes must take particular care to ensure interoperation works correctly. You'll meet many of these occasions in the chapters that follow.

2

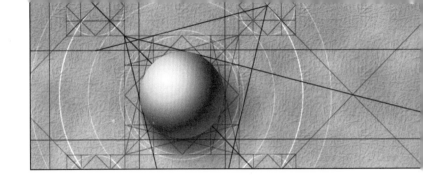

COM+ and .NET

In Chapter 1, you learned that there's a place for COM in your .NET application development toolbox. Likewise, there's a place for COM+ when you're working with .NET. Although COM+ doesn't have as long a history as COM, it's based on COM technology and provides added value that developers still need, even if they're using .NET for most of their development tasks.

In many respects, this chapter continues the story begun in Chapter 1. It takes the next logical step of addressing the need for COM+ in .NET application development tasks. This chapter is an overview—we'll cover most of the issues in this chapter in much greater depth as the book progresses. You'll also learn about two valuable Microsoft Management Console (MMC) snap-ins in this chapter. The value of these tools becomes apparent in later chapters, when you learn how to perform application tasks such as installing a COM+ application.

> **Note** MMC is a container application that holds special COM components known as *snap-ins*. Most snap-ins provide some type of administrative aid, but a developer could create a snap-in to serve just about any purpose. A preconfigured setup that includes one or more snap-ins is called a *console*. You'll find a number of consoles in the Administrative Tools folder of the Control Panel. The two consoles discussed in this chapter help you configure the COM+ Component Services and the .NET Framework.

What Is the Place of COM+ in the .NET World?

Many developers have gotten the idea that .NET is all about Web services and distributed applications that rely on the Internet. In reality, .NET supports this type of development in addition to all other past forms of development. In some cases, using Web services for distributed application development isn't the correct strategy because a company might have a large investment in existing technology or might need the additional security or performance that COM+ can provide. Consequently, COM+ plays an important role in distributed application development.

In many cases, .NET developers will still need the *transactional* or *message-based* application support provided by COM+. These two applications are specific examples of the continued need for COM+ use with .NET—at least for the present.

Database applications that run only on an internal LAN or WAN and need the highest level of reliability make use of the transactional support provided by COM+. A transaction tracks the data as it moves from client to server. Only completed transactions actually appear in the database. Failed transactions are rolled back so that the database remains in a stable state without data corruption.

By using asynchronous data processing, message-based applications eliminate the requirement for sender and receiver to exist at the same time. A recorder creates the message based on data the sender wants to send to the receiver. (In most cases, the client will send data and the server will receive it, but the server can also send data to the client.) *Microsoft Message Queuing Services (MSMQ)* manages the message queue used to hold the message until the recipient can process it. The message queue can appear on the local machine—the remote machine always has a queue to store incoming messages. When a message arrives in the remote queue, a listener alerts the COM+ component to the change in queue status. A player interprets the message content for the component, which then processes the data sent by the sender.

MSMQ helps developers create disconnected applications for independent clients—that is, applications that store data locally until the client has a connection to the server. In short, this technology eliminates the need to use any type of connection while the user is "on the road." The server can also use queues to store messages until it has time to process them. The queue collects messages during peak periods, which the server continues processing during slow times. This technique tends to use server resources more efficiently because the application continues to operate during periods of low activity.

The final reason I discuss in this chapter for using COM+ with .NET applications is the level of security it provides. You'll see as the chapter progresses that COM+ provides *role-based security*, which enables you to set access requirements based on the client's role. For example, you can set security separately for managers and employees. COM+ also allows you to set security at various levels: component, interface, and method. This level of security support is more granular than that which COM provides and overcomes some configuration difficulties developers experienced with COM applications in the past.

COM+ Problems and Improvements

Chapter 1 pointed out a number of issues the developer must face when working with COM. You also learned about DCOM issues and how they affect the distributed programming environment. COM+ relies on both of these technologies, so it shouldn't be too surprising to learn you'll run into the same problems working with COM+ that you do working with either COM or DCOM. For example, making COM+ applications work across an Internet connection through a firewall is just as hard a task as it is with DCOM applications.

COM+ also includes a few problems of its own. As with COM and DCOM, many developers find COM+ daunting to learn. However, COM+ increases the learning curve by adding more functionality. You not only have COM and DCOM issues to worry about, you also have additional concerns such as how to use certain features. Many developers still don't understand how the publish/subscribe model works, and others find role-based security a long leap from COM and DCOM security options.

Another problem is that COM+ tends to change the rules. For example, when working with COM or DCOM, a developer was encouraged to allocate a resource and then hold onto it until every possible need was met. COM+ changes this rule by insisting the developer allocate a resource, use it as quickly as possible for the task at hand, and then release it. In sum, there's a contradiction in the way that COM and COM+ handle the same issue. This problem causes confusion in the developer community—more confusion than even COM and DCOM created.

Note that Microsoft recognized some deficiencies in the COM and DCOM approach when they were creating the COM+ technology and worked to eliminate these deficiencies. Instead of using the straight connection found in COM and DCOM, COM+ relies on *interceptors* (code that captures the communications stream and performs either pre- or post-processing to add functionality to the technology). For example, COM+ relies on interceptors to provide the *role-based security* many developers have found to be a useful alternative to the security COM provided in the past.

One of the more important improvements in COM+ is the management features it provides. You'll learn about COM+ management in the "Using the Component Services MMC Snap-In" section that follows. The short explanation is that you don't need to worry about the registry as much when working with COM+. Most of the administrative tasks you'll perform occur within a GUI or when using specially created installation programs.

Using the Component Services MMC Snap-In

Using the Component Services MMC snap-in is an essential part of the development process for COM+ applications. This snap-in helps you perform the following tasks:

- Install components as part of creating a COM+ application.
- Export an application proxy so that the client can access the component.
- Help the developer or administrator set component security based on the roles users will play in application use.

The Component Services snap-in also provides support for the COM+ publish/subscribe event model. Finally, given the right application setup, the Component Services snap-in will log significant component events for you or you can add event logging support directly into the component. In short, this is the one utility you absolutely must know about to make COM+ applications work.

The next two sections of the chapter discuss the main Component Services areas. We'll begin by looking at the interface for those of you who are new to the MMC snap-in approach to working with administration. Once you have a basic understanding of the interface, we'll discuss what you need to do to install COM+ components on the server. This section includes everything from creating the COM+ application to exporting a proxy for the client's use.

An Overview of the Interface

The Component Services console shortcut appears in the Administrative Tools folder of the Control Panel. Starting this console displays a window similar to the one shown in Figure 2-1. Notice the console includes the Component Services, Event Viewer, and Services snap-ins. Component Services is where you'll manage the COM+ applications you create. Event Viewer helps you to track any significant COM+ events. In most cases, you'll use this area to view any errors the COM+ application records. Finally, Services will help you to work with the various operating system services installed on the target machine.

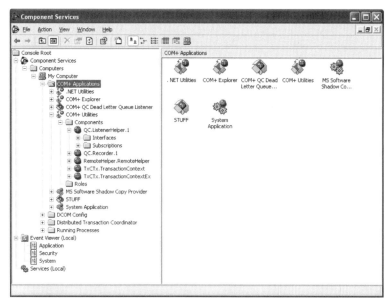

Figure 2-1 Component Services is the main utility that you'll use for installing and managing COM+ components.

As with most MMC snap-ins, in the left (scope) pane Component Services uses a hierarchical display (similar to the one found in Windows Explorer) and a detailed view of the highlighted item in the right (results) pane. Most of the icons in this view have context menus you can access with a right click, just as you would with most Microsoft Windows applications. The context menus tell what tasks you can perform. In short, there isn't anything too unusual about this interface from a usage perspective. If you know how to use Windows Explorer, you'll have a good idea of how to use this MMC snap-in.

Both Event Viewer and Services let you view a single machine. You can choose the machine you want to view by right-clicking the appropriate folder, and then choosing Connect To Another Computer from the context menu. You'll see the Select Computer dialog box as shown in Figure 2-2. The Browse button helps you select any available computer on the network, including servers that you have rights to access. Click OK, and Windows will connect you to the specified computer.

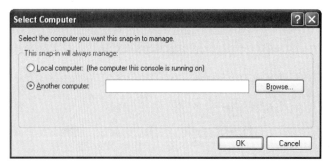

Figure 2-2 The Select Computer dialog box allows you to choose another computer to view.

Component Services allows you to view more than one computer at a time. This feature helps you to move COM+ applications from one machine to another in the same way you'd move files using Windows Explorer. You can add a computer to Component Services by right-clicking the Computers folder, and clicking New and then Computer in the context menu. You'll see an Add Computer dialog box. As with the Select Computer dialog box, you can use the Browse button to find other computers on the network.

The actual content of the Component Services snap-in can vary by operating system version. Figure 2-1 shows the four folders that Windows XP users can access:

- COM+ Applications
- DCOM Config
- Distributed Transaction Coordinator
- Running Processes

Windows 2000 users will normally see the COM+ Applications and Distributed Transaction Coordinator folders (as shown in the WinServer entry in Figure 2-3), which are the two folders we need to discuss in this chapter. Let's begin with the COM+ Applications folder. Servers normally have more default applications than workstations do because they have more COM+ roles to fulfill. Figure 2-3 shows a comparison between the default applications for a workstation (My Computer) and for a server (WinServer). Note that Component Services uses a different icon for a local connection than it does for a remote connection so that you can easily see when you're working with the local machine.

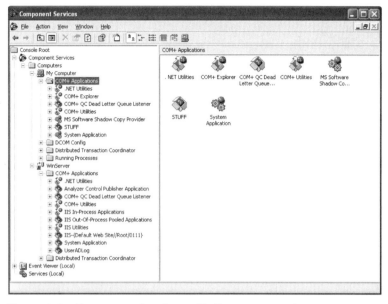

Figure 2-3 Component Services will allow you to work with more than one machine at a time.

COM+ applications contain at least two folders: Components and Roles. A Windows XP installation adds a Legacy Components folder to the mix. Roles are a security requirement for a particular component, interface, or method. We'll talk about roles in the "Adding Security to a COM+ Application" section later in the chapter. For now, let's talk about the construction of COM+ applications from the component perspective.

Components contain one or more interfaces. Each interface contains one or more methods. Methods are what you'll use to access the functionality that the COM+ application provides. You'll often find more components within server applications because servers require more flexibility. However, each of these components will be the same whether found on a workstation or server. In other words, you won't find one version of a component on a workstation and another version on a server—any extra functionality the server requires will appear within a separate component.

Each application level provides property settings that modify that level's behavior. For example, you can set role-based security parameters for a COM+ application at the application, component, interface, and method levels. This means you get a very fine level of control over the behavior of an application. Not every level has the same settings because every level performs a different function within the application hierarchy. The folders directly above each application level allow you to organize that level and change the method of presentation. This includes the choices presented by the MMC snap-in as well as the application itself. In a few cases (where applicable), you'll see a New option on the context menu for the folder that permits you to add a new item. We'll see how this works in the "Creating COM+ Applications and Installing Components" section that follows.

Creating COM+ Applications and Installing Components

Building a COM+ application doesn't require any programming once you create the required components. However, COM+ applications don't just appear on your server because you've created all the required components. You need to use a wizard to create an empty COM+ application. Once you have the application in place, you can add components to it using a different wizard. Each component is added separately; there isn't any way to add them as a group. Windows automatically detects component details to complete the application for you. The purpose of this section is to show you how to perform these two COM+ application creation steps.

As with any component, you have to register your COM+ components. In the past, you relied on the integrated development environment (IDE) to perform the task automatically, used *RegSvr32* to perform the task manually, or included the registration as part of an installation program or other form of automation. When working with .NET applications, you'll rely on the *RegAsm* utility as a replacement for the *RegSvr32* utility. However, the result is the same as when using unmanaged components—the component is still registered in the registry.

In the world of COM+, you don't use any of these registration methods—Windows registers the component for you as part of the process of adding components to a COM+ application. The act of installing a component registers it on a server that it hasn't been registered on before. We'll see in this section that you still need to use the *RegAsm* utility to create a type library for the COM+ wizards to access.

I've created a component for demonstration purposes in this chapter. You don't need to create the component or write any code. All the code for this section appears in the Chapter02\MyMath folder of the companion content. You can download the companion content from the Web at *http://www.microsoft.com/mspress/books/6426.asp*. The purpose of this sample component is to help you learn how the two wizards work. Examples later in the book will show you how to create various types of components you can register using the procedures we'll discuss here.

The following sections show how to use the Component Services MMC snap-in to register and install the *MyMath* component (which includes the *MathFunctions* class). You'll also learn a little about COM+ security and how to export your application to install it on a client machine. The exported application acts as a proxy the client will call to access the component on the server.

Creating the COM+ Application

The first thing we need to do is create a new application for our component. The following procedure shows you how to add a new application to Component Services. (This process is different than those you've used for other component types.)

1. Move the component to a convenient directory on the server. I normally use a central repository for my custom components, but you can use any management scheme you like, including creating special folders for each project you work with. Because of the way .NET components work, you'll need to create a *type library (TLB)* file and register the component in the Global Assembly Cache (GAC) so that the common language runtime can find it.

2. Type **RegAsm MyMath.dll /tlb:MyMath.tlb** at the command prompt in the folder used to hold the component, and then press Enter. This step does register the component, but you'll find that the registration doesn't work as anticipated with COM+. What we need out of this step is the type library.

3. Type **GacUtil -i MyMath.dll**, and press Enter at the command prompt. This step registers the component globally so that the common language runtime can find it when needed. Now we need to register the component with COM+.

> **Tip** During the design and debugging phase of component construction, it pays to create batch (BAT) files that contain the registration and unregistration commands. I usually create one batch file for each purpose. You'll find examples of these two files in the \Chapter02\MyMath\bin\Debug folder of the source code.

4. Open the Component Services console if you haven't done so already.

5. Highlight the COM+ Applications entry, and then click the Action menu and then click Application in the New submenu. You'll see the Welcome To The COM+ Application Install Wizard dialog box.

6. Click Next. You'll see the Install Or Create A New Application page. The Install Pre-built Application(s) option is specifically designed to allow you to install third-party applications. These applications come with an installation file with an MSI extension that contains all the particulars about the application. We won't talk about pre-built applications for most of the applications in this book. Since we're developing our own application, we'll need to use the Create An Empty Application option.

7. Click the Create An Empty Application option. You'll see the Create Empty Application page as shown in Figure 2-4. This page contains a field that holds the name for your application. It also asks you to decide between a library and server application type. In most cases, you'll choose the Server application option because the components you create will execute in a separate process on the server. Library applications execute within the creator's process, which means an errant component can cause the application to fail. In addition, library applications don't support load balancing, remote access, or queued components. Library applications do, however, execute faster because there are fewer process boundaries to cross.

Figure 2-4 Use the COM+ Application Install Wizard to give your application a name and define the application type.

8. Type a name for the application. The example uses *MyMathApp*, but you can use any name you like.

9. Choose between the Server Application and Library Application options. The sample application uses the Server Application option because it allows more complete testing of the component and better protection during debugging.

10. Click Next. You'll see the Set Application Identity page as shown in Figure 2-5. This page helps you choose the identity used to run the component. You'll normally choose the Interactive User option because it allows you to test for role-based security using the identity of the person logged onto the server. The second option, This User, relies on the identity of a specific person. It's handy for situations when you know another server rather than a user will use the component. Using this setting is convenient because the component will always allow the same level of access no matter who makes the request.

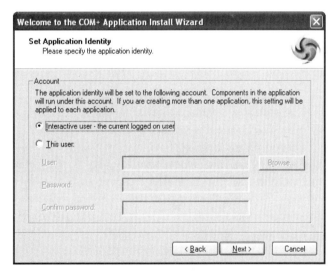

Figure 2-5 You'll use the Set Application Identity page to determine the identity the application uses while running.

11. Choose the Interactive User option, and then click Next. The example will use the Interactive User option because it provides better application security. This setting will augment the role-based security that we'll talk about later. You'll see the final COM+ Application Wizard page.

12. Click Finish. The new application will appear in the list of applications in the COM+ Applications folder. Notice that Windows automatically creates a directory structure you can use for working with the component. We'll use this directory structure in the steps that follow to fully configure the COM+ application for use.

Adding Components to a COM+ Application

The application we've just defined acts as a container for our component. In fact, you could place multiple components within this directory structure—the whole idea is to keep the various applications on the server separate, not necessarily to restrict how you add new components to the server. At the moment, we still don't have the sample component (found in the Chapter 02\MyMath\bin\Debug folder as *MyMath.dll*) installed in Component Services. The following steps will show you how to install the component, even if it isn't registered on the current machine.

1. Open the *MyMathApp* application, and you'll see a minimum of two folders: Components and Roles. (You must highlight the Components folder to add new components to the application.) The Components folder holds any components you want to install for the application. The Roles folder contains security roles you can later assign to the application, an individual component, or a method within the component.

2. Highlight the Components folder, and then use the click Component in the New subfolder of the Action menu to display the COM+ Component Install Wizard dialog box.

3. Click Next. You'll see the Import Or Install A Component page. The Install New Component(s) option helps you to install components you've placed on the server but haven't registered. This is the option you should always use when working with .NET components to ensure you can see all the interfaces and methods they contain. The Import Component(s) That Are Already Registered option helps you to add components that have already been registered on the server. This is the option you'll choose for updates (in which case, the GUID is exactly the same for the new component as it was for the old one) or when the component has been registered for some other reason. For example, you might be using your development machine as the test server. If you use this option with a .NET component, make sure the component contains the *[Guid]* attribute for the class to ensure the GUID remains the same from version to version. Generally, you should avoid this option when working with .NET components to ensure your application works as anticipated. Use the Install New Event Class(es) option to create event classes for subscription use. This particular component installation requires special programming that we'll discuss in Chapter 11.

4. Click Install New Component(s). You'll see the Select Files To Install page like the one shown in Figure 2-6. Although you can install

components that reside on other machines, you'll find that components work more reliably if you place the component on a local server hard drive. (As previously mentioned, you'll probably want to place your custom components in a special place on the server to make them easier to find.) Notice that the folder for the sample component includes both the DLL and TLB files. Always select the TLB file because COM+ won't know what to do with the DLL file.

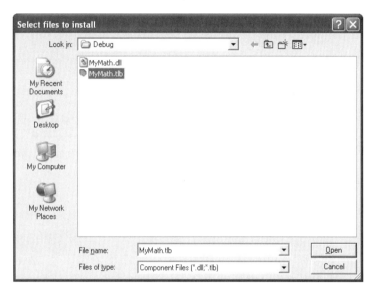

Figure 2-6 Windows will ask for the location of the component you want to install.

5. Find the component file you want to install. The example uses *MyMath.TLB*. Highlight the file, and then click Open to complete the selection process. You'll see the Install New Components page similar to the one shown in Figure 2-7. (You might need to check the Details option to get your dialog box to match the one shown in the figure.) Note that the figure shows what you should see when working with the sample component. The example contains both components and a type library—you'll need both for COM+ applications. Clicking the Add button at this point would allow you to add another file to the list (along with any components the file contains). Our component is also shown as a COM+ component type, and the wizard has found interfaces within the component. (The wizard won't tell you which interfaces have been found at this point—we can hope, it found the ones you wanted to expose.) You need to check all these items as part of the component setup.

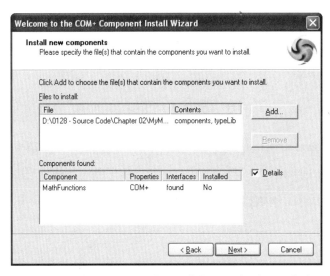

Figure 2-7 Make sure you have all the required parts before you consider the component installation complete.

6. Click Next. You'll see the final COM+ Component Install Wizard page.

7. Click Finish to complete the Install New Component(s) installation process. You'll see the new component added to the right pane of the Component Services window, as shown in Figure 2-8.

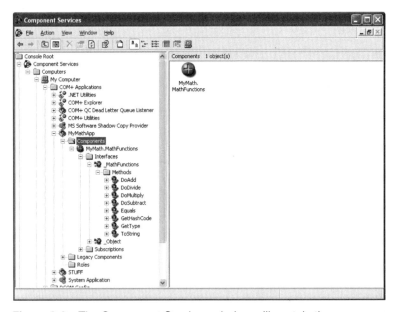

Figure 2-8 The Component Services window will contain the new components you've installed once you complete the COM+ Component Install Wizard.

Adding Security to a COM+ Application

At this point, the COM+ application and an associated component are installed within the Component Services snap-in. However, the component isn't completely operational yet because we haven't installed any security for it. Yes, you can use the component at this point—there isn't any magic about adding security to the COM+ application. However, adding security is essential for creating a COM+ application that works well.

Theoretically, we could get by without adding any security because the application is already protected by the standard Windows security. However, role-based security is one of the features of COM+ that makes life a lot easier for network administrators and developers alike. This is because you can refine the security measures used to protect a component, the interfaces it contains, and the methods required to perform the application's work. Unlike Windows security, where you have to use a one-size-fits-all approach, role-based security allows you to base security on the work a user will perform.

To add role-based security to the component, you'll need to create at least one, and preferably two, roles. We'll call the first role Administrator so that someone logged on as this role will be able to access all the methods within the *MyMath* component. The second role can be any other value, but for this example we'll use User. The User role will be able to access just the four math functions.

1. Highlight the Roles folder, and then click Role in the New submenu of the Action menu to display the Role dialog box.

2. Type a name for the role, and then click OK. For the example, we'll use Administrator for one role and User for the second.

3. Open the Administrators (or Users) folder, and then highlight the Users folder. Click User in the New submenu of the Action menu to display the Select Users Or Groups dialog box shown in Figure 2-9. This is where you'll choose the users that can access components using the Administrator role.

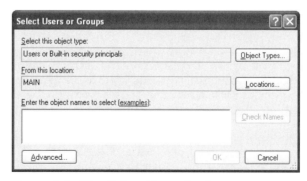

Figure 2-9 The Select Users Or Groups dialog box allows you to choose which users or groups will perform the task specified by the role.

4. Type the names of the users or groups you want to include for each role in the field provided. The example uses the Administrators group for the Administrator role and a test user for the User role. Make sure you separate multiple entries using a semicolon and use the proper form for the entries. If you want Windows to do the work, click Advanced and you'll see a Select Users Or Groups dialog box that will help you find individual users or groups.

5. Click OK. The selected users or groups will get added to the Users folder for the appropriate role in the Component Services window.

6. Repeat steps 1 through 5 for the User role. However, in this case, use your own name, a test user name, or the Users group instead of the Administrators group for the Users folder. Figure 2-10 shows a security setup that would be typical for our scenario. Obviously, any production components you create will have a more complex security setup that allows users to access the components you create in specific roles.

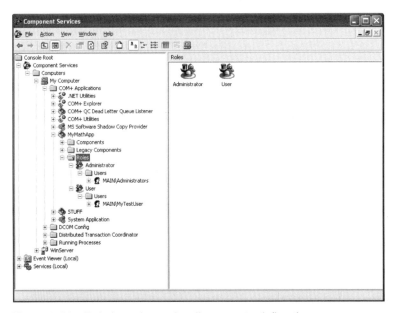

Figure 2-10 Role-based security allows you to define the access a user gets to the methods within a component based on the role that user performs.

I've chosen not to implement any form of security within the *MyMath* component because that would defeat the purpose of using the highly configurable role-based security option. If I had implemented security within the component, any change to the company structure might also mean a change to the code within the component. In most cases, you don't want to add security to your component anymore; you'll want to add security by using the Component Services snap-in.

With this change in methodology in mind, let's see what you'll need to do to add security to the *MyMath* component. First you'll need to enable role-based security. This means making a change at the application level. Right-click the *MyMathApp* entry, and then choose Properties from the context menu. You'll see the MyMathApp Properties dialog box. Choose the Security tab of this dialog box, and you'll see the security options shown in Figure 2-11. This is where you determine what kind of security an application will use.

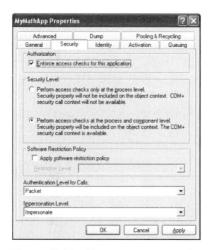

Figure 2-11 You must set security at the application level before you can use role-based security.

> **Caution** You can't use role-based security with library applications. This feature is designed to work only with server applications. Unfortunately, Windows won't protect you from adding role-based security to a library application. This means you could make settings changes that cause an application to stop working for no apparent reason. In other words, this is one setting you should check when you have a malfunctioning library application.

There are actually two settings you need to look at. First make sure you check the Enforce Access Checks For This Application option. This setting enforces security at the component, interface, and method levels. Second make sure you allow access checks at both the process and component levels. You can do this by selecting the second option in the Security Level group shown in Figure 2-11. (The figure shows the Security Level properly configured.) You need to select this option if you plan to use role-based security within your components as well. Otherwise, your components will be limited to whatever security Windows provides at the application level.

Now that we have role-based security enabled at the application level, right-click the *MyMath.MathFunctions* component and choose Properties from the context menu. You'll see the MyMath.MathFunctions Properties dialog box.

As you can see, the MyMath.MathFunctions Properties dialog box helps you to configure a relatively wide range of component options, including whether the component supports transactions. There are also options for allowing the component to engage in object pooling (normally a good idea with database components) and concurrency. Click the Security tab, and you'll see the Security tab of the MyMath.MathFunctions Properties dialog box, similar to the one shown in Figure 2-12. Notice that both the roles we've created are available for use with this component.

Figure 2-12 Windows will automatically display any roles you've created for a COM+ application at all application levels.

Remember that we have role-based security enabled, but as you can see in Figure 2-12, neither of the role-based security options are checked. With the Security tab of the MyMath.MathFunctions Properties dialog box is set as it is, no one can access the component. What you'll need to do is select the roles that you want to access the component. Let's assume the Administrator role will have full access to this component. Select the Administrator entry, and then click OK to make the change permanent.

Now, let's look at the effect of our decision at a lower level of the application. Right-click the _MathFunctions interface (located in the Interfaces folder for the application), and then choose Properties from the context menu. Click the Security tab, and you'll see the _MathFunctions Properties dialog box. Notice that we still have two options to choose from with regard to role-based security, but that Administrator appears in the Roles Inherited By Selected Item(s) list box. This means you don't have a choice about the Administrator role—anyone in this role already has access to this interface. You'll find that the same rule holds true for methods. In other words, everyone in the Administrators group can access everything this component has to offer. On the other hand, the User role still hasn't been defined.

Right-click the DoAdd entry in the Methods folder, and choose Properties. Click the Security tab. You'll see the same list of inherited roles and defined roles as before. This time, select the User role and click OK. The User role now has access to the *DoAdd()* method. Perform the same task for the other three simple math entries: DoSubtract, DoMultiply, and DoDivide.

Exporting COM+ Applications

As with COM, COM+ applications require a proxy on the client machine. The client sees the proxy as the component. Of course, the proxy merely poses as the component and passes anything the client requests on to the server. The method for creating a proxy in COM+ is different from the DCOM method. You actually create an installation program that helps avoid any messy modifications to the registry. Creating a proxy is relatively easy; the following steps show you how.

1. Open Component Services on the server. Locate the *MyMathApp* application in the COM+ Applications folder.

2. Right click *MyMathApp*, and then choose Export from the context menu. You'll see the Welcome To The COM+ Application Export Wizard dialog box.

3. Click Next. You'll see the Application Export Information page shown in Figure 2-13. This is where you'll choose the name and type of export application created. We need a proxy application, in this case, so that the installation routine will direct the *MyMathApp* requests to the server, not to the local machine.

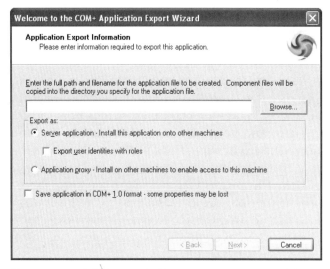

Figure 2-13 Windows will allow you to export your COM+ applications in several formats—including as a proxy application.

4. Type a name for the application you want to create. (The example uses the name *MyMathAppInstall.MSI*, but you can use any name you want.)

5. Choose the Application Proxy option.

6. Click Next. You'll see the final COM Application Export Wizard page.

7. Click Finish. At this point, the application you need is created; all you need to do is install it.

8. Locate the *MyMathAppInstall.msi* file on the client machine. You'll need to install the proxy application on every machine that will use the component in the COM+ application.

9. Right-click *MyMathAppInstall.msi*, and then choose Install from the context menu. An installation dialog will appear for a few moments, and then go away. At this point, you have access to the server-side component through the proxy application. You could create a standard Visual Basic application and use the component without ever seeing the connection between the client and server.

If you open Component Services on the client machine at this point, you'll see that there's a new application named *MyMathApp*. However, this application isn't the full-fledged application found on the server—it's an application proxy. Open the MyMathApp Properties dialog box, and you'll notice you can't change any of the application options. This application is designed to precisely replicate the server application.

Using the .NET Framework Configuration MMC Console

Working effectively with .NET means knowing how to configure the .NET Framework for optimal use. This section of the chapter focuses on the .NET Framework Configuration MMC console. This console helps you manage your .NET components and controls, work with Remoting Services, create a secure environment, and manage configured applications. Each major section of the .NET Framework Configuration console includes a Help screen and at least one link that leads to a task-oriented configuration option, as shown in Figure 2-14. The following sections provide an overview of some of the essential tasks we'll perform in this book.

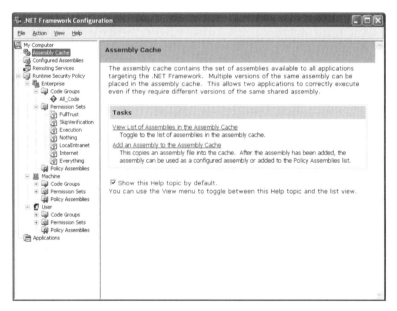

Figure 2-14 Each snap-in for the .NET Framework Configuration console provides a help screen as the starting point.

> **Note** Once you select a link on the Help screen for a particular snap-in, that link remains displayed each time you select the snap-in. To return to the Help screen so that you can select another link, right-click the snap-in entry in the Scope pane and choose View and then Help Topic from the context menu.

Managing Components and Controls

The Assembly Cache snap-in help screen displays two links. The first, View List Of Assemblies In The Assembly Cache, displays a list of assemblies in the GAC, as shown in Figure 2-15. Notice that this list includes the version number and locale information for each assembly. This information is important because sometimes an application requires a specific assembly version or locale. The public key token shows how the assembly is signed. Assemblies with the same public key token are signed by the same individual or company. You can also use this list to copy or delete assemblies in the GAC. Simply right-click the assembly in question and choose the appropriate option from the context menu.

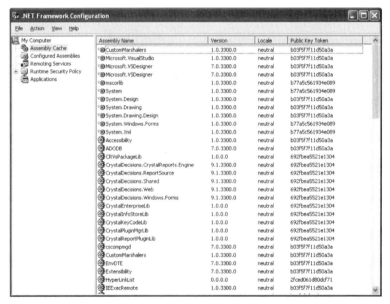

Figure 2-15 Use this list of assemblies to learn more about the content of the GAC.

The Add An Assembly To The Assembly Cache link on the help screen will display an Add An Assembly dialog box. Select the assembly you want to add, and then click Open. If the assembly has a strong name, the snap-in will add it to the GAC for you. Otherwise, you'll see an error message.

The Configured Assemblies snap-in manages the binding policy and codebase of the assemblies in the GAC. You won't see any assemblies in this list for a default .NET Framework installation (at least not as of this writing). However, you can click Configure An Assembly to add an assembly to the list. The following steps show how to configure an assembly.

1. Click Configure An Assembly in the Configured Assemblies Help screen. You'll see the Configure An Assembly wizard. This is where you'll select the assembly to configure. For the purposes of this procedure, I'll use the *MyMath* asssembly added to the GAC earlier in the chapter.

2. Select an assembly to configure. You can manually type the information or click Choose Assembly. When you click Choose Assembly, the snap-in displays the Choose Assembly From Assembly Cache dialog box. Scroll through the list of available assemblies, highlight the one you want to configure, and then click Select. In either case, the Assembly Name and Public Key Token fields will contain the information needed to identify the assembly.

3. Click Finish. The snap-in will add the assembly to the list of configured assemblies. It will then display a Properties dialog box for the assembly.

4. Click the Binding Policy tab to assign a version number binding policy to the assembly if necessary. When an application requests an assembly with a version number within the range you select, the GAC will automatically supply the assembly with the version number you provide.

5. Click the Codebases tab to assign a URI to the assembly if necessary. Whenever an application requests an assembly with a specific version number, the GAC will provide the supplied codebase.

6. Click OK. The assembly is configured.

Whenever you want to view a list of configured assemblies, click the View List Of Configured Assemblies in the Configured Assemblies snap-in. This option displays a list similar to the one shown in Figure 2-15. In this case, however, the list will contain the name of the assembly, the public key token, and the words "yes" or "no" to reflect the status of the binding policy and codebases configuration.

Remoting Services Configuration

The Remoting Services snap-in help screen provides access to just one link, View Remoting Services Properties. Click this link, and you'll see the Remoting Services Properties dialog box. To use this dialog box, select the channel you want to configure. Once you select the channel, adjust the attributes displayed in the attribute list as needed.

Defining a Runtime Security Policy

We'll discuss the issue of security several times throughout the book. However, you need to know a few things about the Runtime Security Policy snap-in at this point. First, these policies affect the common language runtime—not the policies of the system as a whole. This means that using this snap-in helps you modify .NET security without affecting the security of the rest of your machine. Second, notice in Figure 2-14 that this snap-in works at three levels:

- Enterprise
- Machine
- User

The Enterprise level is the most encompassing because it affects everyone who connects to the network. The Machine level affects only the current machine, while the User level affects only a specific user.

Each of these levels includes three folders. The Code Groups folder contains policies that affect the execution of code. For example, if you look at the Machine level, you'll find code groups for each of the zones found in Internet Explorer. Each of these zones will include one or more subzones that also have policies and so on. You can get quite specific about how code runs on a machine using these settings. To modify one of these settings, click the Edit Code Group Properties link.

The Permission Sets folder contains a list of permissions that affect local resources such as files, the network, or hardware. This folder contains entries that group the permissions by area, or you can select the Everything entry to see all the permissions. To see the settings for one of the permissions, right-click its entry and choose Properties from the context menu.

The Policy Assemblies folder contains a list of assemblies that directly affect .NET security. When viewing the contents of this folder, you'll see the assembly name, the version number, and its public key token. There aren't any configuration settings in this folder. You can, however, add or remove assemblies as needed to meet your security needs.

Summary

In this chapter, you've learned about the place of COM+ in the .NET developer's toolbox. It's still an important technology for the developer of distributed applications. In most cases, COM+ complements the capabilities that .NET provides, so combining the two makes sense for the present. Eventually, Microsoft will replace COM+ with something that uses .NET directly, but for now, you still need this technology to make some types of distributed applications work.

You've also learned about two handy MMC snap-ins. Actually, the developer should know about most, if not all, of the MMC snap-ins because they all provide handy administration functions. For example, you'll find the snap-ins provided in the Performance console handy when you want to analyze the performance of your application on various systems. If you haven't already spent time working with the various MMC snap-ins, you might want to do so now. You'll want to have a variety of tools at your disposal as you work through the examples in this book.

Chapter 3 shows you how to use COM components in your .NET application. You'll learn about several tools that come with the .NET Framework that make this job easier. Chapter 3 also helps you understand how .NET interacts with COM. Finally, you'll learn how to build COM components that not only work well with unmanaged applications, but also interact well with managed applications.

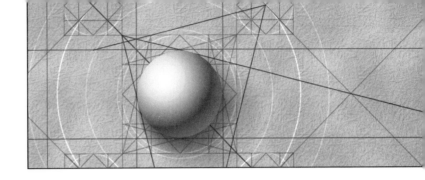

3

Using COM Components in .NET Code

Now that we have looked at the way in which COM and COM+ fit in with the .NET world, we will move on to more specific topics in the next three chapters. To start with, this chapter looks at how COM components can be used in .NET code. Microsoft has taken care to provide backward compatibility in .NET for COM so that existing investment in COM components doesn't have to be abandoned when you move to .NET. The design of .NET makes it possible to use COM components as if they were native .NET components and will even let you use ActiveX controls in the Microsoft Visual Studio .NET Toolbox.

This chapter will show you how to use COM components and ActiveX controls in .NET projects. You'll see how COM coclasses and interfaces are represented in .NET, and how marshaling works between .NET clients and COM components. In the following chapters, you'll see how to use .NET components in COM and COM+ code.

COM Interop: Principles and Mechanisms

The common language runtime needs to have metadata for all the types used in .NET code, including imported COM types. Because metadata is included as part of .NET assemblies, the metadata for COM types must somehow be held in an assembly.

Interop Assemblies

An assembly that represents a COM object to a .NET client or vice versa is called an *interop assembly*. As you've seen, there are two kinds of interop assemblies: Runtime Callable Wrappers (RCWs) that let COM objects be referenced by .NET clients, and COM Callable Wrappers (CCWs) that let .NET components act as COM objects.

There are three ways of producing interop assemblies using tools and classes provided by .NET. These three techniques, listed in order of increasing flexibility, are

- Using the tools provided by Visual Studio .NET
- Using the type library importer tool, TlbImp.exe, which is part of the .NET Framework
- Using the *System.Runtime.InteropServices.TypeLibConverter* class

You'll see how to use each of these later in the chapter.

Each of these three techniques requires that a type library be available from which to generate an interop assembly. What if the type library isn't available, or the interop assembly is incomplete or needs tweaking? In those cases, you can create interop assemblies directly, using suitable attributes in .NET code. The techniques used to do this are covered in Chapter 14, "Working with Predefined Interfaces."

Primary Interop Assemblies

Anyone can produce an interop assembly for a COM type library simply by running TlbImp.exe. If several vendors produced interop assemblies for a commonly used COM component, a client machine could end up with several interop assemblies that differ only in the details of who has produced them. This situation not only clutters machines with multiple copies of functionally identical code, it can also introduce problems. Consider the following scenario:

Two independently developed .NET applications (MyApp and YourApp) both make use of the same COM component and have generated their own interop assemblies. This shared COM component exposes the *IComp* interface.

MyApp exposes a method that needs to be passed an *IComp* reference. If YourApp calls the method, it will pass a reference to its own interop assembly. And this is where the problem rears its head: the two interop assemblies are signed with different keys—one for MyApp and one for YourApp—so .NET regards them as completely different entities. The fact that they are functionally equivalent makes no difference: MyApp will not be happy to be passed a reference to an interop assembly signed by YourApp.

A *primary interop assembly* (PIA) is a unique, master interop assembly that represents a COM component. Only the publisher of a type library can produce an official PIA, so vendors will use this mechanism to distribute interop assemblies that represent their COM types. It is important that only one primary interop assembly is produced for each COM type and that version numbering is strictly enforced. Otherwise, incompatibilities might be introduced. Note that the names and marshaling behavior of PIAs aren't required to exactly match that of the underlying COM object, so they can be changed to make interoperation work more efficiently.

Requirements of PIAs

PIAs must fulfill certain requirements:

- They must include all the COM types defined in the original COM library and maintain the same GUIDs.
- They must be signed with a strong name.
- They must use the *PrimaryInteropAssembly* attribute.
- They must avoid redefining external COM types.
- They can only reference external COM types that are themselves represented by a PIA.

Because they are designed to be used by all clients on a machine, PIAs will normally be installed in the Global Assembly Cache (GAC).

> **Note** You should always use the primary interop assembly provided by the supplier of a COM component, if one is available, rather than producing your own interop assemblies.

Generating Runtime Callable Wrappers

An RCW is an assembly generated using Visual Studio .NET or the .NET Framework that allows a COM component to be used in .NET code. As I mentioned in the section "Interop Assemblies," you can choose from three ways to generate an RCW: by using Visual Studio .NET, by using the TlbImp.exe tool, and by using the *TypeLibConverter* class from code. Each method uses the *type library importer* provided by the .NET Framework in a different way.

In the following sections, I've listed the techniques for generating RCWs in order of increasing flexibility. Visual Studio .NET, the least flexible, provides a simple way to add a reference to a COM component to a project, but it does not support all the options that TlbImp.exe gives you. Using *TypeLibConverter* from code gives you the most flexibility, at the expense of increased complexity.

> **Note** This section covers the generation and use of RCWs for non-UI COM components. The use of ActiveX controls in the Windows Forms designer is covered toward the end of the chapter in the section "Using ActiveX Controls with .NET."

Using Visual Studio .NET

Visual Studio .NET 2003 will create an RCW for COM components for Visual Basic .NET, Visual C#, and managed C++ projects.

> **Note** Visual Studio .NET 2002 won't create RCWs for managed C++ projects. If you're using the older version, you'll have to use the TlbImp.exe tool, as described in the following section.

You can create an RCW using the following steps:

1. Open Solution Explorer.
2. Right-click on either the solution name or the References folder, and select Add Reference from the context menu.
3. This will display the Add Reference dialog, through which you can add references to both .NET and COM components.
4. Select the COM tab, highlight the component you want to use in the listbox, and then click Select. If the component isn't listed, use the Browse button to search for the type library. You can select more than one component at a time.
5. When you've chosen the components you require, click OK.

The RCW will be generated, and an entry will be added to the project References folder. If you look at the properties for the new reference, you will see that the assembly name starts with *Interop.* and contains a namespace with the same name as the type library.

Details of what is placed in the interop assembly, and how COM types are represented, are covered in the section "How COM Entities Are Converted" later in the chapter.

Using the TlbImp.exe Tool

The command line Type Library Importer tool, TlbImp.exe, is provided as part of the .NET Framework and is not dependent on Visual Studio .NET. Because TlbImp.exe provides more options for generating interop assemblies than Visual Studio .NET, it can be used if you need more control over generating RCWs.

> **Note** You need to have your path correctly set up to run .NET Framework tools from a console window. If you are running Visual Studio .NET, you can open a console with the path correctly set by going to the Visual Studio .NET or Visual Studio .NET 2003 entry on the Start menu and selecting the Visual Studio .NET Command Prompt item from the Visual Studio .NET Tools menu.

TlbImp.exe converts type libraries to interop assemblies, and it always converts a whole type library at a time, which means you cannot use TlbImp.exe to selectively convert types from within a library.

Simple Use of TlbImp.exe

The simplest way to use TlbImp is to provide the name of the type library file:

```
tlbimp mytype.tlb
```

This action will produce an RCW with the same name as the type library and with a DLL suffix. If you're using type information that is merged into a COM DLL, TlbImp will detect that the output file would overwrite the input file and will stop with an error message.

Use the */out* option to specify the name of the RCW:

```
tlbimp mytype.tlb /out:myrcw.dll
```

Using TlbImp.exe Options

Table 3-1 summarizes the options that can be used with TlbImp.exe. Several options are concerned with signing the generated RCW. I'll discuss these options later in the chapter.

Table 3-1 Options Used with the TlbImp.exe Tool

Option	Description
/*asmversion:*number	Specifies the version number to be given to the assembly. A version number of 1.0.0.0 will be used by default if this argument is not specified.
/*delaysign*	Signs the resulting assembly using delayed signing, in which the assembly isn't properly signed until late in the development process. See the "Delayed Signing" section later in the chapter for more details.
/*help* or /?	Displays help for the command.
/*keycontainer:*containername	Signs the assembly with the key pair found in the specified key container. See the "Signing Assemblies" and "Installing Assemblies into the GAC" sections later in the chapter for more details.
/*keyfile:*filename	Signs the assembly with the key pair found in the specified key file. See the "Signing Assemblies" and "Installing Assemblies into the GAC" sections later in the chapter for more details.
/*namespace:*name	Specifies the namespace for the assembly.
/*nologo*	Runs the command without any startup banner.
/*out:*file	Specifies the name for the output file. By default, the name is the type library name given in the IDL.
/*primary*	Produces a primary interop assembly, indicating the assembly was produced by the publisher of the COM component. Primary interop assemblies must by signed with a strong name. See the "Generating and Installing Primary Interop Assemblies" section later in the chapter for more details.
/*publickey:*file	Signs the assembly with the specified public key. This option is used for testing and delayed signing. See the "Delayed Signing" section later in the chapter for more details.
/*reference:*file	Gives the name of a file to be used to resolve references to types defined outside the current type library.

Table 3-1 **Options Used with the TlbImp.exe Tool**

Option	Description
/silent	Suppresses the display of success messages.
/strictref	Does not import a type library if the tool cannot resolve all the references within it.
/sysarray	Imports COM-style *SafeArrays* as .NET *System.Array* types.
/transform:name	Transforms metadata as specified by the name parameter. At present, the only name supported is *dispret*.
/unsafe	Produces interfaces without .NET security checks. This should be used only where it is known to be necessary, as it introduces security risks.
/verbose	Displays additional information about the conversion process.

To generate an RCW in the same way that Visual Studio .NET does, use TlbImp with the following options:

```
tlbimp libname.ext /out:Interop.libname.dll /namespace:libname /sysarray
```

Visual Studio .NET will produce an assembly with the same base name as the type library, containing a namespace with the same name as the library. The */sysarray* option causes any references to *SAFEARRAY*s in COM interface methods to be marshaled as .NET *System.Array* types.

Namespaces

The interop assembly will define a namespace, which will be named according to the following rules:

- If neither the */out* nor */namespace* option is specified, the namespace name will be constructed from the input filename, without any extension.

- If the */out* option is specified, the namespace will be constructed from the output filename, without any extension.

- The */namespace* option can be used to override the default namespace generation.

Note that PIAs can contain the *custom* IDL attribute that specifies the namespace to be used in the interop code. This attribute will prevent the namespace from being overridden from the command line. See the section "Importing Libraries" later in the chapter for more details.

Resolving References

COM type libraries can make references to other libraries using the *importlib* IDL statement. By default, TlbImp.exe will try to locate a PIA representing the component. If it can't, it will try to find the location of the type library from the Windows registry and generate an interop assembly for the library. This is a recursive process that is continued until all references have been satisfied.

> **Note** This process, of course, requires that dependent type libraries have been registered. If the dependent type libraries don't have the correct registry entries, the importer will be unable to find them.

If you already know the location of interop assemblies for dependent type libraries, you can specify them using the */reference* option. In this example, *mytype.tlb* contains a reference to a component represented by the interop assembly *Interop.SomeComponent.dll*:

```
tlbimp mytype.tlb /reference:Interop.SomeComponent.dll
```

You can specify as many */reference* options as necessary on the command line.

The */strictref* option can be used to prevent TlbImp.exe from looking in the registry for type library information. If this option is specified, the build will fail if the tool cannot reference components by finding a PIA in the GAC or from a */reference* option on the command line.

```
tlbimp mytype.tlb /strictref
```

The */transform:dispret* Option

COM interfaces commonly use the *[out, retval]* attributes to denote an argument that can be used as a function return value. The */transform:dispret* option is used to determine how such arguments are represented in the RCW. If */transform:dispret* is not specified, *[out, retval]* arguments will be marshaled as *[out]* parameters in the RCW; if it is specified, such arguments will be converted to return values.

> **Note** This option is necessary only for pure *dispinterfaces*. The conversion of *[out, retval]* arguments to return values is automatically carried out for dual and custom interfaces.

As an example, consider the following *dispinterface* definition:

```
[
    uuid(DF8107E9-D9F0-45B6-989B-9226407D8B3B)
]
dispinterface IJAuto {
properties:
methods:
    [id(1)] void Square([in] short val, [out, retval] long* pRet);
};
```

If */transform:dispret* is not specified, the generated RCW contains the following function:

```
// IL function signature in RCW, without /transform:dispret
void Square(int16 val, out int32& pRet);
```

If the option is specified, the function signature looks like this:

```
// IL function signature in RCW, with /transform:dispret
int32 Square(int16 val);
```

Using the *TypeLibConverter* Class

You can use the *System.Runtime.InteropServices.TypeLibConverter* class to create interop assemblies in code in the same way that TlbImp.exe does from the command line.

The *TypeLibConverter* class has three major methods, shown in Table 3-2.

Table 3-2 Members of the *TypeLibConverter* Class

Member	Description
ConvertAssemblyToTypeLib	Takes a .NET assembly and converts it to a COM type library
ConvertTypeLibToAssembly	Takes a COM type library and converts it to a .NET interop assembly
GetPrimaryInteropAssembly	Returns the name and code base of the primary interop assembly that represents a specified type library

This section will use the second method, *ConvertTypeLibToAssembly*, which is the one used by both Visual Studio .NET and TlbImp.exe to generate interop assemblies. The function converts an in-memory type library into an in-memory interop assembly.

> **Note** *ConvertTypeLibToAssembly* has two overloads. I recommend you use the overload that takes a *Version* as the final parameter because the other one is primarily provided for backward compatibility with previous versions of .NET.

Listing 3-1 contains a complete C# sample program that shows how to convert a type library using *ConvertTypeLibToAssembly*. You can find this sample in the Chapter03\ConvertTlb folder in the book's companion content.

```csharp
using System;
using System.Reflection;
using System.Reflection.Emit;
using System.Runtime.InteropServices;
using System.IO;

namespace ConvertTlb
{
    class Class1
    {
        // Define RegKind enum for use in PInvoke declaration
        private enum RegKind {
            REGKIND_DEFAULT=0, REGKIND_REGISTER=1, REGKIND_NONE=2
        }

        // PInvoke declaration to access function in oleaut32
        [DllImport("oleaut32.dll", CharSet=CharSet.Unicode,
                    PreserveSig=false)]
        private static extern void LoadTypeLibEx(
            String strTypeLibName,
            RegKind regKind,
            [MarshalAs(UnmanagedType.Interface)] out Object typeLib);

        [STAThread]
        static void Main(string[] args)
        {
            // Input and output filenames
            string infile, outfile;

            // Process command line arguments
            if (args.Length == 1)
            {
                if (File.Exists(args[0]))
```

Listing 3-1 ConvertTlb.cs

```csharp
            {
                infile = args[0];
                int extPos = infile.IndexOf('.');
                if (extPos != -1)
                {
                    if (infile.ToLower().EndsWith(".dll"))
                    {
                        Console.WriteLine
                            ("Error: output file would overwrite input file");
                        return;
                    }
                    outfile = infile.Substring(0, extPos) + ".dll";
                }
                else
                    outfile = infile + ".dll";
            }
            else
            {
                Console.WriteLine("File {0} not found", args[0]);
                return;
            }
        }
        else if (args.Length == 2)
        {
            if (File.Exists(args[0]))
            {
                infile = args[0];
                outfile = args[1];
                Console.WriteLine("Infile: {0}, outfile: {1}", infile, outfile
);
            }
            else
            {
                Console.WriteLine("File {0} not found", args[0]);
                return;
            }
        }
        else
        {
            Console.WriteLine("Usage: ConvertTlb <typelib> <outfile>");
            return;
        }

        // Call LoadTypeLibEx to load the type library. RegKind_None
        // means that the type library will not be registered in
        // the Windows registry
```

```csharp
        Object typeLib;
        LoadTypeLibEx(infile, RegKind.REGKIND_NONE, out typeLib);

        // Check the call worked
        if(typeLib == null)
        {
            Console.WriteLine("LoadTypeLibEx failed.");
            return;
        }

        // Create a TypeLibConverter and an event handler for events
        // raised during the conversion
        TypeLibConverter converter = new TypeLibConverter();
        ConversionEventHandler eventHandler =
                    new ConversionEventHandler();

        // Call ConvertTypeLibToAssembly on the loaded library
        AssemblyBuilder asm = converter.ConvertTypeLibToAssembly(
            typeLib, outfile, 0, eventHandler,
            null, null, null, null);

        // Save the interop assembly
        asm.Save(outfile);
    }
}

// Define an event handler class for use by the converter
public class ConversionEventHandler : ITypeLibImporterNotifySink
{
    public void ReportEvent(ImporterEventKind eventKind,
                                int eventCode, string eventMsg)
    {
        Console.WriteLine("Event msg: " + eventMsg);
    }

    public Assembly ResolveRef(object typeLib)
    {
        Console.WriteLine("ResolveRef called");
        return null;
    }
}
```

The program first imports the extra namespaces used by the program:

- *System.Reflection* (needed for the definition of the Assembly type)
- *System.Reflection.Emit* (needed for the definition of *AssemblyBuilder*)
- *System.Runtime.InteropServices* (needed for *TypeLibConverter*, *DllImportAttribute*, and *ITypeLibImporterNotifySink*)
- *System.IO* (needed for the File class)

The *ConvertTlb* class itself starts by defining the *Reg_Kind* enum; I'll discuss the purpose of this enumeration shortly. This is followed by a prototype for the *LoadTypeLibEx* function, which is needed so that the Platform Invoke mechanism can be used to execute it.

> **Note** Platform Invoke is a mechanism for using functions in Win32 DLLs from managed code. Using Platform Invoke is covered in Chapter 12, "Interacting with Unmanaged Code."

The *Main* function in the class starts by building input and output filenames from the command line arguments, as follows:

1. If there are two arguments, use them as the input and output filenames.
2. If there is only one argument, use it as the input filename. For the output filename, use the input filename with any extension replaced with *.dll*.

Note that when a single argument is given, the code checks that the output file won't overwrite the input file. If the user gives two filenames explicitly, the program assumes they know what they're doing!

Once the filenames have been constructed, the next task is to call the Win32 *LoadTypeLibEx* to load the type library into memory. This function takes three arguments: the path to the type library, a *RegKind* value, and an *Object* reference that *LoadTypeLibEx* hooks up to the opened type library. Note the use of the *out* modifier to show that the final argument is passed by reference.

RegKind is an enumeration used in the Win32 *LoadTypeLibEx* function, and it is defined here for ease of use. This enum is used to govern whether a type library is registered when it is loaded by *LoadTypeLibEx*. The three members are as follows:

- *REGKIND_DEFAULT*, which causes the default *LoadTypeLib* rules to be followed
- *REGKIND_REGISTER*, which causes the type library to be registered when it is loaded
- *REGKIND_NONE*, which prevents *LoadTypelibEx* from registering the type library

> **Note** You should use *LoadTypeLibEx* rather than the older *LoadTypeLib* because *LoadTypeLib* always registers the libraries it loads if a path is not specified for the library.

If the call to *LoadTypeLibEx* works, the *Object* reference will act as a reference to the loaded library. Assuming all is OK, the next task is to create a *TypeLibConverter* object. When importing type libraries using *ConvertTypeLibToAssembly*, you have to provide a reference to an event handler object, an instance of a class that implements the *ITypeLibImporterNotifySink* interface. You'll find you need to do this even if you don't want to act on any notifications: passing a null reference isn't acceptable in this case. The sink interface specifies two methods: *ReportEvent*, which is called when events occur during conversion, and *ResolveRef*, which is called when a reference to another type library needs to be resolved.

In this simple program, *ResolveRef* isn't implemented and *ReportEvent* simply prints the message associated with any report it receives. In a real application, you would need to implement *ResolveRef* to return—or create and then return—an interop assembly for any type libraries referenced from the one being converted. You might want to recursively call *ConvertTypeLibToAssembly* on the value passed in, or use the *GetPrimaryInteropAssembly* method to see whether a PIA exists for the type.

Once the event handler has been created, *ConvertTypeLibToAssembly* can be called to convert the type library. Let's look at the arguments to the function: The first is the reference to the type library loaded into memory, while the second is the filename of the assembly that will be produced. Note that this file isn't written to disk by the call to *ConvertTypeLibToAssembly*; it must be written to disk as a separate step.

The third parameter indicates any flags that are to be specified for the conversion process. The possible values in the *TypeLibImporterFlags* enumeration are shown in Table 3-3.

Table 3-3 Members of the *TypeLibImporterFlags* Enumeration

Member	Description
PrimaryInteropAssembly	Creates a PIA
SafeArrayAsSystemArray	Causes *SAFEARRAY*s to be imported as *System.Array* references
TransformDispRetVals	Imports *[out,retval]* arguments as function returns
UnsafeInterfaces	Suppresses security checks on imported interfaces

In this case, a value of zero is passed because no flags are being specified.

The fourth argument is a reference to the *ITypeLibImporterNotifySink* event handler object, which cannot be null. The fifth and sixth arguments are used to specify key information if you want to sign the generated assembly. If these parameters are null, the assembly will not be signed. The seventh parameter is a *String* that will be used as the namespace for the generated assembly. If this is null, the namespace used will be derived from the name of the type library. The final parameter can be used to specify the version for the generated assembly. If this is null, the version of the type library is used.

The conversion process produces a reference to an *AssemblyBuilder*, a type that represents an assembly constructed in memory. The *Save* method on the *AssemblyBuilder* is then used to write the assembly to disk.

Assemblies and the GAC

To recap briefly, there are two kinds of assembly: private assemblies that are used by a single application, and shared assemblies that can be used by any application. Private assemblies are installed in the same directory as the application using them, and there is no requirement for them to be digitally signed. Shared assemblies must be installed in the GAC, and they must be digitally signed.

You might want to install assemblies in the GAC for several reasons:

- Security: As part of the operating system directory structure, the GAC directories usually have restricted access.

- Location: The GAC is the first place that .NET looks when resolving references to assemblies, so it is the most efficient place to locate them. It is also the one location for assemblies that can be shared by all applications on a machine.

- Versioning: Different versions of the same assembly can be installed side-by-side in the GAC.

The GAC is located under the assembly\GAC subdirectory of your Windows installation directory (for example, C:\Windows\assembly\GAC). The GAC is structured into a number of subdirectories, whose names are generated by a special algorithm.

Note that Windows Explorer knows about the structure of the GAC, so you'll simply see details of assemblies listed directly under the assembly subdirectory, as shown in Figure 3-1. You'll need to look at the assembly directory using some other tool—such as the *dir* command in a console window—to see the finer structure.

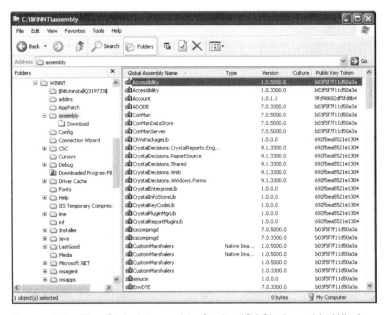

Figure 3-1 The Global Assembly Cache (GAC) viewed in Windows Explorer

Note the two versions of *cscompmgd* in Figure 3-1. You can right-click on an entry in the list and bring up the property pages from the context menu, as shown in Figure 3-2.

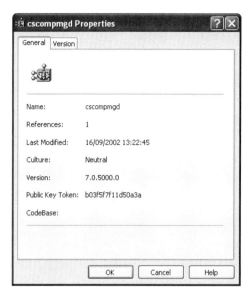

Figure 3-2 Properties of an assembly in the GAC as viewed in Windows Explorer

The properties show that the two versions of this assembly have different version numbers even though they share the same name and public key.

You should never manually copy files into the GAC. Instead, you should use one of the following methods:

- Run the Gacutil.exe tool from the command line. The use of this tool is covered in the "Signing Assemblies" and "Installing Assemblies into the GAC" sections later in the chapter.

- Use an installer that knows about assemblies and the GAC, such as Microsoft Windows Installer (MSI) version 2.0.

- Use Windows Explorer to drop assembly files into the assembly subdirectory.

The Gacutil.exe utility isn't included in the .NET redistributable, so in production scenarios, you are advised to use a suitable installer such as the Microsoft Windows Installer. The Gacutil and drag and drop methods are suitable for use in development and testing.

Strong Names

Assemblies in the GAC are required to have a *strong name*. Private assemblies, which are not required to have a strong name, are identified by three characteristics:

- The simple text name of the assembly
- The version number
- Culture information, if any

This information is sufficient to enable different versions of assemblies to live side-by-side and to maintain culture-specific versions. A strong name adds a public key and a digital signature to these three items. A key can be used as a unique identifier for a company or developer, so it is possible to determine the originator of a signed assembly. The signature is generated from the assembly file using a private key supplied by the originator of the assembly. Strong names bring several advantages to assemblies:

- They guarantee uniqueness for shared assemblies because the key they are signed with will be unique.
- Nobody else can produce a new version of a strong-named assembly unless they have the private key used to sign it.
- They provide an integrity check, with the signature guaranteeing the origin of the assembly and that the assembly has not been tampered with.

Private assemblies can also have strong names, but it is not a requirement. It *is* a requirement that shared assemblies installed in the GAC have strong names.

> **Note** Giving private assemblies strong names will incur overhead because the assembly integrity will be validated by the .NET security mechanism every time it is loaded. Shared assemblies are only validated once, when they are installed into the GAC.

When an application references a strong-named assembly, the referenced assembly's public key is included in the manifest for the application. At run time, this key can be used to verify the integrity of the referenced assembly so that the client code can be sure it's getting the right assembly and that the assembly hasn't been tampered with.

Signing Assemblies

To sign an assembly, first create a key pair using the Strong Name tool, *sn.exe*, which ships with the .NET Framework SDK. The following command will create a private and public key pair, which can be used to sign the assembly:

```
sn -k mykeys.snk
```

When you're using Visual Studio .NET, creating a signed assembly is simple. Every project, whether it is Visual Basic .NET, Visual C#, or managed C++, contains a source-code file called AssemblyInfo (with the appropriate extension). This file contains assembly-related attributes used to edit the metadata that the compiler builds into the assembly upon compilation. One of the entries lets you specify the path to a key file. Here's an example in C#:

```
[assembly: AssemblyKeyFile(@"..\..\mykeys.snk")]
```

One slightly confusing aspect is that different languages handle this in different ways. Visual C# projects include the *AssemblyKeyFileAttribute* in AssemblyInfo.cs as standard. You should specify a path relative to the output directory. In the preceding example, the file would be located in the project directory two levels above the output directory.

Visual Basic .NET does not include the attribute, but you can add it to AssemblyInfo.vb like this:

```
<Assembly: AssemblyKeyFile("..\..\mykeys.snk")>
```

Once again, the path needs to be relative to the output directory, which by default will be *obj/Debug*.

Managed C++ does include the attribute in AssemblyInfo.cpp, so you only need to edit the path.

```
[assembly:AssemblyKeyFileAttribute("mykeys.snk")]
```

Note, though, that for C++ projects the key file path is relative to the project directory, not the output directory.

If you're building an assembly from the command line using the Assembly Linker tool, AL.exe, you can specify the */keyfile* option. The tool expects a keyfile pathname relative to the directory containing the input files. The following example command line will build an assembly named NewAssembly.dll from the module MyModule.mod and sign it with the keypair stored in mykeys.snk:

```
al /out:NewAssembly.dll MyModule.mod /keyfile:mykeys.snk
```

Installing Assemblies into the GAC

The simplest way to install an assembly is to run the *Gacutil.exe* utility with the */i* flag:

```
gacutil /i myassembly.dll
```

There are a few important things to note about using Gacutil:

- Gacutil.exe can be run only by members of the Administrators group.
- If you try to install an assembly that doesn't have a strong name, Gacutil will give the following error message: "Failure adding assembly to cache: Attempt to install an assembly without a strong name."
- The installation fails if the assembly is already in the cache. If you want to overwrite the existing assembly, use the */if* flag instead.

You can uninstall an assembly from the GAC using the */u* flag:

```
gacutil /u myassembly.dll
```

Installation of an assembly using the */i* flag is simple, but there is nothing to prevent someone from removing the assembly when other applications are still depending on it. The */ir* flag can be used to install an assembly and add a reference to its count. This flag needs several parameters to be specified, as shown in the following command line:

```
gacutil /ir myassembly.dll FILEPATH c:\installer.exe "My assembly"
```

This command installs myassembly.dll using the installation application installer.exe. The final string is a description that can be displayed when the contents of the GAC are displayed using the */l* or */lr* flag. See the help for Gacutil for more details of the */ir* option.

An assembly cannot be removed from the GAC using the */u* option if it has outstanding references. The */uf* option can be used to force the removal of an assembly, even if it has outstanding references, unless the assembly was installed using Windows Installer.

Delayed Signing

The keys used to sign real-world production assemblies should be guarded carefully because the private key identifies the assemblies produced by a particular vendor. If someone gains a copy of the private key, he or she can create counterfeit components that will apparently belong to the vendor. For this reason, developers will not usually have access to private keys during the development process. Once development has finished and the assembly is ready to be released, a release build will be made that uses the private key.

Delayed signing (also known as *partial signing*) lets a developer test-sign assemblies, install them in the GAC, and use them, without needing access to the private key. The assembly is signed with the public key only, which lets the assembly use the GAC but doesn't generate a digital signature. Partially signed assemblies cannot be checked for tampering, but that should not be a problem when developing.

To extract the public key from a keypair generated by the SN.exe tool, run it again, specifying the *-p* option:

```
sn -p mykeys.snk mypublickey.snk
```

To use delayed signing in Visual Studio .NET projects, use the public key filename in the *AssemblyKeyFile* attribute and specify *true* for the value of the *AssemblyDelaySign* attribute. Here's an example from a managed C++ project:

```
[assembly:AssemblyDelaySignAttribute(true)];
[assembly:AssemblyKeyFileAttribute("mypublickey.snk")];
```

If you're using the Assembly Linker, specify the public key file for the */keyfile* option and also specify the */delaysign* option.

Generating and Installing Primary Interop Assemblies

From the point of view of .NET, a PIA is simply an assembly marked with the *PrimaryInteropAssembly* attribute. You can generate one by specifying the */primary* option with TlbImp.exe.

You need to ensure when choosing the interop assembly name and the namespace name that they don't conflict with names of existing PIAs. Remember that you can use a custom IDL attribute to specify the namespace for the interop assembly, as described in the section "Importing Libraries" later in the chapter.

Note also that PIAs can only reference other interop assemblies that are also PIAs. If your type library references other components that do not have PIAs, you will have to work around the problem. If the other components are under your control, you can create PIAs for them. If they come from third parties, you might be able to obtain a PIA from the third party. If you can't, you might need to restructure your type library to avoid references to the component. Remember that .NET clients can still *QueryInterface* your component to get interface pointers even if those interfaces are not mentioned in the type library.

PIAs don't have to live in the GAC, so Visual Studio .NET and the .NET Framework use registry entries to locate them. Use the Assembly Registration tool, RegAsm.exe, to install the registry entries needed by PIAs. At its simplest, the command would look like this:

```
regasm myPrimaryAssembly.dll
```

RegAsm adds the following entry to the registry:

```
HKCR\TypeLib\{libid}\major.minor\PrimaryInteropAssemblyName
```

Here *libid* is the GUID of the type library, and *major.minor* represents the version information. This key will have the full name of the assembly as its value, for example

```
cscompmgd, Version=7.0.5000.0, Culture=neutral, PublicKeyToken=b03f5f7f11d50a3a
```

How COM Entities Are Converted

This section describes how the entities that can appear in a COM type library are converted when processed by the type library importer.

Dealing with Attributes

Entities in type libraries can be decorated with many attributes. Some of these are directly equivalent to .NET attributes (for example, the *[in]* and *[out]* directional attributes used on method arguments). Many others have no .NET equivalent, though, so the type library importer will include them in the RCW by using three .NET attributes:

- *TypeLibTypeAttribute* contains details of COM attributes for classes, interfaces, structures, unions, and enumerations.
- *TypeLibFuncAttribute* contains details of COM attributes for interface methods and properties.
- *TypeLibVarAttribute* contains details of COM attributes for fields in structures.

If .NET client code needs to know about the underlying COM attributes, it can use reflection to query these attributes and retrieve the data associated with them.

Importing Libraries

As I mentioned, the basic unit of conversion is the type library, and a single-file interop assembly is produced for each type library processed. If a type library includes references to other libraries, additional interop assemblies might be generated for the included libraries.

If you're using Visual Studio .NET to import components, the name given to the interop assembly will be of the form *Interop.lib_name.dll*, where *lib_name* is the library name. The exact library name depends on the tool used to generate the library. If the library was specified in IDL, the name will be the name associated with the library keyword. If the library was generated by Visual Basic 6, the project name is used as the library name.

You can use the *custom* IDL attribute to specify the namespace that will be used by the type library importer. The *custom* IDL attribute specifies custom behavior using a GUID as its first parameter, which can be recognized by client tools. Here is an example, showing how a namespace can be specified for an interface:

```
// The interface will be placed in the namespace
// MyCompany.MyComponent.IMyInterface
[
  object, dual,
  uuid(3a014c8a-3772-49bb-a8c8-b84d9bf6db72),
  custom(0F21F359-AB84-41E8-9A78-36D110E6D2F9,
              "MyCompany.MyComponent.IMyInterface")
]
interface IMyInterface : IUnknown {
  ...
};
```

The first parameter, *0F21F359-AB84-41E8-9A78-36D110E6D2F9*, shows that this *custom* attribute is defining an interop namespace. You might want to use the *custom* attribute in two cases:

- When you want to prevent the namespace from being overridden during the import process. If a programmer attempts to use the */namespace* option with TlbImp.exe on a type library that uses this attribute, conversion will fail. This is useful when generating PIAs, where the namespace is fixed.

- When specifying a period-delimited namespace for a component. Type library names cannot contain periods, so using the *custom* attribute provides a way to specify a period-delimited namespace for a component.

Importing Data Types

Simple data types are marshaled according to Table 3-4, which shows the types used in IDL and Visual Basic 6. Note that COM value types and reference types (that is, pointers to value types) map to the same .NET type.

Table 3-4 Conversion Between COM IDL, Visual Basic 6.0, and .NET Types

IDL Type	VB6 Type	.NET Type	Remarks
bool	n/a	*System.Int32*	
char, small	n/a	*System.SByte*	8-bit signed integer.
short	*Integer*	*System.Int16*	16-bit signed integer.
int, long	*Long*	*System.Int32*	32-bit signed integer.
hyper, int64, __int64	n/a	*System.Int64*	64-bit signed integer. Types *hyper* and *__int64* become *int64* inside libraries.
unsigned char, byte	*Byte*	*System.Byte*	8-bit unsigned integer. *Byte* is represented as *unsigned char* inside libraries.
wchar_t, unsigned short	n/a	*System.UInt16*	16-bit unsigned integer. Type *wchar_t* is represented as *unsigned short* inside libraries.
unsigned int, unsigned long	n/a	*System.UInt32*	32-bit unsigned integer.
unsigned hyper	n/a	*System.UInt64*	64-bit unsigned integer.
float	*Single*	*System.Single*	Single-precision floating point.
double	*Double*	*System.Double*	Double-precision floating point.
VARIANT_BOOL	*Boolean*	*System.Boolean*	
void*	*Any*	*System.IntPtr*	32-bit integer representing a pointer.
HRESULT	n/a	*System.Int16* or *System.IntPtr*	*HRESULT*s are converted to signed integers because unsigned integers are not CLS-compliant.
SCODE	n/a	*System.Int32*	
BSTR	*String*	*System.String*	
LPSTR	*String*	*System.String*	
LPWSTR	*String*	*System.String*	
VARIANT	*Variant*	*System.Object*	Generic object type.
DECIMAL	n/a	*System.Decimal*	96-bit fixed-point value representing a number.

Table 3-4 Conversion Between COM IDL, Visual Basic 6.0, and .NET Types

IDL Type	VB6 Type	.NET Type	Remarks
DATE	*Date*	*System.DateTime*	
GUID	*n/a*	*System.Guid*	
CURRENCY	*Currency*	*System.Decimal*	
IUnknown*	*Unknown*	*System.Object*	Generic object type.
IDispatch*	*Object*	*System.Object*	Generic object type.
SAFEARRAY(type)	*type()*	*type[]*	Managed array of type.

A quick word about string data types: an *LPSTR* is a null-terminated string of ANSI (single byte) characters; an *LPWSTR* is a null-terminated string of Unicode (multibyte) characters; a *BSTR* is a length-prefixed string of Unicode characters and is used to represent strings in COM, especially those passed to and from Visual Basic 6. All of these map to the .NET *System.String* type.

Handling *void** Arguments

You might have noted from the table that a *void** pointer is not converted to a *System.Object* reference. The reason for this is that a *void** pointer can point to anything—code or data—and this would not be a safe conversion. You obviously need to know what the pointer represents before you can do anything with it.

System.IntPtr is a CLS-compliant type that represents a generic pointer—a *void** pointer, in C++ terms. The type is called *IntPtr* because it is an integer type large enough to hold a pointer, in the same way the *Int32* is an integer type large enough to hold a 32-bit value. Working with *IntPtr* is a topic that could take several chapters, so this section provides only an overview of how *IntPtr* works and how you work with it.

When the type library importer finds a *void** pointer—or any type it can't marshal—it will represent it with an *IntPtr*. When this happens, you'll see the following warning message:

```
At least one of the arguments for 'xxx' cannot be marshaled by the
runtime marshaler. Such arguments will therefore be passed as a
pointer and may require unsafe code to manipulate.
```

If you're working in managed C++ or Visual Basic .NET, you need to use the methods in the *System.Runtime.InteropServices.Marshal* class to work with *IntPtrs*. If you're programming in Visual C#, you can use the *Marshal* class or a language feature specific to C# called *unsafe code*.

The *Marshal* class contains a number of methods that let you read and write to the memory pointed at by an *IntPtr*. These methods are listed in the Table 3-5.

Table 3-5 *Marshal* **Class Methods for Reading and Writing Using** *IntPtrs*

Method	Description
ReadByte, WriteByte	Read or write a single byte via an unmanaged pointer
ReadInt16, WriteInt16	Read or write a 16-bit integer via an unmanaged pointer
ReadInt32, WriteInt32	Read or write a 32-bit integer via an unmanaged pointer
ReadInt64, WriteInt64	Read or write a 64-bit integer via an unmanaged pointer
ReadIntPtr, WriteIntPtr	Read or write a pointer-sized integer via an unmanaged pointer

Listing 3-2 shows how you would read a 32-bit integer from an *IntPtr* in managed C++. You can find this sample in the Chapter03\ReadPtr folder in the book's companion content.

```
#include <iostream>
using namespace std;

#using <mscorlib.dll>

using namespace System;
using namespace System::Runtime::InteropServices;

void main()
{
    // Allocate memory for an int
    IntPtr ip = Marshal::AllocHGlobal(sizeof(int));
    // Grab the pointer and write to the memory
    int* pInt = (int*)ip.ToPointer();
    *pInt = 43;

    // Read it...
    Int32 n = Marshal::ReadInt32(ip);
    cout << "n is " << n << endl;
}
```

Listing 3-2 ReadPtr.cpp

When the *IntPtr* points to an array, overloads to these methods allow you to write particular elements. The following line of code writes *newValue* at a given byte offset from the location pointed to by *myIntPtr*:

```
Marshal.WriteInt16(myIntPtr, nByteOffset, newValue);
```

IntPtr supports equality and inequality operators so that you can check whether two *IntPtrs* are referring to the same location. In C# and managed C++, you can use the overloaded == and != operators; because Visual Basic .NET doesn't support overloaded operators, you need to call the operator functions explicitly:

```
// C# code
if (myIntPtr1 == myIntPtr2)
   Console.WriteLine("They're pointing to the same place...");

' Visual Basic .NET code
If IntPtr.op_Equality(myIntPtr1, myIntPtr2) Then
   Console.WriteLine("They're pointing to the same place...")
End If
```

You can also perform pointer arithmetic on *IntPtrs*, using the +, -, ++, and -- operators, provided you convert them to the right-size integer type before you do any arithmetic. For example, look at this code:

```
// C# code
// Convert an IntPtr to an integer. For Win32, this will be a
// 32-bit integer
Int32 ip = myIntPtr.ToInt32();

// Create a new IntPtr pointing 10 bytes on
IntPtr newPtr = new IntPtr(ip + 10);
```

If the *IntPtr* is pointing to a string, you can use the *PtrToStringAnsi*, *PtrToStringAuto*, *PtrToStringBSTR*, and *PtrToStringUni* methods to read all or part of the string; these methods will return a .NET *System.String* object. The Auto version reads either ANSI or Unicode, whichever is the platform default. The *StringToHGlobalAnsi*, *StringToHGlobalAuto*, *StringToBSTR*, and *StringToHGlobalUni* perform conversion the other way, taking a *System.String*, writing the data to unmanaged memory in the appropriate format, and returning an *IntPtr*. Note that these functions allocate the unmanaged memory, so client code will need to free the memory after use.

Using *IntPtr* from Visual C#

The *unsafe code* feature in C# lets you specify unsafe blocks of code within which you can declare and use pointers. Such code is called *unsafe* because by using pointers, the programmer can do things that might go against the rules established by the common language runtime. In addition, marking blocks where pointers can be used tells the garbage collector it must not move or collect any objects referred to by pointers while the code in the block is being executed.

> **Note** For the unsafe code feature to work, you also have to specify the /unsafe compilation option. In Visual Studio .NET, you'll find this option on the solution's property pages, under Configuration Properties.

Within an unsafe block, you can operate on pointers much as you would in C++. Here is an example that shows an unsafe block in operation:

```csharp
// A simple reference type that wraps an int
class IntWrapper {
   public int val;

   public IntWrapper(int n) {
      val = n;
   }
}

...

// Allocate four bytes using the Marshal class
IntPtr ip = Marshal.AllocHGlobal(4);

// Create a reference object
IntWrapper iw = new IntWrapper(4);

// Create a value object
int n = 5;

// Declare an unsafe block so that pointers can be used
unsafe {
   // Dereference the IntPtr to get a pointer
   int* pi = (int*)ip.ToPointer();
   *pi = 10;

   // A 'fixed' statement lets you get a pointer to a
   // reference type, and means that the garbage collector
   // will not move or collect the underlying object
   fixed (int* pn = &iw.val) {
      *pn = 5;
   }

   // Obtain a pointer to a value object on the stack.
```

```
// This is not garbage collected, so no fixed statement is needed
int* pn2 = &n;
*pn2 = 6;
}
```

You can also, in true C style, use array notation where an *IntPtr* points to an array.

> **Note** For more details on how to use unsafe code in Visual C#, consult a book such as *Inside C#*, Second Edition, by Tom Archer and Andrew Whitechapel, published by Microsoft Press.

Converting Arrays

Arrays in COM are a surprisingly complex topic. This section explains how COM arrays are mapped to .NET arrays and the limitations surrounding such conversions. The first thing to note is that there are two basic types of COM arrays: *SAFEARRAY*s and C-style arrays.

I'll consider both of these types, starting with the *SAFEARRAY*. This type was introduced into COM so that arrays could be exchanged with Visual Basic, which uses array objects that contain bound information as well as data. *SAFEARRAY*s can have any number of dimensions; they also contain details of bounds and can hold any data that can be placed in a *Variant*.

If you import a COM component using Visual Studio .NET, *SAFEARRAY*s will be converted into references to *System.Array* objects.

> **Note** *System.Array* is the base class for all .NET arrays, even the built-in ones that look like they're part of the language. It provides a lot of functionality and can do anything a *SAFEARRAY* can do.

Two consequences of this conversion might not be desirable. First, *System.Array* is typeless, so code needs to discover the type of elements at run time. Second, this class can be awkward to work with because you'll need to use explicit methods and properties (such as *GetValue* and *SetValue*) instead of the shortcuts available with built-in language array types.

The */sysarray* option lets users of TlbImp.exe choose whether or not to import *SAFEARRAY*s as *System.Array* references. If this option isn't specified, the *SAFEARRAY* will be imported as a one-dimensional array of the appropriate type, with a zero lower bound. If the *SAFEARRAY* used by the COM object matches this spec, the default behavior will work fine and generate typed arrays for use in client code. Note that if you have *SAFEARRAY*s that use a lower bound other than zero, these can be imported only as *System.Array* types.

The second basic type of COM array is the C-style array, which is simply a block of memory containing the array data. Unlike *SAFEARRAY*s, C-style arrays contain no extra dimension or bound information. COM supports no fewer than four types of C-style arrays, designed to let the marshaling of array data take place as efficiently as possible. I'll look at each of these four types, starting with fixed-length arrays.

Fixed-length arrays, as the name suggests, have a fixed length, which is specified in IDL using familiar C-style array syntax:

```
HRESULT PassFixed([in] long TwoDArray[3][3]);
```

The import process converts fixed-length arrays to a one-dimensional .NET array, stored in row-major order. The *MarshalAs* attribute is added to the converted array, with the *SizeConst* parameter giving the size of the array. If the array is part of a structure, *MarshalAs* specifies *UnmanagedType.ByValArray*; if the array is a method argument, *MarshalAs* specifies *UnmanagedType.LPArray* (a *Pointer* to an array). The preceding sample IDL would therefore be converted into C# as follows:

```
public void PassFixed(
   [MarshalAs(UnmanagedType.LPArray, SizeConst=9)]Int32[] TwoDArray);
```

Note that the size is nine because the three-by-three two-dimensional array is converted into a one-dimensional array.

Varying arrays let you deal with part of an array; for example, you could pass only elements 10 through 50 of a 100-element array in a method call. Note that varying arrays must use contiguous array elements: you can't leave holes! Varying arrays are specified using combinations of the *[first_is]*, *[last_is]* and *[length_is]* IDL attributes. For example, look at this code:

```
HRESULT PassVarying([in] short start, [in] short length,
         [in, start_is(start), length_is(length)] long arr[100]);
```

There is a problem with importing varying length arrays because these attributes are used to help the generation of efficient proxy/stub marshaling code at the time the IDL is compiled by the MIDL compiler. They aren't runtime attributes, so they aren't included in the type library. This means that the type library importer won't see them, and the array will be converted as a fixed-length array. In the preceding example, the imported method would simply specify a 100-element array for the second argument.

Conformant arrays are arrays whose dimension is specified at run time, via another parameter in the method call, using the *[size_is]* IDL attribute. For example, look at this code:

```
HRESULT PassConformant([in] short size, [in, size_is(size)] long* arr);
```

Note the use of a pointer in the second argument. Once again, the *[size_is]* attribute doesn't appear in the type library, so the pointer will be imported as a pointer to a single instance. You can also define multidimensional conformant arrays, which by default will be converted as *IntPtr*.

> **Note** Pointers involving more than one level of indirection—such as those used when defining a multidimensional conformant array—will be imported as *IntPtr*.

The fourth type of C-style array is the *conformant varying array*, which enables you to pass a part of a dynamic array. As you might expect, these arrays make use of all the attributes I've just mentioned—*[size_is]*, *[first_is]*, *[last_is]*, and *[length_is]*. And once again, because the array attributes do not appear in the type library, they cannot easily be imported.

The workaround for the missing attributes problem involves changing the signature of the generated methods in MSIL. Search for "Editing An Interop Assembly" in MSDN for a description of how to edit these methods in MSIL.

Importing Classes

Importing coclasses is a reasonably straightforward process. The most important thing to note is that two .NET entities are created when COM coclasses are imported:

- A .NET class with the same name as the coclass, with Class appended. So coclass *Person* would be imported as *PersonClass*. This class actually implements the RCW and contains the interface methods the coclass implements.

- A .NET interface with the same name as the coclass. This is known as the coclass interface; it inherits from the coclass's default interface and has no members of its own. Attributes are used to associate the original interface ID (IID) with the .NET interface.

This arrangement is intended to mimic the way Visual Basic 6.0 works. Early versions of Visual Basic wanted to hide the details of COM object implementation from programmers, so it was arranged that the default interface on a coclass would be automatically exposed. The result is that Visual Basic programmers can create an object and directly call default interface methods on it, completely ignoring the fact that COM interfaces exist.

One peculiarity of this mechanism is that you are allowed to use either the RCW class or the coclass interface to instantiate components. Consider the following IDL fragment, which defines a coclass called *MyComponent* that exposes a default interface *IMyInterface*:

```
// Default interface
[
    object,
    uuid(E324E9D1-7A1F-4E8C-AC75-6483B9794F92),
]
interface IMyInterface : IUnknown {
    ...
};


[
    uuid(EDC3200D-4F09-4888-806E-72630ECA54D5),
]
coclass MyComponent
{
    [default] interface IMyInterface;
};
```

When imported, the component will be represented by

- A class called MyComponentClass

- An interface called MyComponent, which inherits from IMyInterface

When you're creating an instance of this coclass, the following two lines of C# code are equivalent:

```
// Creation using the RCW class
MyComponentClass mc1 = new MyComponentClass();

// Creation using the coclass interface
MyComponent mc2 = new MyComponent();
```

Implementing Multiple Interfaces

COM coclasses will often implement more than one interface. The type library importer will generate a class that implements all the interfaces, provided that all the interfaces are specified in the type library. If more than one interface defines a method with the same name and parameter list, generated method names on nondefault interfaces will be prefixed with the appropriate interface name. There is no problem if methods have the same name but different parameter lists, since they will be imported as overloaded methods. Consider the following IDL fragment, which shows a coclass that implements two interfaces, both of which contain a *Print* method:

```
interface IOne : IUnknown {
   HRESULT Print();
};

interface ITwo : IUnknown {
   HRESULT Print();
};

coclass MyComponent
{
   [default] interface IOne;
   interface ITwo;
};
```

When the methods are imported, the RCW will implement them as shown below (using C#):

```
public class MyComponentClass : IOne, ITwo
{
   public virtual void Print();         // Print on default interface
   public virtual void ITwo_Print();    // ITwo
};
```

Importing Interfaces

On import, COM interfaces are converted to .NET interfaces on a one-to-one basis. So that no COM-specific methods are exposed to .NET clients, all *IUnknown* and *IDispatch* methods are removed from the .NET interface.

This means COM interfaces that derive directly from *IUnknown* or *IDispatch* will be imported as .NET interfaces that have no base interface. All other inheritance relationships between COM interfaces will be preserved.

Converted interfaces will be given the *Guid* and *ComInterface* attributes. The *Guid* attribute specifies the original interface IID of the COM interface, while *ComInterface* specifies the type of the original COM interface, which can be one of the following:

- *ComInterfaceType.InterfaceIsDual*, which specifies a dual interface

- *ComInterfaceType.InterfaceIsIDispatch*, which specifies an Automation dispinterface that must be used through late binding
- *ComInterfaceType.InterfaceIsIUnknown*, which specifies a custom interface deriving from IUnknown

The purpose of this attribute is to let .NET know how it should call methods. COM interface methods are called by their offset into the interface's virtual function table. It's important to know how many of the initial entries in the table are taken up with the methods belonging to standard COM interfaces. If the interface derives from *IUnknown*, there will be three such entries, whereas for a dual interface there will be seven (the three belonging to *IUnknown*, plus the four for *IDispatch*).

For example, consider the following pair of COM interfaces:

```
[
    object,
    uuid(8a2b1366-6832-4cfe-b454-b67d1b15965d)
]
interface IAnimal : IUnknown {
    HRESULT Eat();
    HRESULT Sleep();
};

[
    object,
    uuid(815f6162-af6c-45bd-9352-bc28cadfe344)
]
interface IDog : IAnimal {
    HRESULT Bark();
    HRESULT WagTail();
};
```

These would be imported as shown by the following C# code:

```
[
    ComImport,
    InterfaceType(ComInterfaceType.InterfaceIsIUnknown),
    Guid(8a2b1366-6832-4cfe-b454-b67d1b15965d)
]
public interface IAnimal
{
    void Eat();
    void Sleep();
};

[
    ComImport,
```

```
    InterfaceType(ComInterfaceType.InterfaceIsIUnknown),
    Guid(815f6162-af6c-45bd-9352-bc28cadfe344)
]
public interface IDog : IAnimal
{
    void Eat();
    void Sleep();
    void Bark();
    void WagTail();
};
```

Because the COM interfaces are custom interfaces, they are marked as *ComInterfaceType.InterfaceIsIUnknown*. Note how the derived interface contains the base interface methods. Once again, this is done so that the correct offset into the v-table can be calculated when calling the methods.

Importing Methods

Method arguments that are not pointers are passed by value (*ByVal* in Visual Basic .NET), while those that are pointers are passed by reference (*ByRef* in Visual Basic .NET, *ref* in Visual C#). Any pointer with more than one level of indirection (for example, *IUnknown***) will be passed as an *IntPtr* because .NET doesn't support more than one level of indirection.

Methods that use *[out, retval]* parameters will be imported as functions with the appropriate return type. For example,

```
HRESULT Square([in] short n, [out, retval] long* pRet);
```

will be imported into Visual Basic as

```
Public Overridable Function Square(ByVal n As Integer) As Long
```

Importing Properties

COM objects are always accessed via interface methods. Visual Basic programmers, however, are accustomed to using objects that have both methods and properties, so COM interfaces were designed with the ability to expose methods that can be used as properties in client code. Here is a sample property:

```
[propget, helpstring("property X")] HRESULT X([out, retval] SHORT* pVal);
[propput, helpstring("property X")] HRESULT X([in] SHORT newVal);
```

Note how the property methods have the same name. Three attributes can be applied to properties:

- *propget* is used to return a value to the client
- *propput* is used to accept a value from the client
- *propputref* is used to accept an object reference from the client

When properties are imported, a .NET property is created with the same name. The *propget* methods are represented by a .NET method with a *get_* prefix; *propputref* methods are represented by a method with a *set_* prefix. How *propput* methods are converted depends on whether the interface also defines a *propputref* method. If it does, the *propput* is represented by a method with a *let_* prefix; if it doesn't, the prefix will be *set_*.

Here is how the preceding sample property appears in the IL Disassembler, ILDasm.exe:

```
.property int16 x()
{
  .get instance int16 atl1Lib.IFFF::get_x()
  .set instance void atl1Lib.IFFF::set_x(int16)
}
```

.NET properties have two accessor methods, which are used to get and set the property value. You can see how the *propget* and *propput* COM methods are implemented by the *get_x* and *set_x* methods within the property.

Importing Structures, Unions, and Enumerations

Many COM programmers are not aware of the fact that you can declare and use structures, unions, and enumerations within type libraries. These declarations can be made directly in IDL or by using a higher-level program (for example, using Visual Basic 6 to produce an ActiveX control).

Structures

Structures are imported as .NET value types and added to the interop assembly's metadata. Each field of a structure will be represented by a public field in the .NET value type. As an example, here is an IDL struct, together with the resulting .NET type:

```
// An IDL structure
struct Point {
    long x,y;
};

// C# code
public struct Point
{
   public int x;
   public int y;
}
```

If a field within a structure is a reference type (for example, a pointer), the field is imported as an *IntPtr* and marked with the *ComConversionLoss* attribute to show that type information has been lost during the import process.

Unions

IDL lets the COM programmer define unions so that one piece of storage can be represented in more than one way. .NET does not support unions, so they are imported as value types, in a similar way to structs. The type library importer uses two extra attributes—*StructLayoutAttribute* and *FieldOffsetAttribute*—to import the original layout of the union. Both these attributes are defined in *System.Runtime.InteropServices*.

StructLayoutAttribute determines how structures are laid out in memory. The runtime is usually responsible for deciding how best to lay out structures in memory, and the order in which members are laid out might not be the same order in which they are defined. *StructLayoutAttribute* is important in interoperability scenarios, where unmanaged code expects structures to have a fixed layout. The attribute takes one fixed parameter, which determines the layout type. When used for interop, this parameter will take the value *LayoutKind.Explicit* or *LayoutKind.Sequential*. Sequential layout mandates that the members are laid out in sequence, as defined. Packing can be specified to control layout.

Explicit layout is used in conjunction with *FieldOffsetAttribute* and allows the precise position of each member of the structure to be specified. Using an offset of zero for more than one field in a structure makes it possible to mimic an unmanaged union. As an example, consider the following union defined in IDL:

```
// Union composed of a short and a long
[switch_type(short)] union MyData {
    [case(1)] long l;
    [case(2)] short s;
};
```

When converted for use in an interop assembly, the value type produced is equivalent to the following C# code:

```
[StructLayout(LayoutKind.Explicit)]
public sealed struct MyData
{
    [FieldOffset(0)] public Int32 l;
    [FieldOffset(0)] public Int32 s;
}
```

Enumerations

Enumerations are supported in both type libraries and .NET.

> **Note** Enums are defined at the IL level in .NET, so they are supported by all .NET languages and can easily be used across languages.

There is no significant difference between type library and .NET enumerations, so conversion is straightforward. Here is an enumeration defined in IDL:

```
// Enum defined in IDL
typedef [uuid(46e8ae76-fd1f-4f14-a449-74a8b9b1f632)]
enum Colors {
    Red = 1,
    Green = 2,
    Blue = 3
};
```

When converted for use in an interop assembly, this enum is equivalent to the following Visual Basic .NET code:

```
<Guid(46e8ae76-fd1f-4f14-a449-74a8b9b1f632)>
Public Enum Colors
    Red = 1,
    Green = 2,
    Blue = 3
End Enum
```

Constants

Type libraries can also contain constants, but the current version of the type library importer doesn't import such constants. If you need to import constants and are able to modify the type library, you should wrap the constants in an enumeration.

Importing Typedefs

Typedefs in type libraries are imported as the underlying type. For example, consider a type library that defines a typedef *COORDINATE*:

```
[public] typedef int COORDINATE;
```

All arguments of type *COORDINATE* will be imported as type *int*. The converted arguments will have a *ComAliasAttribute* applied to them so that their original type information is not lost. This example shows how a method that took a *COORDINATE* argument would be represented in C#:

```
public void UseCoord([ComAliasName("MyLib.COORDINATE")] Int32 c)
```

If necessary, client code can use reflection at run time to retrieve the typedef name for the argument.

Importing Modules

Type libraries can contain *modules*, which are collections of global methods and constants. Modules are converted into sealed classes when imported, with constants as public members. Here is a simple example of a module containing only constants:

```
// Module defined in IDL
module days {
    unsigned short const MON = 1;
    unsigned short const TUE = 2;
    unsigned short const WED = 3;
    unsigned short const THU = 4;
    unsigned short const FRI = 5;
    unsigned short const SAT = 6;
    unsigned short const SUN = 7;
}
```

When modules are imported, a class equivalent to the following will be constructed:

```
// Imported class (C# code)
public abstract class days {
    public static const unsigned Int16 MON = 1;
    public static const unsigned Int16 TUE = 2;
    public static const unsigned Int16 WED = 3;
    public static const unsigned Int16 THU = 4;
    public static const unsigned Int16 FRI = 5;
    public static const unsigned Int16 SAT = 6;
    public static const unsigned Int16 SUN = 7;
}
```

How to Design COM Components for Use with .NET

If you are the author of a COM component that is going to be used by .NET clients, you can design (or redesign) your component so that it interoperates more smoothly with .NET. This section provides a list of guidelines to help you write components with good interoperability. I've divided the guidelines into five subjects: interfaces, data, error reporting, type libraries, and other considerations.

- Interfaces
    - Avoid manually redefining COM interfaces in managed code. This task consumes time and rarely produces a managed interface compatible with the existing COM interface. Instead, use TlbImp.exe to maintain definition compatibility.
    - Avoid defining methods in a coclass's default interface that have the same names as members of *System.Object* (for example, *Object*, *Equals*, *Finalize*, *GetHashCode*, *GetType*, *MemberwiseClone*, and *ToString*). Methods on the default interface of a component are added to the wrapper class, and if any name conflicts occur, the imported method will override the *System.Object* base class method.
    - Provide ways to explicitly release resources. Many COM components release resources when their reference count drops to zero, which occurs at the final call to *Release*. When used from .NET, however, the RCW holds a reference on the COM object it is managing and typically will not release that reference until it is garbage-collected. The .NET nondeterministic finalization mechanism prevents you from predicting exactly when this will be, so if it is important that resources are freed at a particular point, provide an explicit means to do so.
    - Avoid optional parameters in methods because C# cannot treat them as optional.
    - Use dual interfaces whenever possible because this allows early or late binding from .NET clients.
- Data
    - Use Automation-compatible types where possible. Avoid Variants, asking yourself why you aren't using a more specific type.
    - Avoid using *void** pointers to refer to interfaces. If an interface method can return a pointer to any interface, it is very common to use a *void** pointer to accomplish this:

        ```
        HRESULT GetAnInterfacePointer([in] REFIID theInterfaceId,
                  [out, iid_is(theInterfaceId)] void** pTheInterface
        );
        ```

The second parameter will be marshaled as an *IntPtr*, which is not descriptive or easy to use. It would be better to amend the IDL to use *IUnknown** instead and to specify *[retval]*:

```
HRESULT GetAnInterfacePointer([in] REFIID theInterfaceId,
        [out, retval, iid_is(theInterfaceId)] IUnknown** pTheInter
face);
```

Now the second parameter will be marshaled as a *Guid*, which can then be cast to the appropriate interface type by the client.

- ❏ Use blittable types (which have direct managed equivalents) where possible. Nonblittable types will require conversion during marshaling, and therefore will not perform as well as blittable types.
- ❏ Avoid ANSI strings if possible because it is much more efficient to marshal Unicode string data.
- ❏ Use *SAFEARRAY*s instead of variable-length arrays because of the problems with marshaling IDL arrays explained earlier. Also, wherever possible, use single-dimension arrays with a lower bound of zero. For more details, see the discussion earlier in the chapter in the section "Converting Arrays."
- ❏ Don't define structs with *SAFEARRAY* fields because the importer doesn't support them.

■ Error reporting

- ❏ Avoid returning failure *HRESULT*s for informational purposes. *HRESULT*s are mapped to exceptions so that when an interop assembly receives a failure *HRESULT* from a component, it throws a corresponding *HRESULT*. There is an overhead associated with processing exceptions, but almost no overhead is incurred by the exception handling code when no exception occurs. For this reason, use *HRESULT*s only to signal errors. In addition, *HRESULT*s are processed by the interop assembly, but because successful *HRESULT*s won't result in an exception being thrown, you effectively lose the return value.
- ❏ Always use rich error reporting from COM components, using the *ISupportErrorInfo* and *IErrorInfo* interfaces. Components written in C++ using ATL should have the *ISupportErrorInfo* check box checked on the Options page of the ATL Object

Wizard, and should use the ATL *CComModule::Error* method to return error information using *IErrorInfo*. In Visual Basic 6 code, use the *Error.Raise* method with the optional *Source*, *Description*, *HelpFile*, and *HelpContext* fields:

```
' Raise error 1000, with the source "TheComponent"
' and the specified error message.
' The last two parameters specify a help file
' and help context ID
Err.Raise 1000, "TheComponent", "There has been an error", _
    helpfile.hlp, 100
```

- Type Libraries
  - Provide and register type libraries, so that .NET programmers can use TlbImp to generate interop assemblies. Provide version and locale information in type libraries because this is propagated through to the interop assembly.
  - Avoid defining functions in IDL modules, since these are not imported when creating the interop assembly.

- Other Considerations
  - Implement *IProvideClassInfo*. Methods often contain interface pointers as arguments. The type library importer knows the type of the interface, but the type of the object that implements this interface might not be known. If a component implements *IProvideClassInfo*, the importer can query for type information; this enables it to wrap the interface pointer in a properly typed wrapper.
  - Make as few transitions across the managed/unmanaged boundary as possible because of the cost involved in this transition. This might mean redesigning the interface to your component to make calls more modular.

Responding to COM Events

This section assumes you're familiar with the way in which COM implements events using connection points, as well as the way in which .NET implements events using delegates. A brief overview of the COM mechanism follows, but if you need more information, consult *Inside COM*, by Dale Rogerson (Microsoft Press, 1997).

For more information on delegates and events, consult a book appropriate to your .NET programming language, such as *Inside C#* by Tom Archer or *Programming Microsoft Visual Basic .NET* by Francesco Balena, both published by Microsoft Press.

Connection Points

The COM connection point mechanism provides a standard way for COM clients to receive event notifications from COM objects. A client implements a callback interface on an internal component called an event sink, and the notifying object calls the interface methods as events occur. The source component publishes details of its callback interface or interfaces by marking IDL interfaces with the *[source]* attribute. This attribute indicates that the component acts as a source of calls to the interface rather than implementing the interface and receiving calls.

```
coclass MyObject {
   [default] interface IOne;
   [source] interface MyEvents;
};
```

Source interfaces are commonly dispinterfaces so that they can be handled easily by automation clients.

Connection points are implemented using two interfaces: *IConnectionPointContainer*, and *IConnectionPoint*. These two interfaces are used as follows:

- The client-side event sink queries a server object for *IConnectionPointContainer*. If the object returns an interface pointer, it is a sign that the coclass supports connection points.

- The sink uses methods on *IConnectionPointContainer* to locate the *IConnectionPoint* interface representing a specific event source interface. Since a server can support multiple outgoing interfaces, a client must match its sink to the interface identifier (IID) of a particular connection point interface.

- Once it has obtained the correct connection point object, the event sink calls *IConnectionPoint::Advise* to register its sink interface pointer. The event source holds the connection (and raises events to it) until the client breaks the connection by calling *IConnectionPoint::Unadvise*.

Handling Events from a COM Source

When the type library importer sees an interface marked with the *[source]* attribute, it generates the necessary delegates in metadata that you use in your managed client. In fact, the importer can generate several classes and interfaces to implement the connection point to the .NET transition:

- A .NET interface equivalent to the COM source interface, which has an *_Event suffix*. This interface contains the same members as the COM interface but is declared as a .NET interface.

- A delegate for each method on the source interface. These methods have an *_EventHandler* suffix.

- A class with a *_SinkHelper* suffix. This class implements the .NET interface so that .NET clients don't see the underlying COM connection-point mechanism.

- A class with an *_EventProvider* suffix. This class deals with talking to the COM component's IConnectionPointContainer interface and obtaining an IConnectionPoint interface.

> **Note** Not all of these classes and interfaces show up in the Object Browser.

Events Example

You handle events from a COM component exactly as you handle events from a .NET component. As an example, I'll show how to handle events from the Internet Explorer ActiveX control, using it as a non-UI COM component in a C# console application. In the next section, you'll see how to use this ActiveX control in Windows Forms applications.

The first step is to create an interop assembly for the component. The Explorer control is housed in shdocvw.dll, which lives in the Windows System32 directory. Once you've created a C# console application in Visual Studio .NET, you can add a reference to the component by the usual method (that is, right-clicking on the solution name and choosing Add Reference from the context menu). You'll find the control on the COM tab, under the name *Microsoft Internet Controls*. Once the interop assembly has been generated, you can examine it in the Object Browser. This is a large component with a number of source interfaces. The names of these interfaces start with *D* and end with *Events*. You can see a number of them in Figure 3-3:

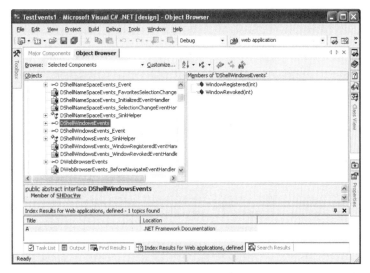

Figure 3-3 The interop assembly for shdocvw.dll, viewed in the Object Browser

The importer has generated the interfaces and classes described in the previous section. For instance, the *DShellWindowsEvents* source interface is represented by the following:

- The *DShellWindowsEvents* and *DShellWindowsEvents_Event* interfaces.

- The *DShellWindowsEvents_EventProvider* and *DShellWindows-Events_SinkHelper* private classes. Note that the Object Browser doesn't show the *EventProvider* class.

- The *DShellWindowsEvents_WindowRegisteredEventHandler* and *DShellWindowsEvents_WindowRevokedEventHandler* delegates, which handle the events in client code.

Listing 3-3 contains a sample program that uses the interop assembly to open an Internet Explorer window and navigate to a URL. You can find this program in the Chapter03\TestEvents1 folder in the companion content.

```csharp
using System;
using SHDocVw;

namespace TestEvents1
{
    class Class1
    {
        // References to interfaces on the Explorer object
        static private InternetExplorer exp = null;
        static private IWebBrowserApp brw = null;

        // Event handlers for Explorer events
        static void OnTitleChange(String s)
        {
            Console.WriteLine("Explorer event: Title changed to {0}", s);
        }

        static void OnDownloadComplete()
        {
            Console.WriteLine("Explorer event: Download complete");
        }

        [STAThread]
        static void Main(string[] args)
        {
            try
            {
            // Create an Explorer
                exp = new InternetExplorer();

            // Wire up an event handler. The name of the sink event
            // interface is DWebBrowserEvents2.
            DWebBrowserEvents2_DownloadCompleteEventHandler evt =
                new DWebBrowserEvents2_DownloadCompleteEventHandler
                    (OnDownloadComplete);
            exp.DownloadComplete += evt;

            DWebBrowserEvents2_TitleChangeEventHandler evt1 =
                    new DWebBrowserEvents2_TitleChangeEventHandler
                        (OnTitleChange);
            exp.TitleChange += evt1;

            // Navigate to a URL
            brw = (IWebBrowserApp)exp;
            brw.Visible = true;
```

Listing 3-3 TestEvents1

```
            string s = "http://www.microsoft.com";
            object o = null;
            brw.Navigate(s, ref o, ref o, ref o, ref o);

            Console.Write("Hit enter to quit: ");
            s = Console.ReadLine();

            brw.Quit();
        }
        catch(Exception e)
        {
            Console.WriteLine("{0}", e.Message);
            return;
        }
    }
  }
}
```

The program starts by creating an *InternetExplorer* object, using the wrapper class generated by Visual Studio .NET. Before doing anything with this object, I need to hook up event handlers, and I do this using the standard .NET event mechanism. Two source interfaces define events generated by the browser—*DWebBrowserEvents* and *DWebBrowserEvents2*. For this sample program, I've chosen to handle two events from *DWebBrowserEvents2*: *TitleChange*, which is fired when the text in the Explorer title bar has changed, and *DownloadComplete*, which is fired each time the download from a URL completes. The delegates for each of these events has been given a name by the import process, using the standard naming convention: the interface name followed by the event name and the suffix *EventHandler*.

Once the events have been hooked up, I can obtain a reference to the *IWebBrowserApp* interface on the Explorer object and use its standard methods to navigate to a URL. When you build and run the application, you'll see events being reported in the console window. You'll also see that the application serves to show how the import mechanism completely hides COM connection points from the .NET programmer.

Using ActiveX Controls with .NET

The definition of an ActiveX Control is any COM object that implements the *IUnknown* interface and handles its own registry entries on installation and removal. As this includes just about any modern COM object, the definition isn't very useful. In this section, I'll discuss ActiveX controls in the original sense, meaning components (often graphical) that can be used in a form-based programming environment.

GUI applications in .NET are constructed using Windows Forms, and they make use of Windows Forms controls. To the programmer, these controls look a lot like ActiveX controls, but they're implemented using .NET rather than COM. This situation is similar to what happened when ActiveX controls were first released and started to eclipse the existing Visual Basic VBX controls: they looked the same but worked very differently underneath. To ease the transition from traditional Windows GUI applications to .NET applications, Microsoft has made it possible to use ActiveX controls in Windows forms projects.

ActiveX controls are used via an RCW just like any other COM object. However, because they are usually used in Windows Forms projects, the *System.Windows.Forms* namespace contains a special class, *AxHost*, that forms the basis of RCWs used to talk to ActiveX controls. *AxHost* also takes care of interacting with the development environment so that the control wrapper can appear in the Toolbox, be dragged onto forms, and have its properties edited in the normal way.

As with plain RCWs, there are two ways to create an RCW for an ActiveX control, depending on whether you are using Visual Studio .NET or working from the command line:

- If you're using Visual Studio.NET, you can simply add a reference to a COM object as if it were a .NET object. The Visual Studio wizard will automatically generate an appropriate wrapper class derived from AxHost and add a suitable icon to the Toolbox.

- If you're building from the command line, the .NET Framework contains a tool called Aximp.exe, which generates RCWs for ActiveX controls.

Adding an ActiveX Control to the Toolbox

To import an ActiveX control into a Visual Studio .NET Windows Forms project and add it to the Toolbox, do one of two things:

- Use Add/Remove Toolbox Items from the Tools menu.

- Right-click anywhere on the Toolbox, and choose Add/Remove Items from the context menu.

Either of these methods will display the Customize Toolbox dialog, which you can use to add Windows Forms controls and ActiveX controls to the Toolbox.

To add the Web browser control used in the previous section, select the COM Components tab and scroll down until you find the Microsoft Web Browser entry, as shown in Figure 3-4. Make sure that the check box next to the name is selected, and press OK.

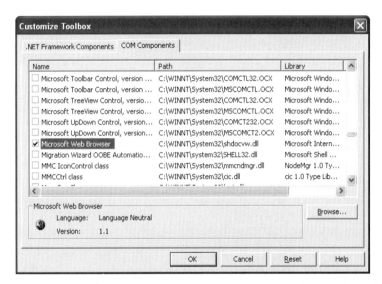

Figure 3-4 The Customize Toolbox dialog, used to add controls to the Visual Studio .NET Toolbox

You'll see that an icon has been added to the end of the list of controls in the Toolbox. Now use the icon to place a browser control on the form. There will be a pause while the control is imported and the wrapper code is generated. You'll find that two new references have been added to the project:

- SHDocVw is the interop assembly.

- *AxSHDocVw* is a wrapper that lets the ActiveX control function as a Windows Forms control.

In the code, you'll find that an object of type *AxSHDocVw.AxWebBrowser* has been created to represent the browser. You can work with the methods and properties of this object in the same way you would with any other Windows Forms control.

Using the Command Line

The Aximp.exe utility generates interop assemblies for ActiveX controls from the command line. Running Aximp against an ActiveX control DLL will generate the same two assemblies that Visual Studio .NET generates: an interop assembly, and a Forms control wrapper with an *Ax* prefix.

```
aximp %systemroot%/system32/shdocvw.dll
```

You can add references to these two assemblies to a Visual Studio .NET project or include them in command line builds using the */reference* flag.

Summary

This chapter described the features that Microsoft has implemented in .NET to allow you to use COM components in .NET applications.

You have seen how *interop assemblies* can be generated by adding a reference in a Visual Studio .NET project, by using the TlbImp.exe utility, or by using the *TypeLibConverter* class from code. The chapter covered the details of how COM types are converted, and introduced some of the issues involved in importing type libraries. You have also seen how ActiveX controls can be used in Windows Forms projects, just as if they were Windows Forms controls. At this point, you should be able to take an existing COM component, and use it in a .NET application.

The next chapter will show you how to do the opposite—to use a .NET component from a COM client. Although this scenario will not be as common as the one we have covered in this chapter, it provides a way to extend COM-based applications using the features available in Visual Studio .NET and the .NET Framework.

4

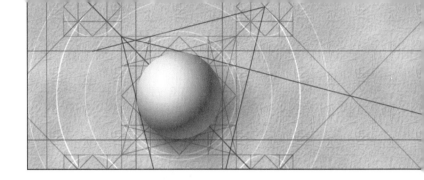

Using .NET Components in COM Applications

Chapter 3 showed you how COM objects can be used in .NET code and how using COM objects facilitates the process of transitioning from COM-based code to .NET applications. This chapter will show how you can also present .NET components as COM objects so that they can be used in COM client code.

The COM Callable Wrapper

You saw in Chapter 3 how the Runtime Callable Wrapper (RCW) wraps COM components to expose them to .NET. This chapter looks at COM Callable Wrappers (CCWs), which are used to wrap .NET components to expose them to COM client code.

There is exactly one COM Callable Wrapper object per .NET object, although the CCW can be used by multiple COM clients at any one time. The .NET object can be directly used by other .NET clients at the same time as it's being used by the CCW, as shown in Figure 4-1.

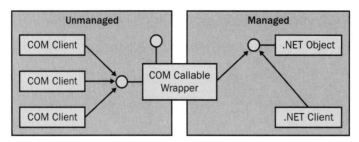

Figure 4-1 A COM Callable Wrapper (CCW) can be used by multiple COM clients.

Because .NET components know nothing of COM or the rules that COM objects must obey, the CCW handles all the low-level operations that must be handled by COM components, which includes handling object identity, object lifetime, and COM interface issues.

Object Identity

COM Callable Wrappers are created on the unmanaged heap. They are created this way so that client code can refer to interface pointers directly and to ensure interface pointers on the CCW obey the COM rules for interfaces (for example, the rule that an object must use the same pointer for an interface throughout the lifetime of the component).

Another identity-related aspect of CCWs is that they expose an *IUnknown* interface, which can be used as the COM identity for the .NET object. The actual .NET component referenced by the CCW is allocated on the managed heap as usual, and the garbage collector can move it around in memory as necessary. Thus, without CCWs, .NET components would break the COM identity rule, which requires an object to return the same *IUnknown* pointer for its lifetime.

Object Lifetime

COM rules state that COM objects should maintain a reference count, which reflects the number of interface pointers being used by clients. When a client has finished with an interface pointer, it signals the fact by calling the interface's *Release* method, which causes the COM object to decrement the reference count. When the reference count drops to zero, no clients hold pointers on the object and the object can terminate itself. Note that it's up to the COM component to manage its own lifetime.

In contrast, the lifetimes of .NET components are managed by the common language runtime, which keeps track of references held by clients. When there are no more client references, the component can be reclaimed by the garbage collector. In the .NET world, it isn't the responsibility of the component to manage its own lifetime.

The CCW acts as a COM object, with a reference count that reflects the interfaces handed out to COM clients. It also holds a reference on the .NET component. When the CCW has no more COM clients, its reference count drops to zero; at this point, it releases the reference it holds on the .NET component.

Standard COM Interfaces on .NET Components

As well as exposing the methods supported by the .NET component, the CCW will also expose a number of common COM interfaces that clients will expect to find on a COM object, as shown in Figure 4-2.

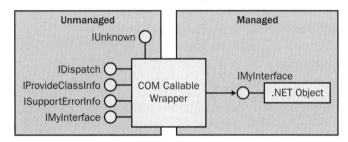

Figure 4-2 A COM Callable Wrapper (CCW) implements a number of standard COM interfaces.

The COM interfaces that are always implemented by a CCW are listed in Table 4-1.

Table 4-1 COM Interfaces Always Implemented by CCWs

Interface	Description
IUnknown	Provides the fundamental lifetime management and interface navigation functionality for COM interfaces.
IDispatch	Provides a mechanism for late binding to objects.
IProvideClassInfo	Provides a way for clients to obtain an *ITypeInfo* interface pointer on an object.
ISupportErrorInfo	Enables client code to determine whether a COM object supports the *IErrorInfo* interface.
IErrorInfo	Provides rich error information. All .NET components support this interface, passing *GUID_NULL* for the ID of the interface that raised the error.
ITypeInfo	Provides type information for the class.

In addition, several other interfaces can be exposed, as listed in Table 4-2.

Table 4-2 COM Interfaces Sometimes Implemented by CCWs

Interface	Description
IDispatchEx	If the .NET component implements the *IExpando* interface, the CCW will implement *IDispatchEx*. This provides an extension to *IDispatch* that allows enumeration, addition, deletion, and case-sensitive calling of members.
IConnectionPointContainer and *IConnectionPoint*	These interfaces will be implemented if the .NET component is a source of events. See the section "Exposing .NET Events in COM" later in the chapter for more details.
IEnumVARIANT	This interface provides a COM mechanism for iterating over collections and will be implemented by the CCW if the .NET component implements the *IEnumerable* .NET interface.

A .NET component can override the standard implementation of any of these interfaces (except *IDispatch* and *IUnknown*) by providing a custom implementation. The CCW will always provide the implementation of *IDispatch* and *IUnknown*.

Custom Interfaces on .NET Components

All access to COM objects is via interface methods. It follows that for .NET components to be exposed as COM components, the methods implemented by the .NET component must be exposed using an interface. How this is done depends on whether the .NET component implements its methods directly or via .NET interfaces.

If a .NET class implements interfaces, those interfaces will be exported as COM interfaces. This process is shown in Figure 4-2, where the .NET component implements *IMyInterface*. This interface is in turn implemented by the CCW and is accessible to COM clients. The conversion process applied to .NET interfaces to expose them to COM clients is detailed in the section "Exporting Interfaces" later in the chapter.

The Class Interface

Where a .NET class implements methods directly, the export process can create an interface through which to make the class methods visible. This interface is called the *class interface*, and by default the export process will generate a pure dispatch interface (a *dispinterface*) as the class interface. The name of this interface will be the name of the class with a leading underscore (for example *_Car* for a class called *Car*).

The type of interface generated for the class interface, and even determining whether it is generated at all, can be controlled by using the *ClassInterface* attribute on .NET classes. Examples in the section "Generating and Using COM Callable Wrappers" later in the chapter will show this attribute in use, as well as show what the generated class interface looks like.

Problems with Using the Class Interface

Although using the class interface makes it easy for .NET programmers to expose .NET components as COM components, you need to be aware of possible problems.

The COM interface rules state that an interface is immutable once it has been defined—it must not change its layout or composition. The class interface, however, is generated automatically from the .NET class definition, so the layout and composition of the interface could change if the makeup of the class is changed.

COM client code is normally written to assume that interfaces won't change, so if the evolution of a .NET component causes changes in the generated class interface, this could end up breaking client code. To get around this problem, switch off the generation of a class interface and define .NET interfaces for the methods you want exposed to COM.

In addition, you should beware of caching the dispatch IDs (*dispIds*) assigned to members in class interfaces. If the layout of the class changes, the dispIds assigned to members might change as well. This isn't a problem for late-bound clients, which discover dispIds at run time, but it might break client code that relies on compile-time caching of IDs.

The way around this problem is to apply the *ClassInterfaceType.Auto-Dispatch* attribute to the interface. This technique generates a dispinterface for the class interface, but it prevents the description of the dispatch interface from being placed in the type library. The lack of interface information in the type library means that client code cannot cache dispIds at compile time.

> **More Info** These problems with dispatch IDs mean that the class interface is most useful for purely late-bound COM clients, such as scripting languages. These clients always query for the dispatch IDs of interface members at run time, so it doesn't matter to them whether these IDs have changed.

Finally, if you do use the class interface, be careful using dual class interfaces (specified using the *ClassInterfaceType.AutoDual* attribute). A description of the interface will appear in the generated type library, which could encourage client code to cache dispIds. In addition, client code can break when dual interfaces are used if changes are made to the base class of the .NET component.

Generating and Using COM Callable Wrappers

There are several steps involved in exporting a .NET component so that it can be used from COM:

1. Add any necessary attributes to the .NET code.
2. Build the assembly.
3. Optionally, create a type library.
4. Sign it with a strong name.
5. Provide the requisite COM-related registry entries.

Each of these steps is discussed in the sections that follow.

Using COM-Related Attributes

This section discusses how attributes are used to control the way in which .NET types are exposed as COM components.

The *ClassInterface* Attribute

The *ClassInterface* attribute governs how the class interface is generated for a type. The *ClassInterface* attribute takes a *ClassInterfaceType* as its one parameter. The *ClassInterfaceType* member used determines the type of class interface created. The members of the *ClassInterfaceType* enumeration and their associated class interfaces are listed in Table 4-3.

Table 4-3 **Members of the *ClassInterfaceType* Enumeration**

Member	Description
AutoDispatch	A pure dispatch interface will be used as the class interface. This type of interface supports only late binding from COM clients.
AutoDual	A dual interface will be used as the class interface. This type of interface can support both early and late binding from COM clients.
None	No class interface will be created when the class is exported.

The *Auto* prefix to *AutoDispatch* and *AutoDual* emphasizes that the runtime automatically generates the interface details.

When you generate a dual class interface by specifying *ClassInterfaceType.AutoDual*, a full interface definition is placed in the type library, complete with autogenerated dispIds. For example, consider this class in Visual Basic .NET:

```
' A VB.NET class that inherits from System.Object by default
Imports System.Runtime.InteropServices
<ClassInterface(ClassInterfaceType.AutoDual)> _
Public Class Class1
    Public Function Square(ByVal n As Integer) As Long
        Return n * n
    End Function

    Public Sub Sub1()
    End Sub
End Class
```

The class interface generated for this class will contain all the class members:

```
[
   odl, uuid(FEDF4CC0-E0ED-3DC4-ABE7-E5B4BBC78D84),
   hidden, dual, nonextensible, oleautomation,
   custom(0F21F359-AB84-41E8-9A78-36D110E6D2F9, ExportVb.Class1)
]
interface _Class1 : IDispatch {
   [id(00000000), propget,
         custom(54FC8F55-38DE-4703-9C4E-250351302B1C, 1)]
   HRESULT ToString([out, retval] BSTR* pRetVal);
   [id(0x60020001)]
   HRESULT Equals([in] VARIANT obj,
         [out, retval] VARIANT_BOOL* pRetVal);
   [id(0x60020002)]
   HRESULT GetHashCode([out, retval] long* pRetVal);
   [id(0x60020003)]
   HRESULT GetType([out, retval] _Type** pRetVal);
   [id(0x60020004)]
   HRESULT Square(
         [in] long n, [out, retval] int64* pRetVal);
   [id(0x60020005)]
   HRESULT Sub1();
};
```

Note how the interface definition also includes all the members of the *System.Object* base class. Remember that including the dispIds in the type library might be problematical if the class layout changes and client code caches dispIds.

The coclass generated for *Class1* uses the class interface as the default interface and also contains a class interface for the *Object* base class. As the following code shows, all coclasses that represent .NET types will contain the _*Object* interface because they all derive from *System.Object*:

```
[
  uuid(3FB70B8A-01EE-3728-AF80-802D1E3A2726),
  version(1.0),
  custom(0F21F359-AB84-41E8-9A78-36D110E6D2F9, ExportVb.Class1)
]
coclass Class1 {
  [default] interface _Class1;
  interface _Object;
};
```

ClassInterfaceType.AutoDispatch creates a dispinterface in the type library, but it omits the definitions of the interface methods. This means the interface can only be used late bound, using the *GetIdsOfNames* and *Invoke* methods on *IDispatch* to discover and invoke methods. As an example, if the *ClassInterfaceType* is changed to *AutoDispatch* on the Visual Basic .NET class in the previous example, the following class interface definition is generated:

```
[
   odl, uuid(FEDF4CC0-E0ED-3DC4-ABE7-E5B4BBC78D84),
   hidden, dual, oleautomation,
   custom(0F21F359-AB84-41E8-9A78-36D110E6D2F9, ExportVb.Class1)
]
interface _Class1 : IDispatch {
};
```

ClassInterfaceType.None prevents a class interface from being generated for a class. This is useful when all methods are exposed via implemented interfaces, in which case there is no requirement for an interface to represent the class itself. Consider the following Visual Basic .NET class, which exposes one function via an interface:

```
Public Interface IMyInterface
    Function Square(ByVal n As Integer) As Long
End Interface

<ClassInterface(ClassInterfaceType.None)> _
Public Class Class2
    Implements IMyInterface

    Public Function Square(ByVal n As Integer) As Long _
      Implements IMyInterface.Square
```

```
      Return n * n
   End Function
End Class
```

The export process will create a coclass and interface definition as follows:

```
[
  odl, uuid(1C60158D-625D-3699-9F90-22653CF8F6F3),
  version(1.0), dual, oleautomation,
  custom(0F21F359-AB84-41E8-9A78-36D110E6D2F9, ExportVb.IMyInterface)
]
interface IMyInterface : IDispatch {
    [id(0x60020000)]
    HRESULT Square([in] long n, [out, retval] int64* pRetVal);
};

[
  uuid(0D499842-1CF8-30A5-9504-8EBDA1E5C055),
  version(1.0),
  custom(0F21F359-AB84-41E8-9A78-36D110E6D2F9, ExportVb.Class2)
]
coclass Class2 {
    interface _Object;
    [default] interface IMyInterface;
};
```

Note how the coclass does not have a class interface, and how the coclass's default interface is now *IMyInterface* rather than the class interface.

The *InterfaceType* Attribute

The *InterfaceType* attribute controls how a .NET interface is exposed to COM as a dispinterface, a dual interface, or an *IUnknown*-derived custom interface. The use of this attribute is covered in the section "Exporting Interfaces" later in this chapter.

The *Guid* and *ProgId* Attributes

These two attributes can be used to override the generation of default GUID and progID values for exported .NET types. GUIDs will automatically be generated for classes and interfaces that are exposed to COM, unless you chose to specify a particular GUID using the *Guid* attribute, as shown in the following Visual Basic .NET code fragment:

```
<Guid(f7291cfb-6b3a-40e7-a9a7-fc4c444a0a08)> _
Public Class MyExportedClass
   ...
End Class
```

A progID will also normally be generated, based on the namespace and typename, but there are restrictions on COM progIDs. For instance, they must be fewer than 40 characters long and not contain any punctuation other than periods. If the names of the namespaces and types you want to export would generate invalid progIDs, you can use the *ProgId* attribute to specify a valid alternative:

```
<Guid(f7291cfb-6b3a-40e7-a9a7-fc4c444a0a08), ProgId("MyStuff.Exported")> _
Public Class MyExportedClass
   ...
End Class
```

The *ComVisible* Attribute

The *ComVisible* attribute is used to control the visibility of .NET assemblies, interfaces, classes, and class members when a type library is produced. By default, public classes and class members are exported to the type library. By using *ComVisible*, the type library exporter can be prevented from exporting selected symbols or classes, as shown in the following Visual Basic .NET example:

```
' This method will not be visible to COM clients
<ComVisible(False)> _
Public Sub Sub1()
   ...
End Sub
```

Applying *ComVisible(false)* to an assembly hides all the types within that assembly. If you do this, you can then use *ComVisible* to make selected types within the assembly visible. Applying *ComVisible(false)* to a type hides all the members of that type, and you cannot selectively make members visible using *ComVisible(true)*. Applying *ComVisible(false)* to an interface means that the type doesn't support it as far as COM is concerned (that is, *QueryInterface* calls for the interface will fail).

The *AutomationProxy* Attribute

Although many COM components will use a custom proxy/stub dynamic-link library (DLL) for marshaling, you can delegate this task to a built-in system marshaler known as the *Automation marshaler* or *Universal marshaler*. The *AutomationProxy* attribute can be applied to assemblies as well as classes and interfaces, and it governs whether the Automation marshaler is used. The default is for a custom proxy to be used, but by using *AutomationProxy* with a *true* argument, the Automation marshaler can be chosen:

```
' This Visual Basic .NET class will use the Automation marshaler
```

```
<AutomationProxy(True)> _
Public Class MyClass
    ...
End Class
```

The *IDispatchImpl* Attribute

When you're exposing .NET types to COM using dual interfaces or dispinterfaces, something has to provide an implementation for the standard *IDispatch* interface methods. There are two alternatives: COM can be asked to supply one via the *CreateStdDispatch* API, or the runtime can use its own implementation. The internal implementation uses reflection where possible, so a type library is seldom required. Note that there are some minor differences in operation between the internal implementation and the COM implementation, which is designed for maximum compatibility with existing COM client code. As an example, the internal implementation will let you pass a signed integer where an unsigned one is expected, which the COM version will not do.

The default behavior is to use the internal implementation provided by the runtime, but if you find problems using late-bound Automation interfaces that you suspect are due to the *IDispatch* implementation, you can use this attribute to try using the COM *IDispatch* implementation.

By using the *IDispatchImpl* attribute, you can control which implementation is used by providing one of the following values as the parameter to *IDispatchImpl*:

- *IDispatchImplType.CompatibleImpl* means that a COM-supplied implementation will be used. The runtime will pass the type information for the object to the *CreateStdDispatch* API.

- *IDispatchImplType.InternalImpl* means that the runtime's own implementation will be used. This is the default.

- *IDispatchImplType.SystemDefinedImpl* means that the runtime will choose which implementation will be used, and has the same effect as specifying *InternalImpl*.

Here's an example showing how to use this attribute with a Visual C# class:

```
// This class will use the COM IDispatch implementation
[IDispatchImpl(IDispatchImplType.CompatibleImpl)]
public class MyClass
{
    ...
}
```

The *ComRegisterFunction* and *ComUnregisterFunction* Attributes

When registering a .NET assembly for COM use, the export process adds a standard set of COM-related registry entries. If you need to place custom information in the registry when a .NET class is exported, you can use the *ComRegisterFunction* attribute to specify a shared function (static function in C++ and C#), which will be called when the assembly is registered. This gives a .NET type a way to participate in the registration process. Here's an example in Visual Basic .NET:

```
Public Class ExportedToCom
    <ComRegisterFunction()> _
    Public Shared Sub TheRegistrationFunction(t As Type)
      ...
    End Sub
End Class
```

The function has a single argument of type *Type*, which is used to denote the type of object for which registration is required. As you will see later in the section "Hosting Windows Forms Controls in ActiveX Containers," this argument is used for obtaining details of the assembly to be registered. You can manipulate the registry using the *Registry* and *RegistryKey* classes in the *Microsoft.Win32* namespace.

It is a requirement that COM types handle both the insertion and removal of their registry data, so if you implement a registration function using *ComRegisterFunction*, you must also implement a matching method that removes the registry entries and tag it with the *ComUnregisterFunction* attribute. Once again, the function is shared and takes a *Type* as its argument:

```
Public Class ExportedToCom
    <ComRegisterFunction()> _
    Public Shared Sub TheRegistrationFunction(t As Type)
      ...
    End Sub

    <ComUnregisterFunction()> _
    Public Shared Sub TheUnregistrationFunction(t As Type)
      ...
    End Sub
End Class
```

Creating a Type Library

Creating a type library for a .NET component is an optional step because some COM components don't provide one. There are three ways to create a type library:

- Use the type library exporter tool, TlbExp.exe.
- Use the assembly registration tool, RegAsm.exe.
- Use the *System.Runtime.InteropServices.TypeLibConverter* class.

Command-Line Tools

The TlbExp.exe tool is run from the command line to generate type libraries from .NET assemblies. The command line has the general form

```
tlbexp assemblyFile [options]
```

where *assemblyFile* is the name of a file containing an assembly. Table 4-4 shows the options that can be used with this command.

Table 4-4 Flags Supported by TlbExp.exe

Option	Description
/help or */?*	Provides help on the options supported by the tool.
/names:file	Allows the user to control the capitalization of names in the generated type library by specifying a text file. Each line of the file should contain a name that occurs in the type library.
/nologo	Runs the tool without a startup banner.
/out:file	Specifies the name of the output type library file. If omitted, the tool uses the assembly name with a *.tlb* extension. Note that the assembly name might not be the same as the name of the file containing the assembly.
/silent	Suppresses the output of informational messages.
/verbose	Displays a list of referenced assemblies for which type libraries also need to be generated.

If the file myfile.dll contains an assembly called *MyType*, the following command line will generate a type library called *MyType.tlb*:

```
tlbexp myfile.dll
```

The */out* option can be used to specify the output filename:

```
tlbexp myfile.dll /out:myfile.tlb
```

RegAsm.exe is used to register .NET components as COM objects, and it can also be used to generate a type library. The command line has the general form

```
regasm assemblyFile [options]
```

where *assemblyFile* is the name of a file containing an assembly. Table 4-5 shows the options that can be used with the RegAsm.exe command.

Table 4-5 **Flags Supported by RegAsm.exe**

Option	Description
/codebase or */c*	Creates a codebase entry in the registry. This can be used to locate assemblies that aren't installed in the Global Assembly Cache (GAC). If the assembly is installed in the GAC, you don't need to use this option. Note that */codebase* can be used only on assemblies that have strong names.
/help or */?*	Provides help on the options supported by the tool.
/nologo	Runs the tool without a startup banner.
/regfile:file or */r:file*	Causes RegAsm.exe to generate a .reg file that contains the registry entries for the class. No changes will be made to the registry when this flag is used. Note that this option cannot be used in conjunction with the */tlb* or */u* option.
/silent or */s*	Suppresses the output of informational messages.
/tlb[:file] or */t[:file]*	Causes RegAsm.exe to generate a type library for the assembly. If no filename is specified, the assembly name will be used as the base for the type library filename.
/unregister or */u*	Causes RegAsm.exe to remove the registry entries for the classes found in the assembly.
/verbose	When used in conjunction with the */tlb* option, RegAsm.exe displays a list of referenced assemblies for which type libraries also need to be generated.

As an example of RegAsm.exe usage, if the file myfile.dll contains an assembly called *MyType*, the following command line will register the assembly and generate a type library called *MyType.tlb*:

```
regasm myfile.dll /tlb
```

The */tlb* option can be used to specify the output filename:

```
regasm myfile.dll /tlb:myfile.tlb
```

Using *TypeLibConverter*

The *System.Runtime.InteropServices.TypeLibConverter* class can be used to generate a type library from within code, using the *ConvertAssemblyToTypeLib* method. The Visual C# example program in Listing 4-1 shows how this method can be used to create a type library from a simple console application. You can find this code in the Chapter04\Converter folder of the companion content. The companion content can be downloaded from the Web at *http://www.microsoft.com/mspress/books/6426.asp*.

```csharp
using System;
using System.Reflection;
using System.Reflection.Emit;
using System.Runtime.InteropServices;

// Define a managed equivalent for the ITypeLib interface
[
    ComImport,
    Guid("00020406-0000-0000-C000-000000000046"),
    InterfaceType(ComInterfaceType.InterfaceIsIUnknown),
    ComVisible(false)
]
public interface ITypeLibInterface {
    void CreateTypeInfo();
    void SetName();
    void SetVersion();
    void SetGuid();
    void SetDocString();
    void SetHelpFileName();
    void SetHelpContext();
    void SetLcid();
    void SetLibFlags();
    void SaveAllChanges();
}

public class Converter {
    public static void Main() {
        // Create assembly, converter and callback objects
        Assembly asm = Assembly.LoadFrom("Account.dll");
        TypeLibConverter converter = new TypeLibConverter();
        ConversionEvents eventHandler = new ConversionEvents();

        // Do the conversion
        ITypeLibInterface typeLib =
                (ITypeLibInterface)converter.ConvertAssemblyToTypeLib(
                    asm, "MyTypeLib.tlb", 0, eventHandler);

        // Save the library
        typeLib.SaveAllChanges();
    }
}
```

Listing 4-1 Converter.cs

```
public class ConversionEvents : ITypeLibExporterNotifySink {
  public void ReportEvent(ExporterEventKind eventKind,
                          int eventCode, string eventMsg) {
    Console.WriteLine("Event: " + eventMsg);
  }

  public Object ResolveRef(Assembly asm) {
    // Resolve the reference here and return a correct type library
    return null;
  }
}
```

If you have read Chapter 3, you'll notice that using *ConvertAssemblyToTypeLib* parallels the use of the *ConvertTypeLibToAssembly* method to import COM type libraries for use in .NET code. The function returns a reference to an object that implements the COM *ITypeLib* interface, so you need to define an equivalent .NET interface to act as the return type. Note that the name of the interface isn't significant, as long as it has the correct interface ID. Note also the attributes on this interface:

- *ComImport* shows this interface has been previously defined in COM so that .NET doesn't regard it as a completely new .NET interface definition.

- *Guid* specifies the interface ID for the *ITypeLib* interface.

- *InterfaceType* defines the interface as being derived from *IUnknown*.

- *ComVisible* says this interface should not be visible to COM in the event that the assembly containing the interface definition is exported as a type library.

The *TypeLibConverter* class will fire events during conversions, and you need to supply an object to act as a sink for these events. Note that you cannot pass a null reference for this parameter. The callback class must implement the *ITypeLibExporterNotifySink* interface, with its two members *ReportEvent* and *ResolveRef*. *ReportEvent* will be called whenever an event is generated by the conversion process, and in this example simply prints a message. If a reference is found to another assembly, *ResolveRef* will be called so that the callback object can return a reference to the correct type library for the assembly. In this example, there are no embedded references, so this function can return null.

The *ConvertAssemblyToTypeLib* method takes four arguments: an *Assembly* object representing the assembly, a string representing the name of the generated type library, optional flags to control the export process, and a reference to a callback handler. Note that the conversion process doesn't save the type library information in the file, so it is necessary to call *SaveAllChanges* once conversion has finished.

Signing the Assembly

.NET component assemblies must be signed with a strong name if they are to be used as COM components. Signing assemblies with strong names has been covered in detail in Chapter 3, in the section "Assemblies and the GAC."

Registering the Component

COM uses entries in the registry to obtain information about component location and capability. For a .NET component to be usable by COM, you need to ensure that the correct COM-related registry entries are available. There are three ways you can do this:

- If you are using Visual Studio .NET, you can use the Register For COM Interop option in the Project Settings dialog to automatically register a component. This option is shown in Figure 4-3.

- Use RegAsm.exe, from the command line. This option was discussed in the last section.

- Use the *System.Runtime.InteropServices.RegistrationServices* class to register the assembly from code.

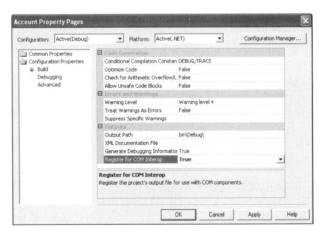

Figure 4-3 Setting the Register For COM Interop option to True will cause a component to be registered for use by COM clients.

The *System.Runtime.InteropServices.RegistrationServices* class can be used to register and unregister components by means of its *RegisterAssembly* and

UnregisterAssembly methods. These two methods are simple to use because they only need to be passed a reference to an *Assembly* object. The *RegisterAssembly* method takes a second argument that can be used to create a codebase entry in the registry, which enables the CLR to locate components that aren't registered in the GAC. The following code fragments show how these methods can be called in Visual Basic .NET:

```
' Load an assembly
Dim asm As [Assembly]
asm = [Assembly].LoadFrom("MyAssembly.dll")

' Create a registration object and register the assembly
Dim rs As new RegistrationServices()
rs.RegisterAssembly(asm, AssemblyRegistrationFlags.None)
```

Using .NET Components from COM Client Code

From the perspective of the programmer, using .NET components in unmanaged code is exactly the same as using other COM components: the same mechanisms are used to access the COM type information and create instances of coclasses.

The difference between using COM components and .NET components lies in the way the .NET components have to be registered before use. The following example will show how to register a .NET component, and then how to use it in COM client code.

The Sample Component

The *LittleString* class exposes a simple string type to COM clients. The class stores a string internally, and implements the *ToUpper*, *ToLower*, and *SubString* methods, delegating the operations to the members of *System.String*. Listing 4-2 contains an example in Visual C#. You can find this sample in the Chapter04\LittleString folder in the book's companion content.

```
using System;
using System.Runtime.InteropServices;

// Auto-generated GUID, dual interface
[InterfaceType(ComInterfaceType.InterfaceIsDual)]
public interface IString {
    string Text { get; set; }
```

Listing 4-2 LittleString.cs

```csharp
// Auto-generated GUID, no class interface
    string ToUpper();
    string ToLower();
    string SubString(int start, int length);
}

[ClassInterface(ClassInterfaceType.None)]
public class LittleString : IString
{
        private string text;

        // Default constructor needed by COM
    public LittleString()
    {
    }

    // Accessor for the text
    public string Text {
        get {
            return text;
        }
        set {
            text = value;
        }
    }

    public string ToLower() {
        return text.ToLower();
    }

    public string ToUpper() {
        return text.ToUpper();
    }

    public string SubString(int start, int length) {
        return text.Substring(start, length);
    }
}
```

There are several things to notice about this code:

- The methods are defined in the *IString* interface, which is implemented by the *LittleString* class. Since all the COM-visible methods are implemented using an interface, the class doesn't need to have a class interface.

- The class has a default constructor, which is necessary if instances are to be created by COM.
- The class provides a property with a setter, which enables the text of the string to be set after the instance has been created.
- A dual class interface has been provided so that early-bound client code can use the type.
- By default, the version information is specified as *1.0.** in the AssemblyInfo.cs file, which leaves it up to Visual Studio .NET to choose the last two parts of the version and generate a new pair of values each time the assembly is recompiled. To prevent this, I've fixed the version number to be *1.0.1.1*. This will make it easier for clients that specify a CLSID when creating instances.

Installing the Component for COM Use

.NET types that are to be used from COM need to be installed in the GAC, which requires the component to have a strong name. Use the SN.exe tool to create a keypair file, and put it in the project directory:

```
sn -k theKey.snk
```

Open AssemblyInfo.cs, and edit the *AssemblyKeyFile* attribute to contain the filename. Remember to set the path to point two levels above, to the project directory:

```
[assembly: AssemblyKeyFile(@"..\..\theKey.snk")]
```

Now build the project to create the assembly DLL. From a Visual Studio .NET Command Prompt window, use RegAsm.exe to register the component and create a type library:

```
regasm LittleString.dll /tlb:LittleString.tlb
```

Then use the *GACUTIL.EXE* tool to install the assembly in the GAC:

```
gacutil -i LittleString.dll
```

The assembly is now registered and installed in the GAC.

> **Note** If you rebuild the assembly, you'll need to reinstall the component in the GAC. If you forget to do this, client code will end up using an old version of the component.

Looking at the Type Library

Opening the type library in the COM/OLE Object Viewer shows that the type library contains the following entries for the coclass and *IString* interface:

```
[
    odl, uuid(A1B26B91-9565-3D0D-9DEC-DC3B2AE594FA),
    version(1.0), dual, oleautomation,
    custom(0F21F359-AB84-41E8-9A78-36D110E6D2F9, IString)
]
interface IString : IDispatch {
    [id(0x60020000), propget]
        HRESULT Text([out, retval] BSTR* pRetVal);
    [id(0x60020000), propput]
        HRESULT Text([in] BSTR pRetVal);
    [id(0x60020002)]
        HRESULT ToUpper([out, retval] BSTR* pRetVal);
    [id(0x60020003)]
        HRESULT ToLower([out, retval] BSTR* pRetVal);
    [id(0x60020004)]
        HRESULT SubString(
            [in] long start, [in] long length,
            [out, retval] BSTR* pRetVal);
};

[
    uuid(BE9CE00E-2318-3B47-AC22-CA58C97EEAA9),
    version(1.0),
    custom(0F21F359-AB84-41E8-9A78-36D110E6D2F9,
                        LittleString.LittleString)
]
coclass LittleString {
    interface _Object;
    [default] dispinterface IString;
};
```

You can see how the *LittleString* coclass doesn't have a class interface and uses *IString* as the default interface. It also exposes the *_Object* class interface for the *System.Object* class. Strings are passed as *BSTR*s so that they can easily be used by COM clients.

Using the Class in COM Code

The sample program in Listing 4-3 shows how this class can be used from unmanaged Visual C++ code, using the COM compiler support included with Visual C++ 6. You'll find this code in the Chapter04\UseNetControl folder in the book's companion content.

```cpp
#define _WIN32_DCOM
#include <iostream>
using namespace std;

// Include definitions of basic Windows types
#include <wtypes.h>

// Import the type library
#import "littlestring.tlb" no_namespace named_guids

int main()
{
   CoInitializeEx(0, COINIT_MULTITHREADED);

   try
   {
      // Create the smart pointer
      IStringPtr sp(__uuidof(LittleString));
      cout << "Created object" << endl;

      // Set the text
      sp->PutText("hello");

      // Convert it to upper case
      _bstr_t bs = sp->ToUpper();

      cout << "Text is " << bs << endl;
   }
   catch(_com_error& ce)
   {
      cout << "com error: " << ce.ErrorMessage() << endl;
   }

   CoUninitialize();

   return 0;
}
```

Listing 4-3 UseNetControl.cpp

The important part of this code is the *#import* directive, which tells the compiler to read a type library and create a wrapper class that can be used to access a COM object. In this example, I've copied the type library to the C++ project directory, but you can use a relative or absolute path instead. The *IStringPtr* object creates a COM object based on the CLSID it is given as its argument: here, it is actually an interface pointer on the CCW that is being returned. Once the object has been created, it can be used like any other COM object.

Exporting Metadata to Type Libraries

This section describes how .NET entities, including interfaces, classes, and methods, are converted when exported to a type library.

Exporting Assemblies

A .NET assembly is converted into a single type library. It is a one-to-one mapping, and you cannot split an assembly over more than one type library. You will always get the same type library regardless of the way it has been produced from the assembly (for example, using the TlbExp.exe tool or the *ConvertAssemblyToTypeLib* class).

> **Note** Assembly names often contain periods (for example, *System.Runtime.InteropServices*). Because the assembly name is often used as the base name for the type library and periods are not allowed in type library names, any periods in the assembly name will be converted to underscores during export.

Assemblies are fully identified by a strong name, which consists of the assembly name, version number, public key, and locale information. Type libraries, on the other hand, are identified by three items:

- A GUID, called the library ID (or LIBID)
- An optional locale identifier (or LCID)
- A version number

The LIBID is constructed from the assembly name and public key information. You must use the public key because there might be two assemblies with the same name, signed with different keys, that need to be mapped onto different type libraries. A given assembly name and public key always yields the same LIBID. If you want to use a specific LIBID, you can override the default by using the *Guid* attribute on the assembly.

Version information is passed from the assembly to the type library, but because COM supports only a two-part version number (in contrast to an assembly's four-part version number), only the major and minor parts of the version are preserved. For example, an assembly with version number 1.22.5.123 will produce a type library with version 1.22.

The assembly locale information is converted to an LCID; if there is no locale information, an LCID of zero will be used in the type library.

If an assembly has the *AssemblyDescription* attribute, the description will be used to provide a *HelpString* for the type library.

Exporting Namespaces

.NET types will lose their namespace information when exported. For example, the class *MyNamespace.MyClass* will be exported simply as *MyClass*. This can lead to problems if two classes have the same name but live in different namespaces, as you see here:

```
namespace Outer {
   // Enum in Outer namespace
   public enum Seasons
   {
       Spring, Summer, Autumn, Winter
   }

   namespace Inner {
      // Enum in Outer.Inner namespace
      public enum Seasons
      {
          Spring, Summer, Autumn, Winter
      }
   }
}
```

In this case, the export process will prefix the generated typenames with namespace information so that the two enums will be called *Outer_Seasons* and *Outer_Inner_Seasons*. Although this transformation will make the code work correctly when called from COM, the type names won't match those in the original .NET code, thus leading to possible confusion for COM programmers.

> **Note** Namespace prefixes are not used if there is no name clash.

Exporting Classes

By default, every class in an assembly is converted into a coclass. The *ComVisible* attribute can be used to prevent .NET classes from being exported to the type library, as shown in the following C# sample code:

```
// Classes are exported by default
public class ExportedToCOM
{
    ...
}

// This class will not be exported
[ComVisible(false)]
public class NotExportedToCom
{
    ...
}
```

The generated coclass will be given an automatically generated GUID unless you specify one using the *Guid* attribute:

```
// Specify a GUID for the coclass
[Guid(4a79399a-bf0f-4208-9512-aa3a438bd67a)]
public class MyComClass
{
    ...
}
```

Abstract classes and interfaces will have their definitions in the type library marked with the *noncreatable* attribute. Concrete classes that don't have a default constructor will also be marked *noncreatable* because COM needs to be able to call a default constructor to create instances.

Inheritance disappears when the type library is generated because there is no inheritance of coclasses. A coclass will expose its own interfaces, plus all the interfaces exposed by its base classes, as shown in the following Visual C# example:

```
// Base inherits from Object by default, and implements interface IOne
class Base : IOne
{
}

// Derived derives from Base, and exposes a dual
// class interface
[ClassInterface(ClassInterfaceType.AutoDual)]
public class Derived : Base
{
}
```

The coclass for the *Derived* class will look like this:

```
coclass Derived
{
  interface IOne;
  interface _Object;
}
```

The coclass exposes the *IOne* interface from the base class. The *_Object* interface represents an interface to the *Object* class; this interface will be generated for all .NET types, since everything inherits from *Object* eventually.

Exporting Interfaces

COM interfaces derived from .NET interfaces will contain the same methods and properties as the original .NET interface.

As with classes, a GUID will be generated automatically to represent the COM interface ID (IID) during the export process. You can override the default *IID* generation by using the *Guid* attribute, as the following C# code fragment shows:

```
[Guid(db568ac0-0c40-40ca-b8dc-9badf68588fc)]
interface IMyInterface
{
  ...
}
```

> **Note** The automatically generated interface ID is derived from the interface name and the complete signatures of all the methods defined by the interface. If you alter any method signatures, or reorder the methods in the interface definition, you'll get a different IID generated. The names of individual methods are not used, so you can change method names without affecting the IID.

Choosing Interface Types

When exporting .NET interfaces, COM dual interfaces are generated by default, as they provide the greatest flexibility for COM clients. You can control the type of interface produced by using the *InterfaceType* attribute. This attribute takes one of the members of the *ComInterfaceType* enumeration, listed in Table 4-6, as a parameter:

Table 4-6 Members of the *ComInterfaceType* Enumeration

Member	Description
InterfaceIsDual	The .NET interface is exposed to COM as a dual interface. This is the default value.
InterfaceIsIDispatch	The .NET interface is exposed to COM as a dispinterface. Such interfaces can be used only via late binding.
InterfaceIsIUnknown	The .NET interface is exposed to COM as a custom interface. Such interfaces can be used only via early binding.

The following Visual C# example shows how to use the *InterfaceType* attribute:

```
' A COM dispinterface will be generated when this interface is
' exported to a type library
[
    InterfaceType(ComInterfaceType.InterfaceIsIDispatch),
    Guid("ACDA141C-A24C-4499-B16E-A95A48A24484")
]
public interface IBase
{
    void BaseMethod();
}
```

Interfaces and Inheritance

Interfaces can, and often do, form an inheritance hierarchy, as shown in the following C# example, where *IDerived* inherits from *IBase*. Any class that implements *IDerived* will have to implement the cumulative interface defined by both *IDerived* and *IBase*:

```
namespace InterfaceInherit
{
    // A base interface, which will be exported as a dual interface
    // by default. A GUID has been specified using the Guid attribute.
    [Guid("ACDA141C-A24C-4499-B16E-A95A48A24484")]
    public interface IBase
    {
        void BaseMethod();
    }

    // IDerived derives from IBase
    [Guid("5DE99C74-D1F1-451d-A509-F8ACCD54BB2E")]
    public interface IDerived : IBase
    {
```

```csharp
    void DerivedMethod();
    long Square (int val);
}

// The class has to implement the methods of both IBase and
// IDerived. Since all the methods I want to expose to COM are
// implemented via interfaces, a class interface is not needed
[
  ClassInterface(ClassInterfaceType.None),
  Guid("682C25B2-5FC8-4b50-903B-2F8B2972F1DC")
]
public class TheClass : IDerived
{
    public TheClass()
    {
    }

    // IDerived Members

    public void DerivedMethod()
    {
    }

    public long Square(int val)
    {
        return val*val;
    }

    // IBase Members

    public void BaseMethod()
    {
    }
}
}
```

When such a hierarchy is exported to a type library, the inheritance hierarchy is necessarily flattened because COM isn't object oriented and doesn't support interface inheritance at run time. A dual interface might appear to be derived from *IDispatch* in Interface Definition Language (IDL), but this means only that it contains the *IDispatch* methods in its vtable. It doesn't mean a dual interface *is IDispatch* in the object-oriented sense.

For the example above, you end up with the following items when the interfaces and class are exported to a type library:

- An *IBase* interface that derives from *IDispatch*
- An *IDerived* interface that derives from *IDispatch*
- A coclass that implements both interfaces

The IDL that follows shows how this appears in the type library. You can see how the relationship between the two interfaces has disappeared, and how they are regarded as completely separate:

```
[
   odl, uuid(ACDA141C-A24C-4499-B16E-A95A48A24484),
   version(1.0), dual, oleautomation,
   custom(0F21F359-AB84-41E8-9A78-36D110E6D2F9,
          InterfaceInherit.IBase)
]
interface IBase : IDispatch {
   [id(0x60020000)] HRESULT BaseMethod();
};

[
   odl, uuid(5DE99C74-D1F1-451D-A509-F8ACCD54BB2E),
   version(1.0), dual, oleautomation,
   custom(0F21F359-AB84-41E8-9A78-36D110E6D2F9,
          InterfaceInherit.IDerived)
]
interface IDerived : IDispatch {
   [id(0x60020000)] HRESULT DerivedMethod();
   [id(0x60020001)] HRESULT Square([in] long val,
                    [out, retval] int64* pRetVal);
};

[
   uuid(682C25B2-5FC8-4B50-903B-2F8B2972F1DC), version(1.0),
   custom(0F21F359-AB84-41E8-9A78-36D110E6D2F9,
          InterfaceInherit.TheClass)
]
coclass TheClass {
   interface _Object;
   [default] interface IDerived;
   interface IBase;
};
```

If an exported class has a class interface, it will be made the coclass's default interface. If a class doesn't have a class interface, the default interface will be the first one implemented by the class. In this case, the default interface is *IDerived*.

Exporting Methods

COM interface method parameters have directional attributes that inform the marshaling code in which direction parameters need to be marshaled. The following bullet points summarize how parameters of .NET methods are represented in COM interface methods:

- Reference types that are passed by value are marked as *[in]* parameters.

- Types that are passed by reference are marked as *[in,out]* parameters.

- Pointers (as used in C# unsafe code and managed C++ code) are also marked as *[in,out]* parameters.

You can apply the *In* and *Out* attributes to .NET parameters, and this will affect how they are represented when the type is exported. As you might expect, .NET *In* parameters are marshaled as COM *[in]* parameters, *Out* parameters are marshaled as *[out]*, and parameters that have both *In* and *Out* attributes are marshaled as *[in,out]*.

COM methods return *HRESULT*s, so .NET methods are converted in such a manner that function return values are represented as *[out, retval]* parameters, and the return type is converted to an *HRESULT*. The following example shows how a Visual C# function would be represented in a type library:

```
// Function that returns a long
public long Square(int n)

// Resulting IDL
HRESULT Square([in]long n, [out,retval]int64* pRetVal);
```

> **Note** The *PreserveSig* attribute can be used to prevent this transformation from taking place so that the signature of the COM method matches that of the .NET method.

If .NET methods don't use *HRESULTs*, what values get returned when .NET methods are executed by COM clients? If no error occurs, the runtime will return *S_OK*. If an exception is thrown by the .NET code, the runtime will return an *HRESULT* that depends on the exception thrown. A large number of possible *HRESULTs* can be returned (over 60 in total), and the most common ones are summarized in Table 4-7. For a full list, consult the .NET Framework Developer's Guide in the online help, under the topic "HRESULTs and Exceptions." Note that some *HRESULT* values can be mapped onto more than one .NET exception class; the table shows only the most common .NET exception classes for each *HRESULT*.

Table 4-7 Conversion Between .NET Exceptions and COM *HRESULT*s

Exception Type	HRESULT	Numeric Value
ArgumentException, InvalidEnumArgumentException	COR_E_ARGUMENT or E_INVALIDARG	0x80070057
ArgumentNullException	COR_E_NULLREFERENCE or E_POINTER	0x80004003
ArgumentOutOfRangeException	COR_E_ARGUMENTOUTOFRANGE	0x80131502
ArithmeticException	COR_E_ARITHMETIC or ERROR_ARITHMETIC_OVERFLOW	0x80070216
ArrayTypeMismatchException	COR_E_ARRAYTYPEMISMATCH	0x80131503
DivideByZeroException	COR_E_DIVIDEBYZERO	0x80020012
Exception	COR_E_EXCEPTION	0x80131500
FileNotFoundException	COR_E_FILENOTFOUND or ERROR_FILE_NOT_FOUND	0x80070002
FormatException, CookieException, UriFormatException	COR_E_FORMAT	0x80131537
IndexOutOfRangeException	COR_E_INDEXOUTOFRANGE	0x80131508
InvalidCastException	COR_E_INVALIDCAST or E_NOINTERFACE	0x80004002
IOException	COR_E_IO	0x80131620
MissingMemberException	COR_E_MISSINGMEMBER	0x80131512
NotImplementedException	E_NOTIMPL	0x80004001
NotSupportedException	COR_E_NOTSUPPORTED	0x80131515
OutOfMemoryException	COR_E_OUTOFMEMORY or E_OUTOFMEMORY	0x8007000E
SecurityException	COR_E_SECURITY	0x8013150A
SystemException, InvalidPrinterException, SoapException, SqlTypeException	COR_E_SYSTEM	0x80131501

Overloaded methods in .NET classes pose a problem because COM doesn't support the concept of overloading of interface methods. To overcome this, the exporter will generate unique method names by adding a suffix to each method name, consisting of an underscore and a numeral. The numeral starts at two and is incremented by one for each additional overloaded method, as shown in the following Visual C# example:

```
// C# overloaded methods
int MyMethod(int val);
int MyMethod(int val1, int val2);
int MyMethod(double d);

// COM interface methods
HRESULT MyMethod([in]long val, [out,retval]long* pRetVal);
HRESULT MyMethod_2([in]long val1, [in]long val2,
                   [out,retval]long* pRetVal);
HRESULT MyMethod_3([in]double val, [out,retval]long* pRetVal);
```

Note that these names are generated automatically when the type is exported, and methods aren't guaranteed to retain the same numerical suffixes in subsequent type library generations.

Exporting Properties

Properties, with their get and set methods, are a fundamental feature of .NET languages and can be defined in both classes and interfaces. COM also supports properties, using the *[propget]* and *[propput]* attributes on interface methods. Here's how the type library exporter handles exporting properties:

- Property get methods become interface methods with the *[propget]* attribute.

- Property set methods become interface methods with the *[propput]* attribute.

- Properties without a get or a set method are ignored.

- If the property type is a class or interface, the property set method will become an interface method with the *[propputref]* attribute, giving it an added level of indirection.

To show you how this works, here is a Visual C# class that implements two properties. One of them is of type *double*, while the other is of class type:

```
namespace props
{
    [ClassInterface(ClassInterfaceType.AutoDual)]
    public class Worker
    {
        public Worker(Worker bs)
        {
            theBoss = bs;
```

```csharp
        }

        private Worker theBoss;
        private double thePittance;

        public Worker Boss
        {
           get
           {
              return theBoss;
           }
           set
           {
              theBoss = value;
           }
        }

        public double Salary
        {
           get
           {
              return thePittance;
           }
           set
           {
              thePittance = value;
           }
        }
    }
}
```

When exported to a type library, the resulting interface looks like this:

```
[
  odl, uuid(2A33C1A5-B38A-36DB-B370-5C3F7AAA0E5F),
  hidden, dual, nonextensible, oleautomation,
  custom(0F21F359-AB84-41E8-9A78-36D110E6D2F9, props.Worker)
]
interface _Worker : IDispatch {
    // Methods inherited from Object have been omitted
    [id(0x60020004), propget]
        HRESULT Boss([out, retval] _Worker** pRetVal);
    [id(0x60020004), propputref]
        HRESULT Boss([in] _Worker* pRetVal);
    [id(0x60020006), propget]
        HRESULT Salary([out, retval] double* pRetVal);
    [id(0x60020006), propput]
        HRESULT Salary([in] double pRetVal);
};
```

The get methods have been converted into *[propget]* methods, the set method for the *double* property has been converted to a *[propput]* method, and the set method for the *Worker* property has been converted to a *[propputref]* property.

Any public fields exposed by .NET types are also converted into *[propput]* and *[propget]* methods when the type is exported. Read-only fields are represented by a *[propget]* method.

Exporting Data Types

The type library exporter will convert .NET types to suitable unmanaged types during the export process. This is more complex than importing data types when using COM components in .NET because .NET components can use a greater range of data types than are available for COM interfaces.

Table 4-8 shows the corresponding .NET, COM IDL, and Visual Basic types for some of the most common data types.

Table 4-8 Conversion Between .NET, COM IDL, and Visual Basic 6 Types

.NET Type	IDL Type	VB6 Type	Remarks
System.Boolean (when used as a parameter)	*VARIANT_BOOL*	*Boolean*	
System.Boolean (when used as a field in a structure)	*long*	*Long*	
System.Byte	*unsigned char*	*Byte*	
System.Int16	*short*	*Integer*	
System.Int32	*long*	*Long*	Can also be marshaled as an *IDL HRESULT* by using the *MarshalAsAttribute*.
System.Int64	*int64*	*n/a*	
System.IntPtr	*long*	*Long*	
System.UInt16	*unsigned short*	*n/a*	Unsigned types aren't supported by Visual Basic.
System.UInt32	*unsigned long*	*n/a*	Can also be marshaled as an *IDL HRESULT* by using the *MarshalAs* attribute.
System.UInt64	*uint64*	*n/a*	
System.Single	*single*	*Single*	
System.Double	*double*	*Double*	

Table 4-8 Conversion Between .NET, COM IDL, and Visual Basic 6 Types

.NET Type	IDL Type	VB6 Type	Remarks
System.String (used as a parameter)	*BSTR*	*String*	
System.String (used as a field in a structure)	*LPSTR*	*String*	
System.DateTime	*DATE*	*Date*	
System.Guid	*GUID*	n/a	
System.Decimal	*DECIMAL*	n/a	Can be marshaled to Visual Basic as a *Currency* by using the *MarshalAs* attribute.
System.Object (used as a parameter)	*VARIANT*	*Variant*	
System.Object (used as a field in a structure)	*IUnknown**	n/a	
Arrays of a given type	*SAFEARRAY(type)*	*type()*	

Note that for some types the marshaled type will be different depending on whether they're used as parameters or as fields in structs. You can also vary the way some types are marshaled by using the *MarshalAs* attribute. This advanced interop feature is discussed in Chapter 13, "Advanced Interaction."

Exporting Value Types

.NET value types are exported as IDL structs. You'll need to use the *StructLayout* attribute with the *LayoutKind.Sequential* argument to fix the layout of the members so that it isn't altered by .NET. Here is an example struct coded in C#:

```
[StructLayout(LayoutKind.Sequential)]
public struct MyStruct
{
   public int valOne;
   public int valTwo;
   public void Method1(int a)
   {
      valOne = valTwo = a;
   }
}
```

The corresponding COM type in the type library looks like this:

```
typedef [uuid(4D469648-1406-3683-BADA-580CE600EE2E), version(1.0),
   custom(0F21F359-AB84-41E8-9A78-36D110E6D2F9, ExportTest.MyStruct)
```

```
]
struct tagMyStruct {
   long valOne;
   long valTwo;
} MyStruct;
```

You can see how the value type has been represented by an IDL struct. Note also that the generated struct contains only data members; methods will not be exported.

> **Note** The *custom* IDL attribute was introduced in Chapter 3. It provides a way to specify the namespace that will be used for this COM type if it is imported back into .NET using the *TlbImp.exe* tool.

Exporting Enumerations

Enumerations are converted into COM enumerations in the generated type library. Since it is a COM requirement that names of enumeration members be unique, the exporter will generate unique names by adding the name of each member of the enumeration as a prefix to the enumeration name itself. For example, consider the following .NET enumeration coded in C#:

```
public enum CompassPoint
{
   North = 0,
   East = 90,
   South = 180,
   West = 270
}
```

The generated COM enum will look like this:

```
typedef [uuid(9371DAC5-C4FA-3B40-8822-90CE107AD8F9), version(1.0),
   custom(0F21F359-AB84-41E8-9A78-36D110E6D2F9, ExportTest.CompassPoint)
]
enum {
   CompassPoint_North = 0,
   CompassPoint_East = 90,
   CompassPoint_South = 180,
   CompassPoint_West = 270
} CompassPoint;
```

You can see that each name has been prefixed with *CompassPoint_* to generate a unique identifier.

How to Design .NET Components for Use with COM

If you are writing a .NET component that you know will be used by COM clients, you can take certain steps to make interoperation as smooth as possible.

Provide a Default Constructor

COM objects are created without any initialization parameters being passed to them; in effect, COM coclasses only ever have default constructors. Any .NET type you expose to COM must therefore have a default constructor. If you also want to provide constructors with parameters for use by .NET clients, you'll need to make sure you provide the same functionality to COM clients by supplying a default constructor plus one or more initialization methods.

Avoid Using Static and Overloaded Methods

Static methods aren't exported to COM type libraries, so you should avoid using them because they won't be COM-visible. Note that you can see static methods using the .NET reflection mechanism, but this requires you to know .NET programming. Programming .NET reflection falls outside the scope of this book.

Overloaded methods get exported to COM with unique names identified by a numeric suffix, as was explained in the section "Exporting Methods" earlier in the chapter. This can be confusing for COM clients because the names of the methods in the type library won't match up with the documented names of the original .NET methods. In addition, changing the .NET class and re-exporting the type library might result in different names being generated, which can break existing clients.

Be Aware of Possible Naming Problems

You can run into problems in several areas with the names you use in .NET assemblies and types. For example, it's common sense not to use names that are significant in COM, such as *IUnknown* or *BSTR*.

In addition, don't differentiate members of types based solely on case. Type libraries aren't case sensitive, so the differences between members differentiated in this way can be lost or give rise to apparently overloaded methods.

Assembly Naming

When type libraries are imported into Visual Basic 6 or unmanaged Visual C++ code, the tools might create a namespace based on the library name found in the type library. Because the library name is created from the assembly name during the export process, you should choose an assembly name that gives rise to a sensible library name.

If you're using Visual Studio .NET, you can set the assembly name from the solution property dialog. The name of the output file will be based on the assembly name, so choosing an assembly name of *MyProject.MyComponent* will result in the creation of an assembly called *MyProject.MyComponent.dll*. Since type library names cannot contain periods, the generated library name will be *MyProject_MyComponent*. You might want to avoid the use of long, descriptive assembly names for assemblies that are going to be exported to COM, to make it easier for clients to use the resulting type library.

Method-Naming Conflicts

Be careful not to define methods that have the same names as those in the *IUnknown* or *IDispatch* interface. In other words, avoid using the following names:

- *QueryInterface*
- *AddRef*
- *Release*
- *GetTypeInfoCount*
- *GetTypeInfo*
- *GetIdsOfNames*
- *Invoke*

If you define a method name that clashes with one of these, the type library exporter will deal with it in the usual way, by creating a COM interface method with a numeric suffix (for example, *GetTypeInfo_2*).

Avoid Altering Interfaces

A fundamental principle of COM is that once an interface has been defined, it shouldn't be changed in any way that will affect users of the interface. This means not adding methods, not removing methods, not changing method signatures, and not changing the order of the methods within an interface definition.

.NET classes and their clients are more able to cope with change than COM interfaces and clients. You can also change .NET type definitions—for instance, reordering the methods within a class—without breaking client code. If you're going to expose a .NET class to COM, you need to ensure you don't make changes to the class that will cause problems to COM clients. Treat the public interface to exported .NET classes as you would COM interfaces, providing a new version number if you make any potentially breaking change.

> **Note** COM clients can see only the public members of .NET classes, so you can change private and protected members without compromising COM safety.

Define Event Source Interfaces

If you want your .NET class to fire events that can be handled by COM clients, define event-source interfaces in managed code and attach them to .NET classes using the *ComSourceInterfaces* attribute. This procedure is discussed in more detail in the "Exposing .NET Events in COM" section later in the chapter.

Use of Attributes

.NET components use attributes to provide data about types above and beyond what the programming language can convey. For example, to show that a class is serializable, it is tagged with the *Serializable* attribute:

```
[Serializable()]
public class MyClass
{
...
}
```

You can also create your own custom attributes, which are used in exactly the same way.

Finding out what attributes a class possesses requires writing code that uses reflection; reflection provides a run-time query of an object's capabilities. You can use reflection from COM clients, but this will normally require late binding to the .NET object. Such code is difficult to write and requires knowledge of how the .NET reflection mechanism works.

Other object-oriented languages that don't support attributes use a different technique. An interface with no members can be used to *tag* a class as having a particular property. For example, in C++ making a class serializable might be implemented like this:

```
// Dummy interface
class ISerializable
{
};

class MyClass : public ISerializable
{
   ...
};
```

You can use a simple cast at run time to find out whether an object inherits from *ISerializable*. This might be a better way to expose attributes to COM clients because *ISerializable* will be exported as an interface and can be discovered by a simple call to *QueryInterface*. Interface methods can be used to provide the same information that can be obtained from custom attributes by reflection.

Provide *HRESULT*s

.NET code signals errors by throwing exceptions, and the interop mechanism passes these to COM clients as *HRESULT*s. Although the .NET coding guidelines recommend that you use the exception classes predefined in the .NET Framework, you can define your own exception types if you need to pass information. If you define your own custom exception classes, you'll need to include an *HRESULT* so that it can be passed to COM. You can include an *HRESULT* by using the protected *HResult* property inherited from the *Exception* base class.

> **Note** You'll need to create a suitable value for the *HRESULT*. All *HRESULT*s not originating from Microsoft must start with 0x8004 (representing a *FACILITY_ITF* error), and the last four hex digits must be greater than 0x200.

Use Versioning Correctly

The type library exporter will automatically generate GUIDs for type libraries, coclasses, and interfaces. These GUIDs are based on the assembly name, the version, and the public key; if the assembly doesn't have a public key, the GUID will be based only on the name and the version.

When you develop projects in Visual Studio .NET, whether they are in Visual C#, managed C++, or Visual Basic .NET, they contain an AssemblyInfo source file that contains the definitions of attributes that will be applied to the assembly. One of these is the *AssemblyVersion* attribute, which appears in C# code like this:

```
[assembly: AssemblyVersion("1.0.*")]
```

The * in the version number tells Visual Studio .NET to automatically generate the last two parts of the version number. These two parts will change with every rebuild of the assembly. This means that every time the assembly is exported, the generated GUIDs for coclasses, interfaces, and the type library might be different because they are based in part on the version number.

To provide fixed GUIDs for exported COM entities, you have two alternatives. The first is to provide an explicit version number in the *AssemblyVersion* attribute, and the second is to provide explicit GUIDs for coclasses and interfaces using the .NET *Guid* attribute.

Hosting Windows Forms Controls in ActiveX Control Containers

Windows Forms controls are the .NET equivalent of ActiveX controls: self-contained components, normally with a user interface, that implement the right architecture for plugging into a suitable container. In the case of Windows Forms controls, the container is a Windows Forms form; in the case of an ActiveX control, the container will be an ActiveX container. Given that the two types of components are performing the same logical task, you might want to use them interchangeably. Interoperation is possible but only to a limited extent, as explained below.

Windows Forms controls can be used as ActiveX controls, but they might not work in all ActiveX containers. Being an ActiveX container is not a binary *either-or* matter, and some containers might not implement all the functionality that it is possible to provide. For this reason, the wrapper that lets Windows Forms controls work as ActiveX controls is designed to work with Internet Explorer. Internet Explorer is not yet a .NET application, but it needs to be able to host Windows Forms controls seamlessly; hence, the built-in support. This means that if you export a .NET control, you'll be able to use it on a Web page in Internet Explorer, but it might not work in other ActiveX containers, such as Visual Basic 6. It might work correctly, but Microsoft gives no guarantees.

Registry Entries

To export a Windows Forms control to work in a container other than Internet Explorer, you'll need to add extra registry entries, as explained in the following paragraphs.

Identifying a Control

ActiveX controls are identified in the registry in two ways. The older way, which dates from the days when a COM component was either an ActiveX control or a plain component, is to add a *Control* subkey to the CLSID for the Windows Forms control. As the capabilities of COM components got more complex, the *Implemented Categories* key was introduced to list the categories to which a component belonged. *Implemented Categories* is a subkey of the control's CLSID, and it has subkeys that identify the capabilities of the component. For ActiveX controls, the subkey you need to add has the name *{40FC6ED4-2438-11CF-A3DB-080036F12502}*. This GUID is known as *CATID_Control*, and unfortunately you have to use the GUID itself rather than its name. You might need to identify a control using both of these methods, although older containers will need only the first entry.

Type Library Entries

The type library for the exported control needs to be registered, and the *TypeLib* subkey of *CLSID* must be set to refer to the library GUID. A *Version* subkey needs to be added to the control's *CLSID* entry, and its value should be set to the version number of the exported type library.

Miscellaneous Entries

The control *CLSID* key should have a subkey called *MiscStatus*, which holds the *OLE Miscellaneous Status Bits*. These bits comprise a collection of flags that detail the capabilities of embeddable COM components, and you *OR* members of the Windows *OLEMISC* structure together to obtain the value you want. The members of the structure are shown in the following listing:

```
typedef enum tagOLEMISC
{
   OLEMISC_RECOMPOSEONRESIZE = 1,
   OLEMISC_ONLYICONIC = 2,
   OLEMISC_INSERTNOTREPLACE = 4,
   OLEMISC_STATIC = 8,
   OLEMISC_CANTLINKINSIDE = 16,
   OLEMISC_CANLINKBYOLE1 = 32,
   OLEMISC_ISLINKOBJECT = 64,
   OLEMISC_INSIDEOUT = 128,
```

```
    OLEMISC_ACTIVATEWHENVISIBLE = 256,
    OLEMISC_RENDERINGISDEVICEINDEPENDENT = 512,
    OLEMISC_INVISIBLEATRUNTIME = 1024,
    OLEMISC_ALWAYSRUN = 2048,
    OLEMISC_ACTSLIKEBUTTON = 4096,
    OLEMISC_ACTSLIKELABEL = 8192,
    OLEMISC_NOUIACTIVATE = 16384,
    OLEMISC_ALIGNABLE = 32768,
    OLEMISC_SIMPLEFRAME = 65536,
    OLEMISC_SETCLIENTSITEFIRST = 131072,
    OLEMISC_IMEMODE = 262144,
    OLEMISC_IGNOREACTIVATEWHENVISIBLE = 524288,
    OLEMISC_WANTSTOMENUMERGE = 1048576,
    OLEMISC_SUPPORTSMULTILEVELUNDO = 2097152
} OLEMISC;
```

Many of the possible values are inapplicable to Windows Forms controls, so it wouldn't be useful to explain the entire structure here. A sensible set of values to *OR* together comprises *OLEMISC_INSIDEOUT*, *OLEMISC_RECOMPOSEONRESIZE*, *OLEMISC_ACTIVATEWHENVISIBLE*, and *OLEMISC_SETCLIENTSITEFIRST*, which gives a value of 131457.

Example: Hosting a Windows Forms Control in Internet Explorer

This section shows you how a simple Windows Forms control can be used in Internet Explorer. The control is called TimeBox, a simple compound control that combines a text box with a button. The user is supposed to enter a time into the control in the format hh:mm:ss. Pressing the button to the right of the control will insert the current time. Listing 4-4 contains the Visual C# code. You can find this sample in the Chapter04\TimeBox folder in the book's companion content.

```
using System;
using System.Collections;
using System.ComponentModel;
using System.Drawing;
using System.Data;
using System.Windows.Forms;

namespace TimeBox
{
    public class TimeBox : System.Windows.Forms.UserControl
    {
        private System.Windows.Forms.TextBox textBox1;
```

Listing 4-4 TimeBox.cs

```csharp
private System.Windows.Forms.Button button1;
/// <summary>
/// Required designer variable.
/// </summary>
private System.ComponentModel.Container components = null;

public UserControl1()
{
   // This call is required by the Windows.Forms Form Designer.
   InitializeComponent();

   // TODO: Add any initialization after the InitComponent call

}

/// <summary>
/// Clean up any resources being used.
/// </summary>
protected override void Dispose( bool disposing )
{
   if( disposing )
   {
      if( components != null )
         components.Dispose();
   }
   base.Dispose( disposing );
}

#region Component Designer generated code
/// <summary>
/// Required method for Designer support - do not modify
/// the contents of this method with the code editor.
/// </summary>
private void InitializeComponent()
{
   this.textBox1 = new System.Windows.Forms.TextBox();
   this.button1 = new System.Windows.Forms.Button();
   this.SuspendLayout();
   //
   // textBox1
   //
   this.textBox1.Location = new System.Drawing.Point(8, 8);
   this.textBox1.Name = "textBox1";
   this.textBox1.Size = new System.Drawing.Size(176, 20);
   this.textBox1.TabIndex = 0;
```

```csharp
            this.textBox1.Text = "";
            //
            // button1
            //
            this.button1.Location = new System.Drawing.Point(192, 8);
            this.button1.Name = "button1";
            this.button1.Size = new System.Drawing.Size(24, 23);
            this.button1.TabIndex = 1;
            this.button1.Text = "...";
            this.button1.Click += new System.EventHandler(this.button1_Click);
            //
            // UserControl1
            //
            this.Controls.Add(this.button1);
            this.Controls.Add(this.textBox1);
            this.Name = "UserControl1";
            this.Size = new System.Drawing.Size(224, 40);
            this.ResumeLayout(false);

        }
        #endregion

        // Property to return the time as a string
        public string Time {
            get {
                return textBox1.Text;
            }
        }

        private void button1_Click(object sender, System.EventArgs e) {
            // puts the time into the textbox
            DateTime dt = DateTime.Now;
            textBox1.Text = dt.Hour.ToString() + ":"
                          + dt.Minute.ToString() + ":"
                          + dt.Second.ToString();
        }
    }
}
```

No special processing is needed to use a Windows Forms control with Internet Explorer. When using .NET components with other programs, you've seen how you need to create a type library to represent the component as a COM object. The aim is to let Windows Forms controls be used in Internet Explorer just as easily as ActiveX controls, so Internet Explorer itself will create an appropriate CCW when it loads the HTML page.

To use this control with Internet Explorer, place an *<object>* tag within the HTML.

```
<object id="TimeBox1"
classid="http:TimeBox.dll#TimeBox.TimeBox"height="300" width="500" VIEWASTEXT>
</object>
```

Note the form of the *classid* attribute specified for the control. This isn't the traditional COM CLSID you usually provide for an ActiveX control. Since Internet Explorer knows about .NET assemblies and how to generate wrappers, the Uniform Resource Identifier (URI) specifies the name of the assembly DLL, a pound sign, and the fully qualified name of the control class. Internet Explorer will use this URI to locate the assembly and automatically generate a CCW for the *TimeBox* class.

> **Note** The *<object>* tag provides a way to embed ActiveX controls and Java applets in HTML pages. For ActiveX controls, the *classid* parameter provides the CLSID (class ID) for the ActiveX control; if this control is registered on the machine where Microsoft Internet Explorer is being run, an instance will be created using the installed DLL. If the control is not installed, the DLL will be downloaded from the server, and temporarily installed on the client machine.

Exposing .NET Events in COM

.NET uses a delegate-based event model, while COM uses connection points. The discussion that follows assumes you are familiar with the way in which COM implements events using connection points, as well as the way in which .NET implements events using delegates. A brief overview of the COM mechanism was presented in the "Responding to COM Events" section in Chapter 3, but if you need more information, consult *Inside COM*, by Dale Rogerson (Microsoft Press, 1997).

For more information on delegates and events, consult a book appropriate to your .NET programming language, such as *Inside C#*, by Tom Archer, or *Programming Microsoft Visual Basic .NET*, by Francesco Balena, both published by Microsoft Press.

As explained in Chapter 3 in the section "Responding to COM Events," these mechanisms are logically similar and intended to fulfill the same requirements but they use completely different implementations. If a .NET component is going to act as a source of events that COM clients can consume, the .NET component needs to implement some additional code that lets it simulate the COM connection-point mechanism.

Using Explicit Source Interfaces

A typical .NET class defines events using delegates and events. For example, a class representing a bank account could define an event that is called whenever the interest rate changes:

```
// Visual C# example
public class Bank
{
   public event RateChangeHandler RateChange;
   ...
};
```

.NET events defined in this way cannot easily be exposed to COM. The problem is that the event definition within the class will be exposed as part of the class interface, and it will be implemented as a pair of methods with *add* and *remove* prefixes:

```
[id(0x6002004)] HRESULT add_RateChange([in]
                        _RateChangeHandler* value);
[id(0x6002005)] HRESULT remove_RateChange([in]
                        _RateChangeHandler* value);
```

While this mimics the way that .NET clients hook event handlers to event sources, a COM client has no way to create a suitable *RateChangeHandler* object and pass it as an argument, given that *RateChangeHandler* needs to be a managed type.

The solution is to define an explicit event-source interface. This interface can then be linked to a class using the *ComSourceInterfaces* attribute, and the type library exporter will use it to implement COM connection-point access to the exported .NET object. Here's the sequence of events you need to follow:

1. Create a source interface that defines the events to be exposed to COM clients.
2. Use the *ComSourceInterfaces* attribute to tell the type library exporter that this interface is a source interface for an exported class.
3. Build the assembly.
4. Generate a type library using TlbExp.exe or an equivalent method.
5. Use the type library with COM client code.

> **Note** As you'll see in the example that follows, implementing a source interface doesn't preclude implementing .NET events on the same class. This means COM and .NET clients can both use events on the same .NET class.

The example in Listing 4-5 defines a class that represents a bank account, which exposes a single event that is fired when the interest rate on the account changes. You can find this sample in the Chapter04\Account folder of the book's companion content.

```csharp
using System;
using System.Runtime.InteropServices;

namespace Bank
{
    // Interface to allow COM clients to use events.
    // Define it as a pure dispatch interface
    [
      Guid("ef81a831-fa49-4ede-b70b-08f2e9d602b2"),
      InterfaceType(ComInterfaceType.InterfaceIsIDispatch)
    ]
    public interface IAccountEvents {
       void NewRate(double val);
    }

    // Delegate for rate change event
    public delegate void RateDelegate(double val);

    // Export the Account class, exposing IAccountEvents
    // as a source interface
    [ComSourceInterfaces(typeof(IAccountEvents))]
    public class Account {
       private static double interestRate = 0;

       // Define the event
       public event RateDelegate NewRate;

       public Account() {
       }

       public double Rate {
          get {
             return interestRate;
          }
```

Listing 4-5 Account.cs

```
        }
        // Fire the event
        public void SetRate(double d) {
            NewRate(d);
        }
    }
}
```

The *IAccountEvents* interface defines the source interface for the *Account* class. It is exposed as a dispinterface—as are most source interfaces—and defines one method. The *Account* class defines a single event, based on the delegate *RateDelegate*, which can be used by .NET clients. The source interface is attached to the *Account* class using the *ComSourceInterfaces* attribute, which takes as its parameter a *Type* object representing the source interface. The *SetRate* method will fire the method when it is called.

Consuming Events in Visual Basic 6

It's simple to consume .NET events in COM-based code. As an example, here is how you could use the *Account* component in Visual Basic 6.

Create a project, and then use the References item on the Project menu to bring up the References dialog, as shown in Figure 4-4. If the *Account* class has been registered correctly, you'll see an entry for it in the list. Check this entry before pressing OK.

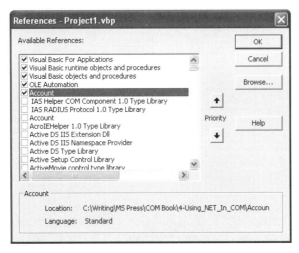

Figure 4-4 A correctly registered class will appear in the References dialog box.

This will add a reference to the class to the project. You can check what has been added by using the F2 key (or the Object Browser item on the View menu) to bring up the Object Browser window, as shown in Figure 4-5. You can see that the class exposes one event, shown by the lightning symbol:

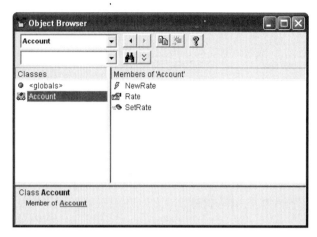

Figure 4-5 The Object Browser shows added classes and their related events.

You can test the *Account* component with some very simple code:

```
Dim WithEvents acc As Account.Account

Private Sub acc_NewRate(ByVal val As Double)
    MsgBox "New account rate is " & val
End Sub

Private Sub Form_Load()
   On Error GoTo errLab
   Set acc = New Account.Account

   acc.SetRate (5#)

   Exit Sub
errLab:
   MsgBox "Error:" & Err.Description
End Sub
```

The first line creates an *Account* object that is going to act as a source of events. The *acc_NewRate* function is a handler that will be called when the event is fired, and this is done in the *Form_Load* function once the object has been created. If you build and run the code, you'll find the message box is displayed as the form is loading at the start of the program.

Summary

In this chapter, you've seen how .NET components can be used by .NET clients. Exposing .NET types to COM is more restrictive—and more work—than importing COM types mainly because .NET types have a much richer structure and integrate in more complex ways than COM types.

COM Callable Wrappers can be produced for .NET types, and these wrappers provide all the behavior COM client code will be expecting. Methods on .NET types are exposed via COM interfaces. .NET interfaces will be converted and exposed as COM interfaces, and if a class doesn't expose its methods using interfaces, a class interface will be constructed through which class methods will be exposed. .NET events can also be handled by COM clients that expect a connection-point style of interaction, provided that the .NET component correctly exposes source interfaces. The final part of the chapter showed that you can use .NET Windows Forms controls as ActiveX controls, but that this is guaranteed to work correctly only in Internet Explorer.

5

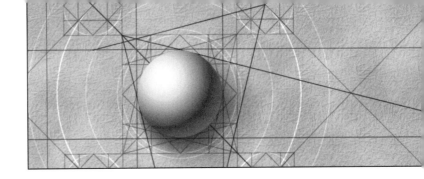

An Overview of COM+ Coding for .NET

In Chapter 4, you learned techniques for making your .NET components accessible to unmanaged applications through COM. You can use many of these same techniques, with a little augmentation, to make your .NET components work in the COM+ environment as well. The purpose of this chapter is to provide you with the knowledge required to understand the relationship between COM, DCOM, COM+, and .NET. Understanding these relationships is important if you want to create a functional COM+ application.

Remember that COM+ relies on COM and DCOM (Microsoft Distributed Component Object Model) to provide part of its functionality. COM is the source of component technology, while DCOM provides the *remote procedure call (RPC)* functionality. The first two sections of this chapter explore the relationship between the two. The chapter will also discuss how *Microsoft Message Queuing (MSMQ)* fits within the *COM+ Queued Components*. Using message queuing can greatly enhance the flexibility of your application and allow it to process data asynchronously.

The final portion of the chapter discusses some COM+-specific issues you need to consider when working with .NET components. For example, the communication with COM+ is two way, so you need to know how to accept as well as send information to COM+. In general, you'll find that the hardest thing to understand is the communication—specifically, how it occurs—because .NET performs part of the work for you in the background.

COM+ Begins with COM

From a client-side component-creation perspective, COM and COM+ are about the same. Despite all the hype to the contrary, you can create a component using either form of the technology. In fact, COM+ is merely an augmentation of existing COM technology when it comes to working with components. The important thing to remember is that COM+ is a true superset of COM, so you lose nothing by using COM+ in place of COM in your applications. Consequently, the information you learned about using COM in .NET in Chapters 3 and 4 also applies to working with COM+. Of course, COM+ deals exclusively with components and not controls, so you need to consider only component interoperability issues.

You'll find that the .NET environment reacts somewhat differently from a COM+ application because this application type installs differently. For this reason you should develop your application with a two-machine setup—one machine is the server, and the other is the client. When you install the proxy application on the client machine, you'll find it doesn't include some features of a standard COM setup because it doesn't need them. The action takes place on the server, not on the client, so the client needs only a pointer to the server. The next section describes some interoperability issues of using COM+ applications with .NET.

In addition to .NET differences, COM and COM+ have some differences that you need to consider when developing your application. For example, the design goals for COM+ are different than those for COM, so naturally, the two technologies work somewhat differently. It's important to know about these differences as you attempt to move a component from COM to COM+—otherwise, you'll run into problems before you even begin to work with .NET. The following sections describe these differences.

A Look at COM+ Interoperability

Unlike COM, COM+ interoperability begins at the server. You create the COM+ application using the component as we did in the "Creating COM+ Applications and Installing Components" section of Chapter 2. Once you export the proxy, you install it on the client machine. For a developer, this means installing the proxy on your workstation. Once you have the proxy installed, you'll be able to view the COM+ application using the Component Services console.

At this point, you use the component just as you would any other component within the .NET IDE. In general, the material in the "Generating Runtime

Callable Wrappers" section of Chapter 3 applies to obtaining a reference to the component. However, you need to consider several special issues when working with COM+ applications. The most important issue is that you're working with a proxy generated on another machine.

Chapter 3 discussed three methods for gaining access to a COM component. The easiest method to use when working with a COM+ application is the integrated development environment (IDE)—otherwise, you'll need to locate the local copy of the type library to use with TlbImp.exe or the *TypeLibConverter* class. If you choose one of these other methods, you'll need the application ID. Right-click the application entry in the COM+ Applications folder of the Component Services console, and choose Properties from the context menu. Select the General tab, and you'll see a dialog box similar to the one shown in Figure 5-1.

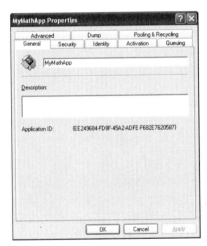

Figure 5-1 You'll need the Application ID to locate the components for the COM+ application on your local drive.

The Application ID field is the one that you're interested in because COM+ uses this GUID to keep the components from each application separate. Append this information to the Program Files\ComPlus Applications\ path, and you'll have the path to your components. In this case, the complete path would be Program Files\ComPlus Applications\{EE249684-FD8F-45A2-ADFE-F682E7620587}. This folder holds a copy of your component and the type library. Make sure you don't move or otherwise change the component or type library when you use it.

We'll also see in Chapter 9 that interoperability requires some interesting component planning. The problem is one of getting COM+ to recognize the component. The base class for your component makes a difference. Consequently, we'll discuss components created with the following base classes:

- Object
- Component
- ServicedComponent

Of the three, the *ServicedComponent* class provides the greatest flexibility. A component based on the *Object* or *Component* class will have limited flexibility and present problems for Windows 2000 developers. However, a component based on the *ServicedComponent* class can present problems of its own. For example, you'll find it difficult to create an application proxy if you install the component using the RegSvcs.exe utility.

As we saw in Chapter 2, creating a simple component results in a COM+ component addition that includes only the methods found in the *Component* class and those found in the *Object* class. This includes the *Equals()*, *GetHashCode()*, *GetType()*, and *ToString()* methods. All this type of component requires is that you add the *[ClassInterface(ClassInterfaceType.AutoDual)]* attribute.

> **Tip** Whenever you create a component for COM+, you should include the *[Guid]* attribute. Whenever COM+ registers your component as part of the installation process, it makes a registry entry. The common language runtime creates a GUID at random unless you define the *[Guid]* attribute. Cleaning up the registry after a development session can become quite time consuming. Using the same GUID all the time means you'll spend less time cleaning and more time developing.

When you design a component based on the *Component* class, you need to add a few more bits of code. Listing 5-1 shows a component that you'll find in the Chapter05\MyMath (Component) folder in the companion content. You can get the companion content at the book's Web site: *http://www.microsoft.com/mspress/books/6426.asp*.

```csharp
using System;
using System.Runtime.InteropServices;
using System.ComponentModel;

namespace MyMath
{
   /// <summary>
   /// A simple class that shows the four basic math functions.
   /// </summary>
   [Guid("0C4340A2-C362-4287-9A03-8CDD3D1F80F6"),
    ClassInterface(ClassInterfaceType.AutoDual)]
   public class MathFunctions : Component
   {
      /// <summary>
      /// Add two Int32 values together.
      /// </summary>
      /// <param name="Value1">The first number.</param>
      /// <param name="Value2">The second number.</param>
      /// <returns>The two numbers added.</returns>
      public Int32 DoAdd(Int32 Value1, Int32 Value2)
      {
         return Value1 + Value2;
      }

      /// <summary>
      /// Subtract one Int32 value from another.
      /// </summary>
      /// <param name="Value1">Initial value</param>
      /// <param name="Value2">Value to subtract</param>
      /// <returns>Value2 subtracted from Value1</returns>
      public Int32 DoSubtract(Int32 Value1, Int32 Value2)
      {
         return Value1 - Value2;
      }

      /// <summary>
      /// Multiply two Int32 values.
      /// </summary>
      /// <param name="Value1">The first number.</param>
      /// <param name="Value">The second number.</param>
      /// <returns>The two values multiplied.</returns>
      public Int32 DoMultiply(Int32 Value1, Int32 Value2)
      {
         return Value1 * Value2;
      }
```

Listing 5-1 MyMath.cs (Component)

```
/// <summary>
/// Divide one Int32 value by another.
/// </summary>
/// <param name="Value1">Initial value.</param>
/// <param name="Value2">Divisor</param>
/// <returns>Value1 divided by Value2</returns>
public Int32 DoDivide(Int32 Value1, Int32 Value2)
{
    return Value1 / Value2;
}
    }
}
```

As you can see, this component requires that you subclass the *Component* class found in the *System.ComponentModel* namespace. Fortunately, this namespace appears in the System.dll file, so you don't need to reference any additional DLLs in your component. Figure 5-2 shows that creating a component using this technique adds the *IComponent* and *IDisposable* interfaces, which include the *add_Disposed()*, *remove_Disposed()*, *Site()*, and *Disposed()* methods. You'll use the *add_Disposed()* and *remove_Disposed()* methods to add and remove event handlers for the *Disposed* event. Notice that there are also two copies of the *Site()* method—one to get the *Site* property value and one to set it.

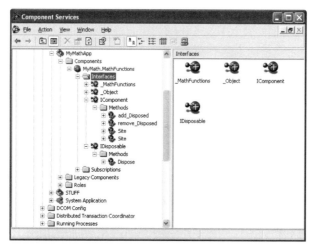

Figure 5-2 Creating a component based on the *Component* class adds the *IComponent* and *IDisposable* interfaces.

Creating a component that subclasses the *ServicedComponent* class gets a little more complex. You need to add a reference to the System.Enterprise-Services.dll. In addition, you need to add the appropriate reference to your code and add some code for the *ServicedComponent* class. Listing 5-2 shows a typical example of the code you need. (You'll find the complete component in the Chapter05\MyMath (ServicedComponent) folder of the companion content.)

```csharp
using System;
using System.Runtime.InteropServices;
using System.EnterpriseServices;

namespace MyMath
{
    /// <summary>
    /// A simple class that shows the four basic math functions.
    /// </summary>
    [Guid("0C4340A2-C362-4287-9A03-8CDD3D1F80F6"),
     ClassInterface(ClassInterfaceType.AutoDual)]
    public class MathFunctions : ServicedComponent
    {
        /// <summary>
        /// Add two Int32 values together.
        /// </summary>
        /// <param name="Value1">The first number.</param>
        /// <param name="Value2">The second number.</param>
        /// <returns>The two numbers added.</returns>
        public Int32 DoAdd(Int32 Value1, Int32 Value2)
        {
            return Value1 + Value2;
        }

        /// <summary>
        /// Subtract one Int32 value from another.
        /// </summary>
        /// <param name="Value1">Initial value</param>
        /// <param name="Value2">Value to subtract</param>
        /// <returns>Value2 subtracted from Value1</returns>
        public Int32 DoSubtract(Int32 Value1, Int32 Value2)
        {
            return Value1 - Value2;
        }

        /// <summary>
        /// Multiply two Int32 values.
        /// </summary>
        /// <param name="Value1">The first number.</param>
        /// <param name="Value">The second number.</param>
        /// <returns>The two values multiplied.</returns>
        public Int32 DoMultiply(Int32 Value1, Int32 Value2)
```

Listing 5-2 MyMath.cs (ServicedComponent)

```
        {
            return Value1 * Value2;
        }

        /// <summary>
        /// Divide one Int32 value by another.
        /// </summary>
        /// <param name="Value1">Initial value.</param>
        /// <param name="Value2">Divisor</param>
        /// <returns>Value1 divided by Value2</returns>
        public Int32 DoDivide(Int32 Value1, Int32 Value2)
        {
            return Value1 / Value2;
        }
    }
}
```

The *System.EnterpriseServices* namespace is especially important to COM+ developers because it provides access to a number of COM+ resources, including the component constructor string. We'll discuss the intricacies of this class later in the book. For now, you need to know that it's also the source of the *ServicedComponent* class. Figure 5-3 shows that this component includes a number of new interfaces, including *IDisposable*, *IManagedObject*, *IRemoteDispatch*, and *System_EnterpriseServices_IServicedComponentInfo*. Your application should never use the methods found in the *IRemoteDispatch* and *System_EnterpriseServices_IServicedComponentInfo* interfaces—they're reserved for .NET Framework use. COM uses the *IManagedObject* interface during component activation and marshaling. Again, you won't normally interact with this interface from an application.

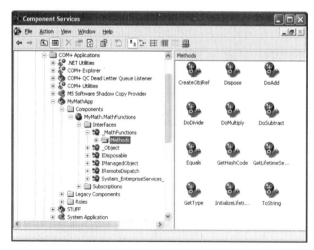

Figure 5-3 Creating a component based on the *ServicedComponent* class adds a number of additional interfaces.

COM+ Design Goals

In Chapter 2, we discussed the reasons you might want to use COM+ for development purposes, even with the features that .NET provides. However, we really haven't discussed the COM+ part of the picture. To understand what you gain by using COM+, you need to understand some of the goals that the design team had in mind when putting COM+ together:

- **Make developing server components as easy as developing client components.** Before COM+, there were a lot of server-specific issues to take care of, such as multiple users hitting a component at the same time. COM+ removes many problems that come with a multiuser environment like the one you find on servers. Of course, the solution is to promote distributed application development.

- **Make it just as easy to develop enterprise applications as it is to develop workgroup applications.** COM+ allows you to create components that will scale to any size. *Load balancing* is a term that you'll hear more and more as companies try to create an environment in which a single programming effort will result in components that continue to work as the company grows.

These two goals define the essential reasons to use COM+. Unlike COM, Microsoft designed COM+ to allow you to create distributed applications that rely on component technology that scales to any size. This COM+ difference will greatly affect how you create applications in the future. In many cases, you'll now create components that applications on the client will use to access data on yet another server.

Let's talk about the client and server situation a little further. COM+ is also part of the Microsoft distributed architecture strategy. Essentially, COM+ is an *n*-tier architecture, where various servers perform specific tasks. Those tasks are just part of a whole application. In other words, a single application on the user's machine might require the services provided by more than one server. One server might have the components that include the basic business logic for the request, another server might access in-memory databases containing things like a list of the states in the United States, and a third server might provide access to the company's main data store. In short, COM+ is the predecessor to the current Web services technology that many companies are considering adopting.

Transactions and COM+

One of the more important reasons to use COM+ is ensuring the integrity of the data you transfer from one machine to another. Anytime two machines talk to each other using any media (cable, wireless, or anything else you can think of), you have to create some type of data exchange protocol. Even if the machines are sitting side-by-side in the same room, there's a chance of losing data because of a bad connection or interference. Given today's distributed environment, there's a much greater chance for lost data, which means that you need some type of transaction technology in place.

Microsoft Transaction Server (MTS) is part of the COM+ universe. MTS is the mechanism by which COM+ guarantees delivery of data from one machine to another. These services not only ensure the data delivery, they also ensure that both the sender and receiver are satisfied with the integrity of the data. The following list provides an overview of the services MTS can provide to COM+:

- **Transactions** A transaction is a single group of instructions the sender or receiver carry out to complete a task. Either a transaction is completed or MTS rolls it back so that the application environment is the same as it was before the transaction started. MTS frees the programmer from managing transactions. All the programmer needs to do is specify that a given set of instructions constitutes a transaction.

- **Resource pooling** Most servers have huge quantities of memory and hard-disk space that components can use to complete tasks. However, given the complex environment in which the developer places components, trying to manage resources is a difficult task to say the least. MTS also features automated resource management. Not only does resource pooling free the programmer from micromanaging system resources, it also ensures each component gets the resources it needs.

- **Security** Getting data from one point to another and ensuring the database records it properly won't do much for you if someone breaks into the connection between the client and server and corrupts the data. As a result, security is one of the more important features that MTS provides.

- **Administration** Managing your MTS setup so that you can get optimum performance from your server is an important task. Microsoft provides a Microsoft Management Console (MMC) snap-in that makes MTS management easier.

As you can see, MTS provides a lot more than just transaction management, although that's its main function. The other services MTS provides merely augment the main function of making sure data gets from one point to another without interruption and that all parties performing operations on that data complete their tasks successfully, or not at all. Without these services, COM+ as a whole would fail because data security is a primary requirement to creating distributed applications.

You won't work directly with MTS in most cases. The *Distributed Transaction Coordinator (DTC)* enables MTS to start transactions on behalf of a component. The DTC also manages transactions that occur on multiple servers. For example, if a component on one server wants to participate in a transaction on another server, the DTC will manage the communication. MTS performs the actual transactional tasks, but the DTC is central to allowing the transaction to occur in the first place. You'll manage the DTC using the Distributed Transaction Coordinator folder elements of the Component Services console shown in Figure 5-4. (In this case, you're seeing the statistics for the server in question.) We'll use this management tool more as the book progresses.

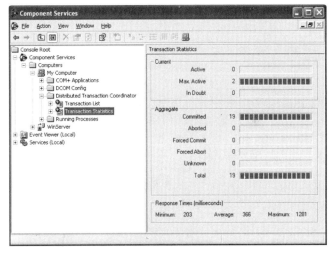

Figure 5-4 Use the Distributed Transaction Coordinator folder elements to manage transactions on a server.

One service that doesn't appear in our list is serialization. This particular feature of MTS ensures that both data and commands arrive at the database in the same order the client created them, even if the network protocol used to transfer the packets of information doesn't guarantee any order of delivery. This means you won't need to worry quite as much about the features provided by the underlying network protocol—at least not when it concerns the order your data will arrive in.

Messages and COM+

COM+ also includes the concept of disconnected applications. A disconnected application is a form of asynchronous processing in which the client and server don't need to exist at the same time. Messaging, a type of e-mail communication, provides the glue required to keep client and server communicating. (The use of message queues isn't precisely the same as e-mail, but the analogy is a good one for understanding how the process works.)

At the heart of this technology is *Queued Components*, which in turn uses *Microsoft Message Queuing (MSMQ)* services. MSMQ is the base stand-alone technology originally introduced for use within Microsoft Windows NT for message-based application development. Queued Components are the new COM+ version of MSMQ that offers a true superset of the older technology. All older MSMQ interfaces are still in place, but now you also have more automation and integration with COM available in Queued Components. Queued Components provides both an application programming interface (API) and a component-based interface for developers. The following list describes some of the benefits of using Queued Components.

> **Note** You'll see MSMQ and Queued Components used throughout the book in an almost interchangeable way. I'll use the term Queued Components whenever I'm talking about a Queued Component–specific feature such as a wizard, while MSMQ will always refer to the underlying technology or an existing feature like a programming API. It's important to see Queued Components as a slightly augmented version of MSMQ that was designed specifically for use with COM+ and not as a new product.

- **Better road-warrior support** In the past, an application that required services from the server or wanted to provide input to the server had to maintain a live connection. Obviously, this is impossible for employees on the road, so companies often had to rely on cumbersome technologies of dubious value that forced the employee to use different methods in different situations. In addition to the problem of getting an employee trained to use more than one data entry and management method, there was a problem with getting the employee to use the right method at the right time.

- **Lower development costs** Older technologies forced the programmer to do more work. Even if the programmer needed to worry only about two data-entry scenarios, that still required twice the amount of code and debugging. In essence, the programmer was writing the same application twice because of a lack of disconnected application tools. Of course, the doubling of data-entry features also resulted in larger applications that required more memory to load. A disconnected application takes only slightly more disk space and memory than a single interface application designed for desktop-only use.

- **No live connection needed** Applications that rely on Queued Components don't care about the current connected state of the application. Data that an application wants to send to the server gets stored in a local message queue if the application can't establish a connection with the server. When the user makes a connection, Queued Components automatically uploads the data in the message queue for the user. In this respect, a Queued Component application acts as an answering machine. A recorder on the client creates the message, a listener on the server alerts the server-side component to the presence of the message, and a player retrieves the message from the queue.

- **Preemptive resource management** The application can also download resources such as database updates or new application functionality from the server before the user attempts to break the connection with the server. This resource management technique helps the user request at least a subset of the data from the server, even though the user might not realize there isn't a connection in place for getting the requested information. The only time the user will notice any difference is if the application needs the data requested immediately and the preemptive resource management module didn't anticipate the need to download it from the server. For example, the application could automatically request the client records needed for the client's appointments the following day based on appointment-book entries. Even if the task didn't get done, as soon as the user establishes a connection, the resource management module can download the requested data in the background. The resource management module can make the request by using messages stored in the user's local queue.

Unlike many other COM+-related services discussed in this chapter, you'll use the Computer Management console to manage the queues on a system, unless you choose to create a custom console for the purpose. Figure 5-5 shows an example of the Computer Management console with the Message Queuing folder displayed. Notice that this folder appears in the Services And Applications folder.

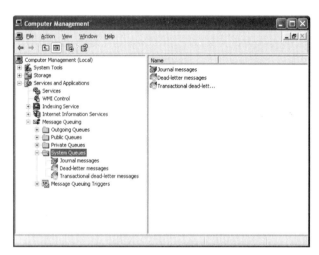

Figure 5-5 Manage the queues for an application using the Message Queuing folder features.

As you can see, MSMQ provides four levels of message queues: Outgoing Queues, Public Queues, Private Queues, and System Queues. We'll use all these queues to create various applications in the book. The System Queues folder is the only folder that actually contains queues when you first install Message Queuing (the name of the option found in the Windows Components Wizard For Windows XP). This queue generally contains messages of a system nature, including messages that MSMQ couldn't deliver. The Outgoing Queues folder contains all messages the local computer will send to the server once a connection is established. The Public Queues folder contains permanent queues that are visible to the public, while the Private Queues folder contains queues that only local applications should see.

Visual Studio .NET makes it almost too easy to use a queue. You can access both local and remote queues using Server Explorer, as shown in Figure 5-6. Notice that you can access all but the Outgoing Queues folder, which makes sense because this folder contains only temporary queues (and only while the client lacks a connection to the server).

Figure 5-6 Use Server Explorer to access local and remote queues.

To add a queue to your application, drag and drop it onto the form. Visual Studio .NET will create a MessageQueue object for you. The properties will contain all the correct pointers for the queue. We'll discuss message queues at length in Chapter 10.

COM+ Services

So far, we've seen that COM+ is an amalgam of various existing technologies. In short, nothing I've said so far is very new. However, the way that COM+ provides a wrapper for making all these technologies work together is a relatively new idea.

Many COM+ concepts we'll discuss are similar to those found in .NET. COM+ is the predecessor to the .NET technologies. Although I haven't mentioned it yet, you should use the remoting features of .NET before you rely on COM+ for managed application requirements. Web services also provide a good alternative to COM+ for Internet applications. In fact, as shown in Figure 5-7, the IDE generates an error if you attempt to directly use a managed component that's part of a COM+ application. There's no reason to pay a double performance penalty for using the component—use it directly as a managed component whenever possible. Of course, disconnected applications are one scenario in which you might want to use managed components in a COM+

application from your managed client—it's a viable application strategy. In addition, you can still use COM+ to make your managed components available to unmanaged clients.

Figure 5-7 Attempting to directly import a managed component that's part of a COM+ application into your application will generate an error message.

COM+ isn't merely a wrapper for existing services, however. It also provides unique services that you won't find in any older Microsoft offerings. The following list provides you with an overview of what these services are. We'll study these features in detail as the book progresses.

- **Events** Applications can receive events generated on the server as if they occurred on the local machine. This means the server-side components you create will have a direct connection to the client. COM+ allows you to use unicast (in which an event is sent to one event sink), multicast (in which an event is sent to multiple event sinks), and unbound (in which an event occurs when client makes contact) events. The unbound event is particularly useful because it can inform a client about conditions on the server after the client performs an initial logon. In other words, every client who logs on to the system will receive the current (dynamic) server status.

- **Security** COM+ relies on MTS for the security of its data in many cases. However, COM+ still has security concerns when instantiated objects on the server need to communicate with a client and there isn't any transaction. In addition, COM+ enables the developer to create queued components—essentially a component in a message. We discussed security issues as part of the "Adding Security to a COM+ Application" section of Chapter 2.

- **Component Load Balancing (CLB)** Large companies normally use more than one server for their data storage needs. Of course, this means the company normally needs to provide access to specific servers to a given user in order to manually balance the server load. Load balancing lets everyone access all the available servers through a router. The router keeps track of how much of a load each server has and balances new requests accordingly. In addition, the router can move current requests from a failed server to the good ones in the cluster without the user even realizing a server failure has occurred.

- **Queued Components** Clients require updates to the components they hold from time to time and, in some cases, will require a new component before they can perform a specific task. In the past, the administrator had to install new components individually on each machine or create cumbersome batch files to do the job. The use of Queued Components helps each client to receive automatic component updates. The administrator doesn't need to do much more than install the component on the server. Because all users have access to the same component, they all receive the update at the same time.

- **Compensating resource manager** Legacy applications require this particular service. It builds a framework around the old server application so that clients can access the application using all the new features COM+ provides. The main goal of this service is to help you maintain your investment in established applications, yet allow the old application to interact with other resources on the server. Of course, this feature comes at the cost of performance, so upgrading your components to .NET is one option you should consider.

- **Administration** COM+ uses an MMC snap-in to provide administrative services for your server-side components. This snap-in lets you manage all COM components and helps you administer all new services COM+ provides. This snap-in also provides a programming interface that allows you to install, configure, and automatically deploy your COM+ components. It relies on the Active Directory catalog to store the attributes for each of the components installed on the server. The COM+ component attributes include transactions, security roles, and activation properties.

- **Publish/subscribe event model** COM+ provides a new event model that helps the developer create applications that don't need to know quite as much about each other. The component publishes events and doesn't care where those events go. An application can subscribe to events without really knowing their source. In between these two applications are component services, which manage the connection between publisher and subscriber.

Understanding the Role of DCOM in COM+

COM has been through a number of changes as Microsoft works to make it fulfill the needs of developers. The Microsoft Distributed Component Object Model (DCOM) was the second step in the evolution of COM. This version of COM helps components and applications communicate over a network no matter how widely separated the participating computers are from each other. In general, DCOM isn't a component technology, it's a binary data transfer technology. Microsoft modeled DCOM after the Open Software Foundation (OSF) distributed computing environment remote procedure call (DCE RPC) specification.

DCOM can communicate over a broad range of network protocols. This includes both the HTTP and TCP/IP protocols used by the Internet. In other words, a component on a laptop in New York could communicate with a server running in Paris and use that server's resources as if the two were in the same room. In addition, DCOM takes care of handling the network protocol details for you so that you can concentrate on the business logic of the component you're designing.

The theory of DCOM is great, but the implementation has proved a little less than stellar, so we now have Web Services for the Internet. Because DCOM is a binary rather than a text-based data transfer technology and because DCOM uses a range of ports in its communication, it has problems getting through the firewalls most companies need to have in place. However, there are ways to make DCOM work for private application communication.

> **Tip** You have quite a few resources at your disposal when it comes to DCOM on the Internet. The best place to start looking for the latest information about this technology is at the Microsoft DCOM Web site at: *http://www.microsoft.com/com/dcom.asp*. This site provides a link to the DCOM specification, books on how to work with DCOM, programming samples, white papers, and links to other Web sites with additional DCOM information. One of the better places to get information about the OSF DCE RPC specification (the underlying technology for DCOM) is at: *http://archive.dstc.edu.au/AU/research_news/dce/dce.html*. This Web site will help you find the specification, frequently asked question (FAQ) sheets for using DCE RPC in a variety of environments, and a list of vendors who support DCE RPC in their products.

Most developers are aware of the DCOMCnfg.exe utility used to configure components for use with DCOM. Essentially, with the DCOMCnfg utility you can tell the local machine where to find the component on a remote machine. The configuration utility also helps you with issues such as security and adding new protocols for data transfer. Microsoft Windows XP uses the Component Services console for this purpose and entering DCOMCnfg.exe at the command line will bring up this console. You'll find a DCOM Config folder similar to the one shown in Figure 5-8 for configuration issues. Right-click the component of interest and choose Properties from the content menu to configure the component.

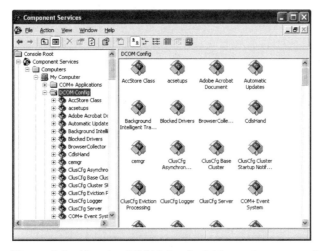

Figure 5-8 Use the DCOM Config folder options to configure components if you use Windows XP.

We won't pursue DCOM development in this book except as it applies to making COM+ work. DCOM is an older technology that a few developers still use. It has lost favor to newer technologies, such as Web services, for most new development. In addition, if you know how to make COM work with .NET, you have a good idea of how to make DCOM work too—at least from a development perspective. With this in mind, the following sections examine some of the inner workings of DCOM and describe how they apply to COM+ application development.

How Does the Connection Work?

In this section, we'll present a bird's-eye view of how DCOM creates and manages a connection between the client and server. You need to understand how this connection works so that you can troubleshoot problems in your own applications. Figure 5-9 contains a block diagram of the flow of data from the client to the server. The list that follows Figure 5-9 describes each of the diagram elements.

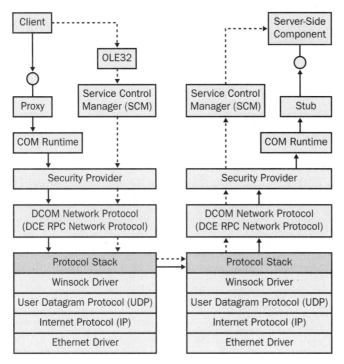

Figure 5-9 A simplified DCOM connection overview block diagram

> **Note** Figure 5-9 assumes a generic component setup. We aren't doing anything fancy here because the idea is to learn how the connection between the client and server works. A real-world component would provide more in the way of functionality and, therefore, would perform a lot more communication to complete a task. The underlying communication technology will remain the same no matter how complex or simple your component is. The only thing that will change is the amount and type of communication between the client and server.

- **Client** Originates requests to the server for resources and support. As far as it's concerned, the component is local and of an unmanaged type.

- **OLE32** DLL containing the methods used to create an instance of an object (along with a wealth of other functionality). There are five methods available for remote object creation: *CoCreateInstanceEx()*, *CoGetInstanceFromFile()*, *CoGetInstanceFromStorage()*, *CoGetClassObject()*, and *CoGetClassObjectFromURL()*. However, if you look at the registry entry shown in Figure 5-10, you'll notice the client will use one of these functions to call Mscoree.dll instead of your component. The Mscoree.dll creates the COM Callable Wrapper (CCW) for your component.

Figure 5-10 The Registry holds the key to understanding how DCOM calls the component.

- **Service Control Manager (SCM)** Creates the initial connection between the client and server. DCOM relies on the SCM only during object creation. This feature is implemented by the *TransportLoad()* method in the Rpcltscm.dll file.

- **Proxy** Creates the server's presence within the client's address space. The operating system creates and manages the proxy, which is a table of interfaces, at the request of the COM runtime. It allows the client to think that the server is local, even though the server is located on another machine. Windows uses a method like *CreateProxyFromTypeInfo()* found in the Rpcrt4.dll file to create the proxy.

- **COM runtime** Includes the operating system elements that host objects and provide client/server communication. The COM runtime is part of any COM-related scenario—both in-process and out-of-process, and local and remote.

- **Security provider** Ensures all parties in the data exchange have the correct rights. The security provider logs the client machine onto the server machine to allow the data exchange to take place. Some security providers will also protect all data transferred between the client and server in some way—usually by using encryption.

> **Note** Windows provides support for several standard security providers for both Internet and local network use. These providers include NT LAN Manager (NTLM, the standard Windows NT security protocol), Kerberos, Distributed Password Authentication (DPA, which is used by CompuServe and MSN), secure channel security services like Secure Sockets Layer (SSL)/ Private Communications Technology (PCT), and third-party Distributed Computing Environment (DCE) providers. The choice of security provider usually depends on the application setup and the media used to transfer the data. In addition, the security provider chosen must work on both client and server.

- **DCOM Network Protocol (DCE RPC Network Protocol)** Defines a protocol (the set of rules) for creating a connection with a remote server for using objects installed on that server. In addition to implementing a component protocol, this block contains all the elements needed to implement the Object Remote Procedure Call (ORPC) specification at an application level. This particular component has several names in the Microsoft documentation—the most popular of which is *DCOM wire protocol*. For the most part, this low-level data transfer protocol is invisible to the .NET developer and you'll never need to worry about it, even if you decide to work with DCOM.

- **Protocol Stack** Provides the low-level connectivity required for the network at various levels. The actual network communication requires more than just one protocol—there are network-related protocols to consider as well. The protocol stack consists of all the protocols required to create a connection between the client and server, including network-specific protocols such as TCP/IP. Figure 5-9 shows a typical protocol stack consisting of a Winsock driver, a User Datagram Protocol (UDP), an Internet Protocol (IP), and an Ethernet driver. The Ethernet network interface card (NIC) actually used to create the physical connection between the client and server doesn't appear in the figure.

- **Stub** Creates the impression of the client's presence within the server's address space. The operating system creates and manages the proxy, which is actually a table of interfaces, at the request of the

COM runtime. As far as the server is concerned, it's working with a local client. Windows uses a method such as *CreateStubFromType-Info()*, which is found in the Rpcrt4.dll file used to create the stub.

- **Server** Instantiates the COM object from which the client has requested services and resources.

Two communication paths are shown in Figure 5-9. The first path (the dotted line) shows how to create an instance of the object. The second path (the solid line) shows the path of normal communication between the client and server. Creating a line of communication between a client and server normally follows these steps.

> **Note** The following discussion follows a pure COM perspective of the DCOM data transfer technique. If you're using a .NET component or client, the .NET interoperability technologies discussed in Chapters 3 and 4 come into play. The point is that .NET creates a seamless method of making DCOM work. As far as DCOM is concerned, it's working with both an unmanaged component and an unmanaged client. Only the common language runtime knows that one or the other (or perhaps both) is a managed version of the code.

1. The client issues one of the five object creation method calls we discussed earlier in the section (in the Ole32.dll bullet item). The call must include both a class ID (CLSID) and a server name (along with any information required to log onto the server). As an alternative, the client can issue a standard call that Ole32.dll will resolve to a remote location based on a registry entry, or the client can use monikers.

2. Ole32.dll calls on the client-side SCM to create a connection to the server machine because it can't service the call locally.

3. The DCOM network protocol creates the required packets to send information from the client to the server.

4. The server-side SCM creates an instance of the desired server-side component and returns a pointer of the object instance to the client. The pointer actually points at the CCW for a managed component.

5. The server-side SCM calls on the COM runtime to create a stub with which the component will interact.

6. The client-side SCM calls on the COM runtime to create a proxy with which the client will interact.

7. The SCM returns a pointer to the proxy to the client. Remember that this pointer belongs to the Runtime Callable Wrapper (RCW) for a managed client, not the actual client.

8. Normal client-side and server-side component communications begin.

Connection-Oriented Data Flow Optimization

Sometimes, the development and placement of a component depends on how much communication is taking place. Consider a situation in which a client needs access to the contents of a database. You could place a component directly on the client machine that would access the database manager, gain access to the required data, and then format it for the user. However, this design would require a lot of network communication because the client would need to constantly communicate with the database manager and send or receive the data.

Splitting the component in two would allow you to reduce the amount of data traversing the network. One component on the client machine could send data requests and format the incoming data. A second component on the server could make the data requests and deliver only the required information to the client. Using this approach would significantly reduce network traffic, enhance both client and server efficiency, and make the user more productive all at the same time.

DCOM performs some connection manipulation on its own. One of the most important changes DCOM will implement automatically is connection optimization. For example, if you have a server-side component that's manipulating a database using OLE DB or ODBC, DCOM will more than likely copy the component to the client and then remove itself from the data stream. Because the connection to the database exists through a third party (normally, a provider), neither the client nor the database manager notice any difference in the performance of the component. However, since DCOM is out of the picture, the component executes more efficiently. Obviously, this is a very specific kind of connection change and DCOM implements it only when the client will see a significant performance gain.

COM+-Specific Issues

We've examined quite a few COM+ issues so far in this chapter. However, most of the discussion has focused on the ways in which COM+ combines older technology and makes it easier to use. The following sections describe issues specific to COM+. We'll discuss the applications you can create, special error-handling considerations, and even a special security class you need to know about.

Application Types

Unlike previous renditions of COM, COM+ supports the idea of a true application type. An application type, in this case, isn't the same as the application types you associate with a client machine. For example, there are no database or spreadsheet application types when talking about COM+. Here's a list of the four COM+ application types:

- Library
- Server
- Proxy
- Preinstalled

Part of the reason for this new direction is that COM+ handles each kind of application differently. For example, COM+ handles the security of a library application differently than the security of a server application. When working with a library application, the object executes in the client process and the component relies on the client's security context. On the other hand, a server application executes out of process. A combination of the component attributes and the client information supplied as part of the component request define the security context.

The following sections will help you better understand how the four application types differ. You need to know about the various COM+ application types to determine what type of application you want to develop.

Server Applications

The server application is an out-of-process server. It executes in its own process and creates its own context. You can access all COM+ services using a server application, and the full resources of the host machine are at your disposal (within the scope of the security settings at least).

You'll create the server application more often than any other COM+ application type because this is the most versatile form of application. Obviously, this application will execute on the server and produce the least amount of network traffic (if you optimize it that way).

Library Applications

A library application represents one of the newest ways to integrate components in an application. The library application executes in the client process. This means that while the library application file physically resides on the server and the server must request its services, the resulting object will execute on the client machine. The client downloads a library application from the server and uses it locally.

Because of the way a library application executes, COM+ places restrictions on the way you can work with it and the services you can access. These restrictions make sense when you think about the client orientation of the library application. Here's a list of the restrictions:

- No remote access support
- Can't use CLB
- Can't use Queued Components

Library applications can use role-based security. However, the client application's access limits the level of access for a library application. In other words, you can't create a component that will provide the client application with more access than it would normally get with its standard security settings. This limitation makes it impossible for a rogue component to damage the system or for users to pry into areas of the server they have no right seeing.

So, what are some of the advantages of library applications compared to standard client-side components? You get most of the same advantages that you would for a COM+ application, but from a client-side perspective. For example, you'll still make component updates at the server, not at the client machine. The server, not the client, still secures access to the component. In fact, the client won't see a copy of the component on disk—the component resides on the server and loads into the client's memory. In short, using library applications allows you to get the best benefits of client-side components without many of the problems that client-side components pose.

Proxy Applications

When working with DCOM, you had to either use the DCOMCnfg utility (Component Services console for Windows XP users) to configure the client machine to access the remote application, or find some method to add the required registry entries through a remote application. Not only was this a difficult and error-prone process, but it required some amount of administrator time for each new client and each new version of the component. In short, the old methodology was time consuming and almost unsafe from an application perspective.

COM+ provides the proxy application type. This isn't a component but a proxy for a component registered on the server. The proxy application runs on the client machine and automatically adds information into the registry about the real component that resides on the server. This component information includes class identification (CLSIDs), program identification (ProgIDs), the remote server name (RemoteServerName), and marshalling information. This combination of entries will allow the client to access the component on the server without additional intervention on the part of the administrator or developer. In short, Microsoft has automated what could otherwise be a time-consuming and error-prone task in COM+.

Preinstalled Applications

COM+ comes with a group of preinstalled applications. Some developers might think these applications are for COM+ use only—many Windows services in the past have worked exactly this way. The opposite is true with COM+—you're now encouraged to use these preinstalled components to make your own programming job easier.

You'll find all the COM+ applications in the COM+ Applications folder of the Component Services console. The number of applications you see partly depends on which optional services you install. For example, there are components related to Queued Components within this folder. Here's a list of the potential COM+ Applications folder entries:

- COM+ QC Dead Letter Queue Listener
- COM+ Utilities
- IIS In-Process Applications
- IIS Out-Of-Process Packed Application
- IIS System Applications
- IIS Utilities
- System Application

Error Handling

Error handling is a special concern for .NET developers using COM+ because COM+ presents a few special issues. The "How to Design COM Components for Use with .NET" section of Chapter 3 recommended using the *HRESULT* value as a means of indicating an error occurred within the component. This technique works fine in only a few cases when working with COM+. In many cases, an *HRESULT* value won't do much for you because the client application might not even be present to receive the error. COM is a local technology, whereas COM+ is a distributed technology, which makes the developer's task of error handling more difficult. You can use the *HRESULT* method if you know the client is going to be present to receive the return value. Otherwise, you need to find another method of error handling and reporting.

First you should try to avoid an extensive requirement for error handling. You need to create components that can recover from as many errors as possible so that error reporting isn't a significant issue. For example, the component should include code for a reasonable number of retries on a database connection before it reports an error. Likewise, it should contain code for internally handling as many resource errors as possible.

You will need to implement some form of error reporting because even a robust component will run into error conditions it can't handle. You could exercise a number of solutions, but the most practical solution is to place an error message in the Event Log to indicate the component experienced a problem. Of course, this creates uncertainty as to when, if ever, someone will actually find the error. The problem for many servers is that the administrator never looks at the Event Log as long as the server is still functional. Adding an email message to the error reporting routine cures this problem.

For every good solution, there's usually a good problem. The Event Log and email message solution suffers from a problem of information overload if the component fails drastically and produces an avalanche of error messages. Placing a limit on the number of error messages a component can generate within a given timeframe can help, but the administrator might still find a pile of messages in his or her inbox. Obviously, there are other solutions to the problem of error reporting for COM+ applications, but the use of the Event Log coupled with an email message works best overall.

Some developers create problems with their components because they're used to developing applications in COM. For example, a developer should never add display code to a COM+ component. The reason is simple. The server is very likely stored in a closet somewhere, and no one will ever look at it. The error message will never convey the information it's supposed to provide and could actually block proper server operation. We'll discuss more errors of this type as the book progresses.

Security

Security is an important issue for any distributed application. COM+ provides a solution in the form of role-based security. You learned how to configure this kind of security in the "Adding Security to a COM+ Application" section of Chapter 2.

The main security interface you need to know about when creating a COM+ component is *ISecurityCallContext*. You'll find the functionality of this unmanaged interface in the *SecurityCallContext* of the *EnterpriseServices* namespace. Don't add a reference to the COM+ Services Type Library to your application to gain access to the *ISecurityCallContext* support. The IDE will allow the addition, but it's important that you use the *SecurityCallContext* class members instead.

The *SecurityCallContext* class provides access to the security data for a particular component in a particular context. What this means to you as a developer is that you determine what role the current user is in and what his or her rights are. The fact that this interface is for a particular context means you can work only with the request associated with this particular instance of the component. In addition, you won't be able to gain information about the component as a whole.

This interface is normally accessible to your COM+ component if the administrator enables role-based security, but you won't always need to use it. The only time you'll need to use the methods of this class is when you decide to handle security within the component rather than allow the administrator to handle security as part of the component's configuration.

You'll normally use the *SecurityCallContext* class methods to learn specific information about the current component context. All this information is contained in the security call context collection—essentially an array of information about the currently executing instance of your component. Here's a list of the information that you can obtain from the security call context collection:

- Number of callers
- Minimum authentication level
- Callers
- Direct caller
- Original caller

In addition to the security call context collection information, the *SecurityCallContext* class helps you to determine whether a caller or user is in a specific role. You'd use this information to either grant or reject requests for access to specific methods within the component. You can also determine whether the administrator has enabled role-based security for this component (vs. being available on the server).

Now that you have a better idea of what the *SecurityCallContext* class can do for you, let's look at the available methods. Table 5-1 provides a list of methods you'll use most often. Table 5-2 provides a list of properties associated with this class. (In most cases, the properties replace method calls used by the *ISecurityCallContext* interface, so you need to look at both tables for comparison.)

Table 5-1 *SecurityCallContext* **Method Summary**

Method	Description
IsCallerInRole	Determines whether the direct caller is in a specified role. This method won't list all roles the caller is in. It merely allows you to determine whether the caller is a member of the role you specify. You can use this method to determine whether a caller should have access to a specific method or resource within the component.
IsUserInRole	Performs essentially the same task as *IsCallerInRole*, but for a specific user. The difference between the caller and a user is that the caller is the one currently using the component. The user call can refer to any user who has access to the server—not necessarily the user making the current call.

Table 5-2 *SecurityCallContext* **Property Summary**

Property	Description
Callers	This property returns one or more *SecurityCallers* objects. Each object describes a specific caller in the list of callers to the component method. Consider this a paper-trail property. This property accesses the *Callers* item in the *ISecurityCallContext* collection in COM+.
CurrentCall	This static property obtains a *SecurityCallContext* object for the current call. Essentially, this is your gateway for gaining access to the information provided by the *ISecurityCallContext* interface.
DirectCaller	This property returns the *SecurityIdentity* object for the direct caller of this method. The direct caller is the last caller in the caller hierarchy list. Use this property to determine whether the last caller in the list has the proper rights to request access to the component. If not, there's little point in continuing to process the request.

Table 5-2 *SecurityCallContext* **Property Summary**

Property	Description
IsSecurityEnabled	This property determines whether the administrator has enabled role-based security for this instance of the component. The method won't determine whether the administrator has enabled role-based security for other instances of the component.
MinAuthenticationLevel	This property returns the security information for the least secure caller in the caller hierarchy. By examining this property, you can determine whether any caller in the caller chain lacks proper credentials for component access.
NumCallers	This property returns the number of callers in the caller list. It accesses the *NumCallers* item in the *ISecurityCallContext* collection in COM+.
OriginalCaller	This property returns the *SecurityIdentity* object for the original caller of this method. The original caller is the first caller in the caller hierarchy list. Use this property to determine whether the first caller in the list has the proper rights to request access to the component. Sometimes the original caller tries to overcome security issues by hiding behind the rights of another caller.

Summary

This chapter has helped you understand three essential elements of COM+ development: COM, DCOM, and Queued Components and how they relate to the .NET components. In most cases, effectively mixing the managed environment of .NET with the unmanaged environment of COM+ comes down to communication. Learning to marshal data as needed and to interpret what you receive from COM+ is important.

Now that you have a better understanding of how COM+ works from the .NET perspective, you'll want to look at your .NET component development plans and determine whether any areas exist that require additional work. For example, you might determine that you need to spend additional time defining the data flow from your managed component to an unmanaged application that calls on COM+ for services. Likewise, your managed application might require additional work to ensure it will interact properly with COM+.

Chapter 6 begins the next section of the book. You'll begin writing applications that put into practice everything you've learned in the book so far. In Chapter 6, you'll learn attributed programming techniques. Attributes are an essential element of the .NET framework, and they've been added to unmanaged areas of Visual C++ as well. The next chapter puts the various attributed programming techniques in focus and helps you create your first COM applications using .NET code.

Part II
Writing COM Code

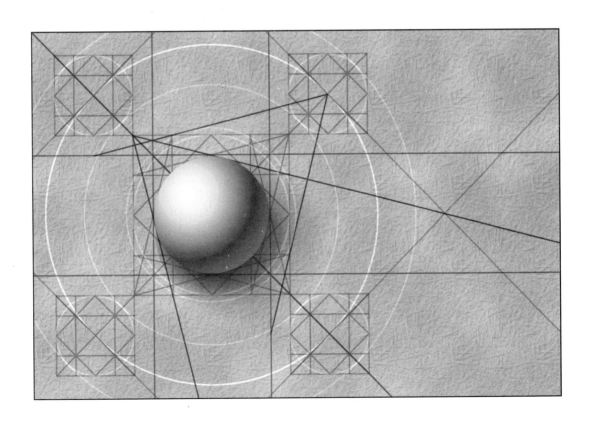

6

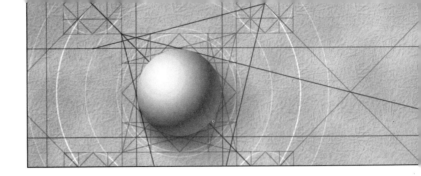

Attributed Programming

The second part of this book switches away from interoperability issues and focuses instead on creating and using COM components by exploiting the new features of Visual C++ .NET. The Active Template Library (ATL) was introduced in Visual C++ 4, and was designed to let C++ programmers create the smallest, fastest, most efficient COM components possible. The library has matured with successive releases of Visual C++ and now provides a very powerful tool for the C++ COM programmer.

Microsoft has introduced many new features into the latest version of ATL, version 7. Most important, though, Microsoft has introduced a new way to write ATL COM components, using *attributed programming*. This innovation makes it possible to write ATL COM components directly in C++, and for many components, developers will no longer have to interact with the Interface Definition Language (IDL) or work with the ATL source code. In fact, the compiler generates the IDL and ATL source code at compile time, so you don't need to look at them at all unless you want to understand what is happening.

This chapter provides an introduction to attributed programming, while Chapter 7 looks at the additions to the latest version of ATL—in particular, the ATL Server classes, which are designed for writing server-side applications for use with Internet Information Server (IIS).

> **Important** Attributed programming is used to create COM components in C++ using the ATL library. That means this chapter has nothing to do with .NET and also assumes knowledge of C++ and ATL programming on the part of the reader. No information in this chapter applies to Visual C# or Visual Basic .NET.

What Are Attributes?

Attributes provide a way to extend C++ without breaking the structure of the language. They define an add-on mechanism that is used to attach extra data to C++ constructs but which doesn't require adding new keywords to the language or altering the way C++ currently works.

> **Important** Attributes are used for several separate tasks in the .NET release of Microsoft development tools: providing metadata for managed types, creating COM objects, creating Web Services and ATL Server code, implementing performance counters, and implementing OLEDB consumers. Although the C++ syntax is the same wherever attributes are used, the tasks are quite different and attributes can work in different ways. For example, COM attributes deal with code generation, whereas metadata attributes provide data that can be used at compile time, run time, or both.

In Visual C++ 6, most COM development in C++ used the ATL library. While ATL produces very small, efficient COM classes, a large proportion of COM objects don't make use of ATL functionality beyond using the wizards to create an ATL skeleton and add methods and properties. The use of ATL for these components is overkill, and the developers of these classes don't need to modify—or even see—the ATL or IDL source code.

The COM-related attributes are designed to simplify the creation of COM components, and it's possible to create many components without seeing any ATL or IDL code at all. Even if you are used to using ATL, attributed programming can increase the productivity of component developers. You can still use

ATL if you need to, but attributes simplify the process of component creation for the many cases where you don't need anything out of the ordinary.

To put it rather simplistically, attributes let you specify in C++ code the same things you previously had to code in IDL or ATL. COM developers don't need to use a different library or learn IDL to create components, and they can do all their development in plain C++. Here's a simple example. To mark a class as the implementation of a COM coclass, use the *coclass* attribute on the class definition:

```
[coclass]
class MyObject
{
    ...
};
```

If you also want to specify the CLSID for the resulting coclass rather than have one generated automatically for you, add the *uuid* attribute:

```
[coclass, uuid(12EA4458-7753-11D2-098A-00C04F37BBFF)]
class MyObject
{
    ...
};
```

When you compile code containing attributes such as *coclass* and *guid*, the compiler automatically generates the ATL and IDL code needed to implement the COM component.

You can apply attributes to nearly any C++ construct, such as interfaces, classes, data members, and member functions. As you read the chapter, you'll find explanations of all the major attributes available to the COM programmer using Visual C++ .NET.

Using attributes replaces the large amount of IDL and registration code required by a COM component with a few concise annotations to class and interface definitions.

> **Note** COM attributes don't change the way COM objects are registered and the way they work, so type libraries and registry entries are still the same as before. Attributes simply provide a simpler and more abstract layer at the C++ code level.

How Do Attributes Work?

Attributes are implemented by *attribute providers*, which are implemented as separate dynamic-link libraries (DLLs). When the Visual C++ compiler recognizes an attribute, the code is parsed and syntactically verified as correct. The compiler then dynamically calls an attribute-provider DLL, which will insert code or make other modifications at compile time; the compiler processes the generated code as part of building the compiled output. The provider that gets called depends on the type of attribute—for example, ATL-related attributes are all implemented by the Atlprov.dll provider. The process is illustrated in Figure 6-1.

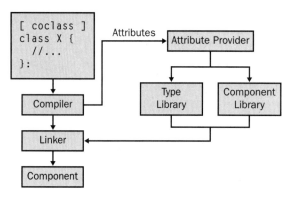

Figure 6-1 An attribute provider works with the compiler to generate code at compile time.

ATL attributes work by inserting ATL code into the project. Attributes don't alter the contents of the source file, and you can see only the injected code in the debugger. If you'd like a copy of the generated code, you can use the /Fx compiler option to generate a file containing the original file with the injected code merged. If you are using Visual Studio .NET, you can find this option on the Output Files pane of the C++ section in the Project Properties dialog. Note that the generated ATL code exists only at compile time, but information about the code needs to be added to debug builds so that it's available to the debugger.

> **Note** As of .NET 1.1, you can't write your own attribute providers. Two providers are used with C++: clxx.dll, which the compiler uses for basic type generation and marshaling; and atlprov.dll for ATL. In fact, it appears unlikely you'll ever be able to write custom providers because they interact with the compiler at a very low level and to write them would require knowing a lot of details about how the compiler works that are unlikely to be made public knowledge.

Using Attributes in C++ Code

In case you haven't used attributes in C++ code in Visual Studio .NET, this section briefly explains attribute syntax and usage. The basic syntax will be familiar to anyone who has done IDL coding.

Attributes can be attached to elements in C++ code by placing square brackets immediately before the element that the attributes apply to:

```
[coclass, uuid(12EA4458-7753-11D2-098A-00C04F37BBFF)]
class MyObject
{
  ...
};
```

In the example, the *coclass* and *uuid* attributes are being applied to the class that follows. If you need to specify more than one attribute, use a comma-separated list. Attributes can take parameters—in the example, *coclass* doesn't take any parameters, while *uuid* takes one, a GUID.

Attribute parameters can be mandatory or optional. Mandatory parameters (also called *positional parameters*) occur first in the argument list. Optional (or *named*) parameters occur after any positional ones, and they use a *name=value* syntax to denote which optional parameters are being specified. This means it doesn't matter in which order named parameters are specified. Here's an example:

```
[ module(dll, uuid = "{1D196988-3060-486E-A4AC-38F9685D3BF7}",
        name = "SimpleObject",
        helpstring = "SimpleObject 1.0 Type Library",
        resource_name = "IDR_SIMPLEOBJECT") ];
```

The module attribute has one positional parameter (*dll*) and four named parameters. The named parameters can be specified in any order.

> **Note** Although it has no bearing on how you use attributes in your C++ code, what you're doing when you specify an attribute is coding a constructor call. Attributes are implemented by classes, and when you attach an attribute to a code element, you're specifying how the attribute object should be created by giving the parameters for the constructor. The attribute object can then be invoked by the compiler or run time to do its job.

As well as using COM attributes, you can also write your own custom attributes for use with C++ classes and members. These have nothing to do with COM and are not used by the compiler. Instead, they're used to provide extra run-time information about types, which can be retrieved using the .NET Framework reflection mechanism. For example, you could create a custom attribute that holds information about the revision history of a class. Writing custom attributes is outside the scope of this book; if you want to know more, read *Programming with Managed Extensions for Microsoft Visual C++ .NET* by Richard Grimes, published by Microsoft Press.

Walkthrough: Creating a Simple COM Component

This section provides a complete walkthrough that shows how to create a simple COM server housed in a DLL by using attributed code and the wizards provided by Visual Studio .NET. After you've created the object, you'll see how to test the component from a console application, and then how to write the same code without using Visual Studio .NET.

Create an ATL project as normal. Select the Application Settings, and note how the Attributed and DLL options are selected by default. Note also how selecting the Attributed option disables the Proxy/Stub Merging, MFC, and Component Registrar Support options. Deselecting the Attributed option causes a nonattributed ATL project to be created and enables the disabled options.

Figure 6-2 The Attributed check box governs whether attributed code will be produced by the ATL Project Wizard.

You'll find the project contains two .cpp files: the normal stdafx.cpp used to handle precompiled header generation, and the source code file for the project, SimpleObject.cpp. Open this file, and you'll find that it contains a stand-alone *module* attribute, similar to the one below:

```
// The module attribute causes DllMain, DllRegisterServer and
// DllUnregisterServer to be automatically implemented for you
[ module(dll, uuid = "{1D196988-3060-486E-A4AC-38F9685D3BF7}",
        name = "SimpleObject",
        helpstring = "SimpleObject 1.0 Type Library",
        resource_name = "IDR_SIMPLEOBJECT") ];
```

The stand-alone *module* attribute is used to generate the standard skeleton code required by an ATL application, including (as the comment says) the registration functions.

Seeing the Inserted Code

The */Fx* (merge inserted code) compiler option can be used to provide a listing that shows the code that has been inserted by the attributes. If you're using Visual Studio .NET, right-click the solution name in Solution Explorer and click Properties to bring up the property pages for the solution. Then expand the C/C++ entry in the list in the left-hand pane, select Output Files from the expanded list, and set the Expand Attributed Source option to Yes. If you're not using Visual Studio, simply add */Fx* to the compiler command line.

Compile the project, and you'll find that a file with a .mrg.cpp extension is produced for each source file, which contains the original source with generated code merged in. Note the comment at the top of the .mrg files: the code in these files might not be exactly the same as that which was generated for the compiler.

If you look in the SimpleObject.mrg.cpp file, you can see the generated definitions for the registration functions, which will look similar to this:

```
#injected_line 7 "c:\\writing\\com book\\simpleobject\\simpleobject.cpp"
extern "C" STDAPI DllRegisterServer(void)
{
    return _AtlModule.DllRegisterServer();
}
#injected_line 7 "c:\\writing\\com book\\simpleobject\\simpleobject.cpp"
extern "C" STDAPI DllUnregisterServer(void)
{
    return _AtlModule.DllUnregisterServer();
}
```

The *#injected* directives show which line in the original file caused this code to be injected.

Further down the .mrg file, you'll see the definition of a module class. Note that the following code has been reformatted to make it easier to read:

```
//+++ Start Injected Code For Attribute 'module'
#injected_line 7 "c:\\writing\\com book\\simpleobject\\simpleobject.cpp"

class CSimpleObjectModule : public CAtlDllModuleT<CSimpleObjectModule>
{
public:
    DECLARE_LIBID(__uuidof(SimpleObject))
};
```

This code defines an ATL module class that is derived from *CAtlDllModuleT<>*. In previous versions of ATL, modules were represented by *CComModule*; in version 7, this functionality has been split between several new classes. You'll find details of these new classes in the "Creating Modules" section later in the chapter.

Adding COM Objects

You add a class to represent a COM coclass by right-clicking the Solution name in Solution Explorer, selecting Add and then Add Class from the context menu. Select the ATL Simple Object icon from the right-hand pane, and click Open. The ATL Simple Object Wizard appears as shown in Figure 6-3. This wizard looks similar to the ATL Object Wizard in Visual Studio 6.

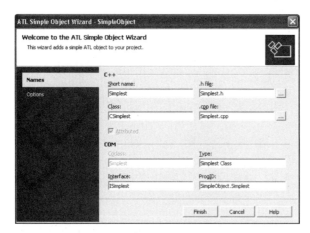

Figure 6-3 The ATL Simple Object Wizard lets you set the names of files, classes, and COM identifiers.

The Options pane shown in Figure 6-4 lets you set the options for your new coclass before it's implemented, and once again it's very similar to the one you are familiar with in Visual Studio 6.

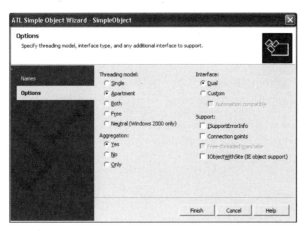

Figure 6-4 The Options pane lets you specify COM properties for the coclass.

Note that one bug from previous versions has been fixed: the free-threaded marshaler option is grayed out when the threading model won't support it.

When the wizard completes, the .h and .cpp files for the implementation class will have been generated and added to the project. You'll also note that there's no IDL file in the project, as everything you would have specified in the IDL is now added using attributes. As you'd expect from an ATL project, the header file Simplest.h contains the definition of the C++ class that implements the coclass, but the code is very different. First, you'll see an interface definition that looks like this:

```
// ISimplest
[
    object,
    uuid("FE19D164-DB7D-4A17-8D99-DFD57FB69E02"),
    dual, helpstring("ISimplest Interface"),
    pointer_default(unique)
]
__interface ISimplest : IDispatch
{
};
```

The COM interface is defined directly in C++, using the __interface keyword. It is qualified with the same attributes that you'd expect to see on the definition of an interface in a COM IDL file.

> **Note** The __interface keyword is used to define both the COM interface and managed .NET language interfaces. The keyword is the same, but the usages are completely different.

Here is the definition of the implementation class:

```
// CSimplest

[
    coclass,
    threading("apartment"),
    vi_progid("SimpleObject.Simplest"),
    progid("SimpleObject.Simplest.1"),
    version(1.0),
    uuid("5BDCE1E1-D79D-41E1-9500-E4ED3E64887A"),
    helpstring("Simplest Class")
]
class ATL_NO_VTABLE CSimplest :
    public ISimplest
{
public:
    CSimplest()
    {
    }

    DECLARE_PROTECT_FINAL_CONSTRUCT()

    HRESULT FinalConstruct()
    {
        return S_OK;
    }

    void FinalRelease()
    {
    }

public:

};
```

This is recognizably an ATL class. It contains familiar items such as the *ATL_NO_VTABLE* and *DECLARE_PROTECT_FINAL_CONSTRUCT* macros, but it doesn't expose any ATL implementation details—such as the ATL base classes—which are provided when the code is injected by the attribute provider at compile time. You'll see what this code looks like shortly.

Once again, you can see information that would have been provided in the IDL file is supplied inline using attributes. This is very useful—for instance, if you want to change, say, the threading model of a component, you need to change only the *threading* attribute on the class definition. With ATL 3, you would have had to change it in the header file and the registration .rgs file.

If you generate a .mrg file and open it, you can see how the class has been generated. One thing you might notice is that even though the component has a dual interface and the interface definition in the Simplest.h file derives from *IDispatch*, the generated class doesn't inherit from *IDispatchImpl*:

```
class ATL_NO_VTABLE CSimplest :
    public ISimplest
,
    /*+++ Added Baseclass */
 public CComCoClass<CSimplest, &__uuidof(CSimplest)>,
    /*+++ Added Baseclass */ public CComObjectRootEx<CComSingleThreadModel>,
    /*+++ Added Baseclass */ public IProvideClassInfoImpl<&__uuidof(CSimplest)>
{
public:
    ...
```

The *coclass* attribute generates its own implementation of *IDispatch*, which you can see if you look further down the listing. If you decide that you want to use the ATL 3 behavior, you can manually derive from *IDispatchImpl*, and the attribute provider will not generate the custom implementation.

> **Note** This is the general principle: attribute providers will not generate code if they see that an implementation already exists. Because of this principle, you can provide custom behavior in a straightforward manner by overriding the attribute provider.

What About IDL?

If all the attributes you used to specify in IDL are now written in the C++ code, is there still an IDL file? The answer is a definite *yes*. The underlying mechanisms of building, registering, and using COM objects haven't changed, so it's still necessary to provide a type library. An IDL file is still needed, then, so that MIDL can compile it into a type library. The file is generated by the compiler from the attribute information in the source code, and you can see it in the project directory once you've done a build. You can open this file, and its content should be familiar. Don't make changes to it, though, because it will be regenerated by the compiler.

The name of the file will be the project name with a prepended underscore—for example, _SimpleObject.idl. If you have a reason to change this, bring up the project properties by right-clicking the solution name in Solution Explorer, choosing Properties, and then looking for the Embedded IDL entry under the Linker section. You can change the Merged IDL Base File Name, but make sure that you don't use the project name, as this can cause generated filenames to clash with others already in the project.

Adding Methods and Properties

You add methods and properties to the coclass by using Class View. If this isn't visible, select Class View on the View menu or press CTRL+SHIFT+C to display it. Expand the component node—which in this case is called *SimpleObject*—and find the *ISimplest* interface symbol. Right-click the interface symbol, click Add and then Add Method to bring up the Add Method Wizard shown in Figure 6-5.

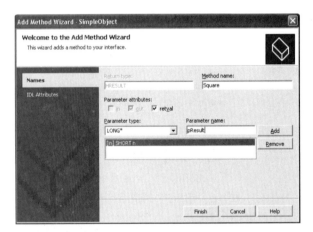

Figure 6-5 Adding a method to an ATL class using the Add Method Wizard

The main difference between the ATL 7 and the ATL 3 wizard is the ability to set parameter attributes rather than having to type them in. You'll also find that the parameter attribute check boxes are sensitive to the parameter type—

that is, if you don't specify a pointer type, the dialog will disable the *out* and *retval* check boxes.

> **Note** Make sure you use the *Add* button to add each parameter, and don't press *Finish* before you've added the final one—otherwise, it won't be added.

The second page of the wizard shown in Figure 6-6 lets you set the IDL attributes for the method.

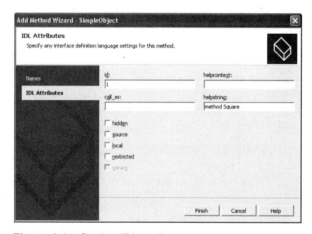

Figure 6-6 Setting IDL attributes using the Add Method Wizard

As you'd expect, this adds a COM method definition to the interface defined in Simplest.h and an implementation method to the *CSimplest* class. Because the interface has been defined as dual, the method has a dispID, which is automatically set to the next available value.

Properties can be added in a similar way, by selecting the Add Property menu item to bring up the Add Property Wizard.

Building the project creates the component DLL and its type library, and it also writes an IDL file using the attributes in the code. Here's a sample IDL file that was produced for a simple component:

```
import "c:\Program Files\Microsoft Visual Studio .NET 2003\
Vc7\PlatformSDK\include\prsht.idl";
import "c:\Program Files\Microsoft Visual Studio .NET 2003\
Vc7\PlatformSDK\include\mshtml.idl";
import "c:\program files\microsoft visual studio .net 2003\
```

```
                vc7\platformsdk\include\dimm.idl";
                import "c:\Program Files\Microsoft Visual Studio .NET 2003\
                Vc7\PlatformSDK\include\mshtmhst.idl";
                import "c:\program files\microsoft visual studio .net 2003\
                vc7\platformsdk\include\docobj.idl";
                import "c:\Program Files\Microsoft Visual Studio .NET 2003\
                Vc7\PlatformSDK\include\exdisp.idl";
                import "c:\Program Files\Microsoft Visual Studio .NET 2003\
                Vc7\PlatformSDK\include\objsafe.idl";

                [
                    object,
                    uuid(FE19D164-DB7D-4A17-8D99-DFD57FB69E02),
                    dual,
                    helpstring("ISimplest Interface"),
                    pointer_default(unique)
                ]
                #line 14 "c:\\writing\\cm\\com book\\attributes\\simpleobject\\simplest.h"
                interface ISimplest : IDispatch {
                #line 16 "c:\\writing\\cm\\com book\\attributes\\simpleobject\\simplest.h"
                    [propget,id(2),helpstring("property X")]
                            HRESULT   X([out,retval] short *pVal);
                    [propput,id(2),helpstring("property X")]
                            HRESULT   X([in] short newVal);
                    [id(3),helpstring("method Square")]
                            HRESULT   Square([in] SHORT n,
                                            [out,retval] long* pResult);
                };


                [ version(1.0), uuid(1D196988-3060-486E-A4AC-38F9685D3BF7),
                    helpstring("SimpleObject 1.0 Type Library") ]
                library SimpleObject
                {
                    importlib("stdole2.tlb");
                    importlib("olepro32.dll");

                    [
                        version(1.0),
                        uuid(5BDCE1E1-D79D-41E1-9500-E4ED3E64887A),
                        helpstring("Simplest Class")
                    ]
                #line 34 "c:\\writing\\cm\\com book\\attributes\\simpleobject\\simplest.h"
                    coclass CSimplest {
                        interface ISimplest;
                    };
                }
```

You can see that—apart from some import declarations and formatting—it is very similar to the ATL IDL files you're used to working with.

Testing the Component

You can easily write a console application to test the component. Listing 6-1 contains an example. You can find this sample in the Chapter06\TestObject folder of the book's companion content. This content is available from the book's Web site at *http://www.microsoft.com/mspress/books/6426.asp*.

```
#include <iostream>
#include "atlbase.h"

// Create wrappers for the component
#import "..\_SimpleObject.tlb" no_namespace

using namespace std;

void main()
{
   CoInitialize(NULL);
   {
      // Create an instance of the object
      CComPtr<ISimplest> pI;
      pI.CoCreateInstance(__uuidof(CSimplest));

      // Call the Square method
      long res = 0;
      res = pI->Square(3);
      cout << "Result is " << res << endl;
   }
   CoUninitialize();
}
```

Listing 6-1 TestObject.cpp

One thing to note here: You might wonder why the code between *CoInitialize* and *CoUninitialize* is placed in a block. It is important that all COM interface pointers be released by the time *CoUninitialize* is called, and placing the code in a block ensures that any *CComPtr* smart pointers have had their destructors called (and thus have released interface pointers they hold) before the call to *CoUninitialize*.

Creating the Server by Hand

You can also create COM servers without using Visual Studio .NET to help create and process the attributed code. Here's how you could create the same simple server using Notepad or another text editor in place of Visual Studio .NET.

Creating the Header File

First, create a header file to contain the *#define* and *#include* directives needed by the project as shown in Listing 6-2. You'll find this file in the Chapter06\HandCrafted folder in the book's companion content.

```
#pragma once
#define STRICT

#ifndef _WIN32_WINNT
    #define _WIN32_WINNT 0x0400
#endif

#define _ATL_ATTRIBUTES
#define _ATL_APARTMENT_THREADED
#define _ATL_NO_AUTOMATIC_NAMESPACE

#include <atlbase.h>
#include <atlcom.h>
#include <atlwin.h>
#include <atltypes.h>
#include <atlctl.h>
#include <atlhost.h>
using namespace ATL;
```

Listing 6-2 Defs.h

This file sets up the environment for the attributed ATL source code. Note the definition of the *_ATL_ATTRIBUTES* symbol, which results in the inclusion of the ATL attribute provider. You need to have this defined whenever you want to use attributes with ATL code. The other two *#define*s are used to create an apartment-threaded component and to prevent the use of a namespace.

Creating the ATL DLL

Next, create a source file for the component, which in this case I've called MyServer.cpp as shown in Listing 6-3. This file is also located in the Chapter06\HandCrafted folder in the book's companion content.

```
#include "Defs.h"

// The module attribute is specified in order to implement DllMain,
// DllRegisterServer and DllUnregisterServer
[ module(dll, name = "MyServer", helpstring = "MyServer 1.0 Type Library") ];
[ emitidl ];
```

Listing 6-3 MyServer.cpp

The file simply contains two ATL attributes. The first attribute, *module*, you've already seen in the Visual Studio .NET example. It causes the generation of the ATL DLL container code, and in this case I'm specifying a minimum number of parameters. I haven't specified a *uuid* attribute, which means that one will be generated automatically by the compiler.

The *emitidl* attribute causes IDL attribute information to be echoed in the IDL file created by the compiler. Save the file, compile it, and run *Regsvr32.EXE* to register the component:

```
cl /LD MyServer.cpp
regsvr32 MyServer.dll
```

The */LD* flag tells the compiler and linker to build a DLL rather than an EXE. When you look at the directory in which you compiled the source, you'll find that IDL and type library files have been generated. Since you didn't specify a name for these files, the type library and IDL files both use the default *vc70* root name; you'll see how to specify a different file name later in the chapter.

Adding Interface and Coclass Definitions

Just as in the Visual Studio .NET example, you add attributes directly to the C++ source code to control the creation of a COM component. To add an interface to the server project, open the source file and add the following definition:

```
// ISimplest
// Note: Replace this uuid with one generated using uuidgen
[
    object,
    uuid("103FF9D9-8BC9-4ea8-8CD4-C1E627D04358"),
    dual, helpstring("ISimplest Interface"),
    pointer_default(unique)
]
__interface ISimplest : IDispatch
{
    HRESULT Square([in] short val, [out, retval]long* pResult);
};
```

The *__interface* keyword is used to define a COM interface. It is different from the *interface* keyword used in ATL 3, which was simply a typedef for *struct*. Using *__interface* imposes COM interface rules on the C++ code—for example, an interface can derive only from another interface (and not from a class or struct) and can contain only pure virtual functions (so no data members, constructors, or destructors). The type of interface to be generated is defined by an attribute. By default, the interface will be custom, but *dual* can be used to specify a dual interface and *dispinterface* to specify an ODL-style dispatch interface.

The members of the interface are added using standard IDL-like syntax, with attributes used to define the direction in which parameters are passed.

The attributed C++ class definition is similar to the IDL interface definition, and all the attributes will be familiar to the ATL programmer. Add the definition of the class to the source code after the interface:

```
// CObject1
[
   coclass,
   threading("apartment"),
   vi_progid("MyServer.Simple"),
   progid("MyServer.Simple.1"),
   version(1.0),
   uuid("15615078-523C-43A0-BE6F-651E78A89213"),
   helpstring("Simple Class")
]
class ATL_NO_VTABLE CObject1 : public ISimplest
{
public:
   CObject1() { }

   // The single method
   HRESULT Square(short val, long* pResult){
      *pResult = val * val;
      return S_OK;
   }

   DECLARE_PROTECT_FINAL_CONSTRUCT()
   HRESULT FinalConstruct()
   {
      return S_OK;
   }

   void FinalRelease()
   {
   }
};
```

The class has the following attributes set:

- *coclass*, which defines this as the implementation of a COM coclass. This must be specified for all coclass implementations.
- *threading*, which specifies the threading model for the coclass.
- *vi_progid*, which specifies the version-independent progID for the class.
- *progid*, which specifies the progID, including version information.
- *version*, which defines the version of the coclass.
- *uuid*, which can be used to specify an attribute if you don't want to use the default generated by the compiler.
- *helpstring*, which is used to define a helpstring for the coclass.

After compiling and registering the component, you can use the same simple console application to test the component.

Basic Attributed Programming

Now that you've seen how to create a COM server by using attributes, this section will examine the use of attributes in more detail and provide a reference to the most commonly used attributes.

Creating Modules

When creating COM code with ATL, you have the choice of using a DLL, an EXE, or a Windows Service as the container for the coclasses. Each of these needs to provide a framework for hosting the coclasses it contains, and this framework is provided for you by the ATL Project Wizard. In previous versions of ATL, this would result in the creation of explicit code. For example, for a COM DLL project, you could see—and edit—the definitions and implementation of the *DllMain*, *DllGetClassObject*, *DllRegisterServer*, *DllUnregisterServer*, and *DllCanUnloadNow* functions, and you could also see and edit the basic IDL library definition.

When using attributes, the stand-alone *module* attribute performs these functions. It generates the skeleton for the appropriate server type, and it defines the IDL library block that will contain the coclass definitions.

The *module* attribute can take a large number of parameters, as shown in Table 6-1.

Table 6-1 Parameters for the *module* Attribute

Parameter	Description
type	Defines the type of module that will be created. The value can be *dll*, *exe*, or *service*, with the default being *dll*.
name	The name of the library block.
uuid	The GUID for the library block. If this parameter is omitted, a GUID will automatically be generated.
version	The version number for the library block. The default value is *1.0*.
lcid	Used to specify the 32-bit Windows National Language Support locale identifier for the library. This attribute identifies the locale for a type library and lets you use international characters inside the library block.
control	A Boolean value specifying whether all the coclasses in the library are controls.
helpstring	The help string for this library block.
helpstringdll	Specifies the DLL to be used for document-string lookups.
helpfile	The name of the help file for the type library.
helpcontext	The help context ID for this type library.
helpstringcontext	Specifies the context ID for a help topic.
hidden	Prevents the entire library from being displayed in a *user-oriented browser*, such as the Visual Basic Object Browser.
restricted	Members of the library cannot be used arbitrarily. This parameter is typically used to prevent access from scripting languages.
custom	Can be used to specify one or more custom attributes, each of which is defined by a GUID and a value.
resource_name	The resource ID of the .rgs file used to register the APPID of the DLL, executable, or service.

Using the *module* Attribute

You cannot use the *module* attribute with a completely empty parameter list. You must provide a minimum of a *name* parameter, in which case defaults will be assumed for all the other parameters:

```
[module(name="MyObject")];
```

This bit of code will define a *library block* in the IDL using the name provided, and it will generate a GUID to represent the library ID and use a default version of 1.0. Here's the library block in the IDL that was generated from the *module* statement:

```
[ version(1.0), uuid(1a7833b4-e38a-32a6-a32e-d4c61bfb3305) ]
library MyObject
{
    importlib("stdole2.tlb");
    importlib("olepro32.dll");
}
```

As well as creating the library block in the IDL file, the inclusion of a *module* attribute also creates a global object to manage the coclasses in the DLL or EXE. In previous versions of ATL, this object was called *_Module* and was of type *CComModule*. In Visual C++ .NET, the functionality provided by *CComModule* has been spread over a number of classes, as listed in Table 6-2.

Table 6-2 ATL Module Classes

Class	Description
CAtlBaseModule	*CAtlBaseModule* exposes data needed by most ATL applications, including the resource instance and the *HINSTANCE* of the module. This class inherits from the *_ATL_BASE_MODULE* structure, which contains module-specific data.
CAtlComModule	*CAtlComModule* implements a COM server module, providing basic registration and deregistration functionality for objects in the module's object map and for type libraries.
CAtlWinModule	*CAtlWinModule* provides support for ATL classes that have GUIs.
CAtlDebugInterfacesModule	*CAtlDebugInterfacesModule* provides support for debugging interfaces. This class is used in any ATL project that has defined the *_ATL_DEBUG_QI* symbol.
CAtlModule	*CAtlModule* provides basic functionality for all module types, including the *Lock* and *Unlock* methods used for threadsafe operation.
CAtlModuleT	*CAtlModuleT* is a template class that derives from *CAtlModule*. It acts as a base class for the following three module classes and contains basic registration functionality.
CAtlDllModuleT	*CAtlDllModuleT* is a template class that derives from *CAtlModuleT*. It provides support for DLL servers, including implementations of the *DllMain* function, plus the four functions always exported by DLL servers (*DllGetClassObject*, *DllRegisterServer*, *DllUnregisterServer*, and *DllCanUnloadNow*).

Table 6-2 ATL Module Classes

Class	Description
CAtlExeModuleT	*CAtlExeModuleT* is a template class that derives from *CAtlModuleT*. It provides support for EXE servers, including parsing the command line, registering and revoking class objects, and managing interaction with the message loop.
CAtlServiceModuleT	*CAtlServiceModuleT* is a template class that derives from *CAtlModuleT*. It provides support for ATL servers implemented as Windows Services, with functionality that includes parsing the command line and installing, registering, and uninstalling the service.

The generated code will contain a module object called *_AtlModule*, which will be of one of the three *CAtlXxxModuleT* types: *CAtlDllModuleT* if the module type was given as *dll* (or if no type was specified), *CAtlExeModuleT* if the module type was given as *exe*, or *CAtlServiceModuleT* if the module type was given as *service*.

> **Tip** You can see the generated code if you use the */Fx* compiler switch, and examine the .mrg file that is created.

In addition, *CAtlExeModuleT* implements a timeout mechanism, which can be used to improve server performance in cases where large numbers of objects are being created and destroyed. The COM rules state that when the last object supported by a server has been destroyed, the server can exit. If the Boolean *m_bDelayShutdown* member of *CAtlExeModuleT* is set to *true*, the server will not shut down until the period specified by *m_dwTimeOut* has expired. The default timeout is 5 seconds.

The *custom* Attribute

This attribute provides a general mechanism for adding metadata to type libraries and can be applied to modules, interfaces, and coclasses. It takes two parameters:

- A GUID that identifies the metadata
- A value, which can be anything that will fit into a *VARIANT*

The GUID used to identify the metadata has no meaning except to clients that are looking for it. Use of this attribute on C++ classes will result in an equivalent IDL custom attribute being added to the IDL and compiled into the type library. Clients must use the type library interfaces (*ITypeLib* and *ITypeInfo*) to retrieve details of custom attributes.

As an example of the use of this attribute, consider the following fragment of Visual C# code, which is generated when a .NET component is being exported for use as a COM object:

```
[
   odl, uuid(FEDF4CC0-E0ED-3DC4-ABE7-E5B4BBC78D84),
   hidden, dual, nonextensible, oleautomation,
   custom(0F21F359-AB84-41E8-9A78-36D110E6D2F9, ExportVb.Class1)
]
interface _Class1 : IDispatch {
  // ...
};
```

For exported .NET components, the *custom* attribute is used to specify the namespace to which the .NET component belongs. When the COM Callable Wrapper (CCW) is created to expose a .NET instance as a COM object, the CCW can find the namespace information from the type library.

Creating Interfaces

In previous versions of ATL, interfaces were defined directly in IDL and implemented in the ATL source class. Wizard support in Visual Studio would add implementation code to the ATL class files, but there were several disadvantages with the way this process worked. First there was often a lot of manual work to be done, especially when adding extra interfaces to a class. Second, doing anything out of the ordinary required a detailed knowledge of IDL. This was unsatisfactory because IDL is a complex and subtle language, requiring extra knowledge and skills on the part of the C++ programmer.

Using attributes, the programmer now codes an interface definition directly in C++, using attributes to provide all the information that would have been given in the IDL file. In many cases, there is a one-to-one mapping between .NET COM attributes and IDL constructs, so if you already know how to construct and edit IDL, you'll be able to quickly transfer to using attributes.

As the previous walkthrough explained, COM interfaces are defined using the new *__interface* keyword. Interfaces defined in this way have the following properties:

- They can inherit from zero or more base interfaces.
- They cannot inherit from a base class.

- They can contain only public, pure virtual methods.
- They cannot contain constructors or destructors.
- They cannot define overloaded functions or operator overloads.
- They cannot contain static methods.
- They cannot contain data members, although pure virtual properties are allowed.
- Methods use the *__stdcall* calling convention.

Note that the *__interface* keyword is not only used for COM interface definitions, it can also be used for defining both managed and unmanaged C++ interfaces. To define a COM interface, you need to apply the *object* attribute to the interface definition, as you also have to do in IDL interface definitions.

```
// A non-COM interface
__interface INonCOM
{
   // Interface definition
};

// A COM interface
[ object ]
__interface ICOM : IUnknown
{
   // Interface definition
};
```

Once the compiler sees the object attribute, it will apply the rules that COM interfaces and interface methods have to follow. For example, since all COM interfaces are based on *IUnknown*, COM interfaces defined using *__interface* must inherit from *IUnknown* or another COM base interface.

Attributes are used to provide information to the compiler to enable it to generate an IDL file for compilation by MIDL. The attributes that can be used with interfaces are shown in Table 6-3, and you will see that they parallel many attributes used in an IDL interface definition.

Table 6-3 Attributes Used with Interfaces

Attribute	Description
async_uuid	Generates both synchronous and asynchronous versions of the interface. A GUID must be provided to be used as the interface ID for the asynchronous interface.
custom	Inserts one or more IDL custom attributes, each of which is identified by a GUID and a value.

Table 6-3 **Attributes Used with Interfaces**

Attribute	Description
dispinterface	Defines an interface as being a pure dispatch interface, only usable by late-bound clients. Dispinterfaces must have *IDispatch* at the top of their inheritance hierarchy.
dual	Defines an interface as being a dual interface, usable by early-bound or late-bound clients. Dual interfaces must have *IDispatch* at the top of their inheritance hierarchy.
export	Indicates that an interface should be included in the IDL. This attribute is not normally needed, as COM interface definitions are automatically included in the generated IDL.
helpcontext	The help context ID for this interface.
helpfile	The help file for this interface.
helpstring	The help string to display for the interface.
helpstringcontext	The help context ID for this interface.
hidden	Adds the hidden IDL attribute to the interface, indicating that it should not be shown in the Visual Basic Object Browser.
library_block	By default, only interfaces that are used in coclass definitions are compiled into the type library. An interface tagged with the *library_block* attribute will be placed in the library block in the IDL, and therefore compiled into the type library regardless of whether it is referenced by a coclass.
local	The local attribute can be used on an interface to cause the MIDL compiler only to create header files.
nonextensible	When applied to an Automation interface, this attribute indicates that the interface cannot be extended at run time.
object	Defines the interface as being a COM interface, as opposed to being a managed or unmanaged non-COM interface. All COM interface definitions will include this attribute.
odl	Marks the interface as an ODL interface. This attribute is supported only for backward compatibility and is not required.
oleautomation	Marks an interface as being compatible with OLE Automation. This means the parameters and return types for methods in the interface must be Automation-compatible.
pointer_default	Specifies the default pointer attribute for pointers used in this interface. This attribute can take one of three parameters: *ptr*, *ref*, or *unique*. These correspond to the equivalent IDL pointer attributes.
restricted	Denotes that an interface cannot be called arbitrarily. This attribute is used to restrict the interfaces that can be used from scripting languages.
uuid	Specifies an interface ID for the interface. If this attribute is not supplied, a GUID will automatically be generated.

Defining Interface Methods

The sample code in the earlier section "Adding Interface and Coclass Definitions" showed how these attributes can be applied to an interface.

An interface is a collection of pure virtual function definitions, but you don't use C++ virtual function syntax to declare them. You declare them as simple function prototypes, and they will be assumed to be public and pure virtual, as shown in the following example:

```
// A COM interface
[object]
__interface ICOM : IUnknown
{
   // Method is assumed to be public and pure virtual
   HRESULT AMethod(int n);
};
```

COM interface methods are required to return *HRESULT*s, and the compiler will issue an error if you try to use any other return type in an interface that has the *object* attribute.

Table 6-4 lists the most common attributes that can be used on methods, parameters and return types.

Table 6-4 Attributes That Can Be Applied to Interface Methods

Attribute	Description
bindable	Indicates that a property supports data binding.
helpstring	Provides a help string for a method.
hidden	Indicates that an interface method should not appear in object browser utilities.
id	Provides a dispatch ID (dispID) for a method.
in	Indicates that a method parameter should be marshaled from the caller to the callee.
local	Denotes a local method for which no marshalling code is generated.
nonbrowsable	Indicates that an interface method should not appear in object browser utilities.
out	Indicates that a method parameter should be marshaled from the callee back to the caller.
propget	Used to label property accessor methods.
propput	Used to label property setting methods.

Table 6-4 Attributes That Can Be Applied to Interface Methods

Attribute	Description
propputref	Used to label a property setting method that uses a reference rather than a value.
ptr	Designates a pointer as a full pointer, which can be null, and can change its value.
retval	Indicates that a method parameter can be used as a function return value. There can be only one *[retval]* parameter, and it must be the last parameter in the method's parameter list.
string	Indicates that an array of, or pointer to, types *char*, *wchar_t*, or *byte* should be treated as a C-style null-terminated string.
synchronize	Causes the method to be synchronized, via calls to *Lock* and *Unlock* placed at the beginning and end of the method code.

Interface methods defined using attributes look similar to their IDL counterparts and use the same rules—for example, *out* parameters must be pointers, and the *retval* parameter must occur at the end of the parameter list. The following code sample illustrates this:

```
// Example attributed interface method
[id(3), helpstring("method Square")] HRESULT Square(
                [in] SHORT val, [out,retval] LONG* pResult);
```

Dispatch Interfaces

Interfaces can be marked with the *dual* or *dispinterface* attributes to show that they can be called by late-bound clients using Automation. All methods in dispatch interfaces must define dispatch IDs (dispIDs) for their methods. These IDs are positive integers.

You use the *id* attribute to assign dispIDs to methods within an interface definition:

```
[id(2)] HRESULT MethodOne();
[id(3)] HRESULT MethodTwo();
```

The compiler will check for duplicate dispIDs, and if any are found, MIDL compilation will fail.

Handling Arrays

You might notice that the list of interface method attributes does not contain any IDL attributes used when passing arrays by pointer (*size_is*, *length_is*, and so on). Although these are not listed as COM attributes, you can still use them when defining methods in COM interfaces, and they will be passed through into the generated IDL. For example, here's the definition of a method that computes the sum of an array of values:

```
HRESULT Sum([in] short nVals, [in, size_is(nVals)] short* pArray,
    [out,retval] long* pSum);
```

Creating Coclasses

The *coclass* attribute is used to mark a class that implements a COM coclass. The attribute can be applied to classes and structs, and it takes no arguments. In its simplest form, it can be used alone, like this:

```
[coclass]
class MyComClass : public ISomeInterface
{
    // ...
};
```

When the *coclass* attribute is applied to a class in an ATL project, the following changes will be made to the class:

- ATL base classes are added.

- If the class inherits from any dual interfaces that are not defined using attributes, these dual interfaces are replaced with the corresponding *IDispatchImpl* class. If a base dual interface is defined using attributes, the interface is not modified in the base class list.

- A COM map is added, listing all interfaces implemented by the target class, all interfaces specified using *com_interface_entry* attributes, and those introduced via *aggregates* attributes.

- An *OBJECT_ENTRY_AUTO* entry is placed in the COM map, which has the effect of entering the class into the COM map, updating the registry, and creating an instance of the object.

The following base classes will be added in the generated code:

- *CComCoClass*, to implement the class factory and aggregation behavior.

- *CComObjectRootEx*, to provide behavior specific to the threading model. If no *threading* attribute is provided, apartment-model threading is assumed.

- *IProvideClassInfo2Impl*, to provide a default implementation of the *IProvideClassInfo* and *IProvideClassInfo2* interfaces. If the *noncreatable* attribute is specified for the class, *IProvideClassInfo2Impl* will not be added as a base class.

These classes provide, among other features, registry entry handling (autoregistration), a class factory, and an *IUnknown* implementation.

The use of the *coclass* attribute also adds a number of member functions to the target class:

- *UpdateRegistry*, to register the class factory for the class.
- *GetObjectCLSID*, to return the component's CLSID.
- *GetObjectFriendlyName*, to return a string of the form "*target_class_name* Object". This function can be explicitly overridden to return another name.
- *GetProgID*, to return a string containing the component's progID.
- *GetVersionIndependentProgID*, to return a string containing the component's version-independent progID.

Table 6-5 lists the attributes that can be used on coclasses.

Table 6-5 Attributes That Can Be Applied to coclasses

Attribute	Description
aggregatable	This attribute denotes that a coclass can be aggregated. See the upcoming "Handling Aggregation" section for more details.
aggregates	This attribute specifies the COM coclasses that a coclass will aggregate. See the upcoming "Handling Aggregation" section for more details.
coclass	Specifies that a C++ class implements a COM coclass.
com_interface_entry	Adds an entry to the *COM_MAP* for the class.
control	Specifies that a coclass implements an ActiveX control.
custom	Adds a custom entry to the type library.
default	Indicates which interfaces should be used as the default interfaces for the coclass.
event_source	Denotes an event source. See the upcoming "Events" section for details on how this attribute is used.
event_receiver	Denotes that this class receives events. See the upcoming "Events" section for details on how this attribute is used.
helpcontext	Provides a context ID within a help file that can be accessed for more help about the class.
helpfile	Provides the name of the help file associated with this class.
helpstring	Provides a help string that can be displayed in object browsers and other end-user tools.

Table 6-5 Attributes That Can Be Applied to coclasses

Attribute	Description
helpstringcontext	Specifies the ID of a help topic in an .hlp or a .chm help file.
hidden	Indicates that this item should not be displayed in object browsers and other end-user tools.
implements	By default, only COM interfaces that are base classes are added to the IDL coclass definition. This attribute forces other interfaces to be added to the IDL definition, even if they are not bases.
implements_category	Adds an implemented category to the *CATEGORY* map for the class. Clients can query this map at run time to determine the categories that are implemented by a class.
licensed	Indicates that this class uses the ActiveX licensing model and must be created using the *IClassFactory2* interface.
noncreatable	Specifies that this class cannot be created by COM. This attribute is normally used on COM types that are created by other methods, such as the C++ *new* operator.
progid	Adds a progID for the class. The parameter to this class is a string containing the progID in the usual *typelib.coclass.version* format.
registration_script	Supplies the path to a registration script (.rgs) file that will be used to register the class. If this attribute is not supplied, a default registration script will be generated. To disable automatic registration, use this attribute with the special path *none*.
requires_category	Adds a required category to the *CATEGORY* map for the class. Clients can query this map at run time to determine the categories that need to be implemented by users of a class.
restricted	Indicates that this coclass cannot be used arbitrarily. This attribute is used to restrict the use of classes by scripting clients.
source	Defines the outgoing (source) interfaces supported by a class. See the upcoming "Events" section for details on how this attribute is used.
support_error_info	Adds support for the *ISupportErrorInfo* interface to the class. See the upcoming "Handling Errors" section for more details.
threading	Specifies the threading model for a class. The parameter for this attribute can be one of the following values: *apartment*, *neutral*, *single*, *free*, or *both*.

Table 6-5 Attributes That Can Be Applied to coclasses

Attribute	Description
uuid	Specifies a CLSID for the class, as a string. If this attribute is not used, a CLSID will automatically be generated for the class.
version	Specifies a version for the class, which will be used to provide the type library block version.
vi_progid	Specifies a progID without a version.

Default Interfaces

COM coclasses support default incoming and outgoing interfaces so that client code—especially Visual Basic 6—can simply create an object without specifying which interface on the object is to be used. These are indicated by applying the *default* attribute to the C++ class, as shown in the following code fragment:

```
[
  coclass,
  default(ITwo)
]
class MyComClass : public IOne, public ITwo
{
  // ...
};
```

If your class implements source interfaces, you can provide a second parameter that specifies the default source interface. If you don't use the *default* attribute, the first base interface will be taken as the default outgoing interface, and the first source interface will be taken as the default source.

Stand-Alone Attributes

A number of COM-related attributes are not applied to classes, interfaces, or methods, but are used as stand-alone attributes. Table 6-6 lists all the stand-alone attributes.

Table 6-6 Stand-Alone Attributes

Attribute	Description
cpp_quote	This attribute is used to pass quoted strings through MIDL compilation into the generated header files. Quotes are stripped from the string before it is inserted into the header file.
custom	Inserts a custom IDL attribute into the IDL file.
emitidl	Determines how IDL generation proceeds. See the upcoming "The *emitidl* Attribute" section for further details.

Table 6-6 Stand-Alone Attributes

Attribute	Description
idl_quote	Some IDL constructs are not implemented via attributes. The *idl_quote* attribute lets you pass unsupported IDL constructs directly into the generated IDL file.
import	Places a *#import* statement in the IDL that causes the inclusion of another .idl, .odl, or header file.
importidl	Merges the content of another .idl file. Any IDL inside the library block of the inserted file is merged into the library block of the file in which the *importidl* attribute occurs. IDL outside the library block will be placed outside the library block of the file in which the *importidl* attribute occurs.
importlib	Imports types from another type library so that they can be referenced in IDL.
include	Causes a *#include* statement to be placed in the IDL after the *import "docobj.idl"* statement.
includelib	Causes an IDL or .h file to be included in the generated IDL after the *importlib* statement. This attribute is repeatable.
module	Declares a module. See the "Creating Modules" section earlier in the chapter for more details.
no_injected_text	Can be used to prevent the compiler from injecting text. This is placed in the merged code generated by the */Fx* compiler option, and ensures that attributes will not be processed a second time if the merge file is compiled.
pragma	This attribute is used to pass a string to the generated header files without any processing by the MIDL compiler. The *pragma pack* attribute can be used to control how the MIDL compiler will pack structures.

Because these attributes are not part of any other C++ construct, they form statements in their own right and will therefore always end with a semicolon when used in code. For example, look at this code:

```
[ module(dll, uuid = "{1D196988-3060-486E-A4AC-38F9685D3BF7}",
        name = "SimpleObject",
        helpstring = "SimpleObject 1.0 Type Library",
        resource_name = "IDR_SIMPLEOBJECT") ];
```

The *emitidl* Attribute

The *emitidl* attribute controls how IDL attributes will be processed. The format of this attribute is shown in the following code fragment:

```
[emitidl(value, defaultimports=boolean];
```

The *value* parameter can take one of four values:

- *true*, meaning that IDL attributes encountered in the code will be processed and added to the generated IDL file. This is the default if this value is omitted.
- *false*, meaning that IDL attributes encountered in the code will not be processed.
- *restricted*, meaning that IDL attributes can be present in a file that doesn't include a *module* attribute. No IDL file will be generated.
- *forced*, meaning that the file must contain a *module* attribute if it also contains IDL attributes.

The *defaultimports* named parameter is optional and takes a Boolean value. If the value is *false*, the standard docobj.idl file (which contains all the Microsoft-defined COM and OLE IDL) will not be implicitly included in the generated IDL. If you want to include any standard IDL files—such as ocidl.idl—you'll have to include them manually.

If the value of *defaultimports* is *true*, docobj.idl will be included. If an .idl file with the same name as an .h file that you *#include* into your source code is found in the same directory as the .h file, the generated .idl file will contain an import statement for that .idl file. Here is an example showing how the *emitidl* attribute can be used:

```
[emitidl(true, defaultimports=true];
```

Handling Aggregation

This section explains how the *aggregatable* and *aggregates* attributes are used to control the aggregation behavior of COM components.

Review of COM Aggregation and Delegation

Before discussing keywords, I'll provide a quick review of COM aggregation and delegation, because the distinctions between the two are often not understood very well by COM programmers. *Delegation* means that one COM object creates another and delegates method calls on one or more interfaces to the created object, as shown in Figure 6-7.

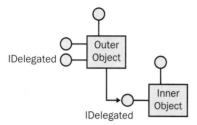

Figure 6-7 COM delegation does not expose the delegated object to the client.

Client code sees only the outer object, and the inner object is *private*. Lifetime and interface management is simple because the inner object is used only by its creator. One of the main advantages of delegation lies in being able to selectively expose functionality from inner objects: you can filter the data being passed to calls or even decide not to expose some interfaces or methods at all. The main disadvantage of delegation is that the outer object has to be written to perform the delegation. Delegation has no special support from ATL because the code needed to work with a delegated object will be different in each case.

If delegation is essentially a code reuse mechanism, *aggregation* is a COM identity trick used to create one *logical* COM object out of two or more *physical* objects. When one COM object aggregates another, it provides the identity—the GUID—for the aggregate, but this time the inner object exposes its interfaces directly to the client. This is shown in Figure 6-8.

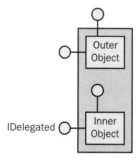

Figure 6-8 COM aggregation exposes aggregated interfaces to the client.

The outer object creates the inner object, and the client—under the impression that it is talking to a single object—talks directly to both of them. This necessitates cooperation between the inner and outer objects to maintain reference counts and handle *QueryInterface* calls. This support is provided by ATL.

The *aggregatable* and *aggregates* Attributes

The *aggregatable* attribute is used to indicate whether a coclass wants to be aggregated. It can take one of three values:

- *allowed*, meaning the coclass can be instantiated as aggregated or stand-alone.
- *never*, meaning the coclass cannot be instantiated as an aggregated object. If an attempt is made to do so, the class factory will return *CLASS_E_NOAGGREGATION*.
- *always*, meaning the coclass must be instantiated as an aggregated object. If an attempt is made to create a stand-alone object, the class factory will return *E_FAIL*.

Here's an example of the attribute in use:

```
[coclass, aggregatable(always)]
class MyClass
{
   // ...
};
```

These values correspond to the *yes*, *no*, and *always* choices presented by the ATL Object Wizard. The default attribute parameter is *allowed*, so you won't see this attribute in the generated code if you choose the *yes* option in the wizard.

The *aggregates* attribute is used to specify one or more objects that are going to be aggregated by a class. For example

```
// This class aggregates instances of the CObject1
// and CObject2 classes
[coclass,
  aggregates(__uuidof(CObject1)),
  aggregates(__uuidof(CObject2))
]
class MyClass
{
};
```

By default, the *aggregates* attribute will add a *COM_INTERFACE_ENTRY_AUTOAGGREGATE_BLIND* entry to the object's interface map, which will expose all the interfaces in the aggregated object. If you don't want to do this, you can use the *com_interface_entry* attribute to specify individual interfaces on aggregated objects, like this:

```
[coclass,
  com_interface_entry(
```

```
        "COM_INTERFACE_ENTRY_AGGREGATE(__uuidof(IAbc), pUnk)")
]
class MyClass
{
   //...
};
```

In this example, the *COM_INTERFACE_ENTRY_AGGREGATE* macro puts an entry in the interface map so that all calls to interface *IAbc* are forwarded to the object whose *IUnknown* pointer is passed as the second parameter. This second parameter will typically be a data member of the class to which the attribute is being applied.

Handling Errors

It is a well-known fact that COM interface methods return *HRESULT*s to indicate status. If you want to return more information than is encapsulated in the standard set of COM *HRESULT*s—the ones you can find in *<winerror.h>*—you should implement the *ISupportErrorInfo* interface, and then use the *AtlReportError* function or the *CComCoClass<>::Error* methods to report errors.

The *support_error_info* attribute is used to implement rich error handling in ATL classes. It can be included in a project by checking the appropriate box in the ATL Object Wizard, and you can also add it by hand to manually written code. The attribute takes as its argument the name of the interface for which error support is to be generated. You can add more than one *support_error_info* attribute if you want to provide rich error information for more than one interface. This will result in the implementation of *InterfaceSupportsErrorInfo*, which contains details of all the interfaces you've named in *support_error_info* attributes. The following example will add rich error support for both the *IOne* and *ITwo* interfaces:

```
[coclass,
  support_error_info("IFoo"),
  support_error_info("IFoo2")
]
class MyClass
{
   //...
};
```

Events

COM provides *connection points* as a standard mechanism for connecting event sources to event sinks. Although they provide a useful standard that can be used between event sources and sinks that have been separately developed, they are expensive (in terms of interface calls) and are therefore normally used only for in-process components.

Attributes can be used to implement connection points by using the *event_source* attribute with the *com* parameter. For example:

```
[coclass, event_source(com)]
class MyClass : public ISomeInterface
{
};
```

Note that *event_source* isn't used only in COM code. This attribute can be used to generate three different kinds of events, depending on the first parameter:

- *com* is used to generate COM connection points.
- *native* is used to generate events using C++ callbacks.
- *managed* is used to generate .NET events and can be used only with managed classes.

Because the syntax is similar for all three types, Microsoft has rather grandly termed this the *Unified Event Model*. As we're dealing with implementing COM objects in this chapter, I'll be considering only the first type.

Adding Event Support

It is easy to add event support if you are creating an ATL object with Visual Studio .NET. Simply check the Connection Points box on the Options page of the ATL Object Wizard. The following paragraphs show you what gets added to an ATL project to support connection points.

The first item that has been added to the generated code is an *event_source* attribute on the implementation class, showing that the class supports COM connection points:

```
[
    coclass,
    threading("apartment"),
    event_source("com"),
    vi_progid("SimpleJ.SimpleK"),
    progid("SimpleJ.SimpleK.1"),
    version(1.0),
    uuid("C57EA18F-2869-4CD8-BB36-7743B63F718E"),
    helpstring("SimpleK Class")
]
class ATL_NO_VTABLE CSimpleK :
    public ISimpleK
{ ...
```

A coclass that implements connection points also has to support a source interface, so you'll see that the wizard has added a dispinterface to the file:

```
// _ISimpleKEvents
[
    dispinterface,
    uuid("5D2B0BD7-5CD8-46E0-9855-2F6B898D0B0C"),
    helpstring("_ISimpleKEvents Interface")
]
__interface _ISimpleKEvents
{
};
```

The *dispinterface* event is associated with the coclass using the __*event* keyword:

```
class ATL_NO_VTABLE CSimpleK :
    public ISimpleK
{
public:
    CSimpleK()
    {
    }

    __event __interface _ISimpleKEvents;
    ...
};
```

This declaration associates *_ISimpleEvents* as a source interface for the class and will also cause the provider to generate a method that you call to fire the event. You can now add the definitions of the event methods to *dispinterface*:

```
__interface _ISimpleKEvents
{
    // Return two values when asked
    [id(1), helpstring("method Values")]
            void Values([in] short x, [in] short y);
};
```

When you compile the project with the */Fx* option set and look at the .mrg file, you'll see the compiler has generated a *Values* method as part of the coclass implementation. To fire this method, you simply call it, and because it has the same name and arguments as the *dispinterface* method, it doesn't matter that the method is hidden from you.

You can also use the __*raise* keyword when firing events:

```
__raise Values(10,10);
```

This keyword "emphasizes the site of an event," to quote MSDN. It is optional and has two effects: it makes it easy to see where events are being raised; and it causes a runtime error if it is used with a function that isn't an event. The second effect helps guard against accidentally calling the wrong function.

Manually Writing COM Event Code

The following code shows how to define a COM class that fires events if you are not using Visual Studio .NET. Listing 6-4 contains the header file, EvtSrc.h, which defines the GUID for a class called *CEventSource*. You'll find this file in the Chapter06\Events\Src folder in the book's companion content.

```
#pragma once

[ dual, uuid("d4efa6dc-bb8f-44f0-88cf-2ae663c76312") ]
__interface IEvents {
   [id(1)] HRESULT Values([in] short nVal1, [in] short nVal2);
};

[ dual, uuid("a3b7fea2-7396-4727-9691-7dc55acca27a") ]
__interface ISource {
   [id(1)] HRESULT Fire();
};

class DECLSPEC_UUID("530DF3AD-6936-3214-A83B-27B63C7997C4") CEventSource;
```

Listing 6-4 EvtSrc.h

CEventSource is a COM class that supports one interface, *ISource*, and one event interface, *IEvents*. The *ISource* interface has one member, *Fire*, which is used to raise the event defined in the *IEvents* source interface. The EvtSrc.cpp file implements this COM class in Listing 6-5. This file is also located in the Chapter06\Events\Src folder in book's companion content.

```
#define _ATL_ATTRIBUTES 1
#include <atlbase.h>
#include <atlcom.h>
#include "EvtSrc.h"

[ module(DLL, name="EventSource", uuid="6E46B59E-89C3-4c15-A6D8-
B8A1CEC98830") ];

[coclass, event_source(com), uuid("530DF3AD-6936-3214-A83B-27B63C7997C4")]
class CEventSource : public ISource {
public:
   __event __interface IEvents;
```

Listing 6-5 EvtSrc.cpp

```
   // This method fires the event
   HRESULT Fire() {
      __raise Values(10,12);
      return S_OK;
   }
};
```

The first thing to note is that to define events in this way, you need to include the ATL header files and define the *_ATL_ATTRIBUTES* preprocessor symbol. The *CEventSource* class defines an event member and uses the optional *__raise* keyword to fire the event when the *Fire* method is called.

You can build this code into a DLL and register the COM coclass by using the following command lines:

```
cl /LD EvtSrc.cpp
regsvr32 EvtSrc.dll
```

In the next section, you'll see how to handle the events raised by this component.

Handling Events

A class that is going to handle connection point events should be created with the *event_receiver* attribute. Like *event_source*, this attribute takes a *com* parameter to show that it wants to use connection points rather than native or managed events. The class also needs to implement the methods in the sink interface, which in practice means defining handler methods that have the same signature. Note that the class does not have to derive from the interface directly; the handler methods will be dynamically hooked up to the source object at run time.

Listing 6-6 shows how to handle the event fired by the *CEventSource* class that was defined in the previous section. You can find this file in the Chapter06\Events\Client folder in the book's companion content.

```
#define _ATL_ATTRIBUTES 1
#include <atlbase.h>
#include <atlcom.h>

#include <iostream>
using namespace std;

#include "..\Src\EvtSrc.h"

// Define a module
[ module(name="EventTest") ];
```

Listing 6-6 EvtClient.cpp

```cpp
// Define an event handler class
[ event_receiver(com) ]
class EventHandlerClass {
public:
   HRESULT Handler1(short nVal1, short nVal2) {
      cout << "Handler1 called with values " << nVal1 << " and "
           << nVal2 << endl;
      return S_OK;
   }

   HRESULT Handler2(short nVal1, short nVal2) {
      cout << "Handler2 called with values " << nVal1 << " and "
           << nVal2 << endl;
      return S_OK;
   }

   // Hook up two handlers to the same event source
   void HookEvent(ISource* pSource) {
      __hook(&IEvents::Values, pSource,
             &EventHandlerClass::Handler1);
      __hook(&IEvents::Values, pSource,
             &EventHandlerClass::Handler2);
   }

   // Unhook the event handlers
   void UnhookEvent(ISource* pSource) {
      __unhook(&IEvents::Values, pSource,
               &EventHandlerClass::Handler1);
      __unhook(&IEvents::Values, pSource,
               &EventHandlerClass::Handler2);
   }
};

int main() {
   // Create COM object
   CoInitialize(NULL);
   ISource* pSource = 0;
   HRESULT hr = CoCreateInstance(__uuidof(CEventSource), NULL,
         CLSCTX_ALL, __uuidof(ISource), (void **) &pSource);
   if (FAILED(hr)) {
      cout << "Error creating CEventSource object: " << hex
           << hr << dec << endl;
      return -1;
   }

   // Create the handler object, and set up the event notification
   EventHandlerClass theHandler;
   theHandler.HookEvent(pSource);
```

```
        // Fire the event
        pSource->Fire();

        // Unadvise
        theHandler.UnhookEvent(pSource);

        CoUninitialize();

        return 0;
}
```

The code defines a class that is going to be used to handle COM events and which is therefore tagged with the *event_receiver(com)* attribute.

Two new keywords are used to handle events: __*hook* and __*unhook*. The __*hook* keyword generates an advise call to the object, telling it to start sending events, while __*unhook* undoes the advise. To use __*hook*, you need to pass three things:

- The address of the event. When handling events from a COM object, this must be the address of an event function on an interface, not on the COM class itself.
- A pointer to the source object.
- The address of the handler function.

Once the call to __*hook* has returned, the handler function will be called each time a *Values* event is fired. To stop being sent events, __*unhook* is called with the same parameters. In this example, two handler functions are hooked to the same event to show it's possible to have more than one handler function for an event.

Compiler Options

There are four linker options that can be used to control the output of IDL and type library files for an attributed COM project. They are listed in Table 6-7 and explained in the following subsections.

Table 6-7 Linker Options Used with Attributed Code

Option	Description
/idlout	Specifies the name of an IDL file in which the compiler will save the IDL generated for the project
/ignoreidl	Specifies that IDL attributes present in the source should not be used to create an IDL file

Table 6-7 Linker Options Used with Attributed Code

Option	Description
/midl	Used to specify the name of a file containing MIDL command-line options
/tlbout	Specifies the name of the type library created by the compiler

Generating IDL

The /idlout and /tlbout options can be used to specify the base names for IDL and type library files. If you don't use either of these options, the linker will use vc70 as the base name for the generated files, creating vc70.idl, vc70.tlb, and so on.

If you just specify /idlout and /tlbout, all the MIDL-generated files (*.tlb, *.idl, *_i.c, *_p.c, and *.h) will take their names from the filename you supply. You can specify both options to generate a type library with a different name to the IDL file. In this case, the IDL file name is used to name all the generated files except the type library.

You use the options on the command line like this:

```
cl /LD MyServer.cpp /link /tlbout:foo.tlb
```

Since /tlbout is a linker option, you need to place it after the /link option.

Suppressing IDL Generation

By default, IDL attributes in source code will be processed and used to create an IDL file, which is then processed by MIDL in the usual way. If you want to suppress the generation of an IDL file for some reason, use the /ignoreidl linker option.

Summary

This chapter has described *attributed programming*, an important upgrade to ATL that makes it much easier to write COM components in C++ using the ATL library. Many ATL developers will find they can now write COM components without having to interact with IDL or the ATL source code.

This chapter has shown you how to apply COM attributes to C++ code, and it has discussed all the common COM-related attributes. You should now be in a position to use attributes to produce COM components more simply than before, while still retaining control over the way in which they are implemented in ATL and represented in a type library.

The next chapter discusses the other major addition to ATL: the set of classes introduced for writing plugins for web servers, which are collectively known as ATL Server. You'll learn which classes form part of the ATL Server library and how to use them to create server applications.

7

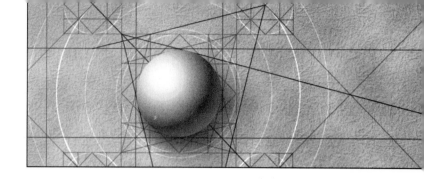

ATL and ATL Server

The previous chapter looked at *attributed programming*, a major new feature for COM programmers that provides a great new way to write COM components using the Active Template Library (ATL). This chapter looks at the ATL library itself, starting with the changes that have been made in the ATL 7.0 release, and introduces the completely new *ATL Server* library.

ATL Server is now one of the three Microsoft C++ libraries, along with the Microsoft Foundation Classes (MFC) library and ATL. MFC is designed for writing desktop graphical user interface (GUI) applications, ATL is designed for writing COM components and ActiveX controls, and ATL Server provides functionality for server-side programming.

Chapter 8 moves away from ATL and looks at how to write components using the .NET Framework.

> **Note** As with Chapter 6, this chapter will be of interest only to C++ programmers because ATL and ATL Server are purely C++ libraries.

Changes in ATL 7.0

A large number of changes have been made to the ATL library since ATL 3.0 was released with Visual Studio 6.0. The changes are too numerous to cover exhaustively in half a chapter, so this section discusses only major changes or those minor changes that are likely to be useful to the programmer. Consult the ATL documentation for a full list and full details.

New Module Classes

The functionality of the *CComModule* class has been divided up among a number of new classes. See the "Creating Modules" section in Chapter 6 for more details of these classes.

Data Handling and Collections

A large number of classes have been added to ATL to help with managing data. These classes can be divided into two groups: classes for managing lists, arrays, and trees; and classes that provide support for collections and enumerators. This section lists the classes that are available and shows how to work with some of the more widely used classes.

Classes for Managing Lists, Arrays, and Trees

The data collection classes that have been added to ATL 7.0 are listed in Table 7-1.

Table 7-1 **Data Collection**

Class	Description
CAtlArray	Implements an array class
CAtlList	Implements a doubly linked list class
CAtlMap	Implements a map class, which contains key-value pairs
CAutoPtrArray	Stores an array of smart pointers
CAutoPtrList	Stores smart pointers in a list
CComSafeArray	Provides a wrapper for the *SAFEARRAY* structure
CComSafeArrayBound	Provides a wrapper for the *SAFEARRAYBOUND* structure
CComUnkArray	Stores COM *IUnknown* interface pointers
CHeapPtrList	Stores a list of heap pointers
CInterfaceArray	Stores an array of COM interface pointers
CInterfaceList	Stores a list of COM interface pointers
CRBMap	Implements a map using Red-Black mapping
CRBMultiMap	Implements a map that can contain multiple keys, using Red-Black mapping

Table 7-1 **Data Collection**

Class	Description
CSimpleArray	Implements a simplified array class for dealing with small numbers of objects
CSimpleMap	Implements a simplified map class for dealing with small numbers of objects

The following sections will show you how to use some of these classes, starting with the arrays.

The *CSimpleArray* Class

The *CSimpleArray* class implements a simple array-like container for managing a small number of objects. *CSimpleArray* is a templated class that takes two template parameters:

```
template <class T, class TEqual = CSimpleArrayEqualHelper<T> >
    class CSimpleArray
```

The first template parameter denotes the type to be stored in the array. The second parameter is optional and is used to specify a class that will be used to test array members for equality. The default class, *CSimpleArrayEqualHelper*, uses *operator=* to test array elements. If the type being stored in the array is a built-in type or defines a suitable *operator=*, you can treat this parameter as optional. If you need to provide special handling for equality, you can provide your own class that implements a single static *IsEqual* method.

CSimpleArray supports a limited range of functionality, as indicated in the following list:

- *Add* and *SetAtIndex* modify the content of the array.
- *Remove*, *RemoveAll*, and *RemoveAt* remove data from the array.
- *Find* locates an element.
- *GetData* gets a pointer to the data held in the object.
- *GetSize* returns the number of elements in the array.
- *operator[]* returns an element.
- *operator=* copies elements between arrays.

The program in Listing 7-1 shows how to use *CSimpleArray*, and how to define a custom equality class. You can find this sample in the Chapter07\SimpleArray folder in the book's companion content. This content can be downloaded from the book's Web site at *http://www.microsoft.com/mspress/books/6426.asp*.

```cpp
#include <iostream>
using namespace std;

#include <atlbase.h>
// Include the header for the simple collections
#include <atlsimpcoll.h>
using namespace ATL;

// Equality helper class
template <typename T> class EqualHelper
{
public:
    static bool IsEqual(const T& t1, const T& t2)
    {
        return t1 == t2;
    }
};

// Specialization of helper class for long*
template <> class EqualHelper<long*>
{
public:
    static bool IsEqual(const long* t1, const long* t2)
    {
        return *t1 == *t2;
    }
};

int main()
{
    // Create an array to hold long*
    CSimpleArray<long*, EqualHelper<long*> > myArray;

    // Add two values
    long l1 = 40000L;
    long l2 = 50000L;

    myArray.Add(&l1);
    myArray.Add(&l2);

    cout << "Element 0 is " << *(myArray[0]) << endl;

    return 0;
}
```

Listing 7-1 SimpleArray.cpp

The array class is going to be used to hold pointers. This means that the default equality comparison class cannot be used because it would simply compare the values in the pointer variables. A template equality class is defined, and then a specialization for *long** is provided, which compares the values behind the pointers correctly.

The *CAtlArray* Class

CAtlArray implements a dynamically expandable array that is more suited to handling large numbers of elements than *CSimpleArray*. Once again, this is a template class that takes two template parameters:

```
template<typename E, class ETraits = CElementTraits<E> >
    class CAtlArray
```

The template class is defined by the type that the array is to hold and by an element traits class that holds the code for working with elements in the array, including methods for moving, copying, comparing, and hashing elements. The default class, *CElementTraits*, is sufficient for simple data types; for more complex types, you can provide your own traits class.

CAtlArray provides more functionality than *CSimpleArray*. The members of the class are listed in Table 7-2.

Table 7-2 Members of the *CAtlArray*

ClassMember	Description
Add	Adds an element to the array
Append	Adds one array to the end of another
AssertValid	Causes the array object to check itself, and throw an exception if its state is invalid
Copy	Copies elements from one array to another
FreeExtra	Removes empty elements from the array
GetAt	Returns an element from the array
GetCount	Returns the number of elements in the array
GetData	Returns a pointer to the first element in the array
InsertArrayAt	Inserts one array into another
InsertAt	Inserts one or more new elements into an array
IsEmpty	Returns true if the array is empty
RemoveAll	Removes all the elements from an array
RemoveAt	Removes one or more elements from an array
SetAt	Sets the value of an element in the array

Table 7-2 **Members of the *CAtlArray***

ClassMember	Description
SetAtGrow	Sets the value of an element, expanding the array if required
SetCount	Sets the size of the array object
operator[]	Returns a reference to an element in the array

The sample program in Listing 7-2 shows how to create and use *CAtlArray*s. You can find this sample in the Chapter07\AtlArray folder in the book's companion content.

```cpp
#include <iostream>
#include <string>
using namespace std;

#include <atlbase.h>
// Include the header for the ATL collections
#include <atlcoll.h>
using namespace ATL;

int main()
{
   // Declare two arrays and initialize them
   CAtlArray<string> strArray1;
   CAtlArray<string> strArray2;

   strArray1.Add(string("one"));
   strArray1.Add(string("two"));
   strArray1.Add(string("three"));

   strArray2.Add(string("giraffe"));
   strArray2.Add(string("zebra"));

   // Insert one array into the other
   strArray1.InsertArrayAt(1, &strArray2);

   // List the array contents
   cout << "Size of array 1 is " << strArray1.GetCount() << endl;
   for (unsigned int i=0; i<strArray1.GetCount(); i++)
      cout << "Element[" << i << "] = " << strArray1[i] << endl;

   return 0;
}
```

Listing 7-2 AtlArray.cpp

> **Note** Unlike the Standard Template Library (STL) and .NET Framework equivalents, there are no iterator classes that work with the ATL data collection classes. If you want to iterate over the elements in a collection, you will have to do it manually.

Support for *SAFEARRAY*s

COM programmers have to use *SAFEARRAY*s when passing array data to and from Microsoft Visual Basic or any other language that wants to use array objects. The problem is that *SAFEARRAY* is a structure, not a class. As such, it has no built-in functionality, and you need to use a number of Win32 API calls to create and manipulate *SAFEARRAY*s. Creating and using these structures can be a complex task, and given that there has been a class for handling *BSTR*s for some time, the provision of a class for handling *SAFEARRAY*s is long overdue.

SAFEARRAY support in ATL 7.0 is provided by two classes: *CComSafeArray*, which wraps the *SAFEARRAY* structure itself, and *CComSafeArrayBound*, which wraps the *SAFEARRAYBOUND* structure used to describe bound information.

Like all the other container classes I've discussed so far, *CComSafeArray* is a templated class that takes two template parameters:

```
template <typename T,
    VARTYPE _vartype = _ATL_AutomationType<T>::type>
class CComSafeArray
```

The first parameter defines the type to be stored in the *SAFEARRAY*, and you can use any Automation-compatible type. The second parameter provides a way to get the type *T* into the *SAFEARRAY* managed by the object. If you're using Automation-compatible types, the default value for this parameter will generate the correct type information.

> **Note** *SAFEARRAY*s can store only data types that can be stored in a *VARIANT*. For a full list of the available types, consult the *CComSafeArray* online help.

The most commonly used members of the *CComSafeArray* class are listed in Table 7-3.

Table 7-3 Members of the *CComSafeArray* Class

Member	Description
Add	Adds an element to the array
Attach	Attaches a *SAFEARRAY* to a *CComSafeArray* object
CopyFrom	Copies data from a *SAFEARRAY* into a *CComSafeArray* object
CopyTo	Creates a copy of a *CComSafeArray* object
Create	Creates a *CComSafeArray* object
Destroy	Destroys a *CComSafeArray* object
Detach	Detaches a *SAFEARRAY* from a *CComSafeArray* object
GetAt	Retrieves a single element from a one-dimensional array
GetCount	Returns the number of elements in the array
GetDimensions	Returns the number of dimensions in the array
GetLowerBound, GetUpperBound	Retrieves bound information
GetSafeArrayPtr	Gets a pointer to the *SAFEARRAY* structure managed by the object
GetType	Returns the type of data stored in the array
IsSizable	Returns true if the *CComSafeArray* is resizable
MultiDimGetAt	Gets the value of an element in a multi-dimensional array
MultiDimSetAt	Sets the value of an element in a multi-dimensional array
Resize	Resizes a *CComSafeArray* object
SetAt	Sets the value of an element in a one-dimensional array
operator[]	Returns a reference to an array element
operator=	Copies the content of one array into another
operator LPSAFEARRAY	Allows a *CComSafeArray* to be used where a *SAFEARRAY* is required

When creating a *CComSafeArray*, you need to specify dimension and bound information. This can be done in several ways: by specifying a lower bound, by using an existing *SAFEARRAY* to initialize the object, or by using a *SAFEARRAYBOUND* structure. The *SAFEARRAYBOUND* structure, which is wrapped by the *CComSafeArrayBound* class, holds details of the lower bound and number of elements for one dimension of a *SAFEARRAY*.

The sample program in Listing 7-3 shows you how to create both one-dimensional and two-dimensional *CComSafeArray*s. You can find this sample in the Chapter07\SafeArray folder of the book's companion content.

```
#include <iostream>
#include <string>
using namespace std;

#include <atlbase.h>
// Include the header for CComSafeArray
#include <atlsafe.h>
using namespace ATL;

int main()
{
    // Create a 1D array with four elements, and a default
    // lower bound of zero.
    CComSafeArray<char> oneDArray(4);

    // Put an 'x' in element 0, a 'y' in element 1, and 'z' in
    // the last two elements
    oneDArray.SetAt(0, 'x');
    oneDArray.SetAt(1, 'y');
    oneDArray.SetAt(2, 'z');
    oneDArray.SetAt(3, 'z');

    for(int i=0; i<oneDArray.GetCount(); i++)
        cout << oneDArray[i] << " ";
    cout << endl;

    // Create a CComSafeArrayBound object for each dimension
    // Set the lower bound to zero in each case
    CComSafeArrayBound bounds[2];
    bounds[0].SetLowerBound(0);
    bounds[0].SetCount(2);
    bounds[1].SetLowerBound(0);
    bounds[1].SetCount(5);

    // Create an array object
    CComSafeArray<int> twoDArray(bounds, 2);

    // Array to hold indices
    LONG index[2];
```

Listing 7-3 SafeArray.cpp

```
    for(i=0; i<2; i++)
    {
        index[0] = i;
        for(int j=0; j<5; j++)
        {
            index[1] = j;
            twoDArray.MultiDimSetAt(index, i*j);
        }
    }

    // Get an element
    index[0] = 2;
    index[1] = 3;
    int val = 0;
    twoDArray.MultiDimGetAt(index, val);
    cout << "Element[2,3] = " << val << endl;

    return 0;
}
```

The first part of the program creates a one-dimensional array of *char*s. Single-dimensioned arrays don't need *SAFEARRAYBOUND* information, so the array object can be created by simply specifying the number of elements required. The *SetAt* method is used to assign values to the array elements; *operator[]* can be used only to retrieve values because it returns a *const* reference.

The second part of the program creates a two-dimensional array, which requires two *CComSafeArrayBound* objects to hold the bounds information for each dimension. The *MultiDimSetAt* and *MultiDimGetAt* functions are used to set and retrieve elements for arrays with more than one dimension.

Support for Collections and Enumerators

COM supports the idea of enumerating a collection of objects using the *IEnum* family of interfaces. These provide a simple and well-known way to iterate over collections, and the *IEnumVARIANT* interface enables COM objects to fit in with the Visual Basic's *foreach* statement.

C++ programmers who are up to speed with the C++ Standard Library will be accustomed to using the Standard Template Library (STL) container classes when they need to implement collections, but the problem is that there has been no easy way to integrate the STL classes with a COM *IEnum* interface implementation. The COM *IEnum* interfaces are summarized in the following list:

- *CComEnumImpl* implements a COM enumerator for data stored in an array.
- *CComEnum* defines a COM enumerator based on an array, inheriting from *CComEnumImpl*.
- *CComEnumOnSTL* defines a COM enumerator based on an STL collection and implements the *IEnumOnSTLImpl* interface.
- *ICollectionOnSTLImpl* provides methods used by collection classes, such as *get_Count*, *get_Item*, and *get__NewEnum*.

Shared Classes

A number of classes are now shared between MFC and ATL. These are listed in Table 7-4 below.

Table 7-4 Parameters for the Module

AttributeClass	Description
CFileTime, CFileTimeSpan	Classes for manipulating absolute and relative date and time values associated with files. Include the header <*atltime.h*>.
CTime, CTimeSpan	Classes for manipulating absolute and relative date and time values. Include the header <*atltime.h*>.
COleDateTime, COleDateTimeSpan	Classes for manipulating OLE date and time values. Include the header <*atlcomtime.h*>.
CPoint, CRect, CSize	Classes that wrap the Windows *POINT*, *RECT*, and *SIZE* structures. Include the header <*atltypes.h*>.
CStringT	A string class. Include the header <*atlstr.h*>.
CSimpleString	A simple string class. Include <*atlsimpstr.h*>.
CStrBufT	Provides automatic resource cleanup for *CStringT* objects. Include the header <*atlsimpstr.h*>.
IAtlStringMgr	The interface to a *CStringT* buffer manager. Include the header <*atlsimpstr.h*>.

Most of these classes are simple to use or have been available in previous versions of the Microsoft Foundation Classes (MFC). The string classes, however, are new, and merit further discussion.

The *CSimpleStringT* Class

Many C++ programmers have become accustomed to using the *CString* class from the MFC library, and have found that ATL provided no suitable replacement. Several new string classes have been introduced that provide the same functionality as *CString*, while not being tied to the MFC library.

CSimpleStringT is the base class. It is a templated class, which takes a template parameter that defines the character set to be used. The template parameter can be one of the following:

- *CSimpleString<char>* for ANSI strings
- *CSimpleString<wchar_t>* for Unicode strings
- *CSimpleString<TCHAR>* to enable the character set to be automatically chosen

This class provides a simple set of base functionality, as shown in Table 7-5.

Table 7-5 Members of the *CSimpleStringT*

ClassMember	Description
Append, AppendChar	Appends another *CSimpleStringT* or a character.
CopyChars, CopyCharsOverlapped	Copies characters, with or without overlapping.
Empty	Clears the data from a *CSimpleStringT*.
GetAt, SetAt	Returns or sets the character at a given position in the string.
GetBuffer, ReleaseBuffer	Returns a pointer to the string buffer, which can then be modified. *ReleaseBuffer* must be called when the buffer is finished with.
GetLength	Returns the length of the string.
GetManager, SetManager	Gets or sets a pointer to the memory manager for the string.
GetString	Returns a const pointer to the buffer.
IsEmpty	Returns *true* if the string is empty.
LockBuffer, UnlockBuffer	Obtains and then relinquishes exclusive use of the character buffer.
SetString	Reinitializes the buffer of a string object.
StringLength	Returns the length of a string. This is a static method.
Truncate	Truncates the string to a given length.

Table 7-5 Members of the *CSimpleStringT*

ClassMember	Description
operator +=	Concatenates onto an existing string.
operator =	Assigns a new value to a string.
operator []	Provides a synonym for *GetAt*. This operator works only on the right hand side of an expression.
operator PCXSTR	Returns a const character pointer of the appropriate type.

Memory Management

Similar to many classes in the STL, the *CSimpleStringT* class does not implement its own memory management, but relies on the user to provide an instance of a memory manager class. Memory manager classes implement the *IAtlStringMgr* interface, which defines methods for handling memory allocation for strings. Separating memory management from the string class makes it possible to simply implement custom memory management, but if you don't need anything special, you can use the *CAtlStringMgr* class, which provides a default implementation of the interface.

The *CAtlStringMgr* class delegates the actual memory management task to a memory allocator class. There are five allocator classes provided by ATL:

- *CCRTHeap*, which uses the *malloc*, *realloc*, and *free* functions.

- *CWin32Heap*, which uses the Win32 heap functions *HeapAlloc*, *HeapRealloc*, and *HeapFree*.

- *CLocalHeap*, which uses the Win32 local heap functions *LocalAlloc*, *LocalRealloc*, and *LocalFree*. Note that these functions are comparatively slow, and you should use the *CWin32Heap* allocator instead.

- *CGlobalHeap*, which uses the Win32 global heap functions *GlobalAlloc*, *GlobalRealloc*, and *GlobalFree*. Note that these functions are comparatively slow, and unless you are required to use the global heap functions (for example, for DDE and clipboard operations), you should use the *CWin32Heap* allocator instead.

- *CComHeap*, which uses the COM memory allocator functions *CoTaskMemAlloc*, *CoTaskMemRealloc*, and *CoTaskMemFree*.

This scheme gives you considerable flexibility when you're considering the data storage needs for string data. If none of the options are suitable, however, you can implement your own allocator classes by implementing the *IAtlMemMgr* interface.

CSimpleStringT Example

Listing 7-4 is a simple example showing the use of *CSimpleStringT*. You can find this sample in the Chapter07\SimpleString folder in the books' companion content.

```cpp
#include <iostream>
using namespace std;

// Includes needed for the ATL string and memory classes
#include <atlsimpstr.h>
#include <atlstr.h>
#include <atlmem.h>
using namespace ATL;

int main()
{
   // The string will be allocated on the heap
   CCRTHeap hm;
   // Create a manager object that uses the heap
   CAtlStringMgr sm(&hm);
   // Create an ANSI string object
   CSimpleStringT<char> s1("hello", &sm);

   cout << "string is '" << s1 << "'"<< endl;
   cout << "length is '" << s1.GetLength() << "'"<< endl;

   s1.SetAt(0, 'H');
   cout << "string is '" << s1 << "'"<< endl;

   return 0;
}
```

Listing 7-4 SimpleString.cpp

The program shows how to use the memory management classes to ensure that string data will be stored on the heap. Although I've shown the creation of the three initial objects as separate steps, you can combine these steps into one statement:

```cpp
CSimpleStringT<char> s1("hello", new CAtlStringMgr(new CCRTHeap()));
```

The *CStringT* Class

CStringT provides a more fully featured string class than *CSimpleStringT* and has the following characteristics:

- *CStringT* objects can grow by concatenation.

- *CStringT* objects follow *value semantics*, which means that you can think of a *CStringT* object as an actual string, not as a pointer to a string.

- You can freely substitute *CStringT* objects for character pointer function arguments.

CStringT inherits from *CSimpleStringT*, which means it inherits the functionality of *CSimpleStringT*—including the ability to customize the memory management for the class. Here's the definition of the class:

```
template< typename BaseType, class StringTraits >
class CStringT : public CSimpleStringT< BaseType >
```

As with *CSimpleStringT*, the *BaseType* parameter can be *char*, *wchar_t*, or *TCHAR*. The *StringTraits* parameter determines whether the class will need the C Runtime Library and where string resources are located. When you use the class with ATL (as opposed to MFC), the *StringTraits* parameter can be one of the following:

```
// The class requires the runtime library
StrTraitATL< char | wchar_t | TCHAR,
        ChTraitsCRT< char | wchar_t | TCHAR> >

// The class does not require the runtime library
StrTraitATL< char | wchar_t | TCHAR,
        ChTraitsOS< char | wchar_t | TCHAR> >
```

For example, the following declaration would define a class that works with Unicode and requires the C Runtime Library:

```
CStringT< StrTraitATL< wchar_t, ChTraitsCRT<wchar_t> > > MyString;
```

To save programmers from having to write such complex template class declarations, a number of combinations of *BaseType* and *StringTraits* have been predefined, as listed in Table 7-6. Note how the *ATL_CSTRING_NO_CRT* preprocessor symbol determines whether C Runtime Library support is provided.

Table 7-6 Predefined *CStringT* Classes

Member	ATL_CSTRING_NO_CRT Defined?	Description
CAtlStringA	No	ANSI character type with CRT support
CAtlStringA	Yes	ANSI character type without CRT support

Table 7-6 Predefined *CStringT* Classes

Member	ATL_CSTRING_NO_CRT Defined?	Description
CAtlStringW	No	Unicode character type with CRT support
CAtlStringW	Yes	Unicode character type without CRT support
CAtlString	No	ANSI and Unicode character types with CRT support
CAtlString	Yes	ANSI and Unicode character types without CRT support

The *CStringT* class adds advanced functionality, such as character manipulation, ordering, and searching. The main member functions of *CStringT* are summarized in Table 7-7.

Table 7-7 Members of the *CStringT*

ClassMember	Description
AllocSysString, SetSysString	Allocates a *BSTR* from a *CStringT* object, or copies data into an existing *BSTR*.
AppendFormat	Appends formatted data to a *CStringT*.
Collate, CollateNoCase	Compares strings using locale information.
Compare, CompareNoCase	Compares strings without using locale information.
Delete	Deletes one or more characters from a string.
Find, ReverseFind	Finds a character or substring, starting from the beginning or end of the string.
FindOneOf	Finds the first matching character from a set.
Format, FormatV	Formats a string using *sprintf* formatting. *FormatV* takes a variable argument list.
FormatMessage	Uses the *FormatMessage* application programming interface (API) to format a message string.
Insert	Inserts one or more characters into a string.
Left, Mid, Right	Extracts the left, middle, or right portions of a string.
LoadString	Loads a string from a Windows resource.
MakeLower, MakeUpper	Converts a string to uppercase or lower case.
MakeReverse	Reverses a string.

Table 7-7 Members of the *CStringT*

ClassMember	Description
Remove	Removes characters from a string.
Replace	Replaces one or more characters within a string.
SpanExcluding	Returns the characters up to the first that matches a specified set.
SpanIncluding	Returns the characters up to the first that does not match a specified set.
Tokenize	Extracts a token from a string, starting at a given position.
Trim, TrimLeft, TrimRight	Trims whitespace from a string.

The *CStringT* class also supports a range of concatenation and assignment operators (=, +=, and +) as well as the comparison operators (==, !=, >, >=, <, and <=).

Predefined Types for Use with *CStringT*

Declaring the correct types for characters and pointers to work with a templated class such as *CStringT* can be complex. A number of character and pointer types have been defined to make this task easier, and they are listed in Table 7-8:

Table 7-8 Predefined Types to Work with *CStringT*

Type	Description
XCHAR	A single character of the same type (*char* or *wchar_t*) as the *CStringT*
YCHAR	A single character of the opposite type to the *CStringT*
PXSTR	A character pointer of the same type as the *CStringT*
PYSTR	A character pointer of the opposite type to the *CStringT*
PCXSTR	A *const* character pointer of the same type as the *CStringT*
PCYSTR	A *const* character pointer of the opposite type to the *CStringT*

CStringT Example

The basic sample program in Listing 7-5 shows how to declare and use a *CStringT*. You can find this sample in the Chapter07\CStringT folder of the book's companion content.

```cpp
#include <iostream>
using namespace std;

// We want the Runtime Library
#undef ATL_CSTRING_NO_CRT

// Include the string class header file
#include <atlstr.h>
using namespace ATL;

int main()
{
   // Create an ANSI string
   CAtlStringA s1("hello");

   cout << "string is '" << s1 << "'"<< endl;
   cout << "length is '" << s1.GetLength() << "'"<< endl;

   // String concatenation
   s1 += "world";

   // Change the first character
   s1.SetAt(0, 'H');
   // Insert a space
   s1.Insert(5, ' ');

   cout << "string is '" << s1 << "'"<< endl;

   return 0;
}
```

Listing 7-5 CStringT.cpp

Undefining the *ATL_CSTRING_NO_CRT* symbol means that the *CAtlStringA* class uses ANSI characters and the C Runtime Library.

String Conversion Classes

ATL has always provided macros to simplify the job of converting between character sets. ATL 7.0 has introduced a new set of classes to replace the ATL 3.0 macros, and these classes provide significant improvements when compared with the old macros. These improvements are summarized in Table 7-9.

Table 7-9 Comparison of String Conversion Macros and Classes

ATL 3.0 Macros	ATL 7.0 Classes
Allocates memory only for conversion on the stack, so it's not good for very large strings.	Uses the heap if the stack is not large enough.
The string is freed when the function containing the macro is exited. The macros are not suitable for use in loops then because memory use grows.	The string is freed when the variable goes out of scope. This means that memory can be freed at the end of each loop iteration.
Cannot be used in exception handlers.	Can be used in exception handlers.
Usually requires *USES_CONVERSION* to be defined.	Never requires *USES_CONVERSION* to be defined.
The meaning of the *OLE* symbol depends on the definition of *OLE2ANSI*.	*OLE* is always equivalent to *W*.

The naming convention for the conversion classes has been changed, and names are now of the form

CSourceType2[C]DestType[EX]

where the source and destination types can be the following:

- *A* to denote an ANSI string.
- *W* to denote a Unicode string.
- *T* to denote a generic string. This will map onto ANSI or Unicode depending on whether the *_UNICODE* symbol is defined at compile time.
- *OLE* to denote an OLE character string. This is now equivalent to W.

The optional parts of the name are *C*, which is used to denote a const destination string, and *EX*, which denotes the extended version. The extended versions take a buffer size as a template parameter and can be used when the default buffer size of 128 characters is not appropriate. For example, *CW2CA* would specify conversion from a wide string to a const ANSI string.

To use the conversion classes, create an object of the appropriate type by using the naming convention. This object can then be used where the appropriate destination type is required. For example take a look at Listing 7-6, available in the Chapter07\AltMacros folder of the book's companion content.

```cpp
#include <windows.h>

#include <iostream>
using namespace std;

#undef ATL_CSTRING_NO_CRT

#include <atlconv.h>
#include <atlstr.h>
using namespace ATL;

void func1(LPSTR lps)
{
    cout << "func1: string is '" << lps << "'" << endl;
}

int main()
{
    // Declare a wide string
    LPWSTR lpws = L"wide string";

    // Create a conversion object to let it be used as an
    // ANSI string. Use the Ex version to specify a 30-character
    // buffer
    CW2AEX<30> ca(lpws);

    // Call a function that expects an LPSTR, passing in the CW2AEX
    // instance
    func1(ca);

    return 0;
}
```

Listing 7-6 AtlMacros.cpp

Security Classes

A number of classes have been added to ATL to help use the Windows security system from within code.

> **Note** This isn't the place to provide details on programming Windows security. For more details on this topic, see Keith Brown's book, *Programming Windows Security*, published by Addison-Wesley, 2000.

Table 7-10 describes the security classes.

Table 7-10 The ATL Security Classes

Class	Description
CAcl	This is the base class for the *CDacl* and *CSacl* classes.
CDacl	This is a class that wraps a DACL (discretionary access control list), and gives access to the ACEs (access control entries).
CSacl	A class that wraps a SACL (system access control list), and gives access to the ACEs.
CSecurityAttributes	This class provides a thin wrapper for the *SECURITY_ATTRIBUTES* structure.
CSecurityDesc	This class provides a thin wrapper for the *SECURITY_DESCRIPTOR* structure.
CSid	This class provides a thin wrapper for the *SID* (security identifier) structure.
CTokenGroups	This class provides a thin wrapper for the *TOKEN_GROUPS* structure.
CTokenPrivileges	This class provides a thin wrapper for the *TOKEN_PRIVILEGES* structure.

A number of global security functions, which are commonly used with the security classes, are provided by ATL. You'll find these summarized in Table 7-11.

Table 7-11 The Global ATL Security Functions

Function	Description
AtlGetDacl, AtlSetDacl	Gets or sets the DACL associated with an object
AtlGetGroupSid, AtlSetGroupSid	Gets or sets the group SID associated with an object
AtlGetOwnerSid, AtlSetOwnerSid	Gets or sets the owner SID associated with an object
AtlGetSacl, AtlSetSacl	Gets or sets the SACL associated with an object
AtlGetSecurityDescriptor	Gets the security descriptor for an object

The sample program in Listing 7-7 shows some of these classes in action and is intended for those who have some experience of programming Win32 security. You can find this sample in the Chapter07\AtlSecurity folder of the book's companion content.

```cpp
#include <iostream>
using namespace std;

// Needed because some features are only available on Windows 2000 and later
#define _WIN32_WINNT 0x0500

// Access rights - defined in <Winnt.h>
#define STANDARD_RIGHTS_ALL           (0x001F0000L)

#include <atlbase.h>
#include <atlsecurity.h>
#include <atlstr.h>
using namespace ATL;

int main()
{
    // Get the SID for a file object, and print details. The
    // AtlGetOwnerSid function takes a name and an object type,
    // and fills in the fields of a CSid object
    CSid sid;
    if (!AtlGetOwnerSid("c:\\temp\\output.cpp", SE_FILE_OBJECT, &sid))
        cout << "Error getting SID" << endl;
    else
    {
        cout << "Account: " << sid.AccountName() << endl;
        cout << "Domain: " << sid.Domain() << endl;
        cout << "SID: " << sid.Sid() << endl;
    }

    // Get the security descriptor for the file object.
    // AtlGetSecurityDescriptor takes a name and an object type,
    // and fills in the fields of a CSecurityDesc object
    CSecurityDesc sd;
    if (!AtlGetSecurityDescriptor("c:\\temp\\output.cpp",
        SE_FILE_OBJECT, &sd))
        cout << "Error getting security descriptor" << endl;
    else
    {
        cout << "Security Descriptor:" << endl;

        // SECURITY_INFORMATION defines the information being
        // set or queried
        SECURITY_INFORMATION si = OWNER_SECURITY_INFORMATION |
```

Listing 7-7 AtlSecurity.cpp

```
                         GROUP_SECURITY_INFORMATION |
                         DACL_SECURITY_INFORMATION |
                         SACL_SECURITY_INFORMATION;

// The ToString function produces a string representation of
// a security descriptor. This string can be converted back
// to a security descriptor using the FromString function.
// Note that ToString is only available on Windows 2000
// and later.
CString cs;
sd.ToString(&cs, si);
cout << cs << endl;

// Get the DACL for the security descriptor, and print some
// details
CDacl dcl;
bool bPresent, bDefault;
sd.GetDacl(&dcl, &bPresent, &bDefault);
cout << "DACL: present=" << bPresent <<
        ", defaulted=" << bDefault << endl;

if (dcl.IsNull()) cout << "DACL is null" << endl;
if (dcl.IsEmpty()) cout << "DACL is empty" << endl;

// Add an Access Control Entry (ACE). First, create a SID
// for the administrator account
CSid sid2("Administrator");

// Add an "allow" entry for this SID to the DACL
if (dcl.AddAllowedAce(sid2, STANDARD_RIGHTS_ALL))
{
   cout << "ACE added OK" << endl;
   // Set the DACL back into the security descriptor. Many of
   // the security functions return a bool value, but SetDacl
   // throws an exception if it fails.
   try
   {
      sd.SetDacl(dcl);
      cout << "DACL added OK" << endl;
   }
   catch(CAtlException& ae)
   {
      cout << "Error setting DACL (" << hex << ae.m_hr
           << dec << ")" << endl;
   }
}
```

```
      else
         cout << "Error adding ACE" << endl;
   }
   return 0;
}
```

Regular Expression Classes

Two classes have been added to ATL to provide regular expression matching for strings. An instance of the *CAtlRegExp* class can be created to represent a regular expression, and the object's *Match* function can then be used to see whether the expression matches strings. Here's an example that will match dates with a dd/mm/yyyy pattern:

```
// Create a regular expression object
CAtlRegExp<> re;

// Provide an expression for it to use. Days and months
// are two digits with leading zeros, years are four digits
// with a leading 1 or 2
REParseError err = re.Parse(
     "[0-9][0-9]/[0-9][0-9]/[12][0-9][0-9][0-9] ");
if (err != REPARSE_ERROR_OK)
{
   cout << "Parse error" << endl;
}
else
{
   // Test it...
   CAtlREMatchContext<> mc;

   // Get a test string
   cout << "> ";
   cin >> buff;

   // See if the string matches the pattern
   if (re.Match(buff, &mc))
      cout << "OK" << endl;
   else
      cout << "Error" << endl;
}
```

CAtlRegExp is a templated class that takes a single *CAtlRECharTraits* template parameter, which is used to define character set–dependent behavior. The default argument will suffice for most purposes, so you can create a *CAtlRegExp* instance using empty angle brackets.

The *Parse* function tells the *CAtlRegExp* object to parse a regular expression and use it for pattern matching. There are a number of error status codes that can be returned from this function, but if all is OK, the function will return *REPARSE_ERROR_OK*.

The *Match* function is used to test strings against the expression currently held by the *CAtlRegExp* object. The second argument to the function specifies a *CAtlREMatchContext* object, which can be used to obtain information about the match. For example, regular expressions can contain match groups that correspond to regions within the expression (such as the day or the month in the preceding example), and the context object can be used to obtain the parts of the string that matched the groups.

Other Changes

The *CAdapt* class has been added to make it easier to work with some ATL and COM classes. Certain classes, such as *CComPtr* and *CComBSTR*, implement *operator&* to return something other than the address of the object. For example, *CComPtr* uses *operator&* to return the address of the interface pointer it is managing.

Many container classes expect to be able to use *operator&* to get the address of the object, so it is not possible to use classes such as *CComPtr* and *CComBSTR* in these containers without modification. The *CAdapt* class hides the *operator&* implementation of the type it wraps, while still exposing the rest of the functionality of the wrapped class. Here is an example, showing how you could construct a list of *CComPtr* objects:

```
// Not good because CComPtr::operator& will cause problems
std::list<CComPtr> ptrList;

// CAdapt fixes the operator& problem, while still giving access
// to CComPtr
std::list< CAdapt<CComPtr> > ptrList;
```

A new static *CreateInstance* method has been added to *CComCoClass*, which provides a simple way to create an instance of a COM coclass, without having to use the COM APIs. For example, if *MyComClass* is an ATL class that inherits from *CComCoClass*, you can create an instance of the class like this:

```
// pIface is a pointer to the interface you require
HRESULT hr = MyComClass::CreateInstance(&pIface);
```

Breaking Changes Since Visual C++ 6.0

Some of the changes that have been made to ATL since Visual Studio 6.0 might break existing code. This section lists some of the most important of these changes. For a full list, consult the ATL documentation.

The ATL DLL that shipped with Visual Studio .NET has been renamed ATL70.dll and is not binary compatible with previous releases. Any source code that uses the ATL DLL will need to be rebuilt to work with ATL 7.0.

The *CComModule* class has been replaced by a number of classes that divide up the functionality. See the "Creating Modules" section in Chapter 6 for more details about these classes.

There are now Unicode and ANSI versions of the *CString* class, named *CStringW* and *CStringA*. If you want to build a Unicode *CString* from an ANSI string or vice versa, the compiler will not allow implicit conversions because the appropriate constructors have been made explicit.

> **Note** The *explicit* modifier can be applied to constructors to prevent them from performing implicit conversions. Such constructors have to be called explicitly.

```
BSTR bstr = SysAllocString(L"Hello");
// This requires an implicit conversion, and will fail
CString str = bstr;
```

There are two ways to perform an explicit conversion. The first is to use the underlying type you require, as in this example:

```
BSTR bstr = SysAllocString(L"Hello");
// This does not require an implicit conversion
CStringW str = bstr;
```

The second is to call the constructor explicitly:

```
BSTR bstr = SysAllocString(L"Hello");
// This does not require an implicit conversion
CString str = CString(bstr);
```

This behavior is controlled by the preprocessor symbol *_ATL_CSTRING_EXPLICIT_CONSTRUCTORS*, which is defined in stdafx.h for ATL projects. If you want, you can undefine this symbol to allow explicit conversions.

Introduction to ATL Server

ATL Server, newly introduced in ATL 7.0, is a set of ATL extension classes designed for server-side programming. Despite the *ATL* in the name, these classes have little to do with COM and have been primarily designed to let C++ developers create three kinds of server-side applications:

- ISAPI extensions
- XML Web Services
- Web applications

To help you build these applications, a large number of classes are provided as part of the ATL Server library, including classes for

- Working with sockets and HTTP
- Handling cookie-based sessions
- Caching session state in memory or to database tables
- Performance monitoring
- Working with SMTP
- Writing SOAP clients and servers
- Handling MIME types, and encoding or decoding using various schemes, such as Base64
- Formatting HTML
- Working with files, including memory-mapped files, and providing *IStream*-like access to files

Discussing all of these in detail would require a book in itself. Therefore, in the sections that follow, I'll introduce you to the architecture of ATL Server, and I will use two of the main application types—Web applications and XML Web Services—to demonstrate the main features of the ATL Server library.

ATL Server Architecture

The ATL Server architecture consists of four main elements:

- A Web server, which passes HTTP requests from clients to ATL Server DLLs

- ISAPI extension DLLs, which are passed requests by the Web server, and which route them to an appropriate Web application DLL
- Web application DLLs, which provide application-specific functionality for handling requests and generating responses
- Server Response Files (SRFs), which are text files that contain the static part of the response

> **Note** If you are familiar with ASP.NET, Server Response Files are analogous to .aspx files, and Web application DLLs are analogous to the code-behind files that implement the ASP application functionality.

An ATL Server project will be made up of one ISAPI extension DLL and one or more ATL Server application DLLs. The ISAPI extension DLL caches the loaded ATL Server DLLs and the parsed SRF files, and it contains a thread pool for handling client requests. The ATL Server application DLLs contain classes for parsing SRF files and replacing SRF file tags with HTML. The architecture of an ATL Server application is shown diagrammatically in Figure 7-1.

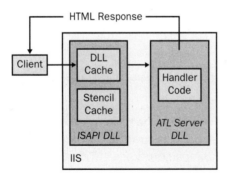

Figure 7-1 The architecture of an ATL Server application

We'll now consider ISAPI extensions, Web application, DLLs, and SRF files in more detail.

ISAPI Extensions

ISAPI (Internet Server API) provides a way to write plug-in DLLs for Microsoft Internet Information Services (IIS). There are two types of ISAPI DLLs: *filters*, which are used by IIS to filter incoming HTTP requests, and *extensions*, which provide functionality for Web applications. In this section, I'm talking only about extensions because ATL Server has no support for writing ISAPI filters.

Although ISAPI extensions have performance and scalability benefits when compared with ASP pages, they have traditionally been hard to write because they have to be coded in C or C++ and use API calls rather than classes. ATL Server makes the task of creating and using ISAPI extensions much easier by splitting off the application-specific functionality and placing it in a Web application DLL.

Web Application DLLs

An ATL Server Web application DLL contains one or more classes that implement *request handler* functions. An SRF file will have one or more Web application DLLs associated with it. Each tag occurring within the SRF file is mapped onto a request handler function in a DLL; when the SRF is processed, the request handler is called, which will usually result in text being echoed to the response stream.

Server Response Files

A Server Response File (an *SRF* file, also known as a *stencil*) is the ATL Server equivalent of an ASP file, in that it contains a mixture of static HTML and tags that will be used to generate custom content at run time. In the case of SRF files, the tags are calls to methods in an ATL Server DLL. The tags, which appear within double curly brackets, are called *replacement tags*. As with ASP pages, the dynamic content is separated from the static layout because the code resides in a Web application DLL.

Browser clients use the URL of an SRF—for example, *http://myserver/myapp.srf*—to connect to the server. The ISAPI DLL is registered as the default handler for SRF files, and it processes the SRF file, making use of the ATL Server Web application DLL to provide dynamic content.

SRF files are often passed in as part of the HTTP request URL, but they can also be held as resources. SRF files contain three types of information:

- The name of the handler class for this SRF and the DLL that houses it
- Static HTML for the returned page
- Placeholder tags in the HTML that are replaced with dynamic content at run time

Here is a simple SRF file that demonstrates the replacement tag syntax:

```
{{handler HelloHandler.dll/Default}}
<html>
<body>
{{Hello}}
</body>
</html>
```

When a client requests the URL of this file, IIS loads the HelloHandler.dll if necessary, and then passes it the request. The SRF file is processed by the *stencil processor* code that is part of ATL Server. Once SRF files have been parsed by the processor, they are cached so that they can be used over again without the need for further parsing. Obviously, if the text in the SRF file is modified, the file will be reprocessed and the cache refreshed.

When the SRF has been processed, the *{{Hello}}* tag results in a call to a method in the DLL, which generates HTML output that is merged with the page.

> **Note** Static content within an SRF file is usually HTML or XML, but it can be any text that doesn't conflict with the formatting used by SRF tags.

SRF Syntax

The syntax of SRF files is simple because there are only six predefined replacement tags. These tags are listed in Table 7-12.

Table 7-12 **Predefined Replacement Tags for SRFs**

Name	Description
codepage	Used to define the code page to be used for processing the file, if the file contains characters that are not part of the ANSI character set.
comment	Places a comment in the SRF file that will be removed during processing. Comments can continue over more than one line, and are placed between *{{//* and *}}* markers.
handler	Identifies a request handler class that will be used to process some or all of the replacement tags within the SRF file. There should be only one handler tag in an SRF file.
include	Inserts the contents of another SRF file.

Table 7-12 Predefined Replacement Tags for SRFs

Name	Description
locale	Used to indicate the locale that should be used for any response generated from the file, from the locale tag onwards.
subhandler	Used to identify a request handler that will be used to process some or all of the replacement tags within a file. There can be more than one subhandler tag in an SRF file.

Handler and Subhandler Tags

Often, all the user-defined replacement tags within an SRF file will be part of a single DLL. A handler replacement tag is placed at the top of an SRF file to name this DLL, using the following syntax:

```
{{ handler path_to_dll/request_handler }}
```

In the handler tag, *path_to_dll* is the path to the handler DLL. This path can be absolute or relative to the directory containing the SRF file. Also in the handler tag, *request_handler* is the name of the request handler within the file that is going to handle the request. You need the name because a handler DLL can contain more than one handler class. Note that the name of the request handler is not necessarily the name of the class within the DLL that implements the handler. Using a separate name allows you to hide code-naming conventions and provide user-friendly names.

> **Note** See the "Writing Web Applications Using ATL Server" section for details of how handler classes are implemented, and how request handlers are named.

There should be only one *handler* tag per SRF file; any subsequent *handler* tags will be silently ignored when the file is processed. Here is an example of a *handler* tag:

```
{{// The following line defines a handler tag }}
{{ handler MyHandler.dll/TheHandler }}
```

The *handler* DLL is MyHandler.dll, which is located in the same directory as the SRF file, and the name of the handler is *TheHandler*.

You can have replacement tags within an SRF file handled by more than one DLL. Any secondary handler DLLs are defined using *subhandler* tags, which use the following syntax:

```
{{ subhandler namespace path_to_dll/request_handler }}
```

As with the handler tag, the *subhandler* tag gives the path to the handler DLL and specifies the name of the request handler within the DLL. It also defines a namespace, which is used to prefix tags within the SRF file so that the processor can tell which DLL should be used to locate the function:

```
{{// The handler tag for the file }}
{{ handler MyHandler.dll/TheHandler }}

{{// A subhandler tag }}
{{ subhandler aux MyOtherHandler.dll/OtherHandler }}

{{// This method is part of TheHandler }}
{{ Method1 }}

{{// This method is part of OtherHandler }}
{{ aux.Method2 }}
```

You can see how the *subhandler* tag defines the *aux* namespace, which is then used to prefix *Method2*. Since *Method1* does not have a prefix, it is taken as being part of *TheHandler*.

Including Files

The *include* tag can be used within an SRF file to include the contents of another file. The included file can be one of three types:

- A file containing static HTML, which is merged with the enclosing SRF file.

- Another SRF file, in which case handlers are loaded as appropriate, and the file is processed in the normal manner.

- An ATL Server Web application DLL. In this case, the file name can contain a query string, which will be passed to the DLL when it is loaded.

Here is an example of how the include tag is used:

```
{{// Include an HTML file }}
{{ include Boilerplate.html }}

{{// Process another SRF file }}
{{ include File2.srf }}
```

Defining Replacement Tags

Replacement tags are added to SRF files to show where dynamic content should be inserted. As I mentioned previously, processing a replacement tag results in calling a method implemented by a handler class in an ATL Server Web application DLL.

The simplest use of replacement tags encloses the name of the tag within double curly brackets. This is used to call handler methods that have no arguments:

```
{{// Call the Welcome method }}
{{ Welcome }}
```

By default, the DLL specified in the handler tag will be used to execute the tag. If you have used subhandlers, you need to specify the name of the subhandler to use a tag that is implemented by the subhandler DLL. The preceding example for defining subhandlers showed how the syntax works.

You can pass arguments to replacement methods by placing them in parentheses after the method name:

```
{{// Pass two arguments }}
{{ AMethod(5, Sunday) }}
```

Arguments are always passed through as strings and will be converted by the handler method. The following section, "Writing Web Applications Using ATL Server," shows how to implement replacement methods that take arguments.

You can use the *if/else/endif* and *while/endwhile* constructs within replacement tags to perform conditional processing. Here is a simple example:

```
{{// Conditional processing }}
{{ if DayIsSunday }}
  Today is Sunday
{{ else }}
  Today is not Sunday
{{ endif }}
```

The key to conditional processing in SRF files is that handler methods always return a status code. If that code is *HTTP_SUCCESS*, the text within the *if* block will be passed to the output stream. In the preceding example, the *DayIsSunday* handler method will return *HTTP_SUCCESS* if the day is Sunday, and the string "Today is Sunday" will be echoed to the output file. If any other value is returned, the string "Today is not Sunday" will be echoed instead.

A *while* loop can be constructed in the same way:

```
{{// Conditional processing }}
{{ while MoreData }}
  <tr><td> {{ GetData }} </td></tr>
{{ endwhile }}
```

In this example, as long as the replacement method *MoreData* returns *HTTP_SUCCESS*, the text within the body of the loop will be repeatedly echoed to the output, which will result in rows being added to a table. Note how the text within the body of the loop calls another replacement method to retrieve the data.

Writing Web Applications Using ATL Server

An ATL Server Web application is the ATL Server equivalent of an ASP.NET application. In ASP.NET applications, .aspx files contain HTML that uses custom tags to execute methods in page handler classes. In ATL Server Web applications, SRF files contain fixed HTML and text, and they use SRF tags to execute methods on handler classes. In both cases, the handler code is supplied in DLLs.

Using Attributes

You can write Web applications using pure C++ code, but two attributes have been supplied that make it easier to write handler classes.

The *request_handler* Attribute

The *request_handler* attribute marks a class as implementing request handler methods and takes a parameter that sets the alias that SRF files will use to identify the handler class:

```
[request_handler("MyHandler")]
class CMyhandler
{
    ...
};
```

If the preceding class was compiled into Handlers.dll, it would be referred to in an SRF file like this:

```
{{// The handler tag for the file }}
{{ handler Handlers.dll/MyHandler }}
```

Using the *request_handler* attribute will normally result in the addition of the ATL Server class *CRequestHandlerT* as a base class and in the addition of a *DECLARE_REQUEST_HANDLER* macro that exposes the class to IIS.

> **Note** I use the word *normally* because *CRequestHandlerT* will not be added as a base class if the attributed class already explicitly implements the *IRequestHandler* interface.

The *CRequestHandlerT* class has several useful members that you might end up using in your handler code. These members are summarized in Table 7-13.

Table 7-13 Commonly Used Members of the *CRequestHandlerT* Class

Member	Description
CheckValidRequest	Override this method if you need to check the validity of the request.
ClearResponse	Clears the response object of any headers and buffered data.
FormFlags	Returns one or more of the ATL Server form flags, which specifies how forms are processed. See below for an explanation of form flags.
HandleRequest	You can override this method to provide your own handling for the HTTP request. For the majority of cases, the default implementation is sufficient.
InitializeChild	Called to initialize the handler when an instance is created during processing a *subhandler* or *include* tag. This method initializes the request and response objects, and calls *ValidateAndExchange*.
InitializeHandler	Called to initialize the handler when an instance is created during processing a *handler* tag. This method initializes the response object, calls *CheckValidRequest*, initializes the request object, and finally calls *ValidateAndExchange*.
MaxFormSize	Returns the maximum size of form that will be accepted. You can override this function if the default value of 48 KB is not acceptable.
ServerTransferRequest	Transfers the request to another handler.
ValidateAndExchange	Override this method to initialize the request handler.
m_dwRequestType	Data member holding the type of the request. The value of this member can be *ATLSRV_REQUEST_STENCIL*, showing that an SRF file was requested; or *ATLSRV_REQUEST_DLL*, showing that a handler DLL was requested; or *ATLSRV_REQUEST_UNKNOWN*.
m_HttpRequest	Returns a *CHttpRequest* object representing the current request.
m_HttpResponse	Returns a *CHttpResponse* object used to write the response to the client.
m_pRequestInfo	Returns a pointer to an *AtlServerRequest* object that holds information about the ATL Server request handling infrastructure. This data will not be used by the majority of users.

The *FormFlags* method is used to return a value that defines how forms will be processed. The following flag values are supported:

- *ATL_FORM_FLAG_NONE* (numerical value 0), which specifies that forms are processed and files will be created
- *ATL_FORM_FLAG_IGNORE_FILES* (numerical value 1), which specifies that attempts to upload files will be ignored
- *ATL_FORM_FLAG_REFUSE_FILES* (numerical value 2), which specifies that attempts to upload files will be treated as an error
- *ATL_FORM_FLAG_IGNORE_EMPTY_FILES* (numerical value 4), which specifies that files of size zero bytes will be ignored
- *ATL_FORM_FLAG_IGNORE_EMPTY_FIELDS* (numerical value 8), which specifies that fields with no content will be ignored

The default implementation provided by *CRequestHandlerT* returns *ATL_FORM_FLAG_IGNORE_FILES*. You can override this method to define other behavior, ORing together values as required.

The *tag_name* Attribute

The *tag_name* attribute establishes the tag name that will be used to call a handler method from within SRF files. Here's an example of a handler function that doesn't take any parameters:

```
[tag_name(name="DoThis")]
HTTP_CODE SomeFunction()
{
    // If all is OK...
    return HTTP_SUCCESS;
}
```

Defining Handler Methods

Handler methods are simply C++ class member functions. These functions can take arguments, but any arguments passed in will need to be converted because HTTP request arguments are always passed as strings. There are three situations to be considered:

- The handler takes no arguments.
- The handler takes one argument that can be parsed automatically.
- The handler takes more than one argument, the argument is of a type that cannot be parsed automatically, or both.

The first case is trivial because there are no arguments to convert. In the second case, if the method takes a single argument that is a *bool*, an integer type (*char*, *short*, *int*, or *__int64*, and their unsigned equivalents), or a floating point type (*float* or *double*), then the conversion from a string will be done automatically. Such methods should be declared to take a pointer of the requisite type, for example,

```
// A handler function that takes a boolean
[tag_name(name="PassABool")]
HTTP_CODE BoolHandler(bool* pArg)
{
    // If all is OK...
    return HTTP_SUCCESS;
}
```

This function could be invoked from an SRF file like this:

```
{{ PassABool(true) }}
```

If the first four characters of the parameter passed in evaluate to *true*—with the comparison being case-insensitive—a Boolean value of *true* will be passed to the handler function. If the parameter cannot be converted for some reason, the conversion process will pass an HTTP error back to the client.

> **Note** Parameters used with replacement tags cannot contain a closing parenthesis character ")". Be careful not to choose a character encoding that results in one of the bytes having the same value as an ANSI closing parenthesis (decimal 41, hex 29).

Using Parsing Functions

If the handler method is going to take a single parameter of a type that isn't automatically parsed, or it's going to take more than one parameter of any type, you'll need to write a parsing function to decode the input data and convert it to a form that can be used by the handler method. The prototype for a parsing function looks like this:

```
HTTP_CODE ParsingFunction(
        IAtlMemMgr* pMemoryManager,
        LPCSTR szArgumentData,
        parameterType** ppArgument
);
```

The first parameter is a pointer to a memory manager object that you use to allocate memory for the converted argument data. The second parameter is the string containing the data from the HTTP request, and the third parameter is a pointer of the appropriate type, through which the function passes the converted value to the handler function.

You link a parsing function to a handler by using the optional second parameter to the *tag_name* attribute:

```
[tag_name(name="DoThis", parse_func="ParsingFunction")]
HTTP_CODE SomeFunction(bool* pb)
{
   // If all is OK...
   return HTTP_SUCCESS;
}
```

The *parse_func* parameter specifies the name of the parsing function, and this function will automatically be called to parse the input data whenever the handler is invoked. If *parse_func* is used, the handler method must take an argument of the same type that will be emitted by the parsing function.

A Sample ATL Server Application

The following example shows how to write a simple ATL Server Web application, which has the following characteristics:

- It has two handler classes, one of which is used as a subhandler.
- It implements handler methods that do not require custom parsing.
- It implements handler methods that do require custom parsing functions.

> **Note** To create and test Web applications, you must have access to a Web server, and have permission to install ISAPI extensions.

Creating the Project

Bring up the New Project dialog box, and in the Visual C++ project types folder select *ATL Server Project*, choosing an appropriate location and name, as shown in Figure 7-2.

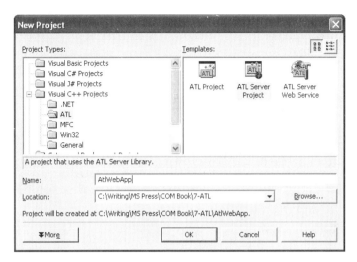

Figure 7-2 Creating an ATL Server Web application project

You can see in the ATL Server Project Wizard dialog box shown in Figure 7-3, that there are a number of project settings that can be used to customize the code and the way it is deployed.

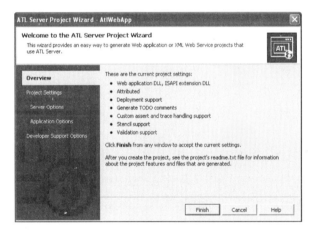

Figure 7-3 The Project Wizard Overview page for an ATL Server Web application project

The default settings will generate attributed code and will automatically deploy the project to a virtual root on the Web server with the same name as the project. The Project Settings page, shown in Figure 7-4, lets you choose how many DLLs are generated. Remember that an ATL Server application consists of one ISAPI extension DLL and one or more ATL Server handler DLLs. You can choose to build these as two separate DLLs, or to merge them into one. You might want to merge them if you have only one Web application DLL.

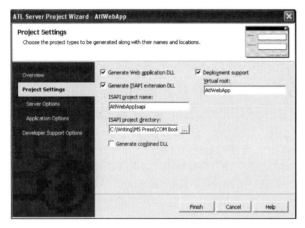

Figure 7-4 The Project Settings page lets you specify how the DLLs will be generated, as well as deployment details.

When you press *Finish* to exit from the wizard, you'll find that two projects have been generated for you, one for each of the ISAPI and Web application DLLs. The interesting code is in the AtlWebApp.h file, which contains the definition of the handler class and its methods:

```
[ request_handler("Default") ]
class CAtlWebAppHandler
{
private:
// Put private members here

protected:
// Put protected members here

public:
// Put public members here

HTTP_CODE ValidateAndExchange()
{
```

```
// TODO: Put all initialization and validation code here

// Set the content-type
m_HttpResponse.SetContentType("text/html");

return HTTP_SUCCESS;
}

protected:
// Here is an example of how to use a replacement
    // tag with the stencil processor.
[ tag_name(name="Hello") ]
HTTP_CODE OnHello(void)
{
m_HttpResponse << "Hello World!";
return HTTP_SUCCESS;
}
}; // class CAtlWebAppHandler
```

The handler class is decorated with the *request_handler* attribute and given a name of *"Default"*. This is the name given to the default handler class within a DLL, and it enables writers of SRF files to specify the default handler in a DLL without having to know a specific handler name. The class defines the *ValidateAndExchange* method, which simply sets the response type to HTML. It also defines a simple replacement tag method named *"Hello"*, which echoes a string to the HTTP response stream. Replacement tag method names often start with *On*, although this is only a convention, and not a requirement.

The project also contains a sample SRF file, which uses the test Hello tag:

```
{{// use MSDN's "ATL Server Response File Reference" to
 learn about SRF files.}}
{{handler AtlWebApp.dll/Default}}
This is a test: {{Hello}}
```

You should test the Web application at this point by building the project. When the build has finished, you should find that a new directory has been created under the Web server's wwwroot directory, and that this new directory contains three files: the two DLLs and the sample SRF file.

Now open a browser window and navigate to the URL of the SRF file. You should see the output displayed in Figure 7-5.

Figure 7-5 The output from the test SRF page that is included in every ATL Server Web application project

Handling Simple Arguments

The following method shows how to implement a handler function that takes a single argument of a type that can be automatically parsed:

```
// A method that uses built-in parsing
[tag_name(name="Square") ]
HTTP_CODE OnSquare(short* pVal)
{
   long result = (*pVal) * (*pVal);
   m_HttpResponse << "Square of " << (*pVal) << " is " << result;
   return HTTP_SUCCESS;
}
```

The method takes an *int** as an argument; because *int* is one of the types that can be automatically parsed, the string parameter passed in with the HTTP request will be converted before the method is called. You can test this method by editing the test SRF file as follows:

```
Testing the square tag: {{Square(3)}}
```

> **Note** You don't enclose arguments in quotes—conversion to strings is automatic.

Implementing Custom Parsing

If you experiment, you'll find that the *Square* method isn't very satisfactory. It uses the *atoi* C Runtime Library function to convert the argument, and one of the properties of this function is that it returns zero if it can't perform the conversion. This means that if you give an invalid argument to the *Square* tag—such as *{{Square(Tuesday)}}*—the *OnSquare* method will be called with an argument of zero. This means that if zero is a valid input value, you can't tell when an invalid argument has been used.

To get around this problem, you can implement a custom parsing function instead of relying on the built-in parsing. The following pair of functions show how to do this:

```
// Parsing function to parse one short value
HTTP_CODE ParseSquareData(IAtlMemMgr *pMemMgr, LPCSTR szParams,
    short **ppDest)
{
    // If any of the parameters are null, fail
    if (pMemMgr == 0 || szParams == 0 || ppDest == 0)
    {
        return HTTP_FAIL;
    }

    // Very simpleminded check...
    for (int i=0; i<strlen(szParams); i++)
    {
        bool bOK = false;
        switch(szParams[i])
        {
        case '-':
            if (i==0) bOK = true;
            else bOK = false;
            break;
        case '+':
            if (i==0) bOK = true;
            else bOK = false;
            break;
        case '0': case '1': case '2': case '3':
        case '4': case '5': case '6': case '7':
        case '8': case '9':
            bOK = true;
            break;
        default:
            bOK = false;
            break;
        }

        if (bOK == false)
        {
```

```cpp
        // Causes 500 - server error
        return AtlsHttpError(500, ISE_SUBERR_STENCIL_PARSE_FAIL);
      }
    }

    // Allocate memory for a short
    *ppDest = (short*)pMemMgr->Allocate(sizeof(short));

    // Convert using atoi because we know the parameter is OK
    **ppDest = atoi(szParams);

    return HTTP_SUCCESS;
}

// A method that uses custom parsing
[ tag_name(name="PSquare", parse_func="ParseSquareData") ]
HTTP_CODE OnSquare2(short* pVal)
{
    long result = (*pVal) * (*pVal);
    m_HttpResponse << "(P)Square of " << (*pVal) << " is " << result;
    return HTTP_SUCCESS;
}
```

The *ParseSquareData* function takes the three parameters that all parsing functions must take: a pointer to a memory manager object, a string containing the data from the HTTP request, and a pointer to receive the converted value. If any of those values is null, the function cannot proceed and a fail status code is returned.

The input string is checked to see that it contains only digits, with an optional leading plus or minus sign. If any other characters are found, the function returns an error status code. The *AtlsHttpError* function builds an HTTP status code out of major and minor parts; in this case, the minor status code shows that parsing a stencil has failed.

If the input string passes the check, enough memory is allocated to hold a *short*. The *atoi* function can be used to convert the string because we know that now a return value of zero represents a real value, rather than an error. The parsing function is then associated with the handler method using the *parse_func* parameter on the *tag_name* attribute.

> **Important** You must allocate memory for the converted argument using the *IAtlMemMgr* pointer because the memory manager will take care of deallocating the memory after use.

If you edit the SRF to invoke the *PSquare* tag and pass an invalid argument, you should see a "Server error" page displayed in the browser.

Writing Web Services Using ATL Server

A Web application is designed to talk to users, typically by sending HTML back to a browser in response to a user request. A *Web service*, on the other hand, is designed to talk to programs rather than clients. In other words, Web services provide a way for a Web server to expose methods that can be called by client code. This means that, unlike Web applications, Web services don't use SRF files because they don't need to merge dynamic content with static HTML and text.

You can implement Web services in two ways:

- Using ASP.NET with .NET programming languages such as Visual C# and Visual Basic .NET, and
- Using C++ and the ATL Server library

Both of these approaches create Web services that have the same functionality, but it's often possible to get much greater efficiency from C++ code.

ATL Server Web Service Architecture

This section is going to look at how Web services are implemented in ATL Server, and then go on to show a sample application.

SOAP and Web Services

You'll hear a lot about SOAP (Simple Object Access Protocol) when people talk about Web services. This section provides an introduction for readers who might not be familiar with the technology.

Web services need to be accessible to as many different types of clients as possible, such as Visual Basic applications, Java applets, or even Unix shell scripts. Existing distributed application technologies—which include DCOM, CORBA, and Java RMI—will connect clients to servers, but they all suffer from drawbacks:

- Some are platform or vendor specific. Think of Microsoft's DCOM, which is pretty much limited to the Windows world.
- Some are language-specific, such as Java's Remote Method Invocation.
- Many are hard to program, requiring considerable investment on the part of the programmer. For example, getting to grips with the details of DCOM and CORBA is not for the faint-hearted!

- Many are hard to administer and debug. DCOM, for example, uses a proprietary binary protocol, and it can be hard to figure out what's happening when something goes wrong.

- Some, such as DCOM, don't work very well over the Internet, where firewalls tend to get in the way of binary communication through particular ports.

SOAP provides a solution to many of these problems. A client using SOAP can invoke a method on a remote host by encoding the details of the method call as a packet of *XML*, and sending it over *HTTP*.

Using HTTP as the protocol has several advantages: it is widely supported, it works well with firewalls, and it makes it easy to host client code on Web pages. Using XML also has advantages—in particular, it is simple to produce and consume XML from almost any language. Using SOAP, it is possible to interact with an ATL Server Web service from a Visual Basic application, a Java applet, or a mainframe application. There is now a SOAP standard from the World Wide Web Consortium (W3C), and SOAP toolkits are available for many languages, including Java, C, and Visual Basic 6.

Using SOAP does have some disadvantages. The main one has to do with the a lack of efficiency: encoding details of a method call in XML might result in several hundred characters being generated, which then have to be sent to the Web service. However, it has been pointed out that for many applications simplicity is preferable to efficiency, and it's always possible to use a more efficient binary protocol, such as DCOM, should the need arise.

The security of XML data has also been perceived to be a problem, but it is quite possible to create secure SOAP communication. One way to approach the problem is to apply security at the HTTP level—using Secure Sockets Layer (SSL), for instance. The problem here is that SOAP is designed so that it can work over different protocols: although most SOAP uses HTTP, there's nothing to stop developers from implementing SOAP-based applications that use other transport mechanisms to shift the XML payload.

You can now secure SOAP communication using two technologies that have been standardized by the W3C: XML Signatures and XML Encryption. Using these, the recipient of a SOAP packet can authenticate the sender and know that the packet hasn't been read or tampered with en route.

The SOAP encoding and decoding is generally invisible to the programmer: it is done as part of the marshaling process that always occurs when data is sent (or method calls are made) across process or machine boundaries. When you are using a Web service from a client such as Visual Basic .NET application, you see nothing of the SOAP communication.

How does a client find out what services Web servers expose? *WSDL* (Web Services Description Language) is an XML format that is used to describe the services offered by a server. A client can request WSDL from a server, and the XML returned will identify the services provided by the server and the set of operations that each service supports. For each operation, the WSDL file describes the format of the request that the client must send for each operation.

WSDL is not designed to be used by humans, but it enables tools such as Visual Studio .NET to construct proxy classes that will talk to Web services on behalf of a client. You will see how to do this in the example later in the chapter.

Implementing Web Services

Now let's look at how Web services can be implemented using ATL Server.

The first step is to create a custom COM interface that defines the methods that the Web service class wants to make available to clients. Here's an example:

```
[ uuid("5DA24F49-9FF5-44B3-A638-C0B3EDBB28D2"), object ]
__interface IMyService
{
   [id(1)] HRESULT Square([in] short nVal,
      [out, retval] long* pResult);
};
```

Remember that the *__interface* keyword is a Microsoft extension used to define interfaces, and that the *object* attribute marks this as being a COM interface. The Web service will expose one method, *Square*, which takes a *short* as an input parameter, and returns a *long*.

> **More Info** Web service methods are defined using a COM interface because COM interface definitions contain all the marshaling details that are necessary to construct the SOAP marshaling code.

The Web service itself is a class that implements the interface. There's nothing special about the implementation, but there are a number of attributes added to the class and its methods that identify it as a Web service. The first attribute to be added is the *request_handler* attribute, which labels that class as being an ATL Server class that can handle external requests.

The *soap_handler* attribute is applied to a class to add the methods necessary for handling SOAP requests, and to expose information about the service via WSDL. The attribute takes a number of parameters, all of which are optional. They are listed in Table 7-14.

Table 7-14 Parameters Used with the *soap_handler* Attribute

Parameter	Description
name	Specifies the name of the Web service. If it is omitted, *"Service"* is appended to the name of the class, and this is used as the Web service name.
namespace	Specifies an XML namespace to which the service class belongs. If it is omitted, the name of the class is used.
protocol	Specifies the protocol used to access this Web service. The only supported value is *"soap"*, which is assumed if the parameter is omitted.
style	Specifies the style of the Web service. The only supported values are *"document"* and *"rpc"*. If omitted, *"rpc"* is assumed.
use	Specifies whether WSDL message parts are encoded or define a concrete schema. If the *"document"* style is used, this parameter must have the value *"literal"*; if the *"rpc"* style is used, this parameter must have the value *"encoded"*.

The *style* parameter of the *soap_handler* attribute determines the type of operation: The *document* style means that the request and response messages contain XML documents. For example, an operation could be sent an *Order* XML document, and return an *Invoice* document; you will typically use XML processing APIs to parse the data sent in document requests. The *rpc* style means that the request message contains details of a method and its parameters, and the response method contains results or error notifications.

> **Note** Note that WSDL is generated on request by a compiler-generated handler, which creates an instance of the handler class to obtain information about SOAP methods and SOAP headers. For this reason, do not assume that the handler class will be instantiated only to handle SOAP requests, and do not perform any lengthy or resource-consuming operations in the constructor.

The *soap_method* attribute is applied to methods within the handler class that are to be exposed to clients. This attribute injects code for parsing SOAP requests. When a SOAP request calls this method, the injected code will do the following:

- Unpack the parameters from the XML request.

- Convert any parameters to appropriate C++ types.
- Call the method.
- Pack the return types into an XML response.
- Return the response packet to the client.

The attribute adds information about the decorated method to the WSDL generated for the Web service.

The *soap_method* attribute can take an optional parameter that specifies the name by which the method will be known to clients; if it is omitted, the method name will be used. You can use the name parameter to hide C++ naming conventions from clients, as shown in the following code:

```
[soap_method("MyMethod")]
HRESULT XyzMethod1()
{
    ...
}
```

Example: Creating a Web Service

This section will demonstrate how to create a Web service using ATL Server.

Open the Visual Studio .NET New Project dialog box, and select the ATL Server Web Service project from the Visual C++ Projects folder, giving it a suitable location and name, as shown in Figure 7-6.

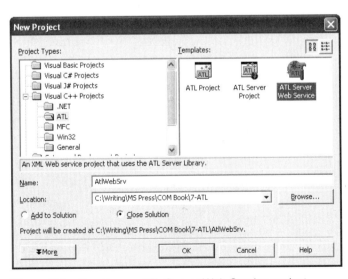

Figure 7-6 Creating an ATL Server Web Service project

ATL Server Web Service applications support many of the same options as ATL Web applications, but if you look at the *Application Options* page, you'll see that stencil support is grayed out when you elect to create a Web service. Once again, you also have the possibility of merging the ISAPI and ATL Server DLLs into one, if you so choose.

The default code produced to implement the service defines a single test *HelloWorld* method, just like the Web application. When you examine the code, though, you'll find that it's implemented very differently.

```
// Interface defining the methods exposed to clients
[ uuid("5DA24F49-9FF5-44B3-A638-C0B3EDBB28D2"), object ]
__interface IMyService
{
[id(1)] HRESULT HelloWorld(
        [in] BSTR bstrInput,
        [out, retval] BSTR *bstrOutput);
};

// Web service class
[ request_handler(name="Default", sdl="GenAtlWebSrvWSDL"),
  soap_handler(
      name="AtlWebSrvService",
      namespace="urn:AtlWebSrvService",
      protocol="soap" )
]
class CAtlWebSrvService :
    public IAtlWebSrvService
{
public:
   [ soap_method ]
   HRESULT HelloWorld(/*[in]*/ BSTR bstrInput,
                   /*[out, retval]*/ BSTR *bstrOutput)
   {
      CComBSTR bstrOut(L"Hello ");
      bstrOut += bstrInput;
      bstrOut += L"!";
      *bstrOutput = bstrOut.Detach();

      return S_OK;
   }
};
```

The method is defined in the *IMyService* interface, and implemented in the *CAtlWebSrvService* class. The class uses the *soap_handler* attribute to provide a *name*, *namespace*, and *protocol* for the Web service.

To add new SOAP methods to the class, you need to manually edit the code because there is currently no wizard support for modifying Web service classes.

Consuming Web Services in C++

Visual Studio .NET makes it simple to consume Web services from C++ projects. Whenever you create a C++ project—even the simplest of Win32 console applications—you'll find that Solution Explorer adds a References folder to the project tree. Right-click on this folder, and choose the Add Web Reference... entry from the context menu. This will display the Add Web Reference dialog box, a as shown in Figure 7-7.

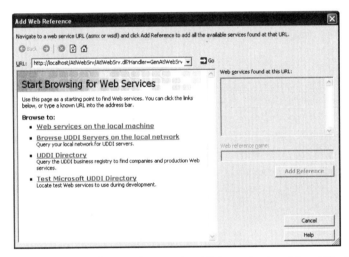

Figure 7-7 Adding a reference to a Web service to a Visual Studio .NET project

You then need to enter a URL that tells the Web service to send back its WSDL description. If the service is named MyService, the URL will look like this:

```
http://localhost/MyService/MyService.dll?Handler=GenMyServiceWSDL
```

You would obviously substitute the correct server name, if the service isn't hosted on the local machine. The Handler argument takes a value of the form Gen*ServiceName*WSDL, where *ServiceName* is the name of the Web service. Click the Go button, and after a pause you should see details of the methods exported by the Web service, as shown in Figure 7-8.

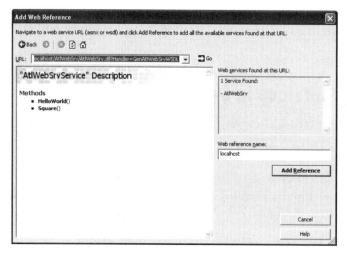

Figure 7-8 The dialog displays the WSDL description of a Web service

If you decide that this is the service you require, you can click the Add Reference button to generate a proxy class and have it added to the project. You will find that a header file called named WebService.h is added to the project, and that this references another header called named localhost.h. Opening the localhost.h header will show you the proxy class that has been generated to talk to the Web service.

To find out what methods you can call, you can either browse the header file code, or use the Class View window to examine the proxy class.

> **Note** If the Class View window isn't already visible, use Ctrl+Shift+C, or use the Class View entry on the View menu.

The program in Listing 7-8 calls a Web service method. You can find this sample in the Chapter07\WebClient folder of the book's companion content.

```
#include <iostream>
using namespace std;

#define _WIN32_WINNT 0x0500

// Include the generated header
#include "webservice.h"
```

Listing 7-8 WebClient.cpp

```
// The namespace created for the service
using namespace AtlWebSrvService;

int main()
{
    // COM must be initialized before using Web services
    CoInitialize(NULL);

    {
        // Create a proxy
        CAtlWebSrvService theService;

        // Call the Web service method
        CComBSTR bResp;
        HRESULT hr = theService.HelloWorld(CComBSTR(L"foo"), &bResp);
        if (FAILED(hr))
        {
            wcout << L"HelloWorld failed (" << hex << hr << dec
                  << L")" << endl;
        }

        // Print the returned string
        wcout << static_cast<const wchar_t*>(bResp) << endl;
    }

    CoUninitialize();

    return 0;
}
```

Note how the *CAtlWebSrvService* object is created within a code block. It's essential for the object to release any COM interface pointers that it holds before the call to *CoUninitialize*. If you don't put the declaration in a code block, the destructor for the *CAtlWebSrvService* object will be called after the call to *CoUninitialize*, and the client program will crash.

Summary

In this chapter, you've seen some of the changes that have been made to the ATL library for version 7.0. A number of new utility classes have been added—

especially in the areas of data structures and string representation—that will provide a lot of new functionality for developers.

ATL Server is a completely new library that is designed for writing server-side code. Based on the same model of templated classes that ATL has used so successfully, ATL Server provides a complete set of classes that cover every aspect of server-side development, including HTTP request handling, handling sessions and cookies, performance monitoring, and security. ATL Server Web applications provide a way to write high-performance C++ server applications that work in a similar manner to ASP.NET.

The next chapter moves away from C++ and ATL, and looks at issues involved in the real-world development of .NET components, such as error handling, security, and performance monitoring.

Part III
Writing COM+ Code

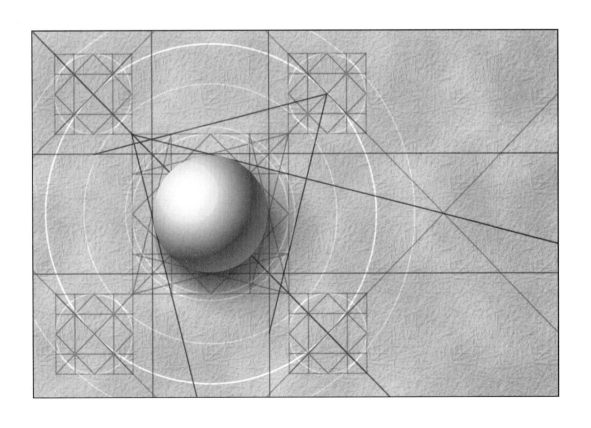

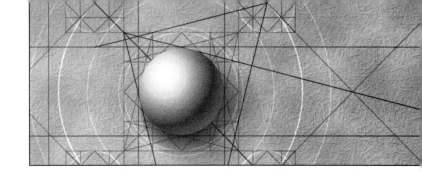

8

A Simple COM+ Example

By now, you know how to create COM component application types. This chapter begins your journey into COM+ application development. We'll experiment with several techniques for developing COM+ applications. The journey is worth the effort, because you'll find that some techniques work better than others do.

After a brief explanation of the importance of GUIDs, the chapter explains how to create a component using the three techniques described in Chapter 5. After you create the component, you'll learn two ways to register it on the server. Exporting the server application as a proxy comes next. The client creation steps and testing procedure are the last two tasks we'll perform. In short, by the time you finish this chapter, you'll know a lot more about how COM+ applications work when you're using a managed component and an unmanaged client. (We'll explore other component and client scenarios in Chapter 9.)

The Importance of Using GUIDs

In Chapter 5, we discussed three techniques for creating managed components that you can use within COM+: simple, derived from the *Component* class, and derived from the *ServicedComponent* class. Before we begin creating components, however, we'll look at an important housekeeping issue for COM+ components. This section helps you understand the necessity of always using the *[Guid]* attribute with components designed for use with COM+.

Using .NET components that lack the *[Guid]* attribute with COM+ could create a mess you never dreamed possible in the registry. A *Globally Unique Identifier (GUID)* provides a method for unmanaged applications to identify your component, as discussed in Chapters 3 and 4. The GUID must remain the same if you want to use any calls that rely on the GUID to instantiate the component. Therefore, the first reason to use the *[Guid]* attribute is to ensure you can document the GUID for unmanaged application calls that require it.

However, the importance of using the *[Guid]* attribute doesn't end with simple identification. Another reason to use the *[Guid]* attribute is to keep your development machine reasonably clean. Every time you register a component, the registration application makes entries in the registry. If you don't assign a GUID to the component, the common language runtime will automatically select a new GUID for you each time. The CLR assigns this GUID randomly, and the GUID won't be the same from registration to registration.

Theoretically, unregistering the component removes the registry entry, but experience shows otherwise. In some cases, developers have ended up with dozens of entries for the same component in the registry, all of which required manual removal. Trying to find all the entries for a complex component is time consuming and error prone. Eventually, the developer will end up formatting the drive and starting from scratch.

COM+ also requires the *[Guid]* attribute for another reason. Imagine that you're using servers in a cluster and that each server has a copy of your component installed on it. If the component doesn't use the *[Guid]* attribute, each server could have a registry entry for the component under a different GUID, which effectively means that each server has a unique version of your component. This little problem makes it impossible for load balancing to work properly because COM will view each component as being different. In sum, even though every server has a copy of the same component, load balancing will see only one copy of the component on one server and won't work as intended.

A Simple Component Example

The simple component has the advantage of being easy to write, using few resources, and providing the smallest number of interfaces to decipher. It truly is a simple way of working with components. This is the technique to use for something like financial calculations or simple data manipulation. It's also one of the easiest ways to learn how to work with COM+ from .NET.

The downside of this development strategy is that the simple component also lacks essential interfaces that the .NET Framework requires to allow certain types of component development. For example, a simple component lacks the *IDisposable* interface, so it can't use unmanaged resources. In fact, it's best to restrict simple component development to situations where an application makes a method call and the component provides a simple reply that doesn't require the use of any unmanaged resource.

Now that you have some idea of why the simple component is one of several good component-building options, let's look at an example. The following sections will take you through the entire process of creating a COM+ application, from building the component to testing the client. Normally, we'll just discuss the essentials for application building, so this is the only time you'll see the whole process at work.

Creating the Simple Component

Listing 8-1 shows a simple component example. In this case, the component performs the desired math operation on two input numbers and returns a result. This is a good example of a simple component because it accepts simple input, provides simple output, and doesn't require use of any unmanaged resources. Note that I removed the comments from the listing in the interest of saving space. You'll find the complete version of the code in the Chapter08\MyMath folder in the book's companion content. You can download the companion content from the book's Web site at *http://www.microsoft.com/mspress/books/6426.asp*.

```
using System;
using System.Runtime.InteropServices;

namespace MyMath
{
    [Guid("EA82646C-2531-42ff-AABF-55028FE0B0B5"),
     InterfaceType(ComInterfaceType.InterfaceIsDual)]
    public interface IMathFunctions
    {
        Int32 DoAdd(Int32 Value1, Int32 Value2);
        Int32 DoSubtract(Int32 Value1, Int32 Value2);
        Int32 DoMultiply(Int32 Value1, Int32 Value2);
        Int32 DoDivide(Int32 Value1, Int32 Value2);
    }

    [Guid("0C4340A2-C362-4287-9A03-8CDD3D1F80F6"),
     ClassInterface(ClassInterfaceType.None)]
    public class MathFunctions : IMathFunctions
    {
        public Int32 DoAdd(Int32 Value1, Int32 Value2)
        {
            return Value1 + Value2;
        }

        public Int32 DoSubtract(Int32 Value1, Int32 Value2)
        {
```

Listing 8-1 MyMath.cs

```
            return Value1 - Value2;
        }

        public Int32 DoMultiply(Int32 Value1, Int32 Value2)
        {
            return Value1 * Value2;
        }

        public Int32 DoDivide(Int32 Value1, Int32 Value2)
        {
            return Value1 / Value2;
        }
    }
}
```

The code for this example is easy to understand. You'll remember from the "Using .NET Components from COM Client Code" section of Chapter 4 that any component you want to export includes an interface. This code begins by defining an interface for the component. Notice the use of the *[Guid]* and *[InterfaceType]* attributes. This chapter already explained use of the *[Guid]* attribute in the "The Importance of Using GUIDs" section.

The *[InterfaceType]* attribute defines how COM interacts with the interface. In this case, the component will provide a dual interface so that both Microsoft Visual C++ and Microsoft Visual Basic applications can access it. More important, the interfaces and methods for the component won't show up in the application folder for the COM+ application in the Component Services console (an administrative tool located in the Administrative Tools folder of the Control Panel) until you add the *[ClassInterface]* attribute.

The class code begins as you might expect. Again, notice the use of the *[Guid]* and *[ClassInterface]* attributes. The *[ClassInterface]* attribute is important because it tells CLR how to interact with the component.

Unlike the example in Chapter 4, this component is encased in a namespace. A local component might not require a namespace because it appears only on a single machine. However, when you begin working with COM+ applications, the probability that someone has named their component the same as your component increases. Consequently, you should encase the component in a namespace to ensure the component name is unique. Of course, this means you also have to add code to the unmanaged application to access the component's type library and provide support for the namespace. Here's a typical entry for Visual C++:

```
// Import the type library and use the associated namespace.
#import "MyMath.TLB" named_guids
using namespace MyMath;
```

Registering the Component on the Server

As mentioned in Chapter 2, you need to register your component on the server before you can use it. Registering the component includes making the appropriate registry entries, creating the COM+ application, and importing the component into the application. Once you perform these three steps, the server knows how to access the component should a client make a request.

Using the GUI Method

There are two methods for registering a component on a server. We explored the GUI method of registering a component in the "Creating COM+ Applications and Installing Components" section of Chapter 2. This is the easiest technique and the one you should use whenever possible. The GUI method provides instant access to all features of the COM+ application and the components that it hosts.

The problem is that this technique works well only on Microsoft Windows XP machines because, in most cases, Windows XP machines have COM+ version 1.5 installed on them. The COM+ 1.0 installation found on Windows 2000 machines can prove problematic. Unfortunately, according to the COM+ 1.5 Web site at *http://msdn.microsoft.com/library/default.asp?url=/library/en-us/cossdk/htm/complusportal_9o9x.asp*, you can't upgrade Windows 2000 machines to COM+ 1.5. This site also explains a number of features that COM+ 1.5 provides. Windows Server 2003 will ship with this newer version of COM+.

Using the RegSvcs Utility

The .NET Framework Services Installation Utility (RegSvcs.exe) helps you register a COM+ application from the command line. To use this utility, you must derive the component from the *ServicedComponent* class. Otherwise, the RegSvcs utility will complain that it can't find a service to register. Here's the usage syntax for the RegSvcs utility:

```
REGSVCS [options] AssemblyName
```

The *AssemblyName* entry contains the name of the DLL you want to register. You must include the DLL extension. Table 8-1 shows a list of the options you can use with this utility.

Table 8-1 *RegSvcs* Utility Options

Option	Description
/? or /help	Displays a help message that contains usage instructions and a typical list of options.
/appdir:<path>	Sets the application root directory to specified path. Normally, RegSvcs assumes you want to use the current directory as the root directory.
/appname:<name>	Uses the specified application name when creating the COM+ application. When working with a .NET component, you can also set this option using the *[ApplicationName]* attribute.
/c	Creates the target application, and displays an error if it already exists. Normally, the RegSvcs utility will simply add a component to an existing application. Because you might want to avoid overwriting an existing application, this switch provides a safety feature of sorts.
/componly	Creates a component entry that configures the component only. The resulting entry won't contain any methods or interfaces. In general, you'll want to avoid this switch when creating standard COM+ applications because you want to provide access to the methods and interfaces.
/exapp	Creates an addition to an existing application. If the application doesn't exist, you'll see an error message. This switch provides a safety feature by installing the component only with other components of the same application. Normally, RegSvcs will create a new application if one doesn't exist.
/extlb	Uses an existing type library instead of creating a new one. The only time to use this switch is if you create a custom type library. Otherwise, using this switch could result in a mismatch between the type library and the component, which means the application will never work as anticipated.
/fc	This is the default application creation switch. It tells RegSvcs to create a new application or use an existing application to install the component.
/nologo	Suppresses the logo output. Useful for batch operations.
/noreconfig	Suppresses reconfiguration of an existing target application. This is a safety switch that prevents RegSvcs from changing the configuration of an existing application.
/parname:<name>	Uses the specified name or ID for the target partition. When working with a .NET component, you can specify this value using the *[ApplicationID]* attribute.
/quiet	Suppresses both the logo output and the success output. Useful for batch operations.

Table 8-1 *RegSvcs* **Utility Options**

Option	Description
/reconfig	Reconfigures the existing target application as needed to add new components. This is the default setting.
/tlb:<tlbfile>	Creates a type library for the application as part of the registration process.
/u	Performs an uninstall of the target application.

You can easily use this utility from a batch file. It always creates a COM+ 1.0 application, so it always works with Windows 2000. However, because RegSvcs creates a COM+ 1.0 application, you lose the benefits of using COM+ 1.5 to build your application. Of course, you'd lose these benefits by using Windows 2000 for your server, so it's not something that most developers will miss until Microsoft Windows Server 2003 is deployed on a number of machines. In general, you'll want to avoid using RegSvcs on Windows XP machines because it doesn't provide the full range of functionality you can obtain by using the GUI method discussed in Chapter 2.

Another disadvantage of using the RegSvcs utility is that it produces a library application you can't export as a proxy. However, you can overcome this problem by manually changing the Activation Type option on the Activation tab of the application Properties dialog box from Library Application to Server Application. Making this change will also modify the security setup and could affect other application settings.

One of the more important issues in using the RegSvcs utility is that it implements any attributes you add to the component. For example, if the RegSvcs utility sees an *[ApplicationName]* attribute in the assembly, it will give the COM+ application that name. The GUI method has the disadvantage of not observing these attributes for the most part, which means you might spend more time manually configuring the resulting application.

Exporting the Application

As with every other COM+ application, you'll need to export a proxy of this application as a minimum. We discussed the basics of this process in the "Exporting COM+ Applications" section of Chapter 2. In general, you can export either a proxy (for use on a client) or a server (for use in a cluster) version of the COM+ application.

You need to consider a few nuances, however, when working with multiple operating system types. Notice the Save Application In COM+ 1.0 Format option at the bottom of the dialog box shown in Figure 8-1. If you're exporting an application from a Windows XP development workstation to a Windows 2000 machine, you'll want to check this box. Otherwise, the installation will fail with an error message.

Figure 8-1 Make sure you select the correct export options for your application.

The export process produces both a Windows Installer (MSI) file and a CAB file. You must place both files on the target machine to install them. Make sure both files appear in the folder you want to use for the application. To begin the installation process, right-click the MSI file and choose Install from the context menu. When the installation process completes, you'll see a new entry in the COM+ Applications folder of Component Services.

Creating the Client

The goal of creating a component (at least in most cases) is to use it eventually in a client. The sample client application discussed in this section enables the user to access all four math functions provided by the *MyMath* component. The client application is named *MyMathTest* and uses a dialog box interface. You'll find the source code for this application in the Chapter08\MyMathTest folder of the source code.

The code for this client looks similar to code you might have created for an application in the past. The code in Listing 8-2 from MyMathTestDlg.cpp contains the essential elements of the client code. It includes only the code for the adding function of the *MyMath* component because the code for the other functions is similar. Note that I've eliminated the normal error-trapping code for the sake of clarity—you'd normally place this code within a *try...catch* statement to ensure that the application traps any errors.

```
void CMyMathTestDlg::OnBnClickedAdd()
{
    IMathFunctions   *pMath;       // Pointer to math object.
    CString          TempString;   // Temporary data string.
    long             Input1;       // Input 1 value.
    long             Input2;       // Input 2 value.
    long             Output;       // Output value.

    // Initialize the COM environment.
    CoInitialize(NULL);

    // Create the object.
    CoCreateInstance(CLSID_MathFunctions,
                     NULL,
                     CLSCTX_ALL,
                     IID_IMathFunctions,
                     (void**)&pMath);

    // Get the input values.
    m_Input1.GetWindowText(TempString);
    Input1 = atoi(TempString.GetBuffer());
    TempString.ReleaseBuffer(-1);
    m_Input2.GetWindowText(TempString);
    Input2 = atoi(TempString.GetBuffer());
    TempString.ReleaseBuffer(-1);

    // Perform the operation.
    Output = pMath->DoAdd(Input1, Input2);

    // Display the result.
    itoa(Output, TempString.GetBuffer(10), 10);
    TempString.ReleaseBuffer(-1);
    m_Output.SetWindowText(TempString);

    // Uninitialize the COM environment.
    CoUninitialize();
}
```

Listing 8-2 A simple component client

The code begins by initializing the COM environment. It instantiates the object next. The IDE creates the *CLSID_MathFunctions* and *IID_IMathFunctions* values as part of importing the MyMath.tlb file. You'll find these values in the MyMath.tlh and MyMath.tli files located in the output folder for this example. Once the code creates the object, it obtains the current input values from the application dialog box. Calling the *DoAdd()* method comes next. The code displays the output value on screen and then uninitializes the COM environment. In short, you won't find anything too surprising in the client code.

The reason the client code looks similar to any client code you created in the past is that the COM+ application proxy appears as a local component. The application creates the same registry entries and acts in all other ways as a standard local COM component. Of course, the component code actually executes on the server, as does any other COM+ component. The .NET component is still called by using the COM Callable Wrapper (CCW). As far as the .NET component is concerned, it's working with a local .NET application—it has no idea that it's actually part of a COM+ application that's servicing the needs of an application on another machine.

Testing the Application

It's time to test the application we've created. The mechanics of this application are simple. Start the client application, enter two numbers, and click one of the four math buttons. Figure 8-2 shows the output of the application when the Add button is pressed.

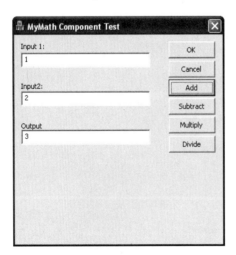

Figure 8-2 The sample application presents the output you'd expect when one of the buttons is pressed.

Depending on your setup, the application could almost feel as if it were using a local component or generating the output value internally. This is the feeling you want a COM+ application to have—the user should not be concerned about where the functionality for an application resides. The fact that the application works and provides the required functionality is all that the user needs.

As a developer, you're probably a little more interested than the user in precisely how this application works. If you used a two-machine setup for testing (always the best choice for COM+ application development), you can verify COM+ application execution on the server. Open the COM+ Applications folder in the Component Services console shown in Figure 8-3. When you click one of the buttons on the client application, you'll notice that the ball within the *MyMathApp* application begins to rotate.

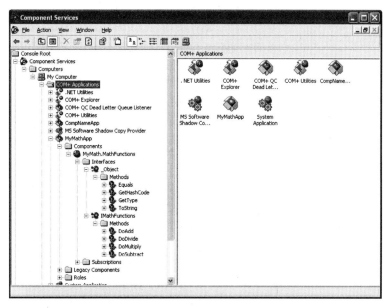

Figure 8-3 Use the entries in the Component Services console to verify COM+ application responses.

If conditions are correct, you'll also be able to track component and even individual method operation from within the console. In most cases, the ball will rotate one time for each call to a component and method. (This example works so quickly you might not actually see the ball rotate for component and method invocations, but later examples will take enough time for you to clearly see the ball rotate.)

At this point, you could also test elements such as security. For example, you could log in as an unauthorized user and attempt to use the COM+ application.

A *Component* Class Example

Components based on the *Component* class include the *IDisposable* interface. The inclusion of this interface adds to the number of things you can do with the component. Instead of performing simple tasks such as math calculations or working within the .NET environment, the component can begin to explore the outside world a little. For example, you can use *PInvoke* to make calls to the Win32 API.

The sample component in this section performs the simple task of obtaining the local computer name by using the *GetComputerNameEx()* Win32 API function. This is an easy function to use, but it demonstrates the power of working with the Win32 API in your .NET applications as needed. Obviously, the .NET Framework already encapsulates much of the functionality found in the Win32 API, so you'll always want to verify that the required information is inaccessible from the .NET Framework before you create a Win32 API solution.

Deriving from the *Component* Class

The component we create in this section will actually have two methods. The first method can return an individual machine name based on the name type input provided by the client. The second method will return all names associated with the computer in a specific order. The sample in Listing 8-3 shows the component code for this example. You can find this code in the Chapter08\CompName folder of the book's companion content.

```
using System;
using System.ComponentModel;
using System.Runtime.InteropServices;
using System.Text;

namespace CompName
{
    /// <summary>
    /// This enumeration contains computer name values that are used
    /// for the GetComputerNameEx() method call.
    /// </summary>
```

Listing 8-3 CompName.cs

```csharp
public enum COMPUTER_NAME_FORMAT
{
    ComputerNameNetBIOS,
    ComputerNameDnsHostname,
    ComputerNameDnsDomain,
    ComputerNameDnsFullyQualified,
    ComputerNamePhysicalNetBIOS,
    ComputerNamePhysicalDnsHostname,
    ComputerNamePhysicalDnsDomain,
    ComputerNamePhysicalDnsFullyQualified,
    ComputerNameMax
};

/// <summary>
/// An interface used to access the ComputerName functions.
/// </summary>
[Guid("AD65E427-A809-4ca0-B408-D364D25D619A"),
InterfaceType(ComInterfaceType.InterfaceIsDual)]
public interface IComputerName
{
    string GetSingleName(COMPUTER_NAME_FORMAT NameType);
    string GetAllNames();
}

/// <summary>
/// This class obtains computer name information from
/// the remote server.
/// </summary>
[Guid("EE24578A-29CC-4554-95F6-C8F4D4F73284"),
ClassInterface(ClassInterfaceType.None)]
public class ComputerName : Component, IComputerName
{
    public ComputerName()
    {
        //
        // TODO: Add constructor logic here
        //
    }

    /// <summary>
    /// Obtains one of many names held by a computer. The precise name
    /// returned is determined by the NameType argument.
    /// </summary>
    [DllImport("Kernel32.dll",
            CharSet=CharSet.Auto,
            SetLastError=true)]
```

```csharp
public static extern Boolean GetComputerNameEx(
    COMPUTER_NAME_FORMAT NameType,
    StringBuilder lpBuffer,
    ref Int32 lpnSize);

public string GetSingleName(COMPUTER_NAME_FORMAT NameType)
{
    StringBuilder  Buffer;     // Buffer used to hold name data.
    Int32          BufferSize; // Size of the data buffer on
                               // return.

    // Initialize the buffer.
    Buffer = new StringBuilder(80);
    BufferSize = 80;

    // Obtain the requested name string.
    if (GetComputerNameEx(NameType, Buffer, ref BufferSize))
        return Buffer.ToString();
    else
        return "No Name Available";
}

public string GetAllNames()
{
    StringBuilder  Buffer;  // Buffer used to hold entire string.

    // Initialize the buffer.
    Buffer = new StringBuilder();

    // Call each name string in turn. Add the name of each string
    // before making the call.
    Buffer.Append("ComputerNameDnsDomain = ");
    Buffer.Append(
        GetSingleName(COMPUTER_NAME_FORMAT.ComputerNameDnsDomain));
    Buffer.Append("\r\nComputerNameDnsFullyQualified = ");
    Buffer.Append(
        GetSingleName
        (COMPUTER_NAME_FORMAT.ComputerNameDnsFullyQualified));
    Buffer.Append("\r\nComputerNameDnsHostname = ");
    Buffer.Append(GetSingleName
        (COMPUTER_NAME_FORMAT.ComputerNameDnsHostname));
    Buffer.Append("\r\nComputerNameMax = ");
    Buffer.Append(
        GetSingleName(COMPUTER_NAME_FORMAT.ComputerNameMax));
    Buffer.Append("\r\nComputerNameNetBIOS = ");
    Buffer.Append(
        GetSingleName
```

```
                    (COMPUTER_NAME_FORMAT.ComputerNameNetBIOS));
                Buffer.Append("\r\nComputerNamePhysicalDnsDomain = ");
                Buffer.Append(
                    GetSingleName
                    (COMPUTER_NAME_FORMAT.ComputerNamePhysicalDnsDomain));
                Buffer.Append("\r\nComputerNamePhysicalDnsFullyQualified = ");
                Buffer.Append(
                    GetSingleName
                    (COMPUTER_NAME_FORMAT.ComputerNamePhysicalDnsFullyQualified))
;

                Buffer.Append("\r\nComputerNamePhysicalDnsHostname = ");
                Buffer.Append
                    (GetSingleName
                    (COMPUTER_NAME_FORMAT.ComputerNamePhysicalDnsHostname));
                Buffer.Append("\r\nComputerNamePhysicalNetBIOS = ");
                Buffer.Append(
                    GetSingleName(COMPUTER_NAME_FORMAT.ComputerNamePhysicalNetBIO
S));

                // Return the result of all the calls.
                return Buffer.ToString();
            }
        }
    }
```

This example has two elements we haven't really touched on in previous chapters. The first is a public enumeration that's helpful in working with the *GetComputerNameEx()* function. Using an enumeration of this type makes it easier for someone using your component to provide the correct input—reducing programming errors and making the code self-documenting in some respects. The *COMPUTER_NAME_FORMAT* enumeration lists the name types that an application can request from the component. The reason that the enumeration is placed at this level is to make it easier for the user to access the enumeration; it also ensures that an unmanaged client, such as a Visual C++ application, will actually see and use the enumeration.

The *IComputerName* interface defines the two methods used for this example. Notice that the *GetSingleName()* method accepts a *COMPUTER_NAME_FORMAT* enumeration value as input. Again, this is simply good coding practice because it ensures the method will receive the input it requires to perform the task.

The *ComputerName* class declaration shows that this case subclasses the *Component* class and implements the *IComputerName* interface. Although the class implements more interfaces, the basic declaration methodology hasn't changed. You still need to add the *[Guid]* and *[ClassInterface]* attributes at a minimum.

This component requires use of a Win32 API function, *GetComputerNameEx()*, to obtain the computer name information the client will request. Notice how this function is declared. You can use this format for many Win32 API calls. The *[DllImport]* attribute will normally require all three arguments presented in the sample code. At a minimum, you must define the DLL where the call is found—this information normally appears in the Visual Studio .NET help file for that function near the bottom of the help topic. You can also find the function calls using the *Depends* utility. In some cases, you'll want to set a specific character set to ensure any string input is in the format required by the function. The *SetLastError* argument ensures the component can retrieve any error information from the function call by using the *Marshal.GetLastWin32Error()* method.

> **Caution** Never use the *SetLastError()* or *GetLastError()* Win32 API function calls in a managed application or component. Because of the way Win32 API function calls are marshaled, there's no way you can know whether these functions will work as anticipated. Always use the *Marshal.GetLastWin32Error()* method to retrieve error information about a Win32 API function call.

Although the *GetComputerNameEx()* function declaration doesn't require the use of the *COMPUTER_NAME_FORMAT* enumeration as input, using this enumeration does make it easier to use the function call. The Int32 value, *lpnSize*, is a value type and is normally passed to the function by value. Because this function returns the final string size in this variable, we need to add the *ref* keyword to pass the value by reference. It's important to look for potential problem areas like this when you create Win32 API function declarations in your code.

The *GetSingleName()* method is the actual workhorse of this component. The code begins by creating a buffer of a specific size to use with the *GetComputerNameEx()* function. Notice the use of a *StringBuilder*, rather than a *String*, as input to the *GetComputerNameEx()* function. Always use a *StringBuilder* object if you expect to receive output from a Win32 API function to ensure the string is marshaled properly. If the *GetComputerNameEx()* function returns *false*, either an error happened or the computer doesn't support the name requested. This component makes things simple by assuming the computer doesn't support the name. However, in a production application, you'd probably want to check for a last error condition to ensure that an error didn't occur. In many cases, the common language runtime won't tell you about Win32 API function call errors unless you specifically request the information.

The *GetAllNames()* method is longer than the *GetSingleName()* method, but it's actually easier to understand. All it does is build a string based on multiple calls to the *GetSingleName()* method. Notice how the *GetAllNames()* method uses a *StringBuilder* object to create the output. This technique is actually more efficient than using a string because the code can modify a *StringBuilder* object. All string objects are re-created for each change, resulting in a performance hit.

Performing the *Component* Class Setup

The setup for this COM+ application is the same as the simple component application discussed earlier in the chapter. The example uses an application name of *CompNameApp*, and we'll export the application as *CompNameAppInstall*. Make sure you export the application as a COM+ 1.0 application if necessary to perform testing on your server setup.

Unlike the simple component created earlier, this component includes support for the *IDisposable* interface. The component must provide this support to work properly when using the Win32 API call. In fact, this component supports the four interfaces shown in Figure 8-4.

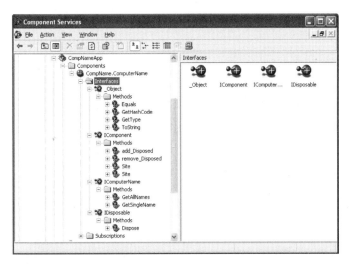

Figure 8-4 A component based on the *Component* class displays four interfaces within the COM+ environment.

Creating the Client

The client for this application will need to test both the single-name and all-name modes of operation. The all-name mode of operation is the easiest to test because it doesn't require any input from the user. For this example, this simplicity means that the all-name mode of operation looks similar to the simple component test code described earlier.

The single-name mode of operation does require a little additional work. The sample in Listing 8-4 from CompNameTestDlg.cpp shows the code you'll need to test the component in this code. You can find the complete source code for this example in the Chapter08\CompNameTest folder of the book's companion content.

```
void CCompNameTestDlg::OnBnClickedSingle()
{
   IComputerName       *pComputerName;    // Component interface pointer.
   _bstr_t             OutputData;        // Output from component.
   COMPUTER_NAME_FORMAT NameType;         // Name Type Enumeration.

   // Initialize the COM environment.
   CoInitialize(NULL);

   // Create the object.
   CoCreateInstance(CLSID_ComputerName,
                    NULL,
                    CLSCTX_ALL,
                    IID_IComputerName,
                    (void**)&pComputerName);

   // Determine which name the user has selected.
   switch (m_Select.GetCurSel())
   {
   case 0:
      NameType = COMPUTER_NAME_FORMAT_ComputerNameNetBIOS;
      break;
   case 1:
      NameType = COMPUTER_NAME_FORMAT_ComputerNameDnsHostname;
      break;
   case 2:
      NameType = COMPUTER_NAME_FORMAT_ComputerNameDnsDomain;
      break;
   case 3:
      NameType = COMPUTER_NAME_FORMAT_ComputerNameDnsFullyQualified;
      break;
   case 4:
```

Listing 8-4 CompName client code

```
         NameType = COMPUTER_NAME_FORMAT_ComputerNamePhysicalNetBIOS;
         break;
      case 5:
         NameType = COMPUTER_NAME_FORMAT_ComputerNamePhysicalDnsHostname;
         break;
      case 6:
         NameType = COMPUTER_NAME_FORMAT_ComputerNamePhysicalDnsDomain;
         break;
      case 7:
         NameType =
COMPUTER_NAME_FORMAT_ComputerNamePhysicalDnsFullyQualified;
         break;
      case 8:
         NameType = COMPUTER_NAME_FORMAT_ComputerNameMax;
   }

   // Get the computer names.
   OutputData = pComputerName->GetSingleName(NameType);

   // Display the output on screen.
   m_Output.SetWindowText(OutputData);

   // Uninitialize the COM environment.
   CoUninitialize();
}
```

This example begins much as the simple component example did. This code initializes the COM environment, and then it creates an instance of the object. The code then uses a switch to determine which option the user selected from the combo box. The combo box *Type* property value is set to *Drop List* so that the user can select only from the authorized options. The switch obtains the current selection using the *GetCurSel()* method and converts that value to a *COMPUTER_NAME_FORMAT* enumeration value. If you look in the TLH file for this application, you'll see the enumeration adds the type name to each of the name values.

One oddity to notice is how the CLR marshals the *StringBuilder* object. To an unmanaged application, this object appears as a *_bstr_t* object. This object encapsulates BSTR values and makes it very easy to work with them in unmanaged code. In this case, all we need to do is use the *SetWindowText()* method to display the text directly on screen.

Once you have the code put together and installed, you can test it using a method similar to the one for the simple component test. The client will call to the server for the information this client provides. Figure 8-5 shows typical output for this application when the user clicks All Names. As before, you'll want to validate that the server is actually called by checking the application activity indicators in the Component Services console.

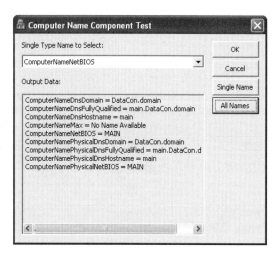

Figure 8-5 Typical output from the application shows a single computer name or all the available names.

A *ServicedComponent* Class Example

Components based on the *ServicedComponent* class are the most flexible method of working with COM+. Using this component strategy usually means a little more coding on your part. In addition, you'll find the resulting component is larger and uses more resources. However, if you want to interact with COM+ fully, this is the only way to go because this method also provides you full access to all COM+ functionality. The vast majority of the COM+ programming examples in this book subclass the *ServicedComponent* class.

This example is the first one in the book to show you the power of the *EnterpriseServices* namespace. This namespace is extremely important to the COM+ application developer because it provides access to most of the COM+ application properties. For example, you'll use the *[ApplicationName]* attribute included with this namespace to assign a name to your application.

One attribute you'll normally include with your application is the *[ApplicationAccessControl]* attribute. This attribute determines whether the COM+ application uses access control checks. If you don't tell the RegSvcs utility that you want to use access control checks, it will assume you do and set them. Here's an example of the *[ApplicationAccessControl]* attribute as used in this example to make access easier:

```
[assembly: ApplicationAccessControl(false)]
```

In this case, the sample component will perform a simple task that demonstrates a powerful COM+ application feature—the constructor string. The developer can use constructor strings within an application to help the administrator configure a COM+ application. For example, you might use the constructor string to indicate the location of a database on the network or allow specialized configuration when the administrator doesn't want to use all the features a component can provide. Another use of the constructor string is registration information. Some companies use this field to hold the product registration number, although there are simpler methods of performing this particular task (such as using the registry to hold the information).

Deriving from the *ServicedComponent* Class

When you derive a component from the *ServicedComponent* class, you need to add the additional attributes mentioned in the introduction to this section. Most of the principles for creating the code are the same. You'll still create an interface that describes the class methods, and you'll still use the various attributes we've discussed in the past such as the *[Guid]* attribute. However, there are subtle differences, as you can see in Listing 8-5:

```
[Guid("BB924921-68D6-4b14-8771-878EDCFEC8B2"),
 InterfaceType(ComInterfaceType.InterfaceIsDual)]
public interface ICheckString
{
    string GetConstructorString();
}

[Guid("93707E2D-7672-4d3f-A8F3-4FB934DB9BE1"),
 ClassInterface(ClassInterfaceType.None),
 ConstructionEnabled(Default="Hello world")]
public class CheckString : ServicedComponent, ICheckString
{
    private string _ConstructorValue;
    public CheckString()
    {
        //
        // TODO: Add constructor logic here
        //
    }

    protected override void Construct(string constructString)
    {
        // Save the value of the constructor string in a
```

Listing 8-5 Obtaining the constructor string

```
      // private variable.
      _ConstructorValue = constructString;
   }

   public string GetConstructorString()
   {
      // Return the current value of the constructor string.
      return _ConstructorValue;
   }
}
```

The first thing you should notice is the addition of the *[Construction-Enabled]* attribute to this example. This attribute tells COM+ to check the *Enable* object construction option and give this entry the default value specified by the attribute constructor ("Hello world" for this example). Also notice that the class itself subclasses *ServicedComponent* and implements the *ICheckString* interface.

The code defines a private variable named *_ConstructorValue*. This variable holds the value of the constructor string. When working with constructor strings, you must override the *Construct()* method, as shown in the listing. In some places in the current documentation, it shows the *Construct()* method as public—the actual implementation is protected as shown. Normally, you'd place code for creating the object in the *Construct()* method. In this case, we simply save the string to the private *_ConstructorValue* variable. The *GetConstructorString()* method returns this string when the client application requests it.

Performing the *ServicedComponent* Class Setup

You can set up this component by using either the GUI or RegSvcs utility methods described earlier in the chapter. If you use the GUI method, you'll obtain the benefits of using COM+ 1.5 under Windows XP. On the other hand, using RegSvcs will create a COM+ 1.0 application. However, using RegSvcs also means that all attributes you define for the component are automatically checked and added to the COM+ application. Figure 8-6 shows the results of using the RegSvcs utility—the results of using the GUI method are the same. The only difference is that the RegSvcs utility application creates a library application (which you can manually change to a server application).

Depending on the method you use to create the COM+ application, you'll want to check and optionally modify the object construction string value for this application. Figure 8-7 shows the Constructor String value that the RegSvcs utility added automatically to the Activation tab of the ConstructString.CheckString Properties dialog box. You can also set this value manually when using the GUI method.

Chapter 8   A Simple COM+ Example   **311**

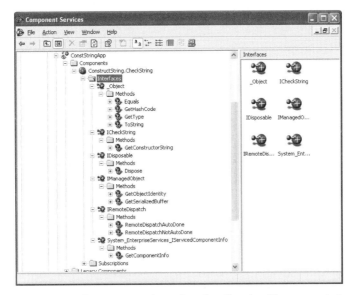

Figure 8-6   Components based on the *ServicedComponent* class show a minimum of six interfaces.

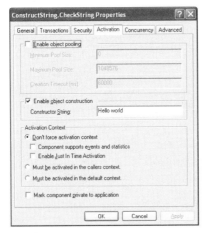

Figure 8-7   You should define a constructor string for this class to see the functionality this feature can provide.

Creating the Client

The client for this example is very simple. All we need to do is create the object and query it for the constructor string value, as shown in Listing 8-6. You'll find this sample in the Chapter08\ConstructStringTest folder in the book's companion content. Notice that in this case all additional code appears in the component. The client code remains simple.

```
void CConstructStringTestDlg::OnBnClickedTest()
{
   ICheckString   *pConstString; // Pointer to ConstString object.
   _bstr_t        Output;        // Temporary data string.

   // Initialize the COM environment.
   CoInitialize(NULL);

   // Create the object.
   CoCreateInstance(CLSID_CheckString,
                    NULL,
                    CLSCTX_ALL,
                    IID_ICheckString,
                    (void**)&pConstString);

   // Perform the operation.
   Output = pConstString->GetConstructorString();

   // Display the result.
   m_Output.SetWindowText(Output);

   // Uninitialize the COM environment.
   CoUninitialize();
}
```

Listing 8-6 Constructor string

When you run this application the first time, you'll see the "Hello world" output shown in Figure 8-8, unless you use some other value for the Constructor String field. In fact, you'll want to test this field by modifying it with other values. The interesting element is that you don't need to stop and start the application to see a change in the constructor string value. The value will change with each request to reflect the actual value of the Constructor String field.

Figure 8-8 This example returns the COM+ application constructor string.

Summary

This chapter has shown you the basic techniques for developing COM+ components using .NET. Each technique has advantages and disadvantages that you'll need to weigh to create precisely the component needed for your application. Using the correct technique makes component building easier and ensures the component will use resources efficiently. You also learned techniques for building the COM+ applications, including two methods for registering the component with the server.

Now that you have a better idea of how to build components for COM+, it's time to look at any projects you need to perform. Ask yourself which of the techniques demonstrated in this chapter will work best for your application. You'll also want to try the various methods to create test projects of your own. Creating a component for COM+ doesn't have to be difficult, but you do want to plan for it.

Chapter 9 demonstrates one of the most practical uses for COM+ applications in today's computing environment—the disconnected application. It's important to understand that the other kinds of applications that COM+ supports are still viable, but that the disconnected application represents the one unique implementation no other technology has replaced. For example, you can replicate many distributed application features of COM+ using technologies such as XML Web Services, but XML Web Services still lacks the means for creating the kind of message-based applications used for COM+ disconnected applications.

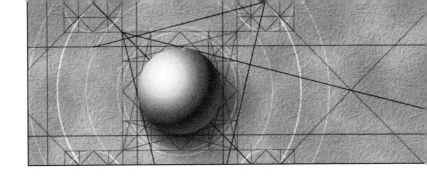

9

Working with Disconnected Applications

In Chapter 8, we discussed how to implement simple COM+ applications. You learned three methods for constructing the components you'll use for COM+ application building blocks. This chapter extends the information you learned in that chapter by showing how to augment the functionality of COM+ with the functionality of Microsoft Message Queuing Services (MSMQ).

Of course, the first thing you'll want to know is how MSMQ adds to the functionality that COM+ provides. All of the communication mentioned in Chapter 8 was synchronous—it occurred in real time. The server and the client had to exist at the same time in order for communication to occur. MSMQ adds an asynchronous processing capability to COM+ applications. This feature helps the developer create applications that work just as well without a connection as they do with a connection. In addition, queued applications can provide a form of load balancing by allowing the server to continue receiving messages even when it doesn't have time to process them immediately.

> **Note** It's impossible to test the applications in this chapter properly using a single machine setup. The point of this chapter is that the client and the server exist on two separate machines. The examples emphasize that you can disconnect the client from the server and the application will still work. If you use a single machine setup to work with the examples in this chapter, you'll miss part of the reason for building this kind of application.

Once you understand how MSMQ relates to the COM+ and .NET environment, we'll begin looking at examples of queued applications. In this case, we'll always create the component using .NET. However, because you don't know whether a particular platform will support .NET, you must look at both managed and unmanaged clients—a topic we'll pursue in this chapter. We'll also discuss what happens when a connection fails so that you understand why disconnected support is so important.

> **Note** This chapter assumes you've already installed the minimum components required for Message Queuing. You'll find this installation option in the Windows Components list of the Windows Components Wizard. Access this wizard by clicking Add/Remove Windows Components in the Add Or Remove Programs applet in the Control Panel. The chapter will use only the minimal setup—you won't need access to the HTTP support provided in newer versions of Windows.

Understanding the Role of MSMQ in this Application

Unlike other, more direct methods of data transfer, MSMQ uses the idea of messages to transfer data and a queue to hold those messages. (A queue is a sort of mailbox for messages.) At a minimum, there's a queue on the server that holds all messages the server components process. Each active component on the server has a separate queue. These components pick up messages from their queue whenever processing on the current message is complete.

In addition to the server queue, some clients also have a queue for local processing. The local queue gets emptied into the server queue anytime there's a connection between the client and the server. In short, messages can be viewed as the packets that normally get carried between client and server on a network. Obviously, this is a simplification of a more complex process, but it helps to start with this perspective of the functioning of MSMQ and the messages that it uses.

The obvious advantage in using MSMQ is that you gain the ability to perform disconnected application handling. The local client queue allows the client to continue processing information even when there's no direct connection to the server for handling the messages. MSMQ handles all message transfers in the background without the user's knowledge. Figure 9-1 shows the relationship between the client and server, and the kinds of queue setups you can expect.

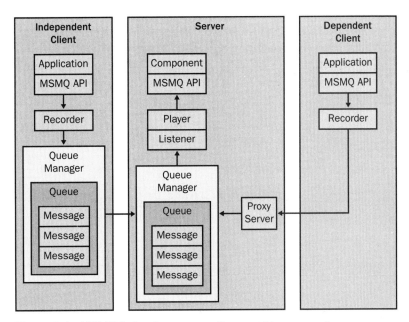

Figure 9-1 MSMQ helps the user continue working even when no connection between the client and server exists.

Notice that there are actually two client types: dependent and independent. Most versions of Microsoft Windows will let you set MSMQ up for either type of operation. However, Microsoft Windows XP creates an independent client—you can't install MSMQ as a dependent client. The main difference between the two types is that the independent client provides its own queue in addition to using the server queue, while the dependent client relies solely on a direct connection to the server.

The two client types have different uses. Obviously, you can't use a dependent client setup for a laptop computer that you intend to use on the road because the dependent client lacks a queue. However, a dependent client setup works for a desktop machine that's located in the same building as a server or on a WAN with a reliable connection. Using a dependent-client setup reduces the disk requirements for using MSMQ and can result in a slight performance boost because the messages appear only in one queue rather than two.

> **Note** The actual performance cost of using MSMQ varies by connection type, client capabilities, server load, and application design. Most developers find that the user doesn't even notice the use of the queue when connected to the server. The performance hit for using a queued application is extremely small. In fact, given that using MSMQ makes it possible to work in disconnected mode, most users are quite happy to have an MSMQ application installed on their system.

We'll discuss the various MSMQ components as the chapter progresses. However, you need to have a basic understanding of what these components do before we get started. As shown in Figure 9-1, three elements are required for establishing and maintaining a message flow between the client and server:

- Recorder
- Listener
- Player

The *recorder* accepts the client output, creates one or more messages based on the content of that output, and then places those messages in the local message or sends them to a proxy server on the server. The local copy of MSMQ accepts the message the client creates and sends it to the server. The server copy of MSMQ places the message in the server's queue. When the *listener* sees a message in the server's queue, it removes the message and gives it to the player. The listener is a configured part of MSMQ. It isn't something MSMQ provides automatically—you need to set up linkage between the listener and the player. Finally, the *player* receives the message, unpacks it, and turns it into data for the server. In some cases, the player has to perform data manipulation to get the data into a format that's acceptable to server-side applications.

> **Note** The message format used by various versions of MSMQ varies. The latest version of MSMQ—the one we'll use in this chapter—relies on XML formatting. Earlier versions of MSMQ relied on a custom data format. This data format affects only the local message storage. Two systems that want to transmit data must agree on the transfer protocol. Consequently, the local data storage issue affects only how you view messages in the various utilities that we'll discuss.

You can look at this process as similar to that used by an answering machine in your home. When someone calls and finds that you're not home, he or she leaves a message by talking to the answering machine instead of talking to you directly. The answering machine stores the message by using any number of methods. When you get home, an indicator on the answering machine tells you that you have one or more messages. Pressing a button on the answering machine normally plays the messages back for you, allowing to you to determine who's called in your absence. As you can see, the idea of disconnected communication isn't new; MSMQ represents a new implementation of an existing idea.

Like COM+, MSMQ can create message traffic that relies on transactions. Generally, you'll use this feature when working with a database or other application that requires a high level of data integrity because transactions do incur a performance penalty. MSMQ applications use a minimum of three transactions for every data transmission, even if it appears that only one transaction occurs. The following list summarizes the transaction events:

- Moving the message between the client application and the local queue

- Moving the message from the local queue and placing it in the server queue

- Removing a message from the server queue and tracking the message's progress on the server

This three-transaction approach makes it a lot less likely that an update will fail due to communication problems, which, in turn, makes the application more reliable. In addition, because a special MSMQ transaction occurs when delivering data from the client to the server, you can be sure each message gets transmitted successfully at least one time.

Throughout this chapter, I'll address the topic of queues in several ways. It's important to know which queue to use for each application need. There are two kinds of queues supported by MSMQ: application and system.

The application queue is created automatically by the application or manually by the administrator. The application uses this kind of queue for messages, administration, reports, and responses.

MSMQ creates the system queues. There are two types: dead letter and journal. *Dead letter queues* store messages the application didn't or couldn't process within a specific timeframe. *Journal queues* contain messages that reflect application, MSMQ, or system events.

Queues can also be public or private. Public queues are available for anyone to use, and the MSMQ Information Service (MQIS) tracks them. Applications normally use private queues for one-to-one communications such as a response from a server on a client machine. You'll learn more about these queues as the chapter progresses.

Creating a Simple Recorder/Player

The first task that any application using MSMQ must perform is creating a message. Earlier in the chapter, you learned about the message flow of an MSMQ application and the construction of a message. Once the queue has a message in it, another application normally retrieves the message and does something with the content.

This section of the chapter shows you the techniques for creating a message recorder and a message player. The message recorder will place a message in the message queue. The message player will retrieve the message and display it on screen. The message will contain a heading, body, and priority level. You can perform a number of other tasks with messages, but this is plenty to start with.

Defining the Message Queue

Before you can send messages to a queue, you have to create the queue. MSMQ allows several methods of creating a message queue. The three most common techniques are

- Define the queue dynamically by using code.
- Let COM+ automatically create the queue for you.
- Create the queue manually by using the Message Queuing snap-in.

We'll take a look at how to perform the third technique, manually creating the message queue by using the Message Queuing snap-in. You'll find this snap-in in the Computer Management console as part of the Services And Applications folder. Within this snap-in, you'll see four folders: Outgoing Queues, Public Queues, Private Queues, and System Queues.

To create the queue for this example, right-click the Public Queues folder and choose New and then Public Queue from the context menu. You'll see a New Object – Public Queue dialog box similar to the one shown in Figure 9-2.

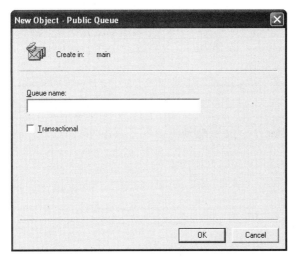

Figure 9-2 Create a queue using the New Object—Public Queue dialog box.

Type the name of the queue, **Temp**, in the Queue Name field. You could also make the queue transactional, but we don't need that feature for this example. Click OK, and the new queue will appear, as shown in Figure 9-3.

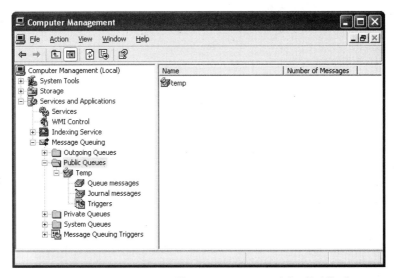

Figure 9-3 The new queue will appear as part of the Public Queues folder.

Notice the organization of the queue. The Queue Messages folder, which contains messages the queue has received, and the Journal Messages folder, which contains messages that indicate events such as delivery failures, are default entries.

The Triggers folder contains a list of applications that react to the messages in the queue. A trigger application can be as simple as a standard Windows application assigned to work with the queue or a COM+ application designed to act as a listener. MSMQ provides several levels of application support. For example, an application can react to the messages in a serialized manner, which means it tests all rules against the message before it moves on to the next message in the queue. You can also choose the level of message retrieval. Some applications might require only the Peeking level of support, while others might require the Retrieval or Transactional Retrieval level.

Accessing the Message Queue

Visual Studio .NET makes it easy to access the queues on any system for which you have access. Simply open a connection to the server in Server Explorer and select the queue you want to use. Figure 9-4 shows a typical example.

Figure 9-4 Creating a queue connection in Visual Studio .NET is as easy as finding it in Server Explorer.

To use the queue, drag it from Server Explorer and drop it into your application. This action creates a *System.Messaging.MessageQueue* object that will appear in the area below the dialog box in the Designer window. The sample application adds two text boxes, a combo box, and some push buttons to send the message. Figure 9-5 shows the test application layout.

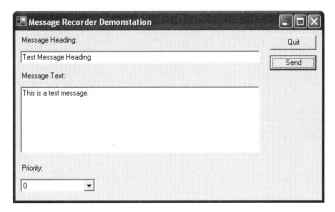

Figure 9-5 The layout of the sample recorder application

Creating the Recorder

Writing the source code for this example is relatively simple because the integrated development environment (IDE) does most of the work for you. Listing 9-1 shows the code you'll need for this example. You'll find the source code in the Chapter 09\Recorder folder of the book's companion content. You can download this content from the book's Web site at *http://www.microsoft.com/mspress/books/6426.asp*.

> **Note** When you add a queue to a project using Server Explorer, the resulting *MessageQueue* object will have a *Path* property value that includes both the machine name and the location of the queue. For example, the source code for this example will include a *Path* property value of **main\Temp**. You must modify the machine name, **main**, to match the name of your server. Otherwise, the path won't point to the proper location on your system. If you are using a two-machine setup, which is the recommended configuration for the examples in this chapter, don't use the generic "." operator. Using the "." operator in the form .\Temp will point the queue to the local machine, which won't test the connection between the two machines.

```
private void btnSend_Click(object sender, System.EventArgs e)
{
    System.Messaging.Message   Msg;   // Message to send.

    // Create the message content.
    Msg = new System.Messaging.Message();
    Msg.Label = txtMessageHeader.Text;
    Msg.Body = txtMessage.Text;
    Msg.Priority = (MessagePriority)cbPriority.SelectedIndex;

    // Send the message.
    TempMQ.Send(Msg);
}
```

Listing 9-1 Creating a message

As you can see from the sample code, sending a message to a message queue isn't hard, especially when compared to the requirements of older versions of Microsoft Visual Studio. All you need to do is create the *Message* object, fill it with data, and then use the *Send()* method of the message queue object to send it to the message queue.

Testing the Recorder

Run the application, change any of the entries that you want, and then click Send. After a second or two, you'll see the message appear in the Public Queues folder. You might have to use the Refresh command to force the message to appear. Once the test message does appear, it will contain the heading in the Label column, the priority in the Priority column, and other information such as a message ID. Figure 9-6 shows a typical entry.

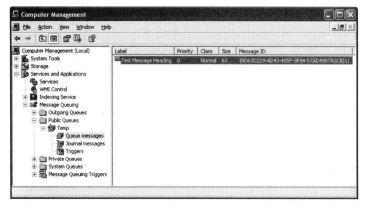

Figure 9-6 After the application sends the message, you'll see it appear in the message queue.

When you double-click the message, a Properties dialog box appears that allows you to see the various message elements. For example, the User tab contains the sending user's name and Security Identifier (SID). You can also learn whether Windows authenticated the message and determine whether the sender encrypted the message. We didn't perform either of these tasks for the example.

The most interesting part of the message is the Body tab. Older versions of MSMQ relied on a custom format to store the message content. You might be surprised to learn that the newest version stores messages in XML format, as shown in Figure 9-7. Using an XML format makes it easier to use MSMQ in a distributed application environment that relies on the Internet for connectivity.

Figure 9-7 The body of the message will appear in XML format rather than the custom format used by older versions of MSMQ.

Creating the Player

At some point, you'll want to retrieve the messages in the queue. You can perform this task by using a number of techniques. The simplest technique is to write an application that looks for the queue, determines whether the queue contains a message, and then displays the content of the message if one exists. That's precisely what the example in Listing 9-2 does.

```
private void btnReceive_Click(object sender, System.EventArgs e)
{
   System.Messaging.Message   Msg;   // Message to receive.

   // Set the queue formatter.
   TempMQ.Formatter = new XmlMessageFormatter(
                      new Type [] {typeof(String)});
```

Listing 9-2 Retrieving a message

```
// Set the queue priority filter.
TempMQ.MessageReadPropertyFilter.Priority = true;

// Get the message.
try
{
   Msg = TempMQ.Receive(new TimeSpan(5));
}

// If the timespan elapses before the message arrives,
// MSMQ will throw an exception.
catch (MessageQueueException MQE)
{
   MessageBox.Show("No Messages to Retrieve\r\n" +
               MQE.Message,
               "Message Error",
               MessageBoxButtons.OK,
               MessageBoxIcon.Error);
   return;
}

// Display the message.
MessageBox.Show("Label: " + Msg.Label +
            "\r\nBody: " + Msg.Body +
            "\r\nPriority: " + Msg.Priority.ToString(),
            "Message Contents",
            MessageBoxButtons.OK,
            MessageBoxIcon.Information);
}
```

The code for retrieving a message is slightly more complicated than the code used to create it. The code begins by creating an *XmlMessageFormatter* object. Remember that MSMQ stores the message in XML format, so you need some way to retrieve the information. As part of defining the *XmlMessageFormatter* object, you must decide which data formats to retrieve. In this case, because the only content the message contains is a string, we need to provide only the *String* type.

To keep the amount of information overload an application has to handle to a minimum, the *System.Messaging.MessageQueue* object automatically filters the content. In some cases, it filters too much content and you need to request that the object send it as part of the message. That's what the *TempMQ.MessageReadPropertyFilter.Priority* property does in this case—setting it to *true* means that the message will contain priority information. (It normally doesn't.)

The *Receive()* method obtains a message from the queue. If you don't specify a *TimeSpan* for the call to wait, it will continue waiting until the queue has a message. Consequently, the call includes this information in the example. If the call returns before the queue contains a message, it will throw a *MessageQueueException* exception. That's why the call appears within a *try...catch* block.

As you can see, the code for displaying the information isn't complex. The *Label* and *Body* properties appear as strings. The *Body* property is a string only because the *XmlMessageFormatter* object converts it for you. The property is actually listed as an object, and you shouldn't assume the message always contains a string (although it does contain one in this case). The code will always need to convert the *Priority* property to a string equivalent. Now that you know how the player works, you can test it. Figure 9-8 shows the output of this example using the default message inputs. Notice that the priority is listed as text, rather than as a number, because the original value is an enumeration.

Figure 9-8 Retrieving the content of a message queue requires a little formatting.

Creating a Simple COM+ Listener/Player

The example in the "Creating a Simple Recorder/Player" section demonstrates the basic principles of MSMQ, but it's not very realistic. While some users might create messages using something similar to the Recorder application, normally an application that's always listening to the queue will receive the messages. Part of the advantage of using a listener is that message processing occurs automatically—no one has to monitor the queue for input.

As with many other aspects of the applications presented in this chapter, you can create a listener in a number of ways. For example, when you create a COM+ application and mark it as queued, the COM+ environment automatically creates a queue and sets up everything for you. We'll look at an example of this listener type later in the chapter. A second type of listener is the one that relies on a trigger. We'll create that type of listener in this section. You'll use the recorder example we created earlier to put messages in the queue, but now this application will automatically remove them.

Creating the Listener/Player Component

The Listener/Player component is similar to the player provided as part of the Recorder application. However, there are important differences. The first difference is that COM+ components normally don't display data on screen. Consequently, the component version will store data in the Event Log. Of course, you could have just as easily sent the data to a database or even to a text file. The second difference is that you don't have a means to create the *MessageQueue* object using the IDE, so the component will have to create this portion of code. Listing 9-3 shows the code we'll use for this example. You'll find the complete source code in the Chapter 09\ListenerPlayer folder of the book's companion content.

```
namespace ListenerPlayer
{
   /// <summary>
   /// This interface provides access to the methods in the
   /// MyPlayer class.
   /// </summary>
   [Guid("140E024D-4145-4cb4-BB3D-E44AA7AF4556"),
    InterfaceType(ComInterfaceType.InterfaceIsDual)]
   public interface IMyPlayer
   {
      void ProcessMessage();
   }

   /// <summary>
   /// The MyPlayer class recives messages from the Temp
   /// message queue using MSMQ and processes them.
   /// </summary>
   [Guid("77510036-E9F5-4536-BA27-925A4FDFA621"),
    ClassInterface(ClassInterfaceType.None)]
   public class MyPlayer : ServicedComponent, IMyPlayer
   {
      public MyPlayer()
      {

      }

      #region IMyPlayer Members

      public void ProcessMessage()
      {
         MessageQueue   TempMQ;   // Message queue.
         Message        Msg;      // Message to receive.
         EventLog       EV;       // Message data storage.
```

Listing 9-3 Creating a Listener/Player component

```
            // Create and initialize the message queue.
            TempMQ = new System.Messaging.MessageQueue();
            TempMQ.Path = "main\\Temp";

            // Set the queue formatter.
            TempMQ.Formatter = new XmlMessageFormatter(
                        new Type [] {typeof(String)});

            // Set the queue priority filter.
            TempMQ.MessageReadPropertyFilter.Priority = true;

            // Create and initialize the event log.
            EV = new EventLog("Application", "Main", "MyPlayer Component");

            // Get the message.
            try
            {
                Msg = TempMQ.Receive(new TimeSpan(5));
            }

            // If the timespan elapses before the message arrives,
            // MSMQ will throw an exception.
            catch (MessageQueueException MQE)
            {
                EV.WriteEntry("No Messages to Retrieve\r\n" +
                        MQE.Message,
                        EventLogEntryType.Error,
                        1001,
                        100);
                return;
            }

            // Display the message.
            EV.WriteEntry("Label: " + Msg.Label +
                        "\r\nBody: " + Msg.Body +
                        "\r\nPriority: " + Msg.Priority.ToString(),
                        EventLogEntryType.Information,
                        1002,
                        100);
        }

        #endregion
    }
}
```

As you can see, this component, like all other COM+ components we've created, includes an interface description. As usual, make sure you define both a *[Guid]* and an *[InterfaceType]* attribute for the interface. This interface includes a single method, *ProcessMessage()*. Notice that the method doesn't return any value (because there is no client) and accepts no input data (because the message should contain everything the method needs).

The *ProcessMessage()* method begins by creating the *MessageQueue* object, *TempMQ*. The process of creating *TempMQ* is simple. All you need to do is instantiate the object and assign a value to the *Path* property. The path information contains the name of the machine on which the queue is found and the name of the queue. As with the player in the Record application, you also need to define values for the *Formatter* and *MessageReadPropertyFilter.Priority* properties.

> **Note** Notice that *TempMQ.Path* points to the **Temp** queue on the **main** machine. You must change the machine name to match the name of your server. For example, if your server's name is WinServer, you would change the *TempMQ.Path* property to **winserver\\Temp**.

Creating the *EventLog* object is next. This task consists of defining a log name, the machine on which the log is stored, and the source of the Event Log entry. In this case, the source is the MyPlayer Component.

> **Note** The code places the *EventLog* object output on a machine named **Main**. You'll need to change this entry to the name of your server. If your server is the local machine, you can also use the "." operator. The "." operator always points to the local machine, rather than to another machine on the network.

Once the code has access to the objects it needs, it attempts to access a message in the queue. Theoretically, it's impossible for the code to throw an exception in this case because the component will never become active unless there's a message to process. However, you'll still want to include the error-trapping code.

Adding an entry to the Event Log requires use of the *WriteEntry()* method. This method accepts the message, an *EventLogEntryType* enumeration value, an event ID, and a category. We'll discuss how these entries work and appear in the Event Log in the "Testing the Listener/Player Application" section of the chapter. For now, you'll need to compile the component.

> **Note** While the name of the component and the method it contains are essential to the remaining portions of the example, the COM+ application name isn't as important. You'll see that the queue triggering (listening) mechanism employed for this example relies on the component program ID and the method name rather than the COM+ application name. However, the example we'll create later in the chapter does rely on the COM+ application name to create the message queue. In this case, you'll want to be careful about how you put the application together and ensure the COM+ application name you create doesn't interfere with any existing queue on the system.

After you compile the component, register it on the server using the Register.bat file found in the Debug folder for the application. Create a COM+ application named TriggerApp, and add this component to it. If you're using a two-machine setup to test the COM+ applications in this book, you'll need to export the application and install it on the client machine. We discussed the mechanics of performing all these tasks in the "A Simple Component Example" section of Chapter 8.

Defining the MSMQ Rule and Trigger

Once you create the ListenerPlayer component, register it, and create a COM+ application for it, you need to create linkage between it and the Temp queue. For this example, we'll use a rule and a trigger to accomplish the task. A rule specifies when to call an application and which application to call. The trigger associates the rule with the queue. Whenever a message arrives in the queue that meets the requirements of the rule, the trigger sends the message to the application. Let's begin by creating the rule.

1. Right-click the Rules folder found within the Message Queuing Triggers folder of Computer Management. Select New and then Rule from the context menu. You'll see a New Rule dialog box.

2. Type a name for the rule. The example uses **Simple Listener/Player**. Type a rule description. The example uses **This is the listener/player used for test purposes**.

3. Click Next. The wizard will show you a blank condition list, as shown in Figure 9-9. The condition list defines when the rule is true. If you don't define any conditions, the rule is always true. To define a new condition, simply select one of the statements from the drop-down list box, type a condition, and then click Add. The example doesn't use any conditions, so the rule is always true.

Figure 9-9 Rules rely on conditions to determine when they become true.

4. Define zero or more conditions as necessary. Click Next. The wizard will ask you to define the application or COM component to invoke when the rule is true, as shown in Figure 9-10. A COM component can include a COM+ application proxy installed on your machine, which is the method we'll use for the example. Figure 9-10 shows the information you'll need to type for the example. In this case, type **ListenerPlayer.MyPlayer** for the Component ProgID, and **ProcessMessage** for the Method Name. Notice that you must include a specific method name as part of the entry.

5. Click Finish. The new rule will appear in the list of rules in Computer Management. (Use Refresh to display it if necessary.)

Figure 9-10 Define the application or COM component you want to invoke when the rule is true.

You can use a single rule with any number of triggers. The association allows one COM+ component to service any number of queues. However, you must create the trigger before anything will happen. The following steps show you how to create a trigger.

1. Right-click the Triggers folder in the queue you want to manage. (Don't use the general Triggers folder found in the Message Queuing Triggers folder.) Select New and then click Trigger in the context menu. You'll see the New Trigger dialog box shown in Figure 9-11.

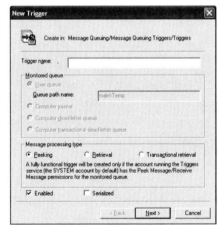

Figure 9-11 Use this dialog box to create a new trigger for a queue.

2. Type a name for the trigger. The example uses **Get All Messages**. Select a Message Processing Type. The example uses Retrieval because the component will retrieve and process messages found in the queue. Finally, select the Enabled option (so that the trigger will begin processing messages), but leave the Serialized option clear (so that the trigger can continue to process messages, even if it hasn't evaluated all the rules for a particular message).

3. Click Next. The wizard will ask you to associate one or more rules with the trigger by moving the rule from the list on the left (Existing Rules) to the list on the right (Attached Rules). Figure 9-12 shows a typical dialog box for this example.

Figure 9-12 Activate the trigger by associating one or more rules with it.

4. Select one or more rules for the trigger. For this example, select the Simple Listener/Player rule.

5. Click Finish. The new trigger will appear in the Triggers folder. (Use Refresh to display it if necessary.) The trigger is set up and ready to use.

Testing the Listener/Player Application

Testing the listener/player application is easy. Begin by creating a new message in the queue using the Recorder application. If you look in Component Services, you'll notice that the TriggerApp application is active. In fact, you might be able to track the activity of the interface and method as well. However, the real test is whether the message ended up in the Event Log.

Open the Event Viewer console, and select the Application log. You should see at least one entry in the list similar to the one shown in Figure 9-13.

Notice that the entry includes the Source, Category, and Event information we defined in the component. The entry type is also correct. The entry also includes the usual time and date information.

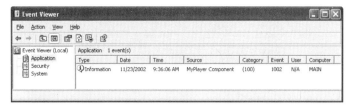

Figure 9-13 The example application creates an Event Log entry similar to the one shown here.

Double-click the Event Log entry so that you can see the associated message. Figure 9-14 shows a typical example for this application. Notice that the Description field contains the message Label, Body, and Priority entries. As you can see, this example demonstrates how easy it is to make manual connections to a queue when needed.

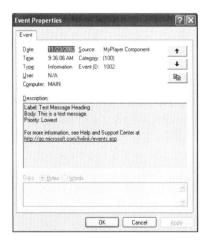

Figure 9-14 Make sure you check the message for proper Label, Body, and Priority entries.

Creating the MSMQ Client Application

In many cases, you'll need to employ MSMQ as part of a larger COM+ application scenario. Consider an order entry system where the user will make the majority of the entries while on the road. In some cases, the user won't have access to a telephone connection, so using a live connection won't always be possible. In short, the application must work the same whether the user is at home or on the road. This scenario is perfect for a combination of COM+ and MSMQ because the application can store the orders in a local queue until the user makes a connection. Once the user does establish a connection, such as at the end of the day, MSMQ will automatically upload the orders to the server. We'll discuss this application scenario later in this section.

Unlike other examples in this chapter, you really need a two-machine setup to see this one work. At one point in the chapter, you'll disconnect one machine from the other to see how the application continues to store updates in the local queue. The only way to see this information is by having two machines so that you can physically disconnect one machine from the other.

This example also takes one shortcut by using the Event Log, rather than a database, for data storage. Generally, the order entry component would require a connection to the database. The component would send the information received in the message to the database. Because this example is concentrating on disconnected application development techniques, using the Event Log is just as useful as creating the connection to the database. The simplified example will clearly show the COM+ development techniques rather than focusing on database application development.

> **Note** This section of the chapter doesn't discuss a few application elements you would need to consider for a complete implementation. For example, the user would probably need a list of client information and the pending orders for those clients. A developer can address this need by downloading client information to the remote machine based on the client visits scheduled for the next day. The information on the client machine would be read-only because the user would need it only for reference.

Designing the Data Encapsulation Component

As part of creating the COM+ application, you need to define a data encapsulation method. Essentially, you're defining a new data type that contains all the information you want to transfer from one machine to another using the message. Listing 9-4 shows the data encapsulation component. You'll find a complete source listing in the Chapter 09\MyDataType folder of the book's companion content.

```csharp
namespace MyDataType
{
   /// <summary>
   /// This interface enables access to the OrderEntry
   /// data members.
   /// </summary>
   [Guid("6B4BF1B5-C7FF-48ee-8D5A-DFA5004E6CF3"),
    InterfaceType(ComInterfaceType.InterfaceIsDual)]
   public interface IOrderEntry
   {
   }

   /// <summary>
   /// This class acts as a data type used to organize
   /// the information for transfer between client and
   /// server.
   /// </summary>
   [Guid("BDB66C95-28D6-4fa0-9AD6-4FD540BC6073"),
    ClassInterface(ClassInterfaceType.None)]
   public class OrderEntry : IOrderEntry
   {
      public String   ClientName;
      public String   ClientID;
      public String   ItemID;
      public String   ItemName;
      public Int32    ItemQty;
      public Decimal  ItemPrice;
   }
}
```

Listing 9-4 Creating a data encapsulation component

As you can see, this is just a fancy way to create a data structure you can use to transfer the data from one machine to another. Interestingly enough, you don't need to register this component on the server. You will have to register it on any machine that uses an unmanaged client to ensure the unmanaged client sends the data in the proper format. Of course, this component must appear in the Global Assembly Cache (GAC) or within the same folder as any managed components or managed applications that use it.

Designing the Message Queue Component

The message queue component builds upon the same principles we've used in other areas of the chapter. However, it adds a few new twists that make it possible to transfer formatted data from one machine to another. Listing 9-5 shows the code for this portion of the example. You'll find a complete source listing in the Chapter 09\OrderEntry folder of the book's companion content.

```csharp
[Guid("F6B0D315-DD16-4659-BE4E-FEF5ED7664B7"),
ClassInterface(ClassInterfaceType.None)]
public class OrderProcess : ServicedComponent, IOrderProcess
{
   public OrderProcess()
   {

   }

   #region IOrderProcess Members

   public void ProcessMessage()
   {
      MessageQueue   TempMQ;   // Message queue.
      Message        Msg;      // Message to receive.
      EventLog       EV;       // Message data storage.
      OrderEntry     OE;       // OrderEntry data.

      // Create and initialize the message queue.
      TempMQ = new System.Messaging.MessageQueue();
      TempMQ.Path = ".\\OrderEntryApp";

      // Set the queue formatter.
      TempMQ.Formatter = new XmlMessageFormatter(
                  new Type [] {typeof(OrderEntry)});

      // Create and initialize the event log.
      EV = new EventLog("Application", ".", "MyPlayer Component");

      // Initialize the OrderEntry object.
      OE = new OrderEntry();

      // Get the message.
      try
      {
         Msg = TempMQ.Receive(new TimeSpan(5));
      }

      // If the timespan elapses before the message arrives,
      // MSMQ will throw an exception.
      catch (MessageQueueException MQE)
      {
         EV.WriteEntry("No Messages to Retrieve\r\n" +
```

Listing 9-5 Creating a message queue component

```
                    MQE.Message,
                    EventLogEntryType.Error,
                    1001,
                    100);
        return;
    }

    // Obtain the data.
    OE = (OrderEntry)Msg.Body;

    // Write the message.
    EV.WriteEntry("Client ID: " + OE.ClientID +
                  "\r\nClient Name: " + OE.ClientName +
                  "\r\nItem ID: " + OE.ItemID +
                  "\r\nItem Name: " + OE.ItemName +
                  "\r\nItem Price: " + OE.ItemPrice.ToString("C2") +
                  "\r\nItem Quantity: " + OE.ItemQty.ToString(),
                  EventLogEntryType.Information,
                  1002,
                  100);
    }

    #endregion
}
```

As you can see, much of the queue interaction is the same. However, the data manipulation is different. Notice that we begin by creating an *OrderEntry* object, *OE*. The code converts the *Msg.Body* property and places the data within *OE*. Once the data is within *OE*, you can access the individual members, as shown in the code. In this case, the code places the data in an Event Log entry, but you could just as easily send the information to a database by placing the entries in a record.

Installing the Message Queue Component

As with all other COM+ applications we'll create, you'll begin this installation by registering the component, creating the COM+ application, and importing the component. For this application, use the name **OrderEntryApp**. The name of the application is important. After you've performed these preliminaries, you'll need to set up the application to use queuing. The following steps show you how.

1. In the COM+ Applications folder in the Component Services console, right-click the OrderEntryApp entry, and select Properties from the context menu. Select the Queuing tab. You'll see an OrderEntryApp

Properties dialog box like the one shown in Figure 9-15. Notice that this dialog box is already set up for use.

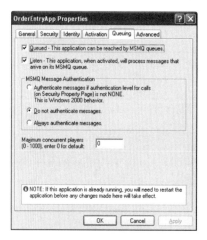

Figure 9-15 The OrderEntryApp Properties dialog box helps you created a queued environment for the application.

2. Click Queued to set up the application for queuing. Click Listen so that the application will listen for new messages in the queue. Select the Do Not Authenticate Messages option—we won't be using security in this example. Your dialog box should look like the one shown in Figure 9-15.

3. Click OK. COM+ will create a new queue for the application. Look in the Message Queuing snap-in and you'll see this new public queue. It has the same name as the COM+ application, which is why the application name is so important. The queue isn't ready to use yet because you need to assign an interface to handle the incoming messages.

4. In Component Services, open the Interfaces folder associated with *OrderEntryComp.OrderProcess*. Right-click *IOrderProcess*, and choose Properties from the context menu. You'll see an IOrderProcess Properties dialog box.

5. Select the Queuing tab, and check the Queued entry. Click OK. The queue is set up now, so you can export the application and install it on the client.

6. Export the application as usual and then right-click the OrderEntryApp entry, and select Start from the context menu. This action starts the application so that it can receive messages from the client.

Designing a Managed Client

This example could use a managed client or an unmanaged client with equal ease. In this case, we'll use a managed client. Listing 9-6 shows the functional client code. You'll find a complete source listing in the Chapter 09\ManagedClient folder of the book's companion content.

```
private void btnSend_Click(object sender, System.EventArgs e)
{
    System.Messaging.Message    Msg;    // Message to send.
    OrderEntry                  OE;     // OrderEntry data.

    // Create the OrderEntry object.
    OE = new OrderEntry();
    OE.ClientID = txtClientID.Text;
    OE.ClientName = txtClientName.Text;
    OE.ItemID = txtItemID.Text;
    OE.ItemName = txtItemName.Text;
    OE.ItemPrice = Convert.ToDecimal(txtItemPrice.Text);
    OE.ItemQty = Convert.ToInt32(txtItemQty.Text);

    // Create the message content.
    Msg = new System.Messaging.Message();
    Msg.Body = OE;

    // Send the message.
    OrderEntryMQ.Send(Msg, "Order Entry");
}
```

Listing 9-6 An example of a managed client

As you can see, this example looks similar to the Send function of the Recorder application we discussed earlier. However, in this case, the code first creates the data object, *OE*. The *Msg.Body* property can accept any object, even custom objects, as input, so sending *OE* is easy. Notice that the code includes a label entry this time because we aren't defining it as part of the message. Either technique will work.

Testing the Application

At this point, you should have the component installed and configured on the server. The client machine should have the proxy application loaded. We've also created a client application to send messages to the server. To test the application, start the client, click Send, and look for the results in the Event Log of the server. You should see the data transferred to the server without any problem.

To better understand this application, you'll want to look at a few other areas. First, look at the Outgoing Queues folder on the client. The first time you run the application, MSMQ creates an outgoing queue for the message traffic that the client generates. This queue includes the name of the server and the server queue, as shown in Figure 9-16. This queue holds the application data until MSMQ can create a connection to the server. Consequently, the client will be unaware that there's no server connection if all it does is send data without waiting for a response.

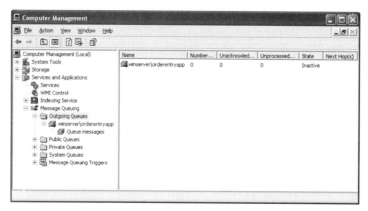

Figure 9-16 The data for a disconnected application resides in the Outgoing Queues folder until MSMQ can send it to the server.

Another area to look at is the actual message sent with this application. Unlike the message shown in Figure 9-7, this entry won't contain simple String entries. You'll notice that the XML includes a data type entry. Each of the data values is encapsulated within an element with the name of the data elements in the class. In short, the XML reflects the packaging we set up earlier rather than the actual data type.

Summary

This chapter has shown you the benefits of mixing MSMQ with COM+ to create applications that work asynchronously. Many of these applications will see use in situations where the client and server might not exist at the same time, such as when a user spends a lot of time on the road. The disconnected application is the most impressive form of this technology but not the only form. We also discussed a number of other uses, such as balancing the server load so that it can continue to work during off-peak hours.

The problem with using this technology is that it comes at a price—a small performance hit. In addition, you have to consider the added complexity of working with MSMQ, versus working directly with the component. That's where the decision point is for the developer. You need to determine whether the benefits of using MSMQ outweigh the potential problems. Sometimes, the best way to learn about the various problems is to build the same simple application twice—once with and once without MSMQ support so that you can see the differences in a controlled environment. In fact, building a double test application is one thing you should try now that you've read this chapter.

Chapter 10 takes you through the process of creating applications that use subscriptions. This form of disconnected application works much the same as any broadcast application you might have worked with in the past, such as the electronic newsletters that are so popular today. The publisher is a component that sends out data but doesn't care where the data goes. The subscriber is a client who receives the data but doesn't really care who published it. In between is COM+, which is managing the publication and subscription process.

10

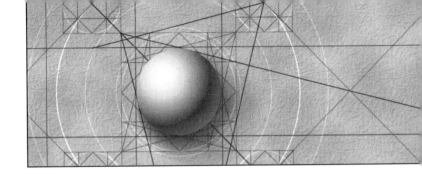

Creating Subscriptions

Just like COM applications, COM+ applications provide the means to react to events. In the world of COM, this technique is the request/reply system. COM+ uses the publish/subscribe system.

The two event-handling techniques share a few of the same concepts, but the implementation is essentially different. The problem with the request/reply system is that the client and server must know about each other—something that isn't always possible when you're working with distributed applications. In addition, when you're using the request/reply system, the client and server must exist at the same time—again, a limitation when working with distributed applications. When you're working with subscriptions, the server publishes an event and the client subscribes to it. In between these two elements is COM+, which handles the data transfer from client to server.

The following sections will help you better understand how subscriptions work with .NET components and clients. In general, you'll find that the common language runtime takes care of all the .NET to COM+ interactions for you as long as you provide the proper attributes and coding functionality in your application. We'll discuss both permanent and transient subscriptions in this chapter. You'll also learn about the techniques required to create a subscription manually (using the Component Services console) and automatically (using application code).

An Overview of the COM+ Catalog

If you've worked at least a little with COM+ using unmanaged components, you know that the information for these components is stored in the COM+ catalog. Using the publish/subscribe method of event handling requires you to know a little more than just this basic piece of information. The COM+ catalog is a special-purpose database that Microsoft Windows uses to store information about the COM+ applications you create. The developer can change every element of that database using standard interfaces and search techniques, as we'll see when working with both the transient and permanent subscription code in this chapter.

As a .NET developer, you must import the COM+ 1.0 Admin Type Library into your component or application to work with the COM+ catalog. The library reference will appear as *COMAdmin* in the References folder. This type library contains a vast number of interfaces and classes, as shown in Figure 10-1. We'll work with only a few of the many classes and interfaces in this book, but it pays to know that the other classes and interfaces exist should you need them for another product. This library encapsulates many of the features that we'll call Component Services throughout this chapter and the remaining COM+ sections of the book.

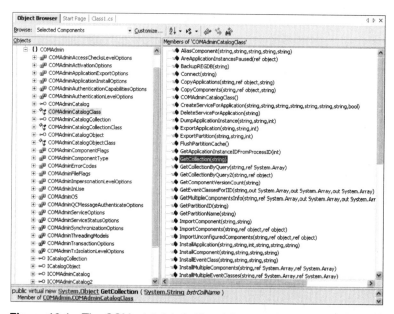

Figure 10-1 The COM+ 1.0 Admin Type Library contains a vast number of classes and interfaces used for COM+ development.

It often helps to look at Component Services when you need to envision what you'll do next with the COM+ catalog. For example, if you need to find information about a specific component, you'll need to find the associated application first, and then locate the component. You'll always use an *ICatalogCollection* object—such as a component or an interface—to access a node within the COM+ catalog. Once you find the object you want to work with, you'll use an *ICatalogObject* object to access individual properties. These two interfaces and a few methods within them are all you'll need to find any piece of information within the COM+ catalog.

Every property can be accessed within the COM+ catalog using the *Value()* method of the *ICatalogObject* interface. You'll access the properties by providing an index value in the form of a keyword. Unfortunately, the development environment won't list these keywords for you, so it takes some research at times to find precisely what you need. The examples in the transient and permanent subscription code sections of the chapter will provide you with keywords for many uses.

There's also the idea of a collection within the COM+ catalog. COM+ collections are the predecessors of the collections commonly used within the .NET Framework, but the two environments have differences you need to know about. When you create an object, you have the equivalent of an empty vessel. Before you can do anything with the object, you need to fill it up. COM+ uses a special method, named *Populate()* for this purpose. As soon as you've identified a unique resource within the COM+ Catalog, you can use the *Populate()* method to retrieve the entire collection of those types of objects.

The *Populate()* method creates a local copy of the object information that you need for working with the COM+ catalog. Any changes you make are on the local copy, and the changes won't affect what anyone else is seeing when making requests of the COM+ catalog until you save the local copy to the global catalog. In addition, the COM+ catalog validates all changes. The COM+ catalog will deny any changes that don't fit within the validation specifications. You'll always use the *SaveChanges()* method of the *ICatalogCollection* interface to make any changes permanent. Make sure you save changes before you move to another area of the COM+ catalog or they'll be lost in many cases.

This is the short overview of the COM+ catalog. You'll learn more about this important COM+ feature as the chapter progresses. For now, you have just enough information to understand the remaining material in the chapter.

What Are Subscriptions?

Distributed applications can't rely on a specific connection existing at any given time—the client and server might not even have a connection. Therefore, the request/reply event system is unlikely to work with a distributed application. The lack of a connection between the client and server forces us to create some new method of handling events. COM+ provides this new event-handling methodology, which is known as the publish/subscribe even system.

In the old setup, there was a client and a server with a direct connection. The client registered an event handler directly with the server. The publish/subscribe event system, on the other hand, uses an intermediary to handle the client/server communication. In short, the publish/subscribe event model has three main elements:

1. The server publishes data through an event class that it registers with Component Services. Once the server publishes data, it's no longer concerned about where the data goes. In other words, the server has no knowledge of which clients receive the data that it publishes.

2. The client subscribes to an event that the server publishes. However, unlike COM client, which registers with the server, the COM+ client registers with the COM+ Catalog. In reality, the client has no idea which server provides the data. All it knows is there's an event it wants to subscribe to. Therefore, we have a server publishing the data and a client subscribing to the data, but we don't have a connection between the two. That's where the event object comes into play.

3. The server creates the event object before firing an event. When the server fires the event, the event object receives it. At this point, the server can terminate if it wants to—it has fired the event, and the event object will handle the details of notifying subscribers. The event object looks through the list of subscribers in the COM+ catalog, and then notifies each subscriber. In short, the event object is the COM+ part of the picture—the intermediary between the server and the client.

At this point, you might be wondering what this three-element method buys you in the way of productivity or reliability. Creating the server is certainly easier. The server doesn't need to provide a request interface or handle client function pointers. All it needs to do is fire an event, nothing more. The subscriber, similarly, needs to know nothing about the server. All it needs to do is implement an interface. This interface has the same name as the server's interface. In short, you can create two components, change components, or even create entirely new functionality using this method without having to change both the client and server. All you need to worry about is implementing an interface with the correct name.

The event object is simple too. All it really contains is stub code (empty functions). The COM+ Event System Service handles the actual event object details. It merely uses the event object you create as a template of the interfaces and methods it needs to handle.

Another advantage of using the publish/subscribe methodology is that you can combine it with Microsoft Message Queuing Services (MSMQ). A COM server (publisher) could queue up changes that would wait until the host computer has time to service them. Likewise, the event object can queue the fired events until the client can pick them up. Consequently, neither the client nor the server has to exist during event handling.

You must consider several subscription issues when working with COM+. The first is the type of subscription you want to create: transient or permanent. The type is determined by the type of registration you want to perform: manual or dynamic. We've already discussed methods for manual component registration in the other COM+ chapters of the book. The following sections describe the two subscription types and the dynamic method of registering a component.

Understanding Transient Subscriptions

Transient applications allow you to make a quick subscription to an event object without spending a lot of time traversing the COM+ catalog. In addition, transient subscriptions won't survive a reboot, which means that applications that fail in the middle of a session won't leave permanent bits of themselves behind. Generally, you'll use transient subscriptions for users on the road or for situations where a connection is easily broken. Because transient subscriptions won't survive a reboot, you can clear them from your system with relative ease.

Understanding Permanent Subscriptions

Permanent subscriptions are located in another part of the COM+ catalog and require a lot more work because you have to first locate the right application. The advantage of a permanent subscription is that it survives reboots and tends to be more efficient for use by long-term applications such as server-based components.

Understanding the Need for Dynamic Registration

Sometimes you don't want to clutter the global assembly cache with components that will see intermittent or temporary use. That's where dynamic registration comes into play. Theoretically, you can place an assembly containing a serviced component in the application folder for a COM+ application. When a client requests services of the component, the component is loaded dynamically. The COM+ applications for a given machine appear in the Program

Files\ComPlus Applications folder. You can find out more about this procedure at *ms-help://MS.MSDNQTR.2003FEB.1033/cpguide/html/cpcondynamicallyregisteringassembly.htm*.

Creating the Event Object

Based on our previous discussions, you know that the first piece of code you should create when creating a publish/subscribe model application is the event object. You need to use this object when creating both the publisher and subscriber. Remember that the event object is the middleman—the go-between for the publisher and subscriber. While the publisher doesn't need to know about the subscriber, and vice versa, they both need to know about the event object. The following sections show how to design and install an event object component.

> **Tip** Sometimes resolving an error requires you to look at configuration issues rather than check your code. In some cases, a developer might have two copies of the same component on a machine. If both components have the same program ID, Windows might choose the older component as part of a client request rather than the new one. Any errors in this older component will give the developer a false impression. Always make sure you unregister and remove older versions of components. Use the OLE/COM Object Viewer (available from the Visual Studio .NET Tools menu) to check for older versions of the component if you suspect an error isn't actually part of your code.

Designing the Component

The event object is the simplest part of the application. Creating the event object is more a matter of configuration than coding. You'll begin by creating a Class Library project with the name SimpleEventObject. Make sure you give your namespace and the default class a name. The example uses a namespace of *SimpleEventObject* and a class name of *SendMsg*. Listing 10-1 shows the source code for the event object. You can find the complete source code in the Chapter10\SimpleEventObject folder of the book's companion content. This content is available from the book's Web site at: *http://www.microsoft.com/mspress/books/6426.asp*.

```
namespace SimpleEventObject
{
   /// <summary>
   /// An interface used to access the SendMsg functions.
   /// </summary>
   [Guid("0E4DB900-60F3-4354-A89A-C90A962F468C"),
    InterfaceType(ComInterfaceType.InterfaceIsDual)]
   public interface ISendMsg
   {
      void FireBroadcastMsg(String strMsg);
   }

   /// <summary>
   /// This class shows how to create a very simple event
   /// object used to create a bridge between a publisher
   /// and a subscriber.
   /// </summary>
   [Guid("6A121716-471A-479f-B1DE-97858FE95483"),
    ClassInterface(ClassInterfaceType.None)]
   public class SendMsg : ServicedComponent, ISendMsg
   {
      public SendMsg()
      {
      }

      /// <summary>
      /// This method acts as a template for the actual
      /// event object.
      /// </summary>
      /// <param name="strMsg">The data we want to send
      /// as a broadcast message.</param>
      public void FireBroadcastMsg(String strMsg)
      {
      }
   }
}
```

Listing 10-1 Simple event object

The code in Listing 10-1 looks short—perhaps too short and too easy. If you're thinking there's an error in the book, you're wrong. All you need to provide for an event object is the prototype of each event you plan to support. COM+ will take care of the implementation of each event, so coding is extremely simple in this case. Notice that the *FireBroadcastMsg()* method has no implementation—the implementation is actually part of the subscriber code.

The event object only provides a prototype. Make sure you compile and register the event object component before you leave this section because you'll need to reference it in other areas of this example.

Installing the Event Object

In Chapter 2, we discussed the method for creating a COM+ application. You use the same process as normal to create the event object application. I named the example SimpleEventApp. Installing the component, however, is different from the process we discussed in Chapter 2. The following steps will show you how to install an event component:

1. In Component Services, create a new COM+ application named SimpleEventApp.

2. Right click the SimpleEventApp\Components folder, and choose New and then Component from the context menu. You'll see a Welcome To The COM Component Install Wizard dialog box.

3. Click Next. You'll see the Import Or Install A Component page shown in Figure 10-2. Notice the Install New Event Class(es) button near the bottom of this dialog box.

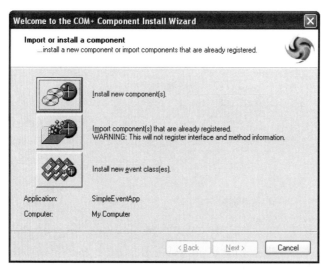

Figure 10-2 The Import Or Install A Component dialog box allows you to install a number of component types.

4. Click Install New Event Class(es). You'll see a Select Files To Install dialog box.

5. Locate the event object type library you want to install (SimpleEventObject.TLB for this example), highlight it, and then click Open. You'll see an Install New Components page like the one shown in Figure 10-3.

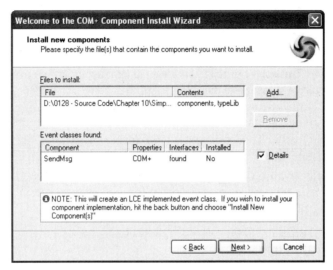

Figure 10-3 The Install New Components page will allow you to check the event object you want to install.

6. Verify the dynamic-link library (DLL) you want to install, and then click Next. You'll see a success page.

7. Click Finish.

The interesting thing about this installation is the result doesn't look much different than the installation we performed in Chapter 2. However, you'll learn later that installing the component as an event class makes a significant difference in how COM+ views the component. Once you create the application on the server, export it as you normally would and install it on the client as a proxy.

Creating the Publisher

The publisher is the entity that fires an event. It can be an application, as in this example, or it can be a component. COM+ doesn't limit your options in this area. The only thing the publisher must do is invoke the method required to fire the event contained within the event object. The sample application fires an event that broadcasts messages to all subscribers. Figure 10-4 shows the simple interface for this portion of the example.

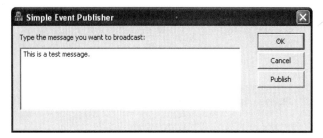

Figure 10-4 The publisher relies on a simple interface to fire an event that broadcasts a message to the subscribers.

As you can see, all you need to do is type a message and click Publish to publish the event. The code for this example looks remarkably similar to the code in Listing 8-6. However, instead of accepting input from the component, this example pushes data to the component in a manner similar to the example in Listing 8-2. You still need to add a reference to the type library for the event object type library, as shown here:

```
// Import the type library and use the associated namespace.
#import "SimpleEventObject.TLB" named_guids
using namespace SimpleEventObject;
```

The publisher—not the subscribers—must reference the event object. Some developers get confused on this issue, and the result is that the publish/subscribe sequence doesn't work as anticipated. Listing 10-2 shows the code to implement the Publish button for this example. You can find the complete listing for this example in the Chapter10\Publisher folder of the book's companion content.

```
void CPublisherDlg::OnBnClickedPublish()
{
    ISendMsg *pSendMsg;   // Pointer to ConstString object.
    _bstr_t  Output;      // Temporary data string.
    CString  Data;        // Data from the message box.

    // Initialize the COM environment.
    CoInitialize(NULL);

    // Create the object.
    CoCreateInstance(CLSID_SendMsg,
                     NULL,
                     CLSCTX_ALL,
                     IID_ISendMsg,
                     (void**)&pSendMsg);
```

Listing 10-2 Simple event publisher

```
    // Send the message.
    MsgText.GetWindowText(Data);
    Output = Data;
    pSendMsg->FireBroadcastMsg(Output);

    // Uninitialize the COM environment.
    CoUninitialize();
}
```

As you can see, the code begins by creating an instance of the object. As usual, the *CLSID_SendMsg* and *IID_ISendMsg* values come from the TLH and TLI files created from SimpleEventObject.TLB during compilation.

Once the code has an instance of the object to use, it obtains the string typed by the user and places it in a *_bstr_t* value, *Output*. The publisher fires the event by calling on the *FireBroadcastMsg()* method with *Output* as an argument. As you can see, the publisher can exit at this point without knowing where the event information has gone (if it goes anywhere at all). If you tried the application now, it would succeed because COM+ doesn't require the presence of a subscriber. The publish/subscribe model allows zero, one, or multiple subscribers.

Creating a Component Subscriber

The easiest type of subscriber to create for this example is a component. Using a component lets you place the subscriber on the server for immediate response. The component will output a message box in this case, which is definitely the incorrect thing to do because no one is usually at the server to see the message box. The example uses this simple approach so that you can obtain instant feedback on the usability of the subscriber. The following sections show you how to design, install, and test this type of subscriber.

Designing the Subscriber Component

Remember that the publisher is firing the event and that the event object manages the event. So far, we don't have anything that actually implements the event. How an application handles an event, even under COM+, is unique for every application. When a user clicks a button on a form, the event handler for that button performs some action—the button component doesn't care what that action is or even that the code has handled it. The same holds true for subscribers. Each subscriber is unique and will handle the event in a unique way. Listing 10-3 shows the code for this subscriber. You'll find the complete listing in the Chapter 10\SubscriberComponent folder of the source code.

```
namespace SubscriberComponent
{
    /// <summary>
    /// This class subscribes to the event object that holds
    /// the message created by the publisher.
    /// </summary>
    [Guid("3162ED10-C74D-4967-BA51-C8EBD10A8D03"),
     ClassInterface(ClassInterfaceType.None)]
    public class SendMsg : ServicedComponent, ISendMsg
    {
        public SendMsg()
        {
        }

        /// <summary>
        /// This method acts as a template for the actual
        /// event object.
        /// </summary>
        /// <param name="strMsg">The data we want to send
        /// as a broadcast message.</param>
        public void FireBroadcastMsg(String strMsg)
        {
            MessageBox.Show(strMsg,
                            "Publisher Message",
                            MessageBoxButtons.OK,
                            MessageBoxIcon.Information);
        }
    }
}
```

Listing 10-3 Component style subscriber

You should notice something almost immediately about the subscriber—it contains no interface description. When you look at the project, you'll notice a reference to the event object, *SimpleEventObject*. The event object provides the interface in this case. Using the interface in this way ensures that the subscriber matches the event object so that the two are compatible.

Note that the namespace for this subscriber is different than the event object. This isn't required, but using a different namespace does make it easier to identify the subscriber. The use of a different GUID for the *SendMsg* class is required. The event object class is different than the subscriber class. In fact, you don't have to use the same names—the only requirement is that the two support the same interface.

The *FireBroadcastMsg()* method contains a simple implementation. The only thing that happens, in this case, is that the event handler displays a message box containing the string passed from the publisher. Obviously, you could set this up to do anything that any other event handler would do.

Installing and Testing the Subscriber Component

You'll create an application and register the subscriber just as you always do when working with COM+. Chapter 2 contains complete instructions for this process. The example uses an application name of SimpleSubscriber. However, when working with a subscriber component, you must create the subscription. The following steps show how:

1. In Component Services, create a COM+ component named Simple-Subscriber and install the SubscriberComponent.

2. Right click the SimpleSubscriber\Components\SubscriberComponent.SndMessage\Subscriptions folder, and choose New and then Subscription from the context menu. You'll see a Welcome To The COM+ New Subscription Wizard dialog box.

3. Click Next. You'll see a Select Subscription Method(s) page like the one shown in Figure 10-5. This is where you choose the methods that you want to use to accept events from a publisher. Notice that all the interfaces and methods the component supports appear in the list. This differs from unmanaged components, where you often see just the interface supported by the component itself.

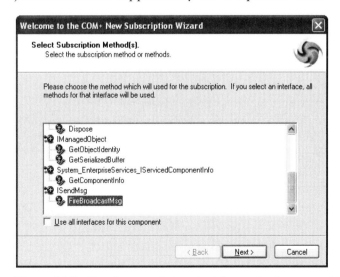

Figure 10-5 The first step is to select the methods you want to receive events.

4. Select just the *FireBroadcastMsg()* method, as shown in Figure 10-5, and then click Next. Windows will search the COM+ catalog for components that publish events that might fulfill your component's needs. Once this search process is complete, you'll see a Select Event Class page like the one shown in Figure 10-6. Notice that the event object we created appears in this dialog box. If you don't see the event object, you need to stop the procedure now and check the previous steps to create the SimpleEventApp application listed earlier in this chapter. Make sure you see the correct event object listed here; otherwise, the example won't work (and neither will your application in real life).

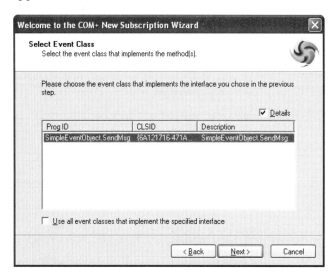

Figure 10-6 Make sure the event object appears in the dialog.

5. Select the *SimpleEventObject.SendMsg* class, and then click Next. You'll see the Subscription Options page shown in Figure 10-7. This is where you'll provide a name for your subscription and enable it. Always enable the subscription unless you don't want to receive events right away.

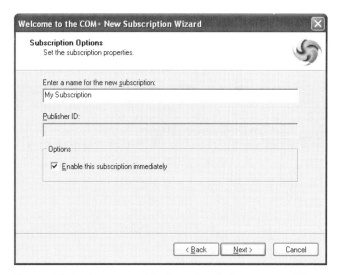

Figure 10-7 Always enable the subscription as part of the configuration process.

6. Type a subscription name (the example uses My Subscription), select the Enable This Subscription Immediately option, and then click Next. You'll see a success message.

7. Click Finish. At this point, you should see a new subscription added to the Subscriptions folder. Figure 10-8 shows a typical example of a subscription.

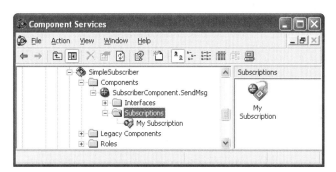

Figure 10-8 The subscription should appear in the Subscription folder once you create it successfully.

You'll need to export the application from the server and install it as a proxy application on the client as normal. At this point, everything is in place to test the first publish/subscribe setup. Start the Publisher application, type a message, and then click Publish. After a few seconds, the server should display a message box containing the text that you typed in the publisher. If you don't see the message box, make sure you enabled the subscriber. Also, verify that both the event object and the subscriber applications are active.

Creating a Dialog-Based Subscriber

In many cases, the subscriber for the events generated by a COM+ application is an application. One of the most common examples is the stock ticker, but you can use subscriber applications for a number of tasks. Any event that you can imagine can become part of a subscriber application solution. For example, it's conceivable that you could create a high-priority e-mail system using such as setup. Administrators could use a subscriber application that provides alerts about server conditions. It's possible that some applications could even provide some type of alarm information for a business or other entity.

The dialog-based subscriber application for this example is going to be a lot more complex than the other elements you've seen so far. The subscriber will need to react to events that the publisher generates. For the sake of simplicity, we'll generate a simple dialog box again with the understanding that you could do a lot more. Subscriber applications normally provide a user interface and the means to interact with the user to filter and otherwise manage the data. The filter is also a requirement for applications that generate a large number of events, such as the stock-ticker application.

The application will also have two different subscribe buttons. The first will create a subscription of the type we discussed in the "Creating a Component Subscriber" section. This first subscription is a permanent subscription because it survives a reboot of the server. It also shows up in Component Services, so you can manage it as you would any other subscription. Components and local applications usually use permanent subscriptions because you want them to be able to get back to work immediately after a server reboot. In addition, because the component is local to the server and the application connects through a LAN connection, there isn't any need to worry about a sudden disconnection.

The second subscribe button will create a transient subscription for the application user who spends time accessing the subscription from the road. A nonlocal application will normally use a transient subscription because it isn't connected the to the server 24 hours a day. In addition, if the server is down for any reason, you don't want to load up the server immediately with client requests after a reboot. In most cases, you want to be sure the server will stay online before you begin accepting requests from remote clients. Finally, clients do disconnect without removing their subscription. Transient subscriptions are easier to remove and are therefore a lot less work for the network administrator.

> **Note** If you haven't removed the subscription created in the "Creating a Component Subscriber" section, you'll want to remove it before you proceed with this section to ensure the message box you see is generated by this application. While it isn't necessary to disable the SimpleSubscriber COM+ application, you might want to do so to keep the test environment clean. Be sure you retain the SimpleEventApp COM+ application because we'll need it for this example.

This example relies on the same component we used in the "Creating a Component Subscriber" section. In this case, we'll use the component locally rather than as part of a COM+ application. To begin this example, you'll need to create a form for a C# client. The example uses an application name of AppSubscribe, but you can use any name desired. Figure 10-9 shows what this form looks like. We'll add code for the buttons in the sections that follow. The complete listing for this example appears in the \Chapter 10\AppSubscribe folder of the source code.

Figure 10-9 Use this client to add and remove subscriptions programmatically.

You'll also need to add a reference to the COM+ 1.0 Admin Type Library to the application, as shown in Figure 10-10. As mentioned in the "An Overview of the COM+ Catalog" section of the chapter, this type library provides the management functions we need to control both permanent and transient subscriptions.

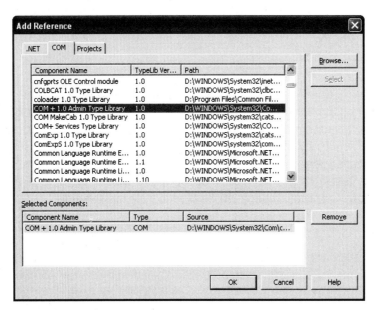

Figure 10-10 Add the COM+ 1.0 Admin Type Library to your application to obtain access to the required management functions.

Before we go on to the subscription-specific code, you need to create some applicationwide variables, initialize one of them in the application constructor, and provide a method for releasing them when the application exits. Not setting these COM objects to null could result in a memory leak in your application (not to mention other problems). Listing 10-4 shows the code used by both subscription techniques.

```
// Declare the administration objects used in this application.
// COM Administrator
private COMAdminCatalogClass    ComAdmin;
// Application Collection
private ICatalogCollection      AppCollection;
// Component Collection
private ICatalogCollection      CompCollection;
// Subscription Collection
private ICatalogCollection      SubCollection;
// A Single Entry Within a Collection
private ICatalogObject          CatalogObject;
// Transient Subscription Identifier
private Object                  TransID;
// Permanent Subscription Identifier
private Object                  PermID;
```

Listing 10-4 Application subscription common code

```
public frmMain()
{
   // Required for Windows Form Designer support
   InitializeComponent();

   // Initialize the administration object.
   ComAdmin = new COMAdminCatalogClass();
}

private void frmMain_Closed(object sender, System.EventArgs e)
{
   // Clean up the COM objects before the application exits.
   TransID = null;
   PermID = null;
   CatalogObject = null;
   AppCollection = null;
   CompCollection = null;
   SubCollection = null;
   ComAdmin = null;
}
```

You'll learn later that accessing the COM+ catalog can mean navigating through three levels of collections: application, component, and subscription. Each of the *ICatalogCollection* objects handles a specific need. In general, you'll want to allocate the number of *ICatalogCollection* objects required for all levels of a given task so that you can easily go to previous levels as needed.

The single *ICatalogObject* object is enough for most applications because you don't want to manipulate more than one catalog level at a time. In addition, it's important not to store a specific object for too long because another application might change it. (This problem can also occur when working with the *ICatalogCollection* objects, but is far less likely to in that situation.)

This application lets you work with both permanent and transient subscriptions. In fact, you can work with them simultaneously if you want. That's why the global variables include two subscription variable identifiers. In general, the code must have these identifiers to determine whether it has found the correct subscription prior to removing it from the subscription list. Now that we have the global concerns taken care of, let's look at the two subscriptions.

Creating a Permanent Subscription

The permanent subscription example has the advantage of creating a visible subscription (one you can verify), and it shows how to parse the COM+ catalog hierarchy. In many cases, it's better to create a permanent subscription first, move the code to the location you want to use for creating a temporary subscription, and make the required temporary subscription changes. (See Listing 10-6 for comparison purposes.) Listing 10-5 contains the code required to parse the COM+ catalog to look for a particular application and a component within that application. The second part of the code creates a new subscription for the target component. You'll find this code in the FrmMain.cs file in the Chapter10\AppSubscribe folder of the book's companion content.

```csharp
private void btnPermanent_Click(object sender, System.EventArgs e)
{
   String    IDVal;    // Temporary PermID

   // Obtain the current application collection and then populate
   // the application collection object with members of that
   // collection.
   AppCollection =
      (ICatalogCollection)ComAdmin.GetCollection("Applications");
   AppCollection.Populate();

   // Locate the application we're interested in subscribing to.
   for (int Counter = 0; Counter < AppCollection.Count; Counter++)
   {
      // Get the current catalog object.
      CatalogObject =
         (ICatalogObject)AppCollection.get_Item(Counter);

      // Determine if this is the correct application.
      if ((String)CatalogObject.Name == "SimpleSubscriber")
      {
         // Obtain the current component collection for the
         // target application.
         CompCollection =
            (ICatalogCollection)AppCollection.GetCollection(
               "Components", CatalogObject.Key);
         CompCollection.Populate();
         break;
      }
   }

   // Locate the target component.
   for (int Counter = 0; Counter < CompCollection.Count; Counter++)
   {
      // Get the current catalog object.
      CatalogObject =
         (ICatalogObject)CompCollection.get_Item(Counter);

      // Determine if this is the correct component.
      if ((String)CatalogObject.Name == "SubscriberComponent.SendMsg")
      {
```

Listing 10-5 A permanent subscription example

```
         // Obtain the subscription collection for the target
         // component.
         SubCollection =
            (ICatalogCollection)CompCollection.GetCollection(
               "SubscriptionsForComponent", CatalogObject.Key);
         SubCollection.Populate();
         break;
   }
}

// Depending on the current subscription status, we'll
// either get a new subscription or free an existing
// subscription.
if (btnPermanent.Text == "Set Permanent")
{
   // Add a new subscription to the permanent subscription
   // collection.
   CatalogObject = (ICatalogObject)SubCollection.Add();

   // Set the catalog object values. This list represents a
   // minimal implementation.
   CatalogObject.set_Value(
      "EventCLSID", "{6A121716-471A-479f-B1DE-97858FE95483}");
   CatalogObject.set_Value("Name", "Permanent Subscription");
   CatalogObject.set_Value("MethodName", "FireBroadcastMsg");
   CatalogObject.set_Value(
      "InterfaceID", "{0E4DB900-60F3-4354-A89A-C90A962F468C}");
   CatalogObject.set_Value("Enabled", true);

   // Save the changes we've made to the transient subscription
   // collection.
   SubCollection.SaveChanges();

   // Change the button caption to match the current subscription
   // status.
   btnPermanent.Text = "Release Permanent";

   // Save the subscription ID for later use.
   PermID = CatalogObject.get_Value("ID");
}

   // We need to release an existing subscription.
else
{
   // Populate the subcollection with existing subscription
   // information.
   SubCollection.Populate();
```

```csharp
        // Check each of the subscription items in turn.
        for (int Counter = 0;
           Counter < SubCollection.Count;
           Counter++)
        {
           // Get the current catalog object.
           CatalogObject =
              (ICatalogObject)SubCollection.get_Item(Counter);

           // See if this is the correct catalog object.
           IDVal = (String)CatalogObject.get_Value("ID");
           if (IDVal == PermID.ToString())
           {
              // Remove the subscription from the list.
              SubCollection.Remove(Counter);
              SubCollection.SaveChanges();

              // Exit the loop.
              break;
           }
        }

        // Change the button caption to match the current subscription
        // status.
        btnPermanent.Text = "Set Permanent";
     }
  }
```

The example begins by creating the *AppCollection* object. Notice that we have to convert the *Object* output of the *GetCollection()* function to an *ICatalogCollection* object. Once the code obtains access to the collection, it uses the *Populate()* method to fill *AppCollection* with the collection data. Failure to populate the collection will cause any operation you try to perform with it to fail. The application will compile just fine, so this particular error is extremely difficult to locate. Just remember that every time your code contains *GetCollection()*, it must also contain *Populate()*.

> **Note** All the *ComAdmin* methods produce plain objects as output, so you'll find that you have to convert almost everything you do. Contrast this to working in the unmanaged environment where the code doesn't need to perform a conversion in most cases. Make sure you perform all required conversions to ensure your code compiles and works properly.

The code uses a *for* loop to look for the application of interest. Most developers might wonder why the code doesn't use a *foreach* statement instead. You'll find that a COM collection is different than a .NET collection in that the COM collection normally lacks a true indexer. The technique shown in the example assures proper application function. Once the code finds the proper application, it creates the *CompCollection* object using the same technique used for the *AppCollection* object. You'll notice that creating the *SubCollection* object follows the same pattern.

At this point, we've parsed the COM+ catalog for an application, and then for a component within the application, and then for the subscription collection for the component. The next step determines whether the application needs to create a new subscription or remove a previously created subscription. The *btnPermanent.Text* value provides a convenient method for assessing this need.

If the application needs to create a new subscription, it begins by using the *Add()* method to create a new *CatalogObject*. The *CatalogObject* is empty at this point—it doesn't point to anything and, in fact, is only a local copy of the object. If the application failed at this point, COM+ would never know the *CatalogObject* existed.

To create a complete *CatalogObject*, the code assigns values to various *CatalogObject* properties using the *set_Value()* method. Some of the values, such as *Name*, are relatively straightforward, and you don't need to worry too much about the value assigned. However, the code must assign a correct value to the *EventCLSID* property. This value comes from the *SimpleEventObject.SendMsg* GUID. If you don't assign a permanent GUID to the object (something that you should always do), you can obtain this GUID from the SimpleEventObject.SendMsg Properties dialog box shown in Figure 10-11. (You can get to this dialog box from within Component Services.) Unlike the subscriptions you might have created for the unmanaged environment, you'll find that the *InterfaceID* and *MethodName* properties also take on new meaning when working with managed components. If you don't assign these values, the component will receive the event but never do anything with it. Finally, the *Enabled* property is essential for transient subscriptions, but you can always use the Subscription Properties dialog box in Component Services to enable a permanent subscription after creating it.

At this point, you have a complete *CatalogObject* entry—one that will work for this application. (You can set other properties, but they aren't essential in this case.) The code makes the subscription complete by using the *SubCollection.SaveChanges()* method. The code also makes the proper change to the *btnPermanent.Text* property and saves the subscription identifier for future use.

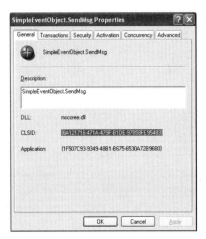

Figure 10-11 Use the SimpleEventObject.SendMsg Properties dialog box to obtain a GUID for your application if no other approach is available.

Let's move on to the process for removing a subscription. The code still parses the COM+ catalog for the application, component, and subscription information. In this case, the code continues by populating the subscription collection so that it can search for the subscription ID saved earlier. The most reliable way to perform this search is to convert both the *CatalogObject.get_Value("ID")* output and the *PermID* value to strings.

Once the code locates the subscription the application created, it removes the subscription from the local copy of the subscription collection using the *Remove()* method. The code saves the changes to the collection using the *SaveChanges()* method. The final step is to set the *btnPermanent.Text* value. As you can see, removing a subscription is much easier than creating it.

Testing the Permanent Subscription

Testing the permanent subscription is relatively easy because you can see the results and perform comparisons to the subscription we created manually. Start the application, and click Set Permanent. After a few seconds, the button caption will change to Release Permanent. Look in Component Services at the SubscriberComponent.SendMsg component subscriptions. Figure 10-12 shows what you'll see if you left the manual subscription in place and added this new subscription using the application.

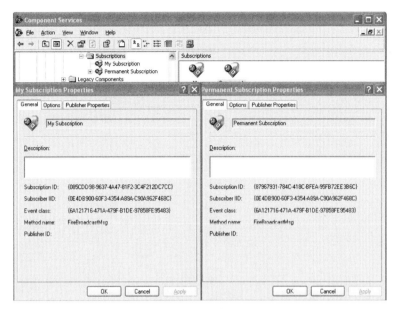

Figure 10-12 Creating a permanent subscription enables you to view and compare the automated and manual subscription methods.

Notice that both subscriptions use the same Subscriber IID, Event Class, and Method Name property values. However, because each subscription is unique, each subscription has a different Subscription ID property value. Select the Options tab in the Permanent Subscription Properties dialog box, and you'll notice that it is set to Enabled. (The Enabled check box in the Options tab of the My Subscription Properties dialog box should be disabled for the following test.)

Use the Simple Event Publisher application to send a message. You'll see the same dialog box as before. The difference is that Permanent Subscription has reacted to this event. To test this hypothesis, click Release Permanent on the Simple Event Application. The Permanent Subscription entry should disappear from Component Services. (Use the Refresh command to refresh the display.) Click Publish in the Simple Event Publisher application and you'll notice the message box doesn't appear because there aren't any active subscribers.

Creating a Transient Subscription

The transient subscription portion of the example relies on a local copy of the component we've used in the past. However, except for the use of the local component, most of the process for creating a subscription is the same. Compare the content of Listing 10-6 with Listing 10-5 and you'll see many similarities.

```
private void btnTransient_Click(object sender, System.EventArgs e)
{
   String   IDVal;    // Temporary TransID

   // Get the transient subscription collection.
   SubCollection =
      (ICatalogCollection)ComAdmin.GetCollection(
         "TransientSubscriptions");

   // Create an object of the correct type.
   SendMsg SM = new SendMsg();

   // Depending on the current subscription status, we'll
   // either get a new subscription or free an existing
   // subscription.
   if (btnTransient.Text == "Set Transient")
   {
      // Add a new subscritpion to the transient subscription
      // collection.
      CatalogObject = (ICatalogObject)SubCollection.Add();

      // Set the catalog object values. This list represents a
      // minimal implementation.
      CatalogObject.set_Value(
         "EventCLSID", "{6A121716-471A-479f-B1DE-97858FE95483}");
      CatalogObject.set_Value("Name", "Transient Subscription");
      CatalogObject.set_Value("MethodName", "FireBroadcastMsg");
      CatalogObject.set_Value(
         "InterfaceID", "{0E4DB900-60F3-4354-A89A-C90A962F468C}");
      CatalogObject.set_Value("SubscriberInterface", SM);
      CatalogObject.set_Value("Enabled", true);

      // Save the changes we've made to the transient subscription
      // collection.
      SubCollection.SaveChanges();

      // Change the button caption to match the current subscription
      // status.
      btnTransient.Text = "Release Transient";

      // Save the subscription ID for later use.
      TransID = CatalogObject.get_Value("ID");
   }

   // We need to release an existing subscription.
   else
   {
```

Listing 10-6 A transient subscription example

```csharp
            // Populate the subcollection with existing subscription
            // information.
            SubCollection.Populate();

            // Check each of the subscription items in turn.
            for (int Counter = 0;
                 Counter < SubCollection.Count;
                 Counter++)
            {
                // Get the current catalog object.
                CatalogObject =
                    (ICatalogObject)SubCollection.get_Item(Counter);

                // See if this is the correct catalog object.
                IDVal = (String)CatalogObject.get_Value("ID");
                if (IDVal == TransID.ToString())
                {
                    // Remove the subscription from the list.
                    SubCollection.Remove(Counter);
                    SubCollection.SaveChanges();

                    // Exit the loop.
                    break;
                }
            }

            // Change the button caption to match the current subscription
            // status.
            btnTransient.Text = "Set Transient";
        }
    }
```

Let's discuss the differences between the two techniques. The first thing you'll notice is that this method doesn't parse the COM+ catalog as much—it simply retrieves the *TransientSubscriptions* collection. The code also creates a local copy of the *SubscriberComponent.SendMsg* object. This object is essential for creating a transient subscription, as we'll see later.

Creating the *CatalogObject* is essentially the same. However, notice that this version of the code creates a value for the *SubscriberInterface* property. The property contains a pointer to the local copy of the *SubscriberComponent.SendMsg* object. The common language runtime automatically creates the proper interface for you, so you don't need to worry about passing the managed object. The *Enabled* property is mandatory for this portion of the example since you can't use Component Services to modify this value.

Testing the Transient Subscription

Testing this portion of the code is easy. Begin by clicking Set Transient in the Simple Event Application window. Send a message using the Simple Event Publisher application. You should see a message box displayed with the published message. Click Release Transient, and send the message again. This time you won't see a message box.

To ensure the permanent and transient subscriptions are truly separate, click both Set Permanent and Set Transient. This step creates two subscriptions. Now publish a message. You'll see one message box from the permanent subscription and a second message box from the transient subscription. (You'll have to dismiss the first message box before you'll see the second one.) Click Release Permanent, and then Release Transient. Publish a message, and you'll notice that no message boxes appear.

Summary

This chapter has shown you various techniques for working with COM+ subscriptions from a .NET component and managed application. Subscriptions are exceptionally useful for tasks such as broadcasting data. As you've learned, a subscription is a technique that a publisher (server) uses to communicate event information to subscribers (clients).

One of the best ways to learn about this technology is to spend time creating simple components that output events of various types. You've learned about the essential transaction types in this chapter, but it helps to spend additional time working with the types of events you expect to use in your production applications.

Chapter 11 moves from the desktop to Web-based applications. Some developers might wonder why it's even necessary to consider this scenario given that many companies are moving to Web services. The Web services technology can replace COM+ in many situations. For example, Web services represent a better way to work with direct, real-time communication needs. However, COM+ still has a lot to offer in this area, and you'll find that Microsoft has enhanced COM+ 1.5 to provide better Web services functionality. In general, any time you need to provide subscription-based or non–real time communication, COM+ is the perfect solution for your Web-based application.

11

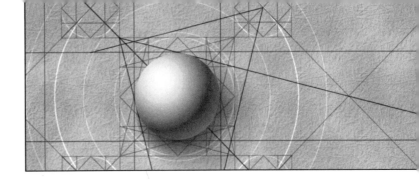

Web Application Scenarios

At some point, you'll want to move an application from the desktop to a Web scenario or create a new application exclusively for a Web environment. You'll find that COM+ is a good choice for some types of Web development. Web sites are becoming increasingly complex as remote users, business partners, and customers ask them to do more for them automatically. The complexity of the new Web pages developers are creating to answer remote access requirements affect remote users. An employee on the road requires full access to company resources, but transferring that data over nonsecure media to a client-side application that doesn't provide great flexibility is a challenge.

We've already looked at several methods for enhancing the remote employee's ability to continue working. For example, the disconnected application in Chapter 9 offers one solution to the problem of keeping employees connected. However, you need to consider what happens if these other solutions won't work for some reason. In some cases, the only real requirement is to provide the remote user with access to information, not the ability to exchange it with the company. In many situations, a Web-based application is the right answer to your application needs. Fortunately, by using COM+ you can augment the capabilities provided by Web-based solutions.

This chapter contains an example of a typical Web-based application that could employ the capabilities COM+ can provide. We're going to create a help-desk type of application that a user on the road can access to resolve problems such as getting orders entered correctly. Such an application could also help the user find small but significant problems on his or her laptop and provide other forms of support as well.

You'll complete this application by learning about four areas of development. The first area is easy—you'll learn about the Microsoft SQL Server 2000 database used for this example. I've already provided everything needed to create it as part of the source code. Help-desk applications often rely on a rule database and an application to perform analysis of a problem the user might be having. Creating the associated analysis component is the second development task. The third development task is creating the Active Server Pages (ASP) script the remote employee will use to interact with the help file and help desk. I chose ASP in this case because the page is so simple and ASP makes it easier to display the code. The fourth development task is to put all the pieces together.

How Do Web-Based Applications Differ?

From a COM+ perspective, Web applications can differ significantly from their desktop counterparts. For example, you'll find that desktop applications are substantially easier to troubleshoot in many cases because all resources required to diagnose the error are local to the application environment (even if the connection exists across a LAN). Web applications also present compatibility problems not found in desktop applications. For example, despite all the time people have spent working on browser compatibility issues, compatibility problems still exist. Where standards do exist, they're often new and untested or poorly worded (leaving some decisions to the imagination of the developer). Creating a stable environment takes more time and is a more significant issue with Web applications.

This section of the chapter discusses some differences between desktop and Web-based COM+ development. We don't intend this section to be a complete list of every problem you'll encounter—think of it more as a listing of the kinds of problems that can occur. In addition, you'll learn a little about the functionality Microsoft continues to add to COM+ to make it a friendlier environment in which to work.

COM+ 1.5 and SOAP

One of the first new features you'll find in COM+ 1.5 is the ability to create a Simple Object Access Protocol (SOAP) setup for your COM+ application. For purposes of discussion, this section relies on the MyMath.dll file discussed in several other chapters (including Chapter 2 and Chapter 5). The version of the MyMath project used for this example appears in the Chapter 11\MyMath folder of the source code.

> **Note** The example in this section will work only on platforms that support COM+ 1.5, such as Microsoft Windows XP and the Windows .NET 2003 server. This example won't work on earlier versions of Windows, including Windows 2000. You must use the MyMath.dll file for this project and not an earlier version. Create the application using the technique found in Chapter 2 rather than the RegSvcs technique. The technique in Chapter 2 creates a COM+ 1.5 application—the RegSvcs technique creates a COM+ 1.0 application, even on platforms that support COM+ 1.5.

You'll begin the project as usual by creating a COM+ application named MyMathApp and installing the MyMath component. Figure 11-1 shows the SOAP configuration setting on the Activation tab of the MyMathApp Properties dialog box. Notice that the figure shows the Uses SOAP option checked and **MyMathMethod** entered in the SOAP VRoot field.

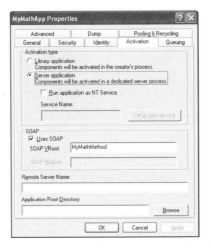

Figure 11-1 Adding support for SOAP to your COM+ application is relatively easy.

When you click Apply, COM+ creates several files for you that become accessible from Internet Information Server (IIS) as an application. Figure 11-2 shows the results of this process. As you can see, the application includes several files and a bin folder.

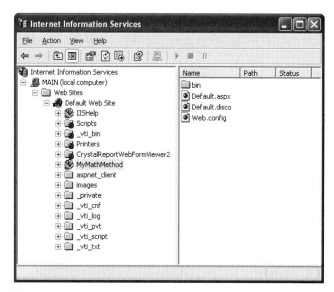

Figure 11-2 Setting the SOAP support options automatically creates some application files for your IIS setup.

Accessing this application displays a simple Web page containing the name of the SOAP application. When you click the MyMath.MathFunctions.soap?WSDL link, you'll see the Web Services Description Language (WSDL) output generated for this application, as shown in Figure 11-3. The WSDL describes the *MyMath.MathFunctions* class and the services it provides.

You can obtain the same output by using the *SoapSuds* utility. This utility accepts various input and generates output using a number of techniques. For this example, it's most convenient to obtain the required information directly from the Web site and place it in an XML file. Here's a typical command line for this utility. (You'll also find the SoapSudsData.bat file in the Chapter 11\MyMath\bin\Debug folder of the source code.)

```
soapsuds -url:http://localhost/MyMathMethod/MyMath.MathFunctions.soap?
WSDL -os:MyMathService.xml
```

Once the Web application is in place, using it is easy. All you need to do is start a new project and create a Web reference by right-clicking the References folder in Solution Explorer and choosing Add Web Reference from the context menu. When you browse to the location that holds the MyMathMethod application, you'll see a list of discovery services for that server. Select the link for the MyMathMethod application and you'll see a service description like the one shown in Figure 11-4. Click Add Reference and your application will have access to this COM+ application through SOAP and the IIS server.

Figure 11-3 The WSDL output of the Web page describes the class and the functionality it provides.

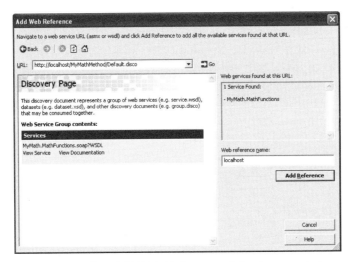

Figure 11-4 The Add Web Reference dialog box can help you locate and use services.

Note that you can always choose to view more information about the features offered by the COM+ application from within the Add Web Reference dialog box. Simply use the same URL you used to view the COM+ application on the Web site using the browser. For example, in the case of this sample application, I used the URL *http://localhost/MyMathMethod/MyMath.MathFunctions.soap?WSDL*. This URL produced the output shown in Figure 11-5.

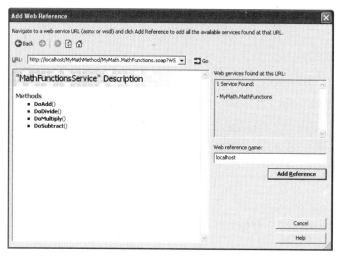

Figure 11-5 You can also view the features provided by an application by using the same URL that the browser provides on the Web site.

A strange thing happens to the *MathFunctions* class as part of its transformation from COM+ application to SOAP application. Figure 11-6 shows that the class now sports two ways of working with the functions. The developer can choose synchronous or asynchronous communication. The SOAP Quick Test application you'll find in the Chapter 11\QuickTest folder of the source code uses both communication methods. You can get the book's companion content from the Web at *http://www.microsoft.com/mspress/books/6426.asp*.

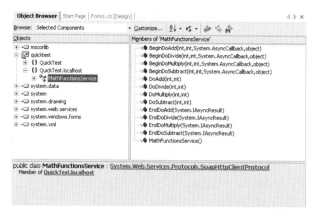

Figure 11-6 The SOAP form of the application has additional functionality not provided by the COM+ version.

This added functionality is a free bonus that you don't have to code. It makes your component just that much easier to use. Listing 11-1 shows the code used with the SOAP Quick Test application.

```
private void btnSynchronous_Click(object sender, System.EventArgs e)
{
   // Get the input.
   int   Input1 = Int32.Parse(txtInput1.Text);
   int   Input2 = Int32.Parse(txtInput2.Text);

   // Create the MathFunctionsService object.
   MathFunctionsService MFS = new MathFunctionsService();

   // Perform a synchronous add.
   int Result = MFS.DoAdd(Input1, Input2);

   // Send the output to the display.
   txtOutput.Text = Result.ToString();
}

private void btnAsynchronous_Click(object sender, System.EventArgs e)
{
   // Get the input.
   int   Input1 = Int32.Parse(txtInput1.Text);
   int   Input2 = Int32.Parse(txtInput2.Text);

   // Create the MathFunctionsService object.
   MathFunctionsService MFS = new MathFunctionsService();

   // Perform an asynchronous add.
   MFS.BeginDoAdd(Input1,
              Input2,
              new System.AsyncCallback(MyCallback),
              null);
}

public void MyCallback(IAsyncResult ar)
{
   // Create the MathFunctionsService object.
   MathFunctionsService MFS = new MathFunctionsService();

   // Obtain the result of the operation.
   int Result = MFS.EndDoAdd(ar);

   // Send the output to the display.
   txtOutput.Text = Result.ToString();
}
```

Listing 11-1 The SOAP Quick Test application

As you can see from the listing, making a synchronous call isn't much different than making a direct call to the COM+ application. (See Listing 8-2 in Chapter 8 for an example of a Visual C++ application that calls the *DoAdd()* method in the MyMathApp COM+ application.) You instantiate the *MathFunctionsService* object and then call the *DoAdd()* method to add the two input numbers. Obviously, the .NET Framework has made it easy for you to make SOAP calls without worrying about the SOAP coding that used to take place.

The asynchronous call is still simple, but it's not quite as straightforward as the synchronous call. The code still begins by instantiating the *MathFunctionsService* object. In this case, the code calls the *BeginDoAdd()* method with the name of the callback method as the third parameter. The *MyCallback()* method follows the format of the *System.AsyncCallback* delegate. The fourth parameter is an optional asynchronous state object you can pass to the callback method—we don't need it in this situation.

The *MyCallback()* method receives an *IAsyncResult* variable, *ar*. This variable actually contains a significant amount of information about the call. However, all we need for this example is the result of the addition. Notice that the code begins by instantiating the *MathFunctionsService* object again. It calls the *EndDoAdd()* method with the *IAsyncResult* variable and converts it to text for display.

COM+ 1.5 and Application Dumps

A new entry on the application Properties dialog box for COM+ 1.5 users is the Dump tab. Figure 11-7 shows what this tab looks like. As you can see, it helps you save a dump of your application to disk. You can load this image of the application into WinDbg for later analysis. (WinDbg, part of the Debugging Tools for Windows, is available on the Web at *http://www.microsoft.com/ddk/debugging/*.) This option is less useful to the managed application developer than it is to the unmanaged application developer, but it's still useful in either case.

Here's the interesting part about this feature. You can set it up to dump the application to disk whenever an error occurs. It won't dump for something minor that you designed your application to handle, but it will create an image for a major fault—normally from an unhandled exception. In sum, this new debugging feature can help create a better environment for your applications. However, it's probably the option of last choice because most developers know that WinDbg isn't an easy debugger to use and definitely won't help much with the managed aspects of your code.

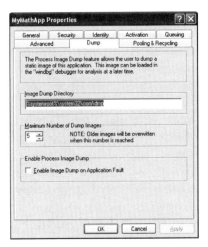

Figure 11-7 Use the Dump tab to save a copy of your application to disk.

You'll want to make a few changes to the setup in most cases. The first change that I make is to modify the Image Dump Directory value. The default setting places the dump in the %systemroot%\system32\com\dmp folder. If I'm at work on an application, I normally place the dump file in a subdirectory of the project folder. Production applications normally have a special folder on the server, so the dump folder also appears in this location.

A second recommended change to the default setup is modifying the Maximum Number Of Dump Images setting. Generally, you'll want a high number for comparison purposes during the development stage—I normally set up my machine for 10 images. Once you have the application debugged, it's unlikely you'll need this feature very often or at all. Given that the average server is a little short on space, clogging the hard drive with extra dumps doesn't make sense. I normally set the number of images to 1, at this point, to save space.

Component Interactions

Many problems developers face are the result of interactions between two application elements. Component interactions can take on a new meaning with Web-based applications. For example, in the application you'll study later in this chapter, there's an ASP script between the client and the server. The ASP script accepts data requests from the client, creates an instance of the required component, formats the data obtained by the component, and outputs it to the client. In short, the client and the server aren't even directly connected. (The same can be said of the SOAP application found in the "COM+ 1.5 and SOAP" section of the chapter—just look at the files shown in Figure 11-2.)

The loss of a direct connection between the client and server can create situations in which the client and server can't communicate well. For example, in preparing the SOAP example for this chapter, I found that an IIS configuration problem caused the MyMath component to fail, although the exact same component works fine when used with a direct COM+ connection. In many cases, the problem is a matter of losing the connection. Because of the way HTML handles components that must be kept alive, the client could lose the context it establishes with the server before the client completes whatever task it needs to accomplish. The point is that you should treat every ASP script query as a new call, even if the Web server keeps the original connection alive.

Scripting also presents other problems. Creating an instance of an object using a script is seldom the same as creating an instance of the same object with a desktop application because of the scripting environment. Consequently, you might find that components won't work at all with your script or that they behave differently than you expect them to. You can get around this problem by thoroughly testing a component during development. Make sure you include scripting tests as part of your test suite. It's also important to make sure the component behaves the same no matter what type of desktop application or script is calling it.

Developers design many components with callbacks in mind. The client makes an initial query, and then the component uses a callback to obtain additional information from the client. Since Web-based applications are unreliable when it comes to communication, it's important to design the component to rely on the client's initial query without any callbacks. In short, always assume the worst-case connectivity scenario and you'll have fewer problems with applications that work fine on the development system but fail when they finally make it to the production system.

Scripting Error Handling

You'll almost certainly rely on scripts, in some way, when working with Web-based applications. In fact, you'll probably need a combination of client-side and server-side scripts to make the application fully functional. Client-side scripts normally don't present much of a problem when it comes to error handling. Either the script works or it doesn't. While the error code the user gets might seem somewhat cryptic, it's usually easy to locate the problem and fix it because client-side scripts are small and usually limited in scope.

Server-side scripts present other kinds of problems. Most scripting languages don't provide error handling. In addition, passing the error information along to the client might prove difficult without a lot of additional coding. Of course, .NET developers have a significant advantage in this area because

ASP.NET provides approximately the same error-handling features that the desktop environment does. In addition, you can use advanced languages such as C# to create your application—a real plus when working with complex applications.

Finally, unlike standard desktop applications or components, many scripting languages provide little access to the event log, denying the developer of even this potential method of recording errors. (Again, using ASP.NET provides the means for creating robust applications that do have access to features such as the event log.) In sum, the developer has to be exceptionally careful when creating the server-side script. Providing range and other non–error producing checks will help reduce problems. If a range or other easily detectable problem is encountered, the script can always provide client feedback in the form of a special Web page.

Fortunately, IIS (at least the versions on Windows 2000, Windows XP, and the Windows 2003 Server) provides rudimentary script-debugging capabilities. Under Windows 2000 you can install this feature separately using the Windows Components Wizard, which is accessed by using the Add/Remove Programs applet in Control Panel. Simply select the Script Debugger option shown in Figure 11-8. For other versions of Windows, you can download the Microsoft Windows Script Debugger from MSDN at *http://msdn.microsoft.com/downloads/default.asp?url=/downloads/sample.asp?url=/msdn-files/027/001/731/msdn-compositedoc.xml*.

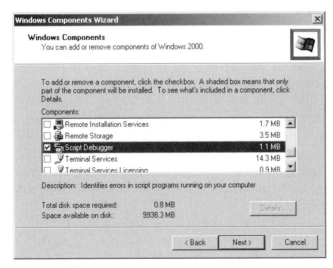

Figure 11-8 Some versions of Windows provide a separate Script Debugger option you can install.

Once you have debugging installed, you'll be able to activate it by clicking Configuration on the Virtual Directory tab of the application Properties dialog box. Select the Debugging tab, and choose the debugging options you want to use. Figure 11-9 shows the required entries. Once you add this feature to your development platform, you'll always be able to debug scripts.

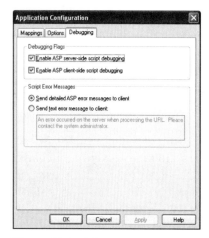

Figure 11-9 IIS provides a script debugger that helps in locating potential problems in your Web-based application scripts.

Human-Language Support

One of the biggest problems you'll run into when working with a Web-based application is the issue of human-language support. The Internet isn't a closed environment. If you plan to make a Web-based application open to the public through the Internet, you'll need to provide support for more than one language.

In many cases, the problem isn't one of translating the content of your Web site. There are many well-understood methods for translating text from one language to another. The main problem is one of application usage. For example, the captions on your application will need to change to support the other languages. You could place the required information in a database that the application could download as needed. The most recently used languages could get stored in a local database or even in the registry.

However, you need to consider even broader issues. For example, the layout of your application must be flexible enough to accommodate the way people normally work, or users will complain the application is difficult to use. This means allowing users to configure the display. While this isn't a problem with most desktop applications, it is a little more difficult with a Web-based application because you don't have control over the position of the various components. In most cases, the best you can do is store the user preferences in a cookie. You can then use the contents of the cookie to configure the display as the application downloads data from the server (or better yet, configure the data at the server).

Accessibility Concerns

Most companies are beginning to realize the importance of making their desktop and Web applications accessible. The creation of new laws requiring accessibility support—such as the Section 508 requirements passed by the US government (*http://www.section508.gov/*)—is one motivation. Sales to those with special needs is another. Enhancing employee productivity is yet another reason companies are making their applications accessible.

When you work with desktop applications, you have good control over the accessibility environment. In fact, the .NET Framework makes it almost too easy to add support for common accessibility features. The user controls these features through the Accessibility Options applet located in the Control Panel. In general, because most of these functions are nearly automatic, COM+ components you create for desktop use are unlikely to change to meet accessibility requirements.

Web applications present new challenges to the COM+ component developer, even if you rely on managed components. For one thing, you no longer have control over the user environment. In addition, the manner in which a particular browser interprets your page is going to be inconsistent with the interpretation by a browser from a different vendor. In many cases, you can avoid adding complicated code to your COM+ application by using smart development techniques for the user interface of your application. For example, the simple act of using Cascading Style Sheets (CSS) can make a significant difference in the complexity of creating an accessible Web application.

Unfortunately, you'll still run into situations where you need to modify the output of the COM+ application to provide additional information to meet accessible application requirements. For example, most accessible application standards require both visual and aural methods of detecting application output. You might find that you need to add extra code to provide the data for both methods.

ASP and Component Communication

One of the ultimate problems with scripting is that you lose the direct connection between the client and the server. The COM+ application might generate an error, but unless the developer who designs the script formats the Web page to pass that error along, the user might never see it. Because a Web-based application normally has a direct connection (you wouldn't create a disconnected application in many cases), it's important to pass any component errors to the client.

Unfortunately, simply passing along the error isn't enough in most cases. The problem is that the user won't know where the problem occurred unless you provide additional information. In most cases, the user will assume an error has occurred locally, unless you make it clear the problem occurred within the component.

Of course, complex applications might have several layers of component calls, and it might be tempting to add code so that the user sees the precise location of the problem. Rather than build overly complex components that do little for the user, it's better to simply report the error as a component error, and then tell the user to contact the network administrator about the problem. An event log entry will allow the network administrator to determine the precise cause of the problem and take steps to fix it.

Defining the Database

As mentioned earlier, the main example for this chapter is a help-desk application, which means we'll need to develop a database. The database will determine what type of information the help-desk application will display. It also determines special component requirements. The database design must consider the following three elements:

- What information you plan to provide to the user
- How you plan to provide the information
- What the formatting requirements are for that data

You can use any database for a help-desk application. For example, if the help-desk application manages a large amount of data, you might want to use a full-fledged database management system (DBMS) such as Microsoft SQL Server 2000. On the other hand, small help-desk applications can rely on something simpler, such as a series of HTML pages accessed through the indexing services provided by IIS. Placing the help pages in a restricted area of the Web site ensures that only authorized personnel can view them and allows you to obtain usage statistics as users make requests.

> **Note** This chapter uses a somewhat compressed set of procedures for building the SQL Server database. These instructions will provide you with all the information required to build the database, associated tables, and indexes, but I'll keep theoretical discussions to a minimum. I also won't talk much about security in this example, but you should always include it as part of your database design. If you want a quick method for creating the database, use the script and delimited text file in the Chapter 11\Scripts and Data folder of the source code. All you need to do to use the script is to load it into a utility such as Query Analyzer and run it.

We'll begin by creating a database for the help desk application. To add a new database, open SQL Server Enterprise Manager and open the hierarchy for the local server. Right-click the Databases folder and choose New Database. Type the name of the database in the Name field, and then click OK to accept the default settings. Double-click the new entry to open it for use. Figure 11-10 shows the details of the HelpMe database. As you can see, this database uses most of the default settings that SQL Server provides. In this case, I decided to allow unrestricted growth and start with a small database size. The reason is simple: a help-desk application will have strictly controlled entries, and the network administrator should be able to keep a close watch on the size of the file. To better control how the file grows, you might want to use the In Megabytes option in the File Growth group. Using this option allows you to specify specific growth intervals for the database.

Figure 11-10 The HelpMe database will use most of the default settings provided by SQL Server.

There's just one table for this example. HelpInformation contains the data the application will display on screen. This includes a help title and associated content, as well as a help topic number used to coordinate various help topics. Figure 11-11 shows the structure of this table. Notice that the TopicNumber field is the primary key for this table.

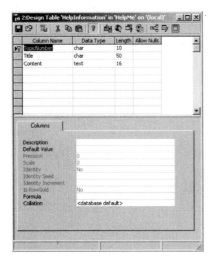

Figure 11-11 A simple table for storing help topics.

Many users will want to search the help desk by topic, so we'll need to add an index to the database. You can add an index to the example for just this purpose. Right-click on the HelpInformation table entry, and choose Manage Indexes from the All Tasks context menu. You'll see a Manage Indexes dialog box like the one shown in Figure 11-12. Notice that this dialog box already contains an index for the primary key and the custom index we'll need for the example.

To create the custom index, click New in the Manage Indexes dialog box to display the Create New Index dialog box. All you need to do is select the Title entry and give the index a name such as TitleSearch. Click OK to create the index, and then click Close to close the Manage Indexes dialog box.

At this point, the design of our table is complete. As you can see, we're using a very simple database design for this application to ensure there are no interactions or other problems to prevent the application from working the very first time. Remember to set security for the table in the example. All you really need to do is ensure you can access the table from an external application.

Figure 11-12 Use the Manage Indexes dialog box to add new indexes to the HelpInformation table.

The final step is creating data for this table. The number of the help title topic has to be unique to ensure the user can individually access each help topic. We'll also want to develop a logical scheme for naming the help topics. The content is the hard part. You need to consider how the client will use the data. For this reason, the text for each Content field entry has to include HTML tags so that the data will appear as the author intended within the target browser. Figure 11-13 shows the sample entries for this example. (See the HelpMe.TXT file for detailed information.)

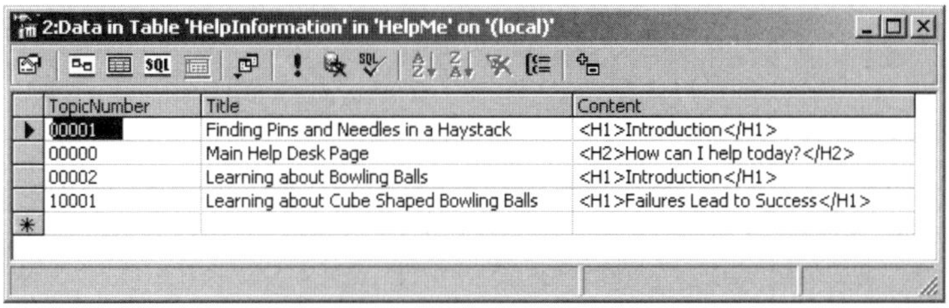

TopicNumber	Title	Content
00001	Finding Pins and Needles in a Haystack	<H1>Introduction</H1>
00000	Main Help Desk Page	<H2>How can I help today?</H2>
00002	Learning about Bowling Balls	<H1>Introduction</H1>
10001	Learning about Cube Shaped Bowling Balls	<H1>Failures Lead to Success</H1>

Figure 11-13 Creating the content for this example means including HTML tags.

> **Tip** Pressing Ctrl+M while in the Data In Table 'HelpInformation' window will allow you to add carriage returns to the end of each line of HTML code. This will make the text more readable when viewed as source code in the browser, making the task of debugging the HTML content easier as well.

Creating the Data Access Component

The COM+ portion of this application comes in the form of a data access component. This component will provide a means for a Web client to access the database. The example doesn't include all the security, integrity, and transactional elements that you'd normally include. However, it does show the mechanics of creating the connection by using a managed component.

Listing 11-2 shows the code for this example. You'll also find the listing in the Chapter 11\HelpAccess folder of the book's companion content. Notice that this example shows how to pass multiple values back to the client—an important technique for anyone who creates components of any complexity. Microsoft Visual Basic developers would replace the C# *ref* keyword with the *ByRef* keyword. The use of the *ref* keyword is required, even though *Strings* are reference variables.

```
[Guid("DF830C4C-7EB0-48ec-BBDE-98DA886AAFCA"),
InterfaceType(ComInterfaceType.InterfaceIsDual)]
public interface IHelpAccess
{
   void GetTitle(ref String strTopicNumber,
                 ref String strTitle,
                 ref String strContents);
   void GetTopic(ref String strTopicNumber,
                 ref String strTitle,
                 ref String strContents);
}

[Guid("C7E5F3CF-043A-439c-8358-3AD9F21FA3A4"),
ClassInterface(ClassInterfaceType.None)]
public class HelpAccess : ServicedComponent, IHelpAccess
{
   public HelpAccess()
   {
   }
```

Listing 11-2 A simple data access component

```csharp
#region IHelpAccess Members

public void GetTitle(ref String strTopicNumber,
                     ref String strTitle,
                     ref String strContents)
{
   SqlConnection  Conn;       // Database Connection
   SqlCommand     Cmd;        // Data Selection
   SqlDataReader  Reader;     // Data Container
   Object         []Data;     // One Row of Data Values

   // Create a connection to the server.
   Conn = new SqlConnection("Initial Catalog=HelpMe;" +
                            "Data Source=WinServer;" +
                            "Integrated Security=SSPI;");

   // Create a command for retrieving the data.
   Cmd = new SqlCommand("SELECT * FROM HelpInformation " +
                        "WHERE Title"="'" + strTitle + "'", Conn);

   // Open the connection and execute the command.
   Conn.Open();
   Reader = Cmd.ExecuteReader();

   // Load the field count from the database.
   Data = new Object[Reader.FieldCount];

   // Determine if the database found the requested information.
   if (Reader.Read())
   {
      // If so, return this information to the user.
      Reader.GetValues(Data);
      strTopicNumber = Data[0].ToString();
      strTitle = Data[1].ToString();
      strContents = Data[2].ToString();
   }
   else
   {
      // Otherwise, return an error message.
      strContents = "Couldn't find the search value: " + strTitle;
      strTopicNumber = "99999";
      strTitle = "Error Finding Value";
   }

   // Close the database connection.
   Cmd.Connection.Close();
}
```

```csharp
public void GetTopic(ref String strTopicNumber,
                    ref String strTitle,
                    ref String strContents)
{
   SqlConnection  Conn;      // Database Connection
   SqlCommand     Cmd;       // Data Selection
   SqlDataReader  Reader;    // Data Container
   Object         []Data;    // One Row of Data Values

   // Create a connection to the server.
   Conn = new SqlConnection("Initial Catalog=HelpMe;" +
                            "Data Source=WinServer;" +
                            "Integrated Security=SSPI;");

   // Create a command for retrieving the data.
   Cmd = new SqlCommand("SELECT * FROM HelpInformation " +
                        "WHERE TopicNumber='" + strTopicNumber +
                        "'", Conn);

   // Open the connection and execute the command.
   Conn.Open();
   Reader = Cmd.ExecuteReader();

   // Load the field count from the database.
   Data = new Object[Reader.FieldCount];

   // Determine if the database found the requested information.
   if (Reader.Read())
   {
      // If so, return this information to the user.
      Reader.GetValues(Data);
      strTopicNumber = Data[0].ToString();
      strTitle = Data[1].ToString();
      strContents = Data[2].ToString();
   }
   else
   {
      // Otherwise, return an error message.
      strContents = "Couldn't find the search value: " +
                    strTopicNumber;
      strTopicNumber = "99999";
      strTitle = "Error Finding Value";
   }

   // Close the database connection.
   Cmd.Connection.Close();
}

#endregion
}
```

The two methods in this component operate essentially the same way. The difference is the value they require as input, the search criteria for the database, and the two values supplied as output. Consequently, I'll describe just one of the methods in the paragraphs that follow.

The code begins by creating a connection to the SQL server. The example uses a simple connection string. You must replace the Data Source value with the name of your own server or the example won't work. Make sure you replace this value in both locations in which it appears (once at the beginning of each method). Normally, you'd check for errors at the end of this call. (In fact, you'd normally perform this operation in a *try...catch* block.)

After the code creates the connection, it creates a command to access the data contained within the database. The formulation of this command is important because it determines the search criteria the database uses to search for the requested data. The code hasn't actually searched for the data yet—it has simply created the command required to perform the task.

At this point, the code opens the connection and executes the command. It still hasn't read the data, but the code has created a *SqlDataReader* object that can perform the task. The *Reader* variable does know the number of fields within the requested table at this point, so the code creates the *Data* array that will hold the information for the requested record upon return from the *Reader.Read()* method call. If the table doesn't contain the requested information, the *Reader.Read()* method returns *false*.

The code is finally ready to retrieve the data values using the *Reader.GetValues()* method. This method places the information from the three fields within the *Data* array. It's important to realize that SQL server doesn't guarantee the data will be returned in any particular order, but it is generally returned in the same order in which the fields appear in the table. When you create complex queries using multiple related tables, always access the field values using specific names rather than the array approach used here. In this case, you'd use the *Reader.GetValue()* method and supply a string containing the requested field name.

Notice that the method returns default values if the database doesn't contain the requested information. At this point, the code closes the database connection and returns the data values to the caller.

Using ASP to Access the Database

The last piece of the application puzzle for this example is the browser support. A browser needs input in the way of HTML and script in order to provide the user with a display. In days past, it would have been possible to create individual Web pages using HTML and links to allow the user to navigate from one portion of the Web site to another. A help-desk application, however, provides too much information of a changeable nature to make individual Web pages a viable solution. That's why you need a combination of HTML, client-side scripting, and server-side scripting to make this type of solution work. As mentioned earlier, I made the design decision to use ASP to provide an easy-to-understand presentation. You could also implement this example using ASP.NET using Code Behind.

This script provides several features that might not be apparent at first. The script allows access to any page in the database using the same URL. The only thing that will change is the variables supplied to the script. If the user passes a *Title* variable, the script will initiate a search of the recordset for a help-desk title. On the other hand, if the user passes a *Topic* variable, the script will initiate a search for that topic number within the recordset. The interface allows the user to save in their Favorites folder help pages that get used a lot, but the use of a consistent URL reduces the chance that broken links will render those Favorites folder entries invalid.

Listing 11-3 contains the ASP code for this example. You can also find the listing in the Chapter 11\SimpleHelpDesk folder of the source code.

```
<%@ Language="VBScript" %>
<HTML>
<HEAD>

<!- Create the help desk object and obtain ->
<!- the current topic or title. ->
<%
    Dim strTopic
    Dim strTitle
    Dim strContents
    Dim DataQuery
    Set DataQuery=Server.CreateObject("HelpAccess.HelpAccess")

    'Determine if we're looking for a title or a topic number.
    'Use the right component method for the type of call.
    If Len(Request.QueryString("Title")) > 0 Then
        strTitle = Request.QueryString("Title")
        DataQuery.GetTitle strTopic, strTitle, strContents
    Else
        strTopic = Request.QueryString("Topic")
        ' Make sure the topic string is set correctly.
        if Len(strTopic) = 0 then
            strTopic = "00000"
        End If
```

Listing 11-3 A simple Help access page

```
        DataQuery.GetTopic strTopic, strTitle, strContents
    End If
%>

<!- Display the current topic title in the titlebar. ->
<TITLE>
    The current topic is: <% Response.Write strTitle %>
</TITLE>

</HEAD>
<BODY ID="ThisPage">

<!-Create a form to display our pushbuttons.->
<FORM NAME="MyForm">

<!- Create the appropriate headings. ->
<H1 ALIGN=center>Welcome to the Help Desk</H1>
<H2 ALIGN=center><B><% Response.Write strTitle %></B></H2>

<!- Display the content. ->
<%
    Response.Write strContents
%>

<!- Provide a place to search by topic. ->
<P><B>Search by Topic:</B><BR>
<INPUT TYPE=text NAME="SearchValue" SIZE=40><P>

<!- Allow the user to search for the topic. ->
<INPUT TYPE=button
       VALUE="Search"
       ONCLICK="window.location.href = 'HelpDesk.asp?Title=' +
                MyForm.SearchValue.value">

<!- Make it easy for the user to get back to the main page. ->
<%
    If Not RTrim(strTopic) = "00000" Then
        Response.Write "<P>Go Back to the "
        Response.Write "<A HREF=HelpDesk.ASP>Main Page</A>"
    End If
%>

</FORM>
</BODY>
</HTML>
```

As you can see, the code begins with the usual HTML tags. One problem ASP.NET solves is the mixture of code and tags shown in this listing. However, given the simplicity of this example, the mixture isn't a problem.

The first scripting task the code will perform is to create three variables to hold the contents of the database fields and make queries. The code also creates an object to hold the *HelpAccess* interface pointer. The *CreateObject()* method instantiates the object and allows the code to make further calls to the component, which will in turn interact with the database we created earlier in the chapter.

The code next determines whether the user has requested the main page by checking for a *Title* variable. If there isn't a title, there must be a *Topic* variable. Even if we're at the main Web page and there isn't any topic number to worry about, the code will create a default topic number value. Notice that the script uses the *GetTitle()* method for a title search and *GetTopic()* for everything else.

After the call to the component completes, we can start displaying information. The title bar will contain the Title field of the table, along with some additional descriptive text. The code uses the *Response.Write()* method to send data to the browser. Because this data is within the <TITLE> tag, it will appear in the title bar.

Creating a form and appropriate headings comes next. Notice that we're using a combination of standard HTML and scripting code here as well.

Finally, the code displays the body of the page. This includes writing the information from the Content field of the database. Remember that this field contains tags that will format the data on screen. Two <INPUT> tags allow us to display a text box and push button for the user to make queries. If this isn't the main Web page, we also want to provide the user with some way to get back to the main Web page. Notice we can use a simple HREF to accomplish this task.

Testing the Application

Testing the example is relatively easy. All you need to do is register the component on the server, place the ASP page in an accessible location of the Web server directory, and point your browser to the correct location. You don't even have to register a proxy on the local machine for this example—all component access occurs on the server.

Figure 11-14 shows the browser output for one of the test pages in the database. Notice that IIS has fully formatted the output. Even the content has the proper formatting because of the tags included within the database table. For example, notice that the word *many* in the description is in bold. Using the database technique presented in this chapter has many advantages because the person creating the content need only access the database, not the Web site.

Figure 11-14 The browser test shows the final output of the Web-based application.

Make sure you perform a reasonable amount of link testing when you initially put the application together. For example, in this case, we'd want to check the ability of the application to get back to the main Web page with a single click, use links that are embedded within the database content, and perform title searches.

Summary

This chapter has helped you learn one way to use COM+ in Web application development. Of course, you can interact with COM+ in a number of other ways. For example, we could have developed the example in this chapter using the SOAP functionality provided with COM+ 1.5. (SOAP functionality isn't available to a COM+ 1.0 user, which means the technique used in this chapter might be the only technique at your disposal.) The point is that COM+ doesn't stop at the desktop—it's a valuable solution for Web applications too.

Now that you have some ideas about how to use COM+ for your next application, it's time to try some of these ideas. Try implementing the example in this chapter for other database application types. For example, simplified versions of contact-management databases often provide a good way to try out COM+ technology because they contain data that's relatively easy to manipulate and check. You'll eventually want to learn how to use a number of data types and how to work with multiple tables. However, you should start small and build your knowledge from there.

Chapter 12 begins a new section of the book. You'll learn about the interoperability requirements for working with COM and COM+. Chapter 12 concentrates on the requirements for using COM. You'll learn about the differences between managed and unmanaged code, how to use P/Invoke in your applications, and about various interoperability concerns for specific languages. In short, Chapter 12 is your introduction to techniques for ensuring you can access everything needed to create complete applications using .NET. Interoperability is an essential part of learning to make COM and .NET work together.

Part IV
Interoperability

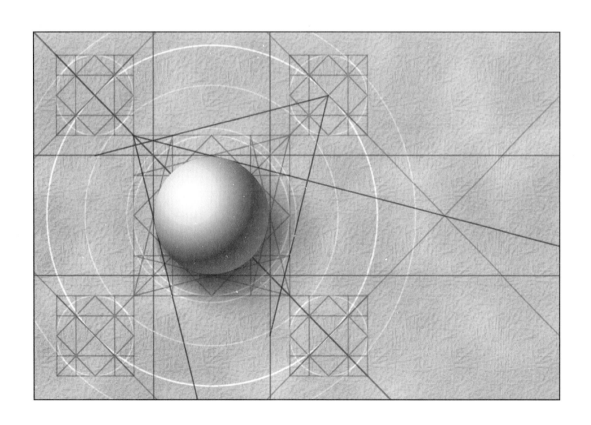

12

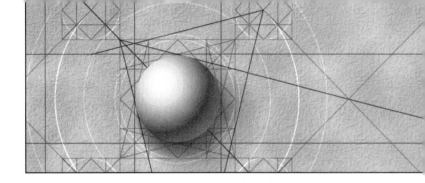

Interacting with Unmanaged Code

This final section of the book addresses interoperability between .NET code and the wider world of Microsoft Windows applications. As you can imagine, .NET code can't live in a vacuum and will have to call (and be called from) code outside the .NET world. Microsoft has put a considerable amount of work into ensuring .NET applications can work simply and effectively with existing Windows code.

This chapter describes the functionality .NET provides for interoperating between *managed code* (which is executed by the common language runtime) and *unmanaged* (or *native*) *code.* In addition to exploring the differences between managed and unmanaged code, this chapter will introduce the Platform Invoke mechanism by which .NET code can interact with unmanaged code. If you've had any experience with using Java JNI (Java Native Interface) to interoperate between Java and C code, you'll see that Platform Invoke is much easier to use.

Interacting with unmanaged code will often involve calling Windows APIs or other functions provided in DLLs. As many of these are C or C++ functions, it is often necessary to pass or receive pointers. Because of the way .NET handles memory, passing pointers to and from unmanaged code can be tricky. To help you accomplish these tasks, this chapter provides an overview of .NET memory management and discusses the language-specific features within C++ and Microsoft Visual C# that are used to work with pointers.

This chapter looks at the basics, and the following chapter will delve more deeply into issues surrounding interoperability and introduce advanced topics.

> **Note** At times, I'll use the term *legacy code*. This word isn't intended to be pejorative. Although it's often used to mean *old-fashioned, out-of-date code*, I'm using the term to mean code you have to use as-is, without being able to rewrite it in .NET. An ActiveX control, for example, might have been written last week, but from the point of view of the .NET programmer, it is legacy code if they have to use it in a .NET project.

Managed and Unmanaged Code

First, let's establish a couple definitions. *Managed code* means code that executes within the .NET environment and is managed by the common language runtime. *Unmanaged code*, also known as *native code*, is ordinary Windows code, which executes outside .NET and doesn't have anything except the operating system controlling it.

The fact that managed code is executed by the runtime has many and far-reaching consequences, particularly in the areas of security and access to resources. What is most important from the point of view of this chapter, however, is the effect the runtime has on memory management.

All memory in managed code is under the control of the common language runtime. Dynamically allocated objects are accessed using references in Microsoft Visual C# and Microsoft Visual Basic .NET, and by using pointers in managed C++. The runtime determines where blocks of memory are allocated and can move them around to manage memory efficiently. The runtime also knows when there are no more references to blocks of memory, and it can reclaim them when the need arises.

The .NET *garbage collector* runs when unused memory needs to be freed up; it can recognize objects that are not being used and reclaim their memory. The garbage collector is discussed in the "Garbage Collection in .NET" section later in the chapter. For now, note that it's usually left up to the system to decide when to do a collection, although a collection can be forced by the programmer by calling the *System.GC.Collect* function.

Unmanaged code, on the other hand, runs outside the .NET environment. This means nothing is responsible for monitoring the execution of unmanaged code or managing memory except the basic mechanisms provided by the operating system. For unmanaged code written in C or C++ (such as the Windows APIs, for example), memory allocation and deallocation is under the control of the programmer. In contrast to .NET, a block of memory always has the same address, and it's up to the programmer to deallocate it when no longer needed.

Manual and Automatic Memory Management

What are the benefits and costs of the automatic memory management provided by a garbage collector compared with the manual method used in C and C++?

Automatic memory management has two main advantages. The first is that you won't get memory leaks because unused memory will always be reclaimed when it's needed. Frequently in C/C++ programs, the programmer will forget to free up memory once it's no longer needed. This results in the program holding on to memory it no longer needs—that is, it has leaked memory. It's common to find C/C++ applications whose memory requirements steadily increase over time because of leaked memory.

The second advantage of automatic memory management is that memory will always be around as long as someone is still using it. If a programmer frees up dynamically allocated memory when it's still required, some other part of the code might try to use memory that has been freed and end up crashing the application. This won't happen if memory is only reclaimed when nobody is using it.

You might wonder why all languages don't use garbage collection. The answer is that manual memory allocation does have some advantages. The first advantage is that it's always possible to know exactly when an object has been destroyed. With garbage collection, you don't know when memory will be reclaimed. The second advantage is that you have control over the amount of memory being used by a process at any one time and can free up memory as soon as it's no longer needed.

Interoperating Between Managed and Unmanaged Code

Because of the differences between .NET code and unmanaged code, a lot of work needs to be done if you are to call unmanaged code from within .NET code.

The .NET Framework provides a set of fundamental data types that can be used by all .NET languages. To pass these data types to and from managed code, they'll need to be *marshaled*. Marshaling is the process whereby method parameters are passed across thread or process boundaries.

Marshaling is done automatically for you for the .NET value types and also for the string type. You'll see later in this chapter how Platform Invoke provides marshaling support and gives you a simple way to access unmanaged functions.

Unmanaged functions often need pointers to objects and data structures, and this has several consequences. The garbage collector compacts memory during a collection run, causing objects to move around during collections. In unmanaged code, pointers are assumed to be fixed, so the runtime must be told not to move the object while it's being used with unmanaged code.

You can define structures in .NET languages, but the runtime reserves the right to lay the structures out in memory in the most efficient way. In other words, you cannot rely on the members of a structure being laid out in memory in the same order as they were defined in the code. This does not matter to .NET client code because the runtime will always access the right member; unmanaged code, on the other hand, assumes the layout of an object in memory matches the definition. For this reason, you can tell .NET that the definition of a structure specifies the layout as well as simply defining the types of the members.

Garbage Collection in .NET

The .NET garbage collector uses references to keep track of allocated memory. When there are no longer any references to an object, the garbage collector marks the object as reclaimable. During a collection, the collector can return to the operating system the blocks of memory used by these reclaimable objects.

The .NET garbage collector uses the Win32 *VirtualAlloc* function to reserve a block of memory for its heap, which is commonly referred to as the *managed heap*. The garbage collector first reserves virtual memory, and then commits the memory as memory requirements grow. The garbage collector keeps track of the address at the end of the managed heap and allocates the next block of memory at this address. By this process, all .NET-managed memory allocations are placed in the managed heap one after another. This method of organization vastly improves allocation time because the garbage collector doesn't have to search through a list of memory blocks for an appropriately sized free block, as normal heap managers do.

Over time, holes begin to form in the managed heap as objects are deleted. When a garbage collection occurs, the collector compacts the heap, filling in holes by moving objects around. This has implications if pointers to managed memory are passed to unmanaged code because the garbage collector might end up moving—or even reclaiming—an object that is being used outside .NET. You'll see later in the chapter how to prevent this from happening.

Generations

In the past, one criticism of garbage collection mechanisms was that they affect the running of an application, often at the least convenient point of execution. Rather than examining every object when a collection occurs, the .NET garbage collector improves performance by dividing objects into *generations*. The garbage collector currently uses three generations, numbered 0, 1, and 2. All newly allocated objects are placed in generation 0. When a collection occurs, objects in generation 0 are examined and unused objects are reclaimed. If this doesn't free enough memory, successively older generations can also be collected.

Objects in generation 0 that survive a managed heap compaction are promoted to generation 1; objects in generation 1 that survive a collection move into generation 2. This use of generations requires the collector to work only with a subset of allocated objects at any one time and therefore decreases the amount of work needed for a collection.

Each generation has a capacity, and a generation will be collected when it becomes full. In .NET Version 1.0, the capacities are 256 KB for generation 0, 2 MB for generation 1, and 10 MB for generation 2. Note that these aren't fixed, and the garbage collector can dynamically adjust these thresholds based on an application's patterns of allocations.

The Large Object Heap

All allocations of 85 KB or larger use a separate heap called the *large object heap*, which is independent from the main managed heap. Using a separate heap for larger objects makes garbage collection of the main managed heap more efficient because collection requires moving memory and moving large blocks of memory is expensive.

In release 1.0 of .NET, the large object heap is never compacted, even when garbage collections occur. This means that if you allocate 5 MB of memory for an object, the large object heap will expand to be 5 MB in size. Even when the object is no longer referenced, the large object heap doesn't decommit the virtual memory and remains at 5 MB. If you allocate a smaller block later on—say 1 MB—the new block will be allocated within the 5 MB allocated to the large object heap. In other words, the large object heap will always grow to hold all the current allocations, but it will never shrink.

Roots

The garbage collector has to know which blocks of memory it can collect. Some collectors use a flag on each allocated block to indicate whether or not the block can be collected. The .NET collector, on the other hand, maintains a tree of references that tracks the objects referenced by the application.

Every .NET application has a set of roots. The root either refers to an object on the managed heap or is set to null. An application's roots include the following:

- Global object pointers
- Static object pointers
- Local variables and reference object parameters
- CPU registers

Figure 12-1 shows a tree of roots for an application. An object that is no longer referenced is not linked into the tree.

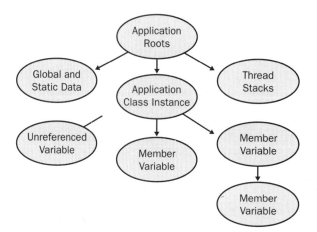

Figure 12-1 The application roots link all the memory used by an application.

An object is *rooted* if at least one parent object holds a reference to it. Before it performs a garbage collection, the collector has to know which objects are still in use. To find these objects, it follows chains of references from the application's roots: every object in a root can reference other objects; these in turn may reference further objects, and so on.

By following these reference chains, the collector can find all the objects that are reachable from the roots. Any objects that do not appear in this list are, by definition, not reachable from any live object. Because these objects cannot be referenced by any application code, it is safe for the collector to release the memory allocated to them. Figures 12-2 and 12-3 show how the heap is compacted during collection and when space allocated to objects that cannot be reached from the roots is reclaimed.

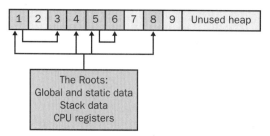

Figure 12-2 Objects 2, 7, and 9 on the managed heap cannot be reached from the application's roots, so they are candidates for garbage collection.

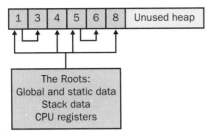

Figure 12-3 After a collection, the heap has been compacted.

Many garbage collectors simply use a flag or a reference count to indicate whether a block of memory is being used. Although that can be more efficient, the .NET approach has an advantage in that it is completely accurate. By following the reference chains from the application roots, the collector ensures that no live objects are collected by mistake.

Objects can be strongly or weakly rooted. A *strongly rooted* object is one to which there is a live reference; the garbage collector will not collect strongly rooted objects. A *weakly rooted* object—also known as a *weak reference*—is one that can be accessed by both the application and the garbage collector. This effectively means that weakly rooted objects can be used until they are collected by the garbage collector. These weakly rooted objects can be useful for data structures that are large but relatively easy to construct. You can create one of these objects and use it; if the garbage collector needs to reclaim memory it will collect the structure, and next time you want to use it, you'll have to rebuild it.

You can find more details of how .NET garbage collection works in the "Garbage Collection" articles Jeffrey Richter wrote for MSDN Magazine, which you can find in the MSDN library at *http://msdn.microsoft.com/msdnmag/find/tech.aspx?phrase=.net*. You might also find useful information in the MSDN article "Production Debugging for .NET Framework Applications," which can be found at *http://msdn.microsoft.com/library/default.asp?url=/library/en-us/dnbda/html/DBGch02.asp*.

Finalization

If a type needs to free up resources—such as sockets or file handles—when instances are destroyed, the programmer can implement *Finalize* and *Dispose* methods for the type.

> **Note** You need these methods only if a type holds unmanaged resources. If a type has references only to other managed types, cleanup will occur automatically.

If implemented for a type, the *Finalize* method is called by the garbage collector when an object is collected. You can't tell when this will happen, so *Finalize* should not be used if it's important *when* resources are freed. When *Finalize* is called, object memory isn't freed until after the next collection, and all child objects are kept alive until that point. In other words, if an object has a finalizer, it will live through one more collection than an object that does not have a finalizer.

The *Dispose* method is part of the *IDisposable* interface. It provides a function that can be called explicitly by the programmer so that an object's resources can be freed at a known point. Resources held by the object will be freed during the call to *Dispose* rather than at the next collection.

When the garbage collector determines which objects aren't reachable from any of the program roots, it places those that have finalizers in the *finalizer queue*. A separate thread is used to walk down this queue, calling *Finalize* on the objects in turn. The programmer has no control over the order in which objects are placed in the queue or when the thread runs. This process has several possible consequences:

- An object could remain in the finalizer queue for some time before its *Finalize* method is called.

- Objects that need to free their resources in a particular sequence might not be able to do so. With this process, you have no idea when finalization will occur relative to other objects in the queue.

- Small objects could hold pointers to large amounts of memory or other resources, and these might not be freed until the object is finalized.

You should not call any methods on other objects in a finalizer, with the exception of base class methods, because you don't know whether the objects you're calling have themselves been finalized yet.

You will often find it far more efficient to implement a *Dispose* method and also provide a finalizer as a backup, in case *Dispose* does not get called. The following sample class definition shows how this can be implemented:

```
class Test : IDisposable {
   private bool bDisposed = false;

   public void Dispose() {
      // Release the resources
      InternalDispose(true);

      // Suppress finalization for this object
      GC.SuppressFinalize(this);
   }
```

```
   protected virtual void InternalDispose(bool bFreeAll) {
      if (bFreeAll) {
         // Free managed resources
      }
      // Free unmanaged resources

      bDisposed = true;
   }

   // Destructor
   ~Test() {
      InternalDispose(false);
   }

   // Methods must check if the object has been disposed
   public void DoSomething() {
      if (bDisposed)
         throw new ObjectDisposedException("Test");
   }
}
```

This class shows a pattern that can be used to construct classes that can be disposed or finalized. The class implements *IDisposable*, which means it needs to provide a public *Dispose* method that takes no parameters. This method should not be declared virtual because derived classes should not be able to override it. Note how *Dispose* calls *GC.SuppressFinalization*. This method removes an object from the finalizer queue and is called here because all resources have been freed, so there is no need for further finalization.

The class also defines a destructor, which will be called when the object is finalized. Both the destructor and *Dispose* use the protected *InternalDispose* method to free up resources. *InternalDispose* takes a Boolean argument. When called by *Dispose*, the argument will be *true* and the method will release all resources held by the object whether they are managed or unmanaged. For managed resources, this will typically be accomplished by calling the *Dispose* method on member objects. If *InternalDispose* is called through the destructor when the object is being finalized, a *false* argument is passed and the method does not attempt to dispose of managed resources, leaving them to be finalized. Derived classes should implement their own *InternalDispose* to free their own resources, and they must call the base class method before returning.

Finally, all class methods must check whether the *bDisposed* flag has been set. If it has, the object is no longer valid for use and an *ObjectDisposedException* should be thrown. Note that the developer has to implement this check in all class methods: there is no way for an object to automatically throw an *ObjectDisposedException* exception.

> ### Destructors in Visual C# and Managed C++
>
> You use the familiar C++ syntax to declare a destructor in both Visual C# and managed C++ classes. These destructors, however, do not operate in the same way as traditional C++ destructors.
>
> You'll find that you cannot override the protected *Finalize* method in Visual C# and managed C++ classes. To provide a finalizer, you implement a destructor in which you implement finalization code. The compiler will convert the destructor into a call to *Finalize*.

Platform Invoke

Platform Invoke (also known as *PInvoke*) is the mechanism by which .NET languages can call unmanaged functions in DLLs. This is especially useful for calling Windows API functions that aren't encapsulated by the .NET Framework classes, as well as for other third-party functions provided in DLLs.

Platform Invoke can be used from any .NET language, and I'll show the basics of invoking unmanaged functions in this section. There are special considerations when using Visual C# or managed C++ to call unmanaged functions, because those languages can use pointers. The two subsections that follow address these specific Visual C# and managed C++ concerns.

Using Platform Invoke involves adding a prototype to your code that uses attributes to tell .NET about the function you're proposing to call. In particular, you need to tell .NET the name of the DLL containing the function, the name of the function, what arguments the function takes, and what the function returns. If you've ever used the *Declare* statement in Visual Basic 6.0 to reference a function in an external DLL, you'll find the way that Platform Invoke operates familiar. Let's look at how Platform Invoke is used from each of the three main .NET languages: Visual Basic .NET, Visual C#, and managed C++.

Using Platform Invoke from Visual Basic .NET

You can use Platform Invoke from Visual Basic .NET in two ways:

- By using the *Declare* statement in a similar way to Visual Basic 6.0
- By applying the *DllImport* attribute to an empty function

Using the *Declare* Statement

The *Declare* statement was present in Visual Basic 6.0, and you can still use it from Visual Basic .NET. The difference is that in Visual Basic .NET the *Declare* statement interfaces with Platform Invoke rather than with a custom Visual Basic mechanism. The following example shows how to use *Declare* to call the Windows *MessageBox* API:

```
Declare Auto Function WinMsgBox Lib "user32.dll" _
Alias "MessageBox" (ByVal hWnd As Integer, _
    ByVal txt As String, ByVal caption As String, _
    ByVal Typ As Integer) As Integer

Sub Main()
    WinMsgBox(0, "Hello", "Testing", 0)
End Sub
```

The *Declare* keyword is followed by one of three values: *Ansi*, *Unicode*, or *Auto*. You'll usually choose *Auto* to let the runtime decide which version of an API to call.

> **More Info** Windows can support more than one type of character encoding—for example, standard Windows 2000 supports both the ASCII (one byte per character) and Unicode (two bytes per character) character encodings. So that code is readily portable between platforms, there needs to be ASCII and Unicode versions of every API function that takes string or character arguments. These versions are identified by an *A* or *W* added to the end of the function name (for example, *MessageBoxW*). You use the root name, such as *MessageBox*, and the compiler decides which underlying function to call based on the character set in use. Although you can specify the version you want, if you use the *Auto* parameter with the *Declare* statement, the compiler will choose the correct version.

The next part of the statement declares either a *Function* or *Sub*, and this is followed by the method name that you're going to use in code—in this case, *WinMsgBox*. Note that this can be the real name of the function and doesn't have to be different. This is followed by the word *Lib* and the name of the DLL that contains the function; this name must be inside double quotes.

The DLL name is optionally followed by an *Alias* declaration. You might want to use another name in your code, and in some cases you might have to. For example, a DLL function might have the same name as a Visual Basic keyword, which means it can't be used as a function name in code. The *Alias* declaration gives the actual name of the function or sub, its arguments and (in the case of functions) its return type.

Using *DllImport*

The *Declare* statement has been provided for backward compatibility with Visual Basic 6.0. In .NET code, it's more usual to use the *DllImport* attribute to access Platform Invoke.

> **Note** The Visual Basic .NET compiler converts *Declare* statements to *DllImport* statements. If you need to use any options available with *DllImport* (described below), you should use *DllImport* directly rather than *Declare*.

Here is the same example, showing how to invoke *MessageBox* using *DllImport*:

```
Imports System.Runtime.InteropServices

<DllImport("User32.dll")> _
Public Shared Function MessageBox(ByVal hWnd As Integer, _
    ByVal txt As String, ByVal caption As String, _
    ByVal typ As Integer) As Integer
End Function

Sub Main()
    MessageBox(0, "Hello again", "Using DllImport", 0)
End Sub
```

When you're using *DllImport*, the function you want to call is implemented as an empty function with the appropriate name, arguments, and return type. This function declaration has the *DllImport* attribute applied to it, which specifies the name of the DLL containing the function. You do not specify a path for the DLL; the runtime will search for it in the normal way, looking in the current directory, the Windows System32 directory, and then along the path.

> **Tip** If the name of the function you want to call clashes with a Visual Basic .NET keyword, you should enclose the function name in square brackets whenever you use it. This will tell the Visual Basic .NET compiler to treat it as a function name rather than a keyword.

Table 12-1 shows parameters that can be provided for *DllImport*.

Table 12-1 Parameters for the *DllImport* Attribute

Parameter	Default	Description
BestFitMapping	*true*	Enables or disables the *best-fit mapping* between Unicode and Ansi characters. When enabled, the interop marshaler will try to find a best match for characters that cannot be directly mapped between Unicode and Ansi.
CallingConvention	*CallingConvention.StdCall*	This parameter is used to show the calling convention of a DLL entry point. The value can be any member of the *CallingConvention* enumeration.
CharSet	*CharSet.Auto*	Indicates how to marshal string data and which entry point to choose when both ANSI and Unicode versions are available. The value can be any member of the *CharSet* enumeration.
EntryPoint	n/a	Specifies the name or ordinal value of the entry point to be used in the DLL. If omitted, the name of the function to which *DllImport* has been applied is taken as the entry-point name.
ExactSpelling	Language dependent. See the "The *CharSet* and *ExactSpelling* Parameters" section for details	Controls whether the compiler will search for *CharSet*-specific entry-point names—for example, *MessageBoxA*.
PreserveSig	*true*	Controls whether conversions are applied to the function signature.

Table 12-1 Parameters for the *DllImport* Attribute

Parameter	Default	Description
SetLastError	*true* in Visual Basic .NET; *false* in other languages	If *true*, indicates that the method being called will call the Win32 *SetLastError* API.
ThrowOnUnmappableChar	*false*	If *false*, unmappable characters are replaced by a question mark (?). If *true*, an exception is thrown when an unmappable character is encountered.

Specifying an Entry Point

The *EntryPoint* parameter can be used to specify the entry point to be used within the DLL. You can use this parameter to specify a function name or an entry point ordinal:

```
' Specify entry point by name
<DllImport("MyDll.dll", EntryPoint="MyFunc")>

' Specify entry point by ordinal. Note the leading #
' sign, which is used to denote an ordinal
<DllImport("MyDll.dll", EntryPoint="#3")>
```

> **More Info** Functions exported from DLLs are usually referred to by name, but it's possible to assign an ordinal number to a function and to use that when calling.

If the *EntryPoint* parameter is omitted, the compiler assumes that the name of the function given in the Platform Invoke prototype is the entry-point name. You can use this parameter to separate the name of the entry point from the name used to call the function.

You will tend to use the *EntryPoint* parameter in two circumstances:

- When the DLL function is called by ordinal number
- When the DLL function does not have a user-friendly name, as is the case with exported C++ member functions

The *CharSet* and *ExactSpelling* Parameters

As I explained earlier, Windows implements two versions of any API function that takes character or string arguments. When you use such an API, the compiler maps the default name (such as *MessageBox*) onto a character set–specific version (*MessageBoxA* or *MessageBoxW*). The *CharSet* parameter controls this mapping process. Its default value is *Auto*, which leaves the compiler to choose which function to call, and there isn't usually any reason to specify any other value.

The *ExactSpelling* parameter controls whether the interop marshaler will perform name mapping. If *false*, the marshaler will convert a default name into a character set–specific version; if *true*, the marshaler will attempt to locate only an exact match for the name given. The default value of *ExactSpelling* is *false* for all languages and character sets, except if *CharSet.Ansi* or *CharSet.Unicode* are used with Visual Basic .NET when the default value is *true*.

The *PreserveSig* Parameter

COM interface methods return *HRESULT*s and can use the *[out,retval]* convention to show that a method can be treated as a function call, with one of the parameters used as the function return value. Methods accessed using Platform Invoke do not normally use *HRESULT*s, so this conversion is not normally needed.

When set to *true*—the default value for Platform Invoke—the *PreserveSig* parameter tells the interop marshaler not to apply the *HRESULT/[out,retval]* conversion to methods.

Handling Errors

Windows API functions use the *SetLastError* API to signal that an error has occurred. Each thread in a Windows application has an error code associated with it, which can be set using *SetLastError* and retrieved using *GetLastError*. Code that uses *SetLastError* must be careful to set a value whether the function succeeds or fails, in case there is a value already set from a previous API call. Client code must be careful to retrieve the error code as soon as possible after making the call, to ensure that it's getting the code that was set by the API. Client code must also remember that the error code is per thread, not per application.

The *SetLastError* parameter to *DllImport* tells the interop marshaler to cache error codes returned by unmanaged functions. The marshaler will call *GetLastError* after the function has executed and cache the value returned. Client code can access this value by calling the *GetLastWin32Error* method.

See the upcoming "Using Platform Invoke from Visual C#" section for a sample program showing how to use *SetLastError* with *DllImport*.

Converting Windows API Parameter Types

Perhaps the main problem with using Platform Invoke is deciding which .NET type to use when constructing the Platform Invoke prototype. Table 12-2 gives the .NET equivalents of the most commonly used Windows data types.

Table 12-2   .NET Equivalents of Windows Data Types

Windows Data Type	.NET Data Type
BOOL, BOOLEAN	*Boolean* or *Int32*
BSTR	*String* (See Chapter 13 for details of string marshaling.)
BYTE	*Byte*
CHAR	*Char*
DOUBLE	*Double*
DWORD	*Int32* or *UInt32*
FLOAT	*Single*
HANDLE (and all other handle types, such as *HFONT* and *HMENU*)	*IntPtr*, *UintPtr*, or *HandleRef* (See the following chapter for a discussion of *HandleRef*.)
HRESULT	*Int32* or *UInt32*
INT	*Int32*
LANGID	*Int16* or *UInt16*
LCID	*Int32* or *UInt32*
LONG	*Int32*
LPARAM	*IntPtr*, *UintPtr*, or *Object*
LPCSTR	*String* (See Chapter 13 for details of string marshaling.)
LPCTSTR	*String*
LPCWSTR	*String*
LPSTR	*String* or *StringBuilder*
LPTSTR	*String* or *StringBuilder*
LPWSTR	*String* or *StringBuilder*
LPVOID	*IntPtr*, *UintPtr*, or *Object*
LRESULT	*IntPtr*
SAFEARRAY	.NET array type (See Chapter 13.)
SHORT	*Int16*
TCHAR	*Char*

Table 12-2 .NET Equivalents of Windows Data Types

Windows Data Type	.NET Data Type
UCHAR	SByte
UINT	Int32 or UInt32
ULONG	Int32 or UInt32
VARIANT	Object
VARIANT_BOOL	Boolean
WCHAR	Char
WORD	Int16 or UInt16
WPARAM	IntPtr, UintPtr, or Object

The marshaling of structures, arrays, and strings is covered in Chapter 13.

Using Platform Invoke from Visual C#

Unlike Visual Basic .NET, Visual C# doesn't have a *Declare* statement, so you have to use the *DllImport* attribute to use Platform Invoke.

The sample program in Listing 12-1 shows how to use Platform Invoke from Visual C# code. See the discussion in the preceding Visual Basic .NET section for details of the parameters that can be used with *DllImport*. You can find this sample in the folder Chapter12\CsLastError in the book's companion content. This content is available from the book's Web site at *http://www.microsoft.com/mspress/books/6426.asp*.

The program calls the *CreateFile* Windows API function to attempt to open a file. If an error occurs, the *FormatMessage* Windows API function is used to print the error message that corresponds to the error code returned by *GetLastWin32Error*.

```
using System;
using System.Runtime.InteropServices;
using System.Text;

namespace CsLastError
{
    class TestPI
    {
        // Flags for use with CreateFile
        // Access modes, from Winnt.h
        const uint GENERIC_READ = 0x80000000;
        const uint GENERIC_WRITE = 0x40000000;
```

Listing 12-1 Class1.cs from the project CsLastError

```csharp
const uint GENERIC_EXECUTE = 0x20000000;
const uint GENERIC_ALL = 0x10000000;

// Creation flags from WinBase.h
const uint CREATE_NEW = 1;
const uint CREATE_ALWAYS = 2;
const uint OPEN_EXISTING = 3;
const uint OPEN_ALWAYS = 4;
const uint TRUNCATE_EXISTING = 5;

// Attribute flags from Winnt.h
const uint FILE_ATTRIBUTE_NORMAL = 0x00000080;

// The Platform Invoke prototype for CreateFile
[DllImport("kernel32.dll",
      CharSet=CharSet.Auto, SetLastError=true)]
public static extern IntPtr CreateFile(
            [MarshalAs(UnmanagedType.LPTStr)]string name,
            uint accessMode, uint shareMode, IntPtr secAtts,
            uint createFlags, uint attributes,
            IntPtr template);

// Flag for use with FormatMessage
public const int FORMAT_MESSAGE_FROM_SYSTEM = 0x00001000;


// The Platform Invoke prototype for FormatMessage
[DllImport("kernel32.dll", CharSet=CharSet.Auto)]
public static extern int FormatMessage(int flags,
            IntPtr source, int messageId,
            int langId, StringBuilder buff,
            int size, IntPtr args);

[STAThread]
static void Main(string[] args)
{
   // See what the current status code is
   int errCode = Marshal.GetLastWin32Error();
   Console.WriteLine(
        "GetLastError when program starts: {0}", errCode);

   // Try to open a file for reading
   IntPtr p = CreateFile(@"c:\temp\test.txt",
                  TestPI.GENERIC_READ, 0, IntPtr.Zero,
                  TestPI.OPEN_EXISTING,
                  TestPI.FILE_ATTRIBUTE_NORMAL, IntPtr.Zero);
```

```csharp
            // Get the status
            errCode = Marshal.GetLastWin32Error();
            Console.WriteLine(
                "GetLastError after call to CreateFile: {0}", errCode );

            // If the status wasn't zero, there is an error
            if (errCode != 0) {
                // Use a StringBuilder to accept an [out] argument
                StringBuilder buff = new StringBuilder(256);
                FormatMessage(TestPI.FORMAT_MESSAGE_FROM_SYSTEM,
                            IntPtr.Zero, errCode, 0,
                            buff, buff.Capacity, IntPtr.Zero);
                Console.WriteLine("Error message: {0}", buff);
            }
        }
    }
}
```

The program starts by defining the flags that are used with the *CreateFile* function. These have been copied from the requisite C header files and converted into C#. This is followed by the prototype for the *CreateFile* API:

```csharp
[DllImport("kernel32.dll",
    CharSet=CharSet.Auto, SetLastError=true)]
public static extern IntPtr CreateFile(
            [MarshalAs(UnmanagedType.LPTStr)]string name,
            uint accessMode, uint shareMode, IntPtr secAtts,
            uint createFlags, uint attributes,
            IntPtr template);
```

The *CreateFile* function can be found in kernel32.dll, and by specifying *CharSet.Auto*, I'm leaving it up to the compiler to sort out which character set to use.

Tip You can find which DLL contains a Windows API function by looking in the Platform SDK online help. At the bottom of the help page for an API function, you'll find the Requirements section; this contains a Library entry that is used to tell C/C++ programmers which link library to use. The root name of this link library is the same as that of the DLL. For example, if the link library is kernel32.lib, you need to specify the kernel32.dll DLL.

We specify the *SetLastError* parameter because this function will use the Windows *SetLastError* API to report error conditions.

The first argument to *CreateFile* is a string, and it has the *MarshalAs* attribute applied to it. This governs how the string is converted when the call is made and will be explained in Chapter 13. You'll also notice that the declaration of *CreateFile* contains several *IntPtr* members. These can be used to represent pointer types when calling unmanaged functions, and they are used for several purposes here:

- The return value from *CreateFile* is a *HANDLE*, which is a *void** pointer, so it can be represented by an *IntPtr*.

- The fourth argument is a pointer to a *SECURITY_ATTRIBUTES* structure. I'm not using this argument when I call the function, so I can specify this as a generic pointer to pass a value of zero when I call the function.

- The final argument is another *HANDLE*, which can be represented by an *IntPtr*.

Note how the function is declared as *extern* so that the compiler knows not to expect an implementation for the function in this class. It also makes sense to declare the function as *static* because the use of the function isn't dependent on an instance of the class.

The next part of the code sets up the Platform Invoke prototype for *FormatMessage*, a Windows API function that can be used to return the error message corresponding to a Windows error code. This function can also be used to construct error message strings from an array of substitution strings. As I'm not using it in this way, there are several arguments that are not used in this program. Once again, *IntPtr*s are used to represent pointer arguments, and this time a *StringBuilder* is used to represent a *String* argument.

In .NET, strings represented by the *String* class cannot be modified, so they aren't suitable for use as output parameters. *FormatMessage* will return a string in the fifth argument, so a *StringBuilder* is used, which will be filled in when the function returns.

The main program tries to create a file that doesn't exist on my machine, so *CreateFile* uses *SetLastError* to set the error code for the thread. Because I specified *SetLastError=true* on the Platform Invoke prototype for *CreateFile*, the interop marshaler caches this value, and I can retrieve it using *Marshal.GetLastWin32Error*. A nonzero value means there is an error, so I use *FormatMessage* to build a string containing the error message, and then print it out.

> **Caution** In .NET code, you should always use the *GetLastWin32Error* function to get the error code. Do not create a Platform Invoke prototype for the Windows *GetLastError* API.

Using Platform Invoke from Managed C++

Platform Invoke is used from managed C++ in a very similar way to the other two languages I've demonstrated. The managed C++ example in Listing 12-2 will illustrate the way in which Platform Invoke is used from C++ by calling the Windows *MessageBox* API and reporting any errors that occur. You can find this example in the Chapter12\InvokeMsgBox folder in the book's companion content.

```cpp
#using <mscorlib.dll>
using namespace System;
using namespace System::Text;

// Needed for interop
using namespace System::Runtime::InteropServices;

// Flags for use with MessageBox
#define MB_OK                   0x00000000L
#define MB_OKCANCEL             0x00000001L
#define MB_ABORTRETRYIGNORE     0x00000002L
#define MB_YESNOCANCEL          0x00000003L
#define MB_NOTAREALFLAG         0x00000999L

// Set up the import
typedef void* HWND;
[DllImport("User32.dll", CharSet=CharSet::Auto, SetLastError=true)]
extern "C" int MessageBox(HWND hw, String* text,
                    String* caption, unsigned int type);

// Flag for use with FormatMessage
const int FORMAT_MESSAGE_FROM_SYSTEM = 0x00001000;

// The Platform Invoke prototype for FormatMessage
[DllImport("kernel32.dll", CharSet=CharSet::Auto)]
extern "C" int FormatMessage(int flags,
            void* source, int messageId,
            int langId, StringBuilder* buff,
            int size, void* args);
```

Listing 12-2 InvokeMsgBox.cpp

```
void main()
{
    String* theText = S"Hello World!";
    String* theCaption = S"A Message Box...";

    // Provide an invalid style parameter
    int nRet = MessageBox(0, theText, theCaption, MB_NOTAREALFLAG);
    if (nRet == 0)
    {
        int nErrCode = Marshal::GetLastWin32Error();
        StringBuilder* pBuff = new StringBuilder(256);
        FormatMessage(FORMAT_MESSAGE_FROM_SYSTEM,
                      0, nErrCode, 0,
                      pBuff, pBuff->Capacity, 0);

        Console::WriteLine("Error from MessageBox: {0}",
                      pBuff->ToString());
    }
}
```

The *MessageBox* API call will return an integer that tells you which button was pressed to dismiss the dialog; a value of zero is returned if there is an error, as you will see if you run the code. The use of *FormatMessage* is almost exactly the same as in the Visual C# example previously shown; the only differences are the use of pointers to managed types and the fact that C++ will allow the use of integer zero for a null pointer and doesn't insist on the use of an *IntPtr*.

Visual C# Concerns

Although C and C++ support the use of pointers, most .NET languages do not. Instead, they use references to access instances of reference types, which only give indirect access to an object and leave the garbage collector free to move the object around in memory.

C# provides a way to work with pointers because Microsoft recognizes several reasons why pointers are useful in C# code:

- You might need to pass pointers to unmanaged functions or COM method calls.

- You might need to interact with a memory-mapped device, which requires I/O to use a particular address.

- References use an extra layer of indirection, so for code that needs maximum efficiency you might want to use pointers.

- You might be converting some code from C or C++ to C# and want to keep as close to the original as possible.

Visual C# code that uses pointers is called *unsafe code* and requires the use of two keywords: *unsafe* and *fixed*. These two keywords were introduced briefly in Chapter 3, and they'll be more thoroughly explained here.

> **Important** Unsafe code results in compiler errors unless the */unsafe* compiler flag is used. If you're using Visual Studio .NET, you can set the unsafe code option on the Configuration Settings tab of the project's Properties Pages dialog box. Command-line compilations should include the */unsafe* flag.

The *unsafe* Keyword

The *unsafe* keyword is used to declare an *unsafe context*. Any operation in Visual C# that involves pointers must take place in an unsafe context. You can use the *unsafe* keyword at several levels in Visual C# code. First you can apply *unsafe* to a class declaration, in which case all the class members are taken to be unsafe. This means that pointers can freely be used within all class methods:

```
public unsafe class UnsafeType
{
   // ...
}
```

You can also apply the keyword to one or more methods within a class:

```
public unsafe void UnsafeMethod()
{
   // ...
}
```

The scope of the *unsafe* keyword is from the point of declaration up to the end of the function; this means you can use pointers as method arguments because the argument list is within the unsafe context.

The third option is to apply *unsafe* to a block of code within a method:

```
unsafe
{
   // Use pointers within this block
}
```

Finally, you can use *unsafe* on Platform Invoke prototype declarations. This is particularly useful when you're calling functions that take pointer arguments because you can specify the pointer type directly and don't have to work out the equivalent managed type. The example in Listing 12-3 shows how to use *unsafe* in this manner. You can find this sample in the Chapter12\CsUnsafe folder of the book's companion content.

```csharp
using System;
using System.Runtime.InteropServices;

public class WinApi {
   // Flags for use with MessageBox
   public static int MB_OK = 0x00000000;
   public static int MB_OKCANCEL = 0x00000001;
   public static int MB_ABORTRETRYIGNORE = 0x00000002;
   public static int MB_YESNOCANCEL = 0x00000003;

   // Note the use of 'unsafe' on the prototype
   [DllImport("User32.dll", CharSet=CharSet.Ansi)]
   public extern static unsafe int MessageBox(int hWnd, char* txt,
              char* caption, int type);
}

class Class1
{
   [STAThread]
   static void Main(string[] args)
   {
      unsafe {
         string sText = "Called from Unsafe Code";
         IntPtr pTxt = Marshal.StringToHGlobalAnsi(sText);
         string sCaption = "Testing...";
         IntPtr pCaption = Marshal.StringToHGlobalAnsi(sCaption);

         int nRet = WinApi.MessageBox(0, (char*)pTxt.ToPointer(),
             (char*)pCaption.ToPointer(), WinApi.MB_OK);
      }
   }
}
```

Listing 12-3 Using *unsafe* on Platform Invoke prototype declarations

The *WinApi* class contains the declaration of the Platform Invoke prototype for *MessageBox*, along with some useful constants. Note how the declaration uses the *unsafe* keyword and how *DllImport* specifies the ANSI character mapping. You'll see why this is necessary very shortly. The second and third arguments for the function can be specified as *char** because the function has been declared as *unsafe*.

Because the function is declared as *unsafe*, it can be called only from within an unsafe context. It would be possible to declare the whole of *Class1* as *unsafe*, but I've chosen to add an unsafe code block to the place where *MessageBox* is actually called. There is a certain amount to be done before the function can be called because of the need to marshal the string arguments. By using pointers, I'm assuming the burden of converting arguments to the right type (for example, *char**) before calling the function; if I had chosen not to use unsafe code, I could have provided a *string* argument and marshaling would have been performed automatically.

String data is passed to this unmanaged function using a pointer. All .NET memory is allocated on the managed heap, which unmanaged applications don't have access to. The unmanaged function expects a pointer to memory it can access, so the string data has to be copied from the managed heap to the unmanaged heap, and this can be done using the *Marshal.StringToHGlobalAnsi* function. This function will take a .NET string, dynamically allocate an appropriately sized amount of unmanaged memory using the Windows *GlobalAlloc* function, and then copy the content of the string into the unmanaged memory.

Note the *Ansi* on the end of the function name. There are also *StringToHGlobalAuto* and *StringToHGlobalUni* versions, but for this example I'm choosing to use the function that converts a string to ANSI (single byte) characters. Using this version means that I need to use the *CharSet* parameter to *DllImport* to tell the interop marshaler to pick the ANSI version of *MessageBox*. If you don't use *CharSet* to specify the ANSI version, the marshaler will pick the Unicode version by default, and this won't display the characters properly.

The *fixed* Keyword

Using references allows the .NET garbage collector to move objects around when it compacts memory during a collection. If you're passing a pointer to a managed object to an unmanaged function, you need to ensure that the garbage collector is not going to move the object while its address is being used through the pointer. This process of fixing an object in memory is called *pinning*, and it's accomplished in Visual C# using the *fixed* keyword. The example in Listing 12-4 shows how to use *fixed*. You can find this example in the Chapter12\CsFixed folder of the book's companion content.

```
using System;

class Class1
{
    // Function to sum the elements in an array
    static unsafe int Sum(int[] arr)
    {
        int result = 0;

        // Pin the array
        fixed (int* pa = &arr[0])
        {
            for(int i=0; i<arr.Length; i++)
                result += *(pa + i);
        }

        return result;
    }

    [STAThread]
    static void Main(string[] args)
    {
        int[] arr = new int[] { 2, 3, 4, 5, 6, 7 };

        Console.WriteLine("Sum = {0}", Sum(arr));
    }
}
```

Listing 12-4 Class1.cs from the CsFixed project

The *Sum* function takes a managed array of *int* as an argument. The *fixed* keyword is used to declare a pointer to a managed variable; declaring a pointer in this way pins the managed variable until the end of the fixed block. Once the end of the block has been reached, the managed variable is unpinned, and the garbage collector is free to move it again.

> **Note** Pinning one element of a managed array will pin the entire array. In more general terms, pinning one member of a type results in the entire instance being pinned. You should, of course, keep objects pinned for as short a time as possible.

The normal C/C++ operators are used to work with pointers: & to take the address of a variable or array element, and * to dereference pointers. Since these operators work with pointers, it is only valid to use them in unsafe contexts. You can also use C-style pointer arithmetic, as shown in the line that increments the *result* variable.

> **More Info** Pointer arithmetic is used to access memory locations in terms of an offset from a starting point. The + and − operators are used to specify whether to move forward or back from the starting point, and the size of the increment or decrement is determined by the pointer type. For example, if *pa* is a pointer to a 4-byte integer, the expression *pa+2* defines an address 8 bytes on from *pa*.

The *stackalloc* Keyword

The *stackalloc* keyword is sometimes used in conjunction with *unsafe*. It allows you to allocate a block of memory on the stack rather than on the heap; because *stackalloc* returns a pointer to the allocated memory, it can be used only in an unsafe context.

Allocating memory on the stack has two effects:

- The memory will automatically be freed at the end of the enclosing block.

- Because the memory is located on the stack, it's not managed by the garbage collector, so it does not have to be pinned.

One advantage of using *stackalloc* is that you can allocate memory to hold an array and access the array elements directly using pointer arithmetic. This will result in much faster array access than using managed array objects. The following function shows how you could declare and use an array using *stackalloc*, and you'll see that you use it in the same way as the *new* operator:

```
public unsafe void MyFunction()
{
    // Stackalloc can only be used in an unsafe context
    int* pa = stackalloc int[100];

    // Use the array
    pa[0] = 10;

    // The memory is deallocated at the end of the function
}
```

Visual C++ Concerns

This section is going to look at interop considerations that apply only to managed C++ code.

Marshaling Argument Types

No marshaling is required between managed and unmanaged types that have the same representation, such as *Int32* and *int*. Other types will need to be converted. Table 12-3 shows how types are represented in the Win32 API, in unmanaged C++, in managed C++, and in the .NET Framework.

Table 12-3 Type Conversion with Platform Invoke

Windows	C++	Managed C++	.NET Framework
HANDLE	void*	void*	IntPtr, UIntPtr
BYTE	unsigned char	unsigned char	Byte
SHORT	short	short	Int16
WORD	unsigned short	unsigned short	UInt16
INT	int	int	Int32
UINT	unsigned int	unsigned int	UInt32
LONG	long	long	Int32
ULONG	unsigned long	unsigned long	UInt32
DWORD	unsigned long	unsigned long	UInt32
FLOAT	float	float	Single
DOUBLE	double	double	Double
BOOL	long	bool	Boolean
CHAR	char	char	Char
LPSTR	char*	[in] String*, [in,out] StringBuilder*	[in] String, [in,out], StringBuilder
LPCSTR	const char*	String*	String
LPWSTR	wchar_t*	[in] String*, [in,out] StringBuilder*	[in] String, [in,out], StringBuilder
LPCWSTR	const wchar_t*	String*	String

Marshaling of structures and arrays is covered in Chapter 13, along with more details of string marshaling.

Pinning

The previous section introduced the concept of pinning—obtaining a pointer to a managed object and telling the garbage collector not to move the object while the pointer is still in scope.

In managed C++, you use the *__pin* keyword to create a pinning pointer from a *__gc* pointer, and the action of creating a pinning pointer pins the object in memory. Listing 12-5 contains an example. You can find this sample in the Chapter12\CppPin folder of the book's companion content.

```cpp
#using <mscorlib.dll>
using namespace System;
#include <iostream>
using namespace std;

// A managed class
__gc class GcClass
{
public:
    int val;
    GcClass(int n) : val(n) {}
};

#pragma unmanaged

void UnmanagedFunction(int* pn)
{
    cout << "n is " << *pn << endl;
}

#pragma managed
void main()
{
    // Create a managed instance
    GcClass* pgc = new GcClass(3);

    // Create a pinning pointer
    GcClass __pin * ppin = pgc;

    // Pass a member to the function
    UnmanagedFunction(&ppin->val);

    // Zero out the pinning pointer
    ppin = 0;
}
```

Listing 12-5 CppPin.cpp

A managed class contains an integer member, whose address I want to pass to an unmanaged function. This means that the address of the managed instance must not change for the duration of the unmanaged function call. I create a pinning pointer, which locks the object in memory, and can then pass the address of a data member to the function. When the pinning pointer is zeroed out—or goes out of scope—the instance will be free to move.

Calling Exported C++ Member Functions

You'll need to take special care when calling functions in DLLs that are class members. When a C++ class member function is compiled, the compiler generates a *mangled name*—a name for the function that encodes its actual name, plus details of the class it belongs to, and its argument and return types. If you use Platform Invoke to call such a function, you'll need to specify the mangled name and use the appropriate calling convention.

Here is an example that shows how to call a C++ member function. First let's look at the declaration of the class and the exported function:

```
class MyClass
{
public:
    int Square(int i) { return i*i; }
};
```

And here is the Platform Invoke prototype you can use to call it:

```
[DllImport("MyDll.dll", EntryPoint="?Square@MyClass@@QAEHH@Z",
    CallingConvention=CallingConvention::ThisCall)]
extern "C" int Square(IntPtr pThis, int i);
```

> **Tip** You can find the exported name of a C++ member function by using the *Dumpbin.exe* utility with the */exports* option to examine the DLL.

The *EntryPoint* parameter gives the exported name of the member function, but the programmer can call it using the more friendly name *Square*. Because the function is a C++ member function but is not static, it needs to be passed a pointer to an object of the appropriate type, which will act as the *this* pointer for the function. You can see the *this* pointer being passed as the first parameter. You also need to choose the correct calling convention: for C++

member functions, this will be the *ThisCall* convention, which assumes that the first parameter in the call will be the *this* pointer.

IJW (It Just Works)

You've seen how Platform Invoke is used to call unmanaged functions from managed code, but many times in managed C++ code this appears to happen automatically. For instance, consider the following class definition:

```
#include <iostream>
using namespace std;

__gc class GcClass
{
public:
   int val;
   GcClass(int n) : val(n)
   {
      cout << "GcClass::ctor" << endl;
   }
};
```

The constructor for the managed class uses unmanaged *iostream* functionality to display a message, without any need for coding Platform Invoke prototypes.

The It Just Works (or IJW) mechanism allows C++ coders to call unmanaged functions in DLLs simply by including the relevant header file and linking with a link library. Because the combination of a header file and link library contains all the information needed by Platform Invoke, in the simplest cases no further work is needed by the programmer.

Simple types will be marshaled automatically, as described in Table 12-3. Sometimes, however, you'll need to marshal data manually. This is especially true where arguments consist of strings, arrays, and structures. Marshaling of these types is covered in Chapter 13.

IJW vs. P/Invoke

Both IJW and Platform Invoke use the same underlying mechanism, but there are some cases when you might prefer one to the other.

The IJW mechanism has several features that might provide an advantage over Platform Invoke in some situations:

- There is no need for Platform Invoke prototypes.

- IJW can be slightly faster than Platform Invoke because the developer will have done any pinning that is needed.
- Marshaling is more explicit, and this can help developers decide on the most efficient marshaling method.
- If you're calling a function more than once, it will be more efficient to marshal the data once and then call it multiple times.

IJW also has some disadvantages:

- Marshaling needs to be specified in code rather than declared by attributes.
- Marshaling code is inline, which might interfere with program logic.
- Marshaling APIs return *IntPtr* for pointers, so extra *ToPointer* calls will be needed to extract the underlying pointer.

The advantages of Platform Invoke can be summarized as follows:

- It works the same way in every .NET language.
- There is no need to write marshaling code.
- It is a simple declarative mechanism.

There are, however, some disadvantages to Platform Invoke:

- Marshaling is performed for every call. This can be wasteful if the same call is being made several times.
- Some functions are not suitable for calling via Platform Invoke. For example, consider an unmanaged function that dynamically allocates memory for a string and returns a *char**. The return type will be mapped onto a *String**, but the caller has no way of deallocating this memory after it has been used. In this case, IJW provides a better mechanism.

C++ is unique in the .NET world, in that it has two separate ways to invoke unmanaged functions. Which method you choose will depend on how you are proposing to use the unmanaged functions that you call.

Summary

This chapter has introduced the Platform Invoke mechanism, which .NET provides to let .NET code call unmanaged functions in DLLs.

Platform Invoke can be used from all .NET languages using the *DllImport* attribute, and you have seen examples of how to do this in Visual Basic .NET, Visual C#, and managed C++. Visual Basic .NET also offers the *Declare* statement as a front end to Platform Invoke, which emulates the Visual Basic 6.0 *Declare* construct. Managed C++ code can use the It Just Works mechanism, which allows C++ developers to call unmanaged functions simply by including header files and linking with the appropriate libraries.

The basics of Platform Invoke presented in this chapter will let you work with a large number of unmanaged functions. Chapter 13 discusses more advanced aspects of interoperability.

13

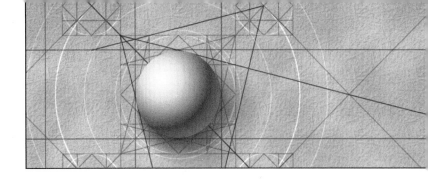

Advanced Interaction

Chapter 12 showed you how to use Platform Invoke to call unmanaged functions defined in dynamic-link libraries (DLLs). For simple functions, the procedures outlined in the previous chapter will work very well, but you will come across cases that demand more advanced techniques.

This chapter will show you how to use unmanaged functions that take string arguments or array arguments, or require pointers to be passed. It will also show you how to pass pointers to managed objects into unmanaged code, and how to specify the path to a Platform Invoke DLL dynamically.

The *MarshalAs* Attribute

You use this attribute to specify how data should be marshaled between managed and unmanaged code when you need to override the defaults. When you're passing a string to a COM method, the default conversion is to a COM *BSTR*; when you're passing a string to a non-COM method using Platform Invoke, the default conversion is to a C-style *LPSTR*. For example, if you want to pass a C-style null-terminated string to a COM method, you will need to use *MarshalAs* to override the default conversion.

You can attach the *MarshalAs* attribute to method parameters and return values, and you always need to specify the type that is to be used for marshaling. The type to be used is represented by a member of the *UnmanagedType* enumeration, whose possible values are shown in Table 13-1.

> **Note** The *MarshalAs* attribute is used in two different scenarios: interacting with COM components using COM interop, and calling unmanaged functions using Platform Invoke. Some of the members listed in the following table will be relevant only to one or other of these scenarios.

Table 13-1 The Members of the *UnmanagedType* Enumeration

Member	Description
AnsiBStr	Used to marshal strings as ANSI *BSTR*s.
AsAny	Determines the type of an object at run time, and marshals the object as the appropriate type.
Bool	Represents a 4-byte Boolean type, equivalent to the Microsoft Windows API *BOOL* type.
BStr	Used to marshal strings as Unicode *BSTR*s. This is the default string marshaling type for string arguments in COM methods.
ByValArray	Marshals an array argument by value. See the "Marshaling Arrays" section that follows for more details.
ByValTStr	Marshals fixed-length character arrays that appear in structures.
Currency	Used to marshal a *System.Decimal* type as a COM currency type instead of as a *Decimal*.
CustomMarshaler	Used to specify a custom marshaler class that will be used to marshal a parameter.
Error	Can be applied to integer types to cause them to be represented as an *HRESULT* in an emitted type library.
FunctionPtr	Represents an integer that can be used as a function pointer. You can use this on a delegate type.
I1	A one-byte integer. This can be applied to managed Boolean arguments to convert them to a one-byte C-style boolean.
I2, I4, I8	Two-, four-, and eight-byte signed integers.
IDispatch	Represents a COM *IDispatch* pointer.
Interface	Represents a COM interface pointer.
IUnknown	Represents a COM *IUnknown* pointer.
LPArray	A pointer to the first element in a C-style array. See the "Marshaling Arrays"" section that follows for more details.

Table 13-1   The Members of the *UnmanagedType* Enumeration

Member	Description
LPStr	Marshals string data as a null-terminated ANSI string.
LPStruct	Represents a pointer to a formatted structure. Used only with Platform Invoke. See the "Marshaling Structs" section that follows for more details.
LPTStr	Represents a platform-dependent string, which will be ANSI on Windows 98 and Windows ME, Unicode on Windows NT, Windows 2000, and Windows XP. This value is used only with Platform Invoke.
LPWStr	Marshals string data as a null-terminated Unicode string.
R4, R8	Represents 4- and 8-byte floating-point values.
SafeArray	Represents a *SAFEARRAY* structure. See the "Marshaling Arrays" section that follows for more details.
Struct	Represents a *VARIANT*.
SysInt, SysUInt	Signed and unsigned integers with platform-dependent size. These will be 4 bytes on 32-bit systems and 8 bytes on 64-bit systems.
TBStr	A length-prefixed, platform-dependent string. This is rarely used.
U1, U2, U4, U8	Represents 1-, 2-, 4-, and 8-byte unsigned integer values.
VariantBool	Represents the OLE *VARIANT_BOOL* type used to represent Boolean values in older COM methods.
VBByRefStr	Represents a string passed by value so that Microsoft Visual Basic .NET can change a string in managed code and have the change propagated back to unmanaged code.

The *MarshalAs* attribute can be applied to a parameter like this:

```
void SomeFunc([MarshalAs(UnmanagedType.LPStr)] string name);
```

The attribute instructs the interop marshaler to marshal the string object as an ANSI null-terminated string.

Marshaling Strings

Strings pose a problem when you're calling unmanaged methods. Most managed types map onto one unmanaged equivalent—for example, a Boolean maps onto a C++ *bool*—but a managed string can map onto several unmanaged types.

When you're calling Windows API functions, a managed string can map onto four unmanaged string types:

- ANSI strings, represented by the *LPSTR* type
- Unicode strings, represented by *LPWSTR*
- System-dependent strings, represented by *LPTSTR*
- COM strings, represented by *BSTR*

> **Note** The system-dependent type, *LPTSTR*, is provided so that the same API function can be used on both Unicode and ANSI systems. *LPTSTR* will be represented by *LPSTR* or *LPWSTR*, depending on whether the ANSI or Unicode version, respectively, of the Windows API function is being called.

The default conversion for managed string arguments depends on the information supplied in the Platform Invoke prototype. As I explained in Chapter 12, the *CharSet* parameter can be used with the *DllImport* attribute to specify which character encoding to use. Table 13-2 summarizes the values that *CharSet* can take and the default values assumed by the .NET programming languages.

Table 13-2 Values for the *DllImport CharSet* Parameter

CharSet Value	Description
Ansi	Marshals strings as ANSI characters. This is the default value for Visual Basic .NET and Microsoft Visual C#.
Auto	Chooses ANSI or Unicode, depending on the target system. The default is ANSI on Windows 98 and Windows ME, and Unicode on Windows NT, Windows 2000, Windows XP, and Windows 2003 Server.
None	This value is obsolete and is equivalent to *CharSet.Ansi*. This is the default value for managed C++.
Unicode	Marshals strings as Unicode characters.

String and *StringBuilder*

When marshaling strings, remember that .NET *System.String* objects are immutable: once created, their content cannot be changed. This means that *System.String* objects can be used only as *[in]* parameters and return values; you should use the *System.Text.StringBuilder* type to represent string arguments that will be marshaled back to the managed caller.

To use a C-style string as a return type from an unmanaged function, you will normally use a managed string, as shown in the following C# code fragment:

```
// Unmanaged function
char* ReturnsAString();

// Platform Invoke prototype
[DllImport("mydll.dll")]
public extern string ReturnsAString();
```

When a return value is marshaled in this way, the interop marshaler will assume that it has to free the unmanaged memory returned by the function once it has created the managed string and initialized it. Occasionally this is not the case: for instance, the *GetCommandLine* API returns a string buffer that is owned by the system and which must not be freed by the caller. In this case, you need to specify an *IntPtr* as the return type. An *IntPtr* is an integer that is large enough to hold a pointer, but the interop marshaler will not automatically treat this as a pointer and will not free the memory it references.

Here is a Visual C# example showing how to return an *IntPtr* and reference the string through the *IntPtr*:

```
// The GetCommandLine API returns a pointer to a buffer
// that is owned by the system, and which must not be
// freed by the caller
[DllImport("kernel32.dll", CharSet=CharSet.Auto)]
public static extern IntPtr GetCommandLine();

// Call GetCommandLine
IntPtr ip = GetCommandLine();
string cmdLine = Marshal.PtrToStringAuto(ip);
```

Note how the *Marshal.PtrToStringAuto* method is used to marshal the data referenced by the *IntPtr* back into a string.

When a string argument to an unmanaged function needs to be marshaled back to the caller, you need to use a *StringBuilder*. In the following example, the *FormatMessage* API builds a string and passes it back in the fifth argument:

```
// The Platform Invoke prototype for FormatMessage
[DllImport("kernel32.dll", CharSet=CharSet.Auto)]
public static extern int FormatMessage(int flags,
            IntPtr source, int messageId,
            int langId, StringBuilder buff,
            int size, IntPtr args);

// Calling the function from C# code
StringBuilder buff = new StringBuilder(256);
FormatMessage(TestPI.FORMAT_MESSAGE_FROM_SYSTEM,
            IntPtr.Zero, errCode, 0,
            buff, buff.Capacity, IntPtr.Zero);
Console.WriteLine("Error message: {0}", buff);
```

A *StringBuilder* object needs to be constructed so that it can be passed to the *FormatMessage* function, and you need to ensure that the object has enough capacity to hold the returned string.

Marshaling Structs

Up to this point, all the Platform Invoke examples have used simple values such as integers and strings. Many unmanaged functions, however, require you to pass structures as arguments.

You can define a managed type that is the equivalent of an unmanaged structure. The problem with marshaling such types is that the common language runtime controls the layout of managed classes and structures in memory. Because you do not reference members by address but by reference, it should not matter to you exactly how the runtime chooses to arrange the type members in memory. The layout does matter, however, when you define a structure that is to be passed to unmanaged code.

The *StructLayout* Attribute

This attribute allows a developer to control the layout of managed types; it is mainly used in interop applications. A *StructLayout* attribute must be initialized with a member of the *LayoutKind* enumeration. The following Visual C# code provides an example:

```
// Use Sequential layout
[StructLayout(LayoutKind.Sequential)]
```

The values defined by the *LayoutKind* enumeration are listed in Table 13-3.

Table 13-3 Values in the *LayoutKind* Enumeration

Member	Description
Auto	The runtime will choose the best layout for the managed type. This value cannot be used on types that are to be used with interop.
Explicit	The position of each member of the type will be specified by using the *FieldOffset* attribute.
Sequential	The runtime will lay out the type members sequentially, in the order in which they are defined.

Three optional parameters can be used with *StructLayout*:

- *CharSet* can be used to specify how string fields within the type are to be marshaled. As with the *DllImport* attribute used by Platform Invoke, this can take the values *Ansi*, *Auto*, or *Unicode*. If *Auto* is specified, the conversion will be platform dependent.

- *Pack* controls the alignment of data fields in memory. The value used with *Pack* must be a value between 0 and 128 that is a power of two. A value of zero indicates the default packing for the platform will be used. If this parameter is not specified, a packing of 4 bytes is used for unmanaged structures (meaning that members can be aligned on boundaries that are multiples of 4 bytes), and 8 bytes is used for managed types.

> **Note** If you don't use packing, structure members will be aligned on *natural boundaries*. This means that members can be placed only at offsets that are a multiple of the member's size—that is, 4-byte integers will be placed at offsets that are multiples of 4, and so on. This can end up leaving unused space in a structure, and packing might help to arrange members more efficiently. When you specify packing, fields align either to their natural boundary or to the pack value, whichever results in the smallest memory use.

- *Size* indicates the absolute size of the type in bytes. This field is mainly used by compiler writers and is not often found in application code.

The following Visual C# code fragment shows how these parameters can be used with *StructLayout*:

```
// Use Sequential layout, with a packing of 8
// and marshal strings as ANSI
[StructLayout(LayoutKind.Sequential), Pack=8,
    CharSet=CharSet.Ansi]
```

Explicit Layout

When you choose explicit layout, you specify the byte offsets of each member of the type, using the *FieldOffset* attribute.

```
// Use Explicit layout in Visual C# code
[StructLayout(LayoutKind.Explicit)]
public struct MyStruct {
   [FieldOffset(2)] public short MemberOne;
   [FieldOffset(5)] public int MemberTwo;
   [FieldOffset(11)] public char MemberThree;
}
```

The memory layout produced by this definition produces a structure 12 bytes in size, which can be seen in Figure 13-1. *MemberOne* occupies two bytes starting at offset 2, *MemberTwo* occupies four bytes starting at offset 5, and *MemberThree* occupies two bytes starting at offset 11.

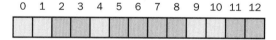

Figure 13-1 Using explicit layout lets a developer control exactly how a structure is laid out in memory.

It should be obvious that the *Pack* parameter isn't applicable when using explicit layout because you are providing all the information necessary for structure layout.

By using an offset of zero for more than one member, you can create a C-style *union*. You can only do this for fields that are blittable types. The following Visual C# example shows how to define a union in this way:

```
// Define a union
[StructLayout(LayoutKind.Explicit)]
public struct MyUnion {
   [FieldOffset(0)] public short arr[2];
   [FieldOffset(0)] public int val;
}
```

Because both members are defined with an offset of zero, they effectively occupy the same memory locations, and the size of the structure is four bytes. For those unfamiliar with C-style unions, this enables you to view the four bytes of memory as either a single *int* or a pair of *short*s.

Handling Nested Structures

Structures are very often built up out of other structures—for example, a *Rectangle* is usually built from two *Point*s. If structures are nested by value, marshaling them is straightforward. Consider the following definitions in C:

```
typedef struct tagPoint
{
  int x,y;
} PNT, *LPPNT;

typedef struct tagRect
{
  PNT p1,p2;
} RCT, *LPRCT;
```

An *RCT* structure contains two *PNT* objects. These can be represented by the following Visual C# structs:

```
// The Point and Rect structures
[StructLayout(LayoutKind.Sequential)]
    public struct Point {
    public int x,y;
}

[StructLayout(LayoutKind.Sequential)]
    public struct Rect {
    public Point p1,p2;
}
```

Note how two *Point* instances can simply be embedded within the *Rect* struct. Using them is also simple. Assume there is an unmanaged C function in a DLL that calculates the area of a rectangle:

```
__declspec(dllexport) int GetArea(LPRCT pRect)
{
    int width =  (pRect->p2.x > pRect->p1.x) ?
                  pRect->p2.x - pRect->p1.x :
                  pRect->p1.x - pRect->p2.x;
    int height = (pRect->p2.y > pRect->p1.y) ?
                  pRect->p2.y - pRect->p1.y :
```

```
                pRect->p1.y - pRect->p2.y;
    return height * width;
}
```

The function simply takes a pointer to a rectangle object and returns its area. A Platform Invoke prototype can easily be constructed and used for this function, as shown in the following Visual C# code fragment:

```
[DllImport("TestInterop.dll")]
public static extern int GetArea(ref Rect rct);
...
Rect r;
r.p1.x = r.p1.y = 10;
r.p2.x = r.p2.y = 15;

int area = GetArea(ref r);
Console.WriteLine("Area is {0}", area);
```

One important point to note about this code is the use of the *ref* keyword, which passes value types by reference rather than by value. It is necessary to use *ref* here because the function is expecting the address of an object.

If a structure contains a pointer to another structure, the situation is slightly more complex. Consider the following two C structures that are used to define a bank account:

```
typedef struct tagPerson
{
    char* firstName;
    char* lastName;
    int age;
} PERSON, *LPPERSON;

typedef struct tagAccount
{
    PERSON* accountHolder;
    char* accountName;
    long accountNumber;
    double balance;
} ACCOUNT, *LPACCOUNT;
```

The *ACCOUNT* class holds a pointer to a *PERSON* object that represents the person owning the account. Using a pointer means, among other things, that one *PERSON* could be associated with several *ACCOUNT*s. To provide a .NET equivalent for use with Platform Invoke, an *IntPtr* should be used to represent the pointer:

```csharp
// The Person structure
[StructLayout(LayoutKind.Sequential, CharSet=CharSet.Ansi)]
   public struct Person {
   public string firstName;
   public string lastName;
   public int age;
}

// The Bank account structure.  Note the use of an IntPtr
// to hold the pointer to the account holder
[StructLayout(LayoutKind.Sequential, CharSet=CharSet.Ansi)]
   public struct Account {
   public IntPtr accountHolder;
   public string accountName;
   public long accountNumber;
   public double balance;
}
```

Note how the *CharSet* parameter is used to set the marshaling type for string members to ANSI; this is needed because the DLL is expecting ANSI characters, but on Windows NT, Windows 2000, and Windows XP systems the default marshaling would use Unicode.

To show how such a structure could be used, suppose that a DLL contains a function that takes a pointer to an account object and returns information about the account in the form of a string:

```c
// Return details for an account, in the form "AccountName (Holder)"
__declspec(dllexport) char* GetAccountDetails(LPACCOUNT acct)
{
   // Allocate a buffer for the return string
   char* buff = (char*) malloc(strlen(acct->accountName) +
      strlen(acct->accountHolder->firstName) +
      strlen(acct->accountHolder->lastName) +
      4);    // terminating null plus two brackets and two spaces

   // Build the return string
   strcpy(buff, acct->accountName);
   strcat(buff, " (");
   strcat(buff, acct->accountHolder->firstName);
   strcat(buff, " ");
   strcat(buff, acct->accountHolder->lastName);
   strcat(buff,")");

   return buff;
}
```

The Platform Invoke prototype is very simple, and the only thing you need to note is that you should use a *ref* parameter so that the address of the *Account* is passed:

```
[DllImport("TestInterop.dll")]
public static extern string GetAccountDetails(ref Account act);
```

Here's a Visual C# example of how you would construct *Person* and *Account* objects and call the function:

```
Person p;
p.firstName = "Fred";
p.lastName = "Smith";
p.age = 45;

Account a;
a.accountName = "Fred's account";
a.accountNumber = 10000;
a.balance = 0.0;

// Allocate memory for a Person
IntPtr ip = Marshal.AllocHGlobal(Marshal.SizeOf(p));

// Marshal the person structure into the memory, but don't delete
// the original
Marshal.StructureToPtr(p, ip, false);

a.accountHolder = ip;

// Make the call
string details = GetAccountDetails(ref a);
Console.WriteLine("Account: {0}", details);

// Free the memory
Marshal.FreeHGlobal(ip);
```

The DLL function is expecting a pointer, and that means the data has to be in unmanaged memory. The *Marshal.AllocHGlobal* method can be used to allocate memory from the unmanaged memory of the process, which is later freed by calling *Marshal.FreeHGlobal*. The Person data is marshaled into the unmanaged memory by calling *Marshal.StructureToPtr*. This method will copy the contents of a managed object into unmanaged memory, performing any necessary marshaling. The third parameter is used to prevent memory leaks.

The *IntPtr* used as an argument could refer to a block of unmanaged memory that itself contains pointers to further unmanaged blocks. If this is the case, these blocks will be orphaned when *StructureToPtr* marshals the new data over the old, resulting in memory leaks. Setting this parameter to *true* will ensure that any existing dynamic memory allocations will be freed up before the call to *StructureToPtr*. In this case, the memory does not contain any pointers, so it is safe to pass *false* as the third argument.

Marshaling Arrays

This section will discuss how to marshal arrays, first when using Platform Invoke and then in COM method calls.

Marshaling Arrays in Platform Invoke

Platform Invoke will take care of the details of marshaling arrays of both blittable and nonblittable types. Arrays are marshaled as *In* parameters by default, which means that the array will be passed by value to the unmanaged function. You can change this behavior by explicitly applying the *In* and *Out* attributes to individual parameters.

Passing Arrays by Value

Many Windows API functions (and third-party DLL functions written in C) will pass array data by value. A typical function signature will look like this:

```
// Pass array by value
void PassArray(short* pArray, int nElements);
```

The first parameter is a pointer to the start of the array, and because a C-style array carries no information about the number of elements it contains, this must be explicitly passed as a second parameter. This function could be used via Platform Invoke in Visual C# as follows:

```
[DllImport("SomeDll.dll")]
public static extern void PassArray(short[] pArray, int nElements);
```

The marshaler will automatically marshal the managed *short[]* array object as an unmanaged C-style array and marshal the values over to the unmanaged function. If you want the function to send values back, you will need to tell the marshaler that it needs to marshal the data in both directions, using the *In* and *Out* attributes:

```
[DllImport("SomeDll.dll")]
public static extern void PassArray(
        [in,out]short[] pArray, int nElements);
```

The unmanaged function can now modify the array elements, and they will be marshaled back to the caller. The unmanaged function cannot, however, change the size of the array.

Passing Arrays by Reference

Arrays can also be passed by reference to unmanaged code:

```
// Pass array by reference
void PassArrayRef(short** ppArray, int* pnElements);
```

In this case, the first parameter is a pointer to a *short**, which means that the *PassArrayRef* function can assign a different value to the *short** at run time. The *pnElements* parameter is also a pointer, which lets the function pass back the number of elements that *ppArray* points to. When you're using Platform Invoke to execute such a function, the first parameter has to be represented by an *IntPtr* because .NET marshaling cannot deal with pointers that have more than one level of indirection:

```
[DllImport("SomeDll.Dll")]
public static extern void PassArrayRef(ref IntPtr ppArray,
    ref int pnElements);
```

Note how the *ref* keyword is used to show that the parameters are being passed by reference. To use this function, you have to marshal the data manually to copy the data into unmanaged memory and create the *IntPtr* needed for the first argument. You also need to marshal the data back into managed memory after the call because Platform Invoke does not know how to deal with the *IntPtr*:

```
// Create and initialize an array
int[] arr = { 1, 2, 3, 4, 5 };
// Get the number of elements for use with Platform Invoke
int nElems = arr.Length;

// Marshal the array into unmanaged memory
IntPtr ip = Marshal.AllocHGlobal(Marshal.SizeOf(int) * nElems);
Marshal.Copy(arr, 0, ip, nElems);

// Call the unmanaged function
PassArrayRef(ref ip, ref nElems);

// Marshal the data back from unmanaged memory
if (nElems > 0) {
    // Create a new managed array
    int[] arr2 = new int[nElems];
    // Copy the data from unmanaged memory
    Marshal.Copy(ip, arr2, 0, nElems);
    // Free the unmanaged memory
    Marshal.FreeHGlobal(ip);
}
```

Marshal.AllocHGlobal allocates unmanaged memory on the Windows heap. The argument is the number of bytes to allocate, and the *Marshal.SizeOf* function can be used to find the size of a managed type or object. *Marshal.Copy* is used to copy the data between managed and unmanaged memory. When the call has been made, the DLL function might have passed back a different buffer, so we need to create a new managed array and copy the data back from unmanaged memory. After copying, the unmanaged memory can be released.

> **Note** If a DLL function allocates memory, you will need to know which mechanism it is using. This example assumes that the Windows *GlobalAlloc* and *GlobalFree* APIs are used; if the COM allocator was used instead, you would have to use calls to *Marshal.AllocCoTaskMem* and *Marshal.FreeCoTaskMem* instead.

Marshaling Arrays in Structures

Unmanaged structures can contain fixed-size embedded arrays, as shown in the following example:

```
struct s1
{
    // An array of 16 longs
    long vals[16];
};
```

When you marshal such an embedded array, you must use the *MarshalAs* attribute to mark the array as *UnmanagedType.ByValArray*, which indicates to the marshaler that it has to pass the array by value. The .NET array declaration will not include any bound information, so you also need to tell the marshaler, by using the *SizeConst* parameter, how many elements it needs to marshal. In Visual C#, you would marshal the preceding example like this:

```
[StructLayout(LayoutKind.Sequential)]
public struct s1
{
    [MarshalAs(UnmanagedType.ByValArray, SizeConst=16)]
        public long[] vals;
}
```

Note that *UnmanagedType.ByValArray* can be used only for embedded arrays.

Marshaling Arrays of Structures

Platform Invoke will happily marshal arrays of structures, with no need for special coding on the managed side. Consider the following unmanaged structure:

```
struct StockItem
{
   long stockNumber;
   int numberInStock;
};
```

This can be represented by the following managed type:

```
[StructLayout(LayoutKind.Sequential)]
public struct StockItem
{
   public long stockNumber;
   public int numberInStock;

   public StockItem(long num, int stk) {
      stockNumber = num;
      numberInStock = stk;
   }
}
```

A constructor is provided to make it convenient to create and initialize instances of the structure. An unmanaged function expects to be passed an array of *StockItem* structures so that it can build a list of items in stock:

```
void SetupStockList(StockItem* pList, int nItems);
```

The Platform Invoke prototype declares an array of *StockItem*s:

```
[DllImport("SomeDll.Dll")]
public static extern void SetupStockList (StockItem[] pList,
   int pItems);
```

The function can be called by simply passing a reference to an array of *StockItem*s:

```
// Create the array of StockItems
StockItem[] theList = {
      new StockItem(123456, 10),
      new StockItem(200001, 3),
      new StockItem(234567, 100),
      new StockItem(301926, 17) };

// Call the function
SetupStockList(theList, theList.Length);
```

Marshaling Arrays in COM Interop

Arrays are more complex to marshal in COM than in Platform Invoke because there are two distinct array types used in COM: C-style arrays and *SAFEARRAY*s.

Passing Arrays to COM

When a .NET object is being used by COM clients, a type library is created to represent the managed object as a COM component. If any exported managed methods contain array parameters, these must be exported in a form that COM can use. We'll consider one-dimensional arrays first. When these are exported, the lower bound is always zero and their size will be known to the marshaler at run time.

The default is to marshal one-dimensional arrays as *SAFEARRAY*s:

```
// Managed function
void MyFunction(short[] theArray)

// Exported definition in type library
HRESULT MyFunction([in] SAFEARRAY(short) theArray)
```

You can use the *MarshalAs* attribute, specifying the type as *UnmanagedType.LPArray*, to marshal the array as a C-style array instead:

```
// Managed function
void MyFunction([MarshalAs(UnmanagedType.LPArray, SizeParamIndex=1)]
short[] theArray, int size)

// Exported definition in type library
HRESULT MyFunction([in] short* theArray, [in] long size);
```

There are several points to note about this code. The *LPArray* type parameter indicates that the array must be passed as a C-style pointer and not as a *SAFEARRAY*. This makes it necessary to tell the marshaler how much data needs to be marshaled, using the second parameter to the *MarshalAs* attribute. I've used the *SizeParamIndex* parameter, which gives the zero-based index of the parameter that will hold the array size at run time. If you've used Interface Definition Language (IDL), you'll recognize this as similar to the IDL *size_is* attribute. If the array is a fixed size, you could also use the *SizeConst* parameter to specify the size.

When a rectangular two-dimensional array is exported to a type library, it is converted to a *SAFEARRAY*, which will contain the bound information for the array:

```
// Managed function
void MyFunction(int[,] arr2d)
```

```
// Exported definition in type library
HRESULT MyFunction([in] SAFEARRAY(long) arr2d);
```

As with one-dimensional arrays, you can also use *UnmanagedType.LPArray* to marshal a managed array as a C-style unmanaged array. Once again, you will need to specify the number of elements using *SizeConst* or *SizeParamIndex* so that the marshaler knows how to marshal the array.

> **Note** You cannot pass ragged arrays (or *arrays of arrays*) to unmanaged code.

Passing Managed Pointers to Unmanaged Code

You will sometimes find that you need to use a pointer to a managed type in unmanaged code. This will normally be a pointer that is passed as an argument to an unmanaged method, but when using C++ you can have managed pointers as members of unmanaged classes. This latter usage is described in the "Using *gcroot* in Managed C++" section that follows.

You know that instances of managed types are controlled by the garbage collector; the reference count on the managed instance reflects the number of clients using the instance, and when the reference count falls to zero the object can be reclaimed by the next garbage collection. Collections can result in objects being moved, but because managed code never deals with the addresses of objects, this does not matter.

When a pointer to a managed object is to be used by unmanaged code, two things must be done:

- The garbage collector must be made aware that there is another reference to the object, even though it cannot *see* the unmanaged client.

- The object must not move or be collected during the time that the unmanaged code is using the managed object. This is done by *pinning* the object: fixing it in memory so that the garbage collector will not move it.

Platform Invoke will handle this for you: when a method takes a managed type as an argument, Platform Invoke will pin the managed object before passing its address to the unmanaged function. This will ensure that the managed object remains at the same address and will not be collected while it is in use in unmanaged code.

The *System.Runtime.InteropServices.GCHandle* (Garbage Collector Handle) class provides a way to use objects safely with unmanaged code when you are not using Platform Invoke. *GCHandle* can be used to provide a *handle* to any .NET object; the handle provides a way to use the managed object in unmanaged code. Table 13-4 shows the members of the *GCHandle* structure.

Table 13-4 The Members of the *GCHandle* Structure

Member	Description
AddrOfPinnedObject	Retrieves the address of a pinned object as an *IntPtr*. This function throws an *InvalidOperationException* if the handle is not a pinned handle.
Alloc	Static method that creates a *GCHandle* to represent a managed object.
Free	Releases a handle. The caller must ensure that this method is called only once on a handle. The method will throw an *InvalidOperationException* if the handle has already been freed or was not initialized.
IsAllocated	Returns *true* if the handle is currently allocated.
Target	Gets or sets the object that this handle represents.

*GCHandle*s are created using the static (*shared* in Visual Basic .NET syntax) *Alloc* method of the *GCHandle* class, as shown in the following fragment of Visual C# code:

```
// Create a normal handle for the managed object myObject
GCHandle gh = GCHandle.Alloc(myObject, GCHandleType.Normal);
```

Four types of handle can be created by *Alloc*. A *normal handle*, *GCHandleType.Normal*, is an opaque handle; this means you cannot take the address of the object to which the handle refers. Normal handles are used when you want to prevent the garbage collector from collecting an object but you do not want to use the object in unmanaged code by taking its address.

A *pinned handle*, *GCHandleType.Pinned*, is similar to a normal handle, but it also allows the address of the object to be taken. For this to work, the object is pinned so that the garbage collector will not move it in memory. Because this reduces the collector's ability to manage its memory, the handle should be freed (via a call to *Free*) as soon as possible. Once you have a pinned handle, you can use the *GCHandle.AddrOfPinnedObject* method to retrieve the object's address.

Note that pinned handles can be produced only for certain types of objects: strings, arrays, and blittable types. You can make managed types blittable by using the *StructLayout* attribute with either the *Explicit* or *Sequential* layout parameters. An *InvalidArgumentException* will be thrown if an invalid type is passed to *Alloc* when creating a pinning handle.

These are the two most common types of handle, but there are two others. A *weak handle*, *GCHandleType.Weak*, is similar to a normal handle, but it does not prevent the underlying managed object from being collected. If the object is collected, the handle will be zeroed out, and this can be tested using the *IsAllocated* property. Finally, a *resurrection tracking handle*, *GCHandleType.WeakTrackResurrection*, will allow the object to be collected, but the handle will not be zeroed out if the object is resurrected. Weak handles will always be zeroed, even if the object is resurrected.

> **Note** Resurrection is a byproduct of the way in which objects are collected by the garbage collector. Chapter 12 described how objects that have finalizers are placed in a special queue; their finalizer methods are run by the finalizer thread, and they are collected the next time the collector runs. When an object is placed in the finalizer queue, it effectively comes back to life—it is resurrected. If the object's finalizer method passes a reference to itself to any other object, the resurrected object will stay alive. You need to be aware, though, that the object's finalizer has already been run and this can cause the object not to behave as expected.

This sample program shows how you can use a *GCHandle* in managed C++ code:

```
#include <iostream>
using namespace std;

#using <mscorlib.dll>
using namespace System;
using namespace System::Runtime::InteropServices;

void main()
{
    // An instance of a managed type
    String* s1 = S"A string";

    // Create a pinned handle
    GCHandle gh = GCHandle::Alloc(s1, GCHandleType::Pinned);
```

```
    // Get the address and cast to a wchar_t
    wchar_t* buff =
      reinterpret_cast<wchar_t*>(gh.AddrOfPinnedObject().ToInt32());

    // Modify the buffer
    buff[2] = L'S';
    wcout << "buffer is '" << buff << "'" << endl;

    // Free the handle
    gh.Free();

    Console::WriteLine("String is {0}", s1);
}
```

A *GCHandle* is represented by an *IntPtr*, so conversion operators are provided to let you convert between the *GCHandle* and *IntPtr* types. A simple cast can be used in Visual C#:

```
// If no handle type is specified, a normal handle is created
GCHandle gh = GCHandle.Alloc(theObject);
IntPtr ip = (IntPtr)gh;
```

In managed C++ and Visual Basic .NET, you need to call the conversion operator method directly:

```
// Managed C++ code
GCHandle gh = GCHandle::Alloc(theObject);
IntPtr ip = GCHandle::op_Explicit(gh);

' Visual Basic .NET code
Dim gh As GCHandle = GCHandle.Alloc(theObject)
Dim ip As IntPtr = GCHandle.op_Explicit(gh);
```

Pinning in Managed C++

Chapter 12 introduced the __pin keyword and explained how it is used in managed C++. Creating a pinned *GCHandle* and using the __pin keyword are both procedures that can be used to pin objects in managed C++ code, but there are differences between them. The first difference is that __pin can be applied to any object type, whereas a pinned *GCHandle* can be created only for strings, arrays, and blittable types.

The second major difference is that the address returned by applying __pin to a *System::String* or *System::Array* object will be different from the one returned by *GCHandle::AddrOfPinnedObject*. The reason for this is that *AddrOfPinnedObject* is intelligent enough to return a pointer to the data buffer inside the string or array object, whereas *__pin* will simply return the address of the object. For other blittable types, *AddrOfPinnedObject* will return the address of the first data member, whereas *__pin* returns the address of the object.

Finally, *__pin* is more efficient than using a *GCHandle* because it is represented by one attribute, whereas creating a *GCHandle* adds the overhead of creating a *GCHandle* instance and calling methods.

Using *gcroot* in Managed C++

Managed C++ is rather unusual among .NET languages in that it allows you to mix managed and unmanaged code within the same application. This feature lets you use managed C++ code as a bridge between managed and unmanaged code.

For example, suppose you have existing C++ code that represents a data feed and fires events when new data arrives. The existing unmanaged code requires client code to implement handler functions and pass the addresses of those functions to the data feed so that they can be used as callbacks. How can you use the data feed code from Visual C# or another .NET language? You can't simply take the address of a C# method and expect unmanaged C++ code to use it as a callback. Even if you could, .NET code expects to use .NET events, not C++ callbacks.

One solution would be to write a managed C++ wrapper class to sit between the unmanaged C++ data provider and the Visual C# client. The managed C++ class implements the callbacks required by the unmanaged code, and its handler functions fire .NET events that can be consumed by Visual C# clients.

One problem with this design is that the unmanaged data provider class will need to hold a pointer to the managed wrapper class so that it can call the callback functions. This is a problem because unmanaged classes cannot contain pointers to managed types:

```
class Unmanaged
{
  Managed* pObj;    // compiler error
  ...
};
```

The reason for this is quite obvious: the unmanaged type is not under the control of the garbage collector, but it holds a reference to a managed type. The collector, then, has no way of knowing when it will be safe to collect the managed object because it cannot tell when the unmanaged object has finished with it.

You saw earlier in the chapter how *GCHandle* can be used to solve this problem. Visual C++ provides a template class, *gcroot*, that wraps a *GCHandle* and makes the handle easier to use. The *gcroot* class is a smart pointer: it takes a managed type as its template parameter and creates a *GCHandle* to represent the managed instance. The smart pointer lets you call managed instance methods through the *GCHandle*, and the handle is destroyed along with the *gcroot* object.

The example in Listing 13-1 shows how *gcroot* can be used. You can find this example in the Chapter13\GcRootDemo folder of the book's companion content.

```cpp
// Include the gcroot header file
#include <gcroot.h>

#using <mscorlib.dll>
using namespace System;
using namespace System::Runtime::InteropServices;

// A managed class
public __gc class Managed
{
   String* name;
public:
   void SetName(String* nm) { name = nm; }
   void SayHello() { Console::WriteLine(S"Hello, {0}", name); }
};

// An unmanaged class that contains a pointer to a managed object
class Unmanaged
{
   gcroot<Managed*> pManaged;
public:

   Unmanaged(Managed* pm, const char* nm) : pManaged(pm)
   {
       pManaged->SetName(nm);
   }

   // Call a function on the managed object
   void Hello() { pManaged->SayHello(); }
};

void main()
{
   // Create a managed object
   Managed* pman = new Managed();
```

Listing 13-1 GcRootDemo.cpp

```
    // Create and initialize an unmanaged object
    Unmanaged unman(pman, "Fred");

    unman.Hello();
}
```

The program defines a managed class that holds a *System::String* as a data member. The *SetName* method provides a way to set the string's value, and the *SayHello* method prints out the current value as part of a message. The unmanaged class uses an instance of *gcroot* to encapsulate a pointer to the managed type, and it uses the *gcroot* instance to call functions on the managed type. Note how an unmanaged *const char** is automatically marshaled to a *System::String* when it is used as the argument to *SetName*.

A closer look at the *gcroot* class shows that it provides the following operations:

- An *operator=* function that allows copying of *gcroot*s

- A conversion operation that allows conversion from the *gcroot* instance to the template parameter type

- The *operator->* function for smart pointer operation

The class makes *operator&* private: client code must not be allowed to take the address of the object and point to it from elsewhere because doing so could have serious consequences for the garbage collector.

Dynamically Loading Platform Invoke DLLs

When constructing a Platform Invoke prototype, you specify the name of the DLL as the first parameter to the *DllImport* attribute, with no path information. The runtime will locate the DLL using the normal DLL location rules: look first in the current directory, and then in the System32 directory, and then along the path.

What if you want to choose the DLL to be used at run time? There are two distinct cases to be considered here, depending on whether you want to specify the path to the DLL named in the Platform Invoke prototype or make a completely dynamic choice of DLL.

Choosing the Path to the DLL at Run Time

The key here is the fact that if a suitably named DLL is already loaded when the external function is executed, Platform Invoke will use the loaded DLL to resolve references. So if you arrange to load the DLL you require before calling a function using Platform Invoke, your chosen DLL will be used rather than another DLL being loaded.

There isn't a method in the .NET Framework for dynamically loading a Windows DLL, so you have to use the *LoadLibrary* Windows API call, which lives in Kernel32.dll. Because this is itself a Windows API call, you need to construct a Platform Invoke prototype for *LoadLibrary* before you can use it. Listing 13-2 is a managed C++ sample program that shows this technique in use. You can find the source for this program in the Chapter13\CppLoadLib folder in the book's companion content.

```cpp
#include "stdafx.h"

#using <mscorlib.dll>
using namespace System;
using namespace System::Runtime::InteropServices;
using namespace System::Text;

// The Platform Invoke prototype for LoadLibrary
[DllImport("kernel32.dll", CharSet=CharSet::Auto, SetLastError=true)]
extern "C" void* LoadLibrary(
    [MarshalAs(UnmanagedType::LPTStr)] String* pLibName);

// Flag for use with FormatMessage
const int FORMAT_MESSAGE_FROM_SYSTEM = 0x00001000;

// The Platform Invoke prototype for FormatMessage
[DllImport("kernel32.dll", CharSet=CharSet::Auto)]
extern "C" int FormatMessage(int flags,
            void* source, int messageId,
            int langId, StringBuilder* buff,
            int size, void* args);

// The DLL to be loaded is called TestDll.dll, but I want to
// specify the path at run time... it isn't in any of the standard
// places
[DllImport("testdll.dll", CharSet=CharSet::Auto)]
extern "C" long Square(short nVal);

void main()
{
    // Load the DLL
    void* pLib = LoadLibrary("c:\\temp\\testdll\\debug\\testdll.dll");
```

Listing 13-2 CppLoadLib.cpp

```
// If there is an error, display the message
if (pLib == 0)
{
    int nErrCode = Marshal::GetLastWin32Error();
    StringBuilder* pBuff = new StringBuilder(256);
    FormatMessage(FORMAT_MESSAGE_FROM_SYSTEM,
                    0, nErrCode, 0,
                    pBuff, pBuff->Capacity, 0);

    Console::WriteLine("Error from LoadLibrary: {0}",
            pBuff->ToString());
    return;
}

Console::WriteLine("Library loaded OK");

// Call the unmanaged function
long lRes = Square(5);
Console::WriteLine("Square of 5 is {0}", __box(lRes));
}
```

The *LoadLibrary* function takes as its only argument a string containing the path to the DLL to be loaded. If the function succeeds, the return value is a handle to the loaded library, which is represented as a *void** pointer; a value of zero indicates the function has failed to load the library. If an error occurs, the *GetLastWin32Error* and *FormatMessage* functions can be used to retrieve the error code and convert it to a message. Once the DLL has been loaded, the Platform Invoke call will use the loaded DLL rather than looking for another one.

One drawback of this method is that the DLL you load must have the same name as the one specified in the Platform Invoke prototype. Because the DLL name must be known at compile time, you cannot use a variable to provide the information at run time.

Fully Dynamic DLL Loading

On occasion, you might need to execute an unmanaged function in a DLL in a completely dynamic manner. Some plug-in architectures allow users to specify a DLL and function to use at run time, so you cannot specify the name of the DLL in a predefined Platform Invoke prototype.

You can, in these situations, load a DLL in a fully dynamic manner by using a .NET Framework feature called *reflection emit*. This advanced feature is used by compiler and tool writers; it provides a way to generate IL code on the fly at run time and either save it to disk or execute it. Reflection emit can be used to create assemblies, modules, and types and is too complex a topic to cover here.

Using Callbacks

Sometimes a DLL function will take a function pointer as one of its arguments; the DLL function can then use the pointer to call back to the client function, thus providing two-way communication. This is a common technique for implementing mechanisms such as event handling and filtering.

> **More Info** Function pointers are used in C and C++ code. A function pointer is the address of a function, and the function can be executed through the pointer. Function pointers are typed, so only addresses of functions with the correct argument list and return type can be assigned to the pointer.

The short C++ program in Listing 13-3 shows a callback in action. You can find this sample in the Chapter13\CppCallback folder of the book's companion content.

```cpp
// Exclude rarely-used stuff from Windows headers
#define WIN32_LEAN_AND_MEAN
#include <windows.h>

#include <iostream>
using namespace std;

// The user-defined callback function
BOOL CALLBACK EWSProc(LPTSTR name, LPARAM lp)
{
   cout << "EWSProc: " << name << endl;
   return TRUE;   // continue enumeration
}

int main(int argc, char* argv[])
{
   // Enumerate window stations
   BOOL bOK = EnumWindowStations(EWSProc, (LPARAM)0);
   cout << "Enum " << ((bOK) ? "OK" : "failed") << endl;

   return 0;
}
```

Listing 13-3 CppCallback.cpp

The *EnumWindowStations* API is used to enumerate the window stations present on a Windows NT, Windows 2000, or Windows XP system. It is typically used to search the list of window stations, looking for one with a particular name.

> **More Info** A window station is a securable object associated with a process, which contains a clipboard, an atom table, and a set of desktop objects. There are three common desktops: the default desktop, the login desktop, and the screen-saver desktop. The default desktop has access to the screen and is used for normal communication with the user. The login desktop is displayed if you press Ctrl+Alt+Del, and the screen-saver desktop is used to run screen savers. The window station for the interactive user is always named Winsta0.

The API takes a pointer to a callback function as its first argument and a user-defined parameter as its second; this second parameter can be anything, but it will often be a string representing the name of the window station that is being looked for. The callback function is called once for each window station; it is passed the name of a window station and the user-defined parameter that was passed to *EnumWindowStations*. If the enumeration is to continue, the callback should return *TRUE*; if no more enumeration is needed, the function should return *FALSE*. Running the program should give output similar to the following, although the number of window stations enumerated—and their names—will vary:

```
EWSProc: WinSta0
EWSProc: Service-0x0-3e7$
EWSProc: Service-0x0-3e4$
EWSProc: Service-0x0-3e5$
EWSProc: SAWinSta
EWSProc: __X78B95_89_IW
Enum OK
```

Although function pointers are peculiar to C and C++ and can't be used directly from other languages, DLL functions that use callbacks can be called from any .NET language using *delegates*. If you haven't met delegates before, you will find a brief description in the following section.

Introduction to Delegates

A *delegate* is the .NET equivalent of a C/C++ function pointer. Delegates have several advantages over function pointers, the main one being that they are language independent, whereas function pointers can be used only from C or C++ code.

In simple terms, a delegate is an object that can call a function for you. Delegates are perhaps most easily explained through an example, so here is a Visual Basic .NET program that shows how to create and use a delegate:

```
Module Module1
    ' Define a delegate to call a trig function
    Public Delegate Function TrigDelegate( _
        ByVal angleInRadians As Double) As Double

    ' A trig function
    Public Function Sin(ByVal angleInRadians As Double) As Double
        Return Math.Sin(angleInRadians)
    End Function

    Sub Main()
        ' Create a delegate bound to the Sin function
        Dim del As New TrigDelegate(AddressOf Sin)

        Dim d As Double = del(1.0)
        Console.WriteLine("Sin of 1.0 radians is {0}", d)
    End Sub
End Module
```

The delegate definition is introduced with the *Delegate* keyword; apart from that, it is a normal function definition. The arguments and return value of the delegate define which functions it will be able to call: in this case, the delegate can call any function that takes a *double* as an argument and returns a *double*.

The delegate is followed by the definition of a trigonometric function that returns the sine of an angle. Notice how the signature of this function matches that of the delegate. To use the delegate, create a new *TrigDelegate* object and pass in the address of the *Sin* function. This binds the function to the delegate and ensures that when the delegate is executed, the *Sin* function will get called. You can now use the delegate in exactly the same way as you would the *Sin* function; the delegate calls the *Sin* function for you, passing in the argument and returning the result.

One characteristic of delegates that distinguishes them from function pointers is that a delegate object can be bound to more than one method at once. On the next page is an example in Visual C# that shows this.

```csharp
using System;

namespace CsDelegate
{
    class Class1
    {
        // Delegate definition
        public delegate double TrigDelegate(double angleInRadians);

        // Two trigonometry functions
        public static double Sin(double angleInRadians) {
            double d = Math.Sin(angleInRadians);
            Console.WriteLine("Sin of 1.0 radians is {0}", d);
            return d;
        }

        public static double Tan(double angleInRadians) {
            double d = Math.Tan(angleInRadians);
            Console.WriteLine("Tan of 1.0 radians is {0}", d);
            return d;
        }

        [STAThread]
        static void Main(string[] args)
        {
            // Create delegates to call Sin and Tan functions
            TrigDelegate delTrig1 = new TrigDelegate(Class1.Sin);
            TrigDelegate delTrig2 = new TrigDelegate(Class1.Tan);

            // Combine the two delegates
            delTrig1 += delTrig2;

            // Execute the delegate
            double d = delTrig1(1.0);
        }
    }
}
```

When the *delTrig1* delegate is executed, the *Sin* and *Tan* methods will both be called, and they will be called in the order in which the delegates were added together.

Using Delegates for Callbacks

Now that you've seen what delegates are and how they work, let's look at how you'd use them to implement callbacks. When calling a function that uses callbacks from unmanaged C++, you supply the name of the function as an argument; in managed code, you simply supply the name of a delegate instance.

The Visual C# program in Listing 13-4 shows how you can provide a callback function using delegates. The application performs the same task as the C++ *EnumWindowStations* example in the previous section, so you can compare how the two approaches work. You can find this sample in the Chapter13\Delegates folder of the book's companion content.

```csharp
using System;
using System.Runtime.InteropServices;

namespace Delegates
{
    class Class1
    {
        // Delegate used to represent callback function
        public delegate Int32 EnumWinStaDelegate(
            [MarshalAs(UnmanagedType.LPTStr)] string name,
            IntPtr lparam);

        // Platform Invoke prototype for EnumWindowStations
        [DllImport("user32.dll", CharSet=CharSet.Auto)]
        public static extern Int32 EnumWindowStations(
                EnumWinStaDelegate callbackfunc, IntPtr lparam);

        // Delegate instance
        static EnumWinStaDelegate del;

        // The callback function that is bound to the delegate
        static Int32 Callback(string name, IntPtr lparam) {
            // Get the string back from the IntPtr
            string sp = Marshal.PtrToStringAuto(lparam);

            if (name.Equals(sp))
                Console.WriteLine(
                    "Found required WinStation: {0}", name);
            else
                Console.WriteLine("WinStation: {0}", name);

            return 1;    // non-zero equates to true
        }

        [STAThread]
        static void Main(string[] args)
        {
```

Listing 13-4 The Class1.cs file from the Delegates sample

```
            // Create the delegate, and bind it to the callback
            // function
            del = new EnumWinStaDelegate(Callback);

            // Call the function, passing in the name of the
            // WinStation we want to look for
            string s = "WinSta0";
            IntPtr ip = Marshal.StringToHGlobalAuto(s);

            Int32 result = EnumWindowStations(del, ip);
            if (result != 0)
               Console.WriteLine("Enum OK");
            else
               Console.WriteLine("Enum failed");

            // Free the memory used to marshal the string
            Marshal.FreeHGlobal(ip);
         }
      }
   }
```

The delegate *EnumWinStaDelegate* is defined to represent the callback function. Looking at the C prototype for the function, you can see that the arguments are an *LPTSTR* and an *LPARAM*. A string can be used for the first argument, with an appropriate *MarshalAs* attribute to control how it is marshaled. An *LPARAM* is simply a pointer, so it can be represented by an *IntPtr*. The Platform Invoke prototype for the *EnumWindowStations* function is simple; you will need to specify *CharSet.Auto* so that the correct character mappings are used for the call and callback.

A delegate object is created at the start of the main program and bound to the callback function; this is equivalent to assigning an address to a function pointer in C++. It is then simply a matter of calling the *EnumWindowStations* function, passing in the name of the delegate, and passing in the name of the user-defined parameter cast to an *IntPtr*. To pass a string as the second parameter, the string needs to be marshaled to a type acceptable to unmanaged code. *Marshal.StringToHGlobalAuto* allocates memory from the Windows heap using *GlobalAlloc*, and then copies the content of the string into unmanaged memory, returning an *IntPtr* that represents the allocated memory. The callback function takes the *IntPtr* and uses *Marshal.PtrToStringAuto* to marshal the unmanaged data back into a string again. This string can then be compared with the one passed in as the first parameter to see whether the named window station can be found.

Garbage Collection Considerations

The previous section showed how to use a delegate to provide a managed equivalent of a callback. Although this is a useful technique, there is a potential problem with this code. The delegate object *EnumWinStaDelegate* is used by the unmanaged function *EnumWindowStations*, and unmanaged code is invisible to the .NET garbage collector. If the unmanaged function is the only code using the delegate, no references are held on the delegate object by managed code. This means the object might get collected if the garbage collector performs a collection. As far as the collector is concerned, the object is unused.

This problem particularly affects delegates because the garbage collector has no way of knowing when unmanaged code has finished with the delegate object. Premature garbage collection doesn't tend to affect COM objects because the COM *AddRef/Release* mechanism provides a way for unmanaged client code to signal that a managed object is no longer required.

Using the *KeepAlive* Method

The *System.GC.KeepAlive* method can be used to prevent an object from being garbage collected, even if there are no references to it in managed code. Here is an example of how it could have been used in the previous example to prevent the delegate object from being prematurely collected:

```
static void Main(string[] args)
{
   // Create the delegate, and bind it to the callback
   // function
   del = new EnumWinStaDelegate(Callback);

   // Call the function, passing in the name of the
   // WinStation we want to look for
   string s = "WinSta0";
   IntPtr ip = Marshal.StringToHGlobalAuto(s);

   Int32 result = EnumWindowStations(del, ip);
   if (result != 0)
      Console.WriteLine("Enum OK");
   else
      Console.WriteLine("Enum failed");

   // Guard the delegate object
   GC.KeepAlive(del);

   // Free the memory used to marshal the string
   Marshal.FreeHGlobal(ip);
}
```

You might think something looks wrong with this code because the call to *KeepAlive* is placed *after* the call to the unmanaged function that uses the object you want to protect. This placement is used because *KeepAlive* is used in a rather unusual manner: Instead of being treated as a normal function call, a *KeepAlive* statement signals to the runtime that the variable passed in as an argument must be kept alive—not garbage collected—until after the *KeepAlive* statement. The bottom line is that we need to place a call to *KeepAlive* after the Platform Invoke call for it to work correctly.

Using the *HandleRef* Type

You'll encounter another circumstance in which you might need to protect against objects being collected at the wrong time. Many resources used or provided by the Windows operating system are represented by *handles*. Examples include files, threads, and registry keys. Sometimes you will need to use .NET objects that wrap these handles, such as a *FileStream* object that wraps a handle to a file. You want to protect against the possibility that the objects that you use to hold these handles in your managed code are garbage collected during the execution of a lengthy Platform Invoke call.

Such handles will often be represented by *IntPtr* objects, as shown by the following Platform Invoke prototype for the Windows *ReadFile* API function:

```
// Visual C# Platform Invoke prototype
[DllImport("kernel32.dll")]
public static extern bool ReadFile(
    IntPtr handle,              // the file handle
    StringBuilder buff,         // buffer to receive data
    int nToRead,                // number of bytes to read
    out int nRead,              // number actually read
    in Overlapped flag          // overlapped structure
);
```

The function could be used like this:

```
// Create a FileStream
FileStream fs = new FileStream("Test.txt", FileMode.Open);
// Create a buffer of 100 characters
StringBuilder buff = new StringBuilder(100);

// Call ReadFile
int numRead = 0;
ReadFile(fs.Handle, buff, 100, out numRead, 0);
```

The *Handle* member of *FileStream* returns the file handle as an *IntPtr* so that it can be passed to *ReadFile*. But the *IntPtr* handle is used only by the unmanaged *ReadFile* function, so there are no managed references to it. It is therefore possible that the handle object would be collected if the garbage collector performed a collection while the call to *ReadFile* is executing.

Although you could use *GC.KeepAlive* to protect the handle, the *System.Runtime.InteropService.HandleRef* type provides a neater alternative for this situation. As the name implies, a *HandleRef* is a type that wraps a handle in a managed object so that the handle has at least one managed reference. You can use a *HandleRef* object wherever you would have used an *IntPtr* to represent a handle. Here is how you would use a *HandleRef* with the call to *ReadFile*:

```
// Create a FileStream
FileStream fstm = new FileStream("Test.txt", FileMode.Open);
// Create a buffer of 100 characters
StringBuilder buff = new StringBuilder(100);

// Create a HandleRef
HandleRef href = new HandleRef(fstm, fstm.Handle);

// Call ReadFile using the HandleRef
int numRead = 0;
ReadFile(href, buff, 100, out numRead, 0);
```

The *HandleRef* constructor takes two arguments: a reference to the managed object to be kept alive, and an *IntPtr* representing the unmanaged handle held by the object. The *HandleRef* object will ensure that the object it is wrapping will not be garbage collected until the *HandleRef* is destroyed.

Performance Considerations

Finally, a word about the performance of Platform Invoke. Each individual Platform Invoke call has an overhead of between 10 and 30 x86 instructions. In addition to this, extra costs will be incurred if parameter data has to be marshaled. There is no marshaling cost between blittable types that have the same representation in managed and unmanaged code (for example, a C++ *int* and a *System.Int32*), but there might be significant cost involved when marshaling other types, such as strings and arrays.

You will get better performance if you have as few Platform Invoke calls as possible, and if these calls marshal as much data as possible.

If you know that there is no possibility that the unmanaged routines you are calling could perform any damaging operations, you can switch off the runtime security checks by using the *SuppressUnmanagedCodeSecurity* attribute. Under normal circumstances, calls into unmanaged code cause a security check to ensure that every routine in the call chain has *UnmanagedCode* permission.

This obviously imposes an overhead on the call, and can be switched off using *SuppressUnmanagedCodeSecurity*. Using this attribute places the burden of security back onto the programmer, and of course, you'll only ever want to use it if you find that security checking is adding unacceptable overheads.

```
// Suppress security checking
[DllImport("MyDll.dll", CharSet=CharSet.Auto),
     SuppressUnmanagedCodeSecurity]
public static extern void SomeFunction();
```

As a final performance tip, note that it is possible to load DLLs and locate routines before any Platform Invoke calls are made. Normally the Platform Invoke prototype is evaluated, DLLs are loaded, and routines located on the first call to a routine. The *System::Runtime::InteropServices::Marshal* class contains two methods that let you preload DLLs for use with Platform Invoke methods: *Prelink* and *PrelinkAll*. The *Prelink* method takes a *MethodInfo* object that describes the method to be invoked by Platform Invoke, and then verifies the Platform Invoke prototype, loads the DLL, and verifies that it contains the requested method. *PrelinkAll* is similar, in that it calls *Prelink* for all the methods on a given class.

Summary

This chapter has shown you some of the complexity that can arise when using Platform Invoke to call unmanaged code. You have seen how to control the way in which strings, arrays, and structures are passed between managed and unmanaged code, and you have been introduced to the *MarshalAs* attribute and its uses.

C++ poses particular problems when interacting between managed and unmanaged code because of its use of pointers. The chapter discussed the use of the *GCHandle* type and the *gcroot* template class, and it showed how you can make sure managed objects will not be collected by the garbage collector when they are being used only in unmanaged code.

Most Platform Invoke calls are defined at compile time, but you saw how to influence the choice of DLL, and I mentioned that it is also possible to completely build a Platform Invoke method at run time.

The next chapter completes our look at interoperability by showing how you can work with predefined COM interfaces by defining managed equivalents.

14

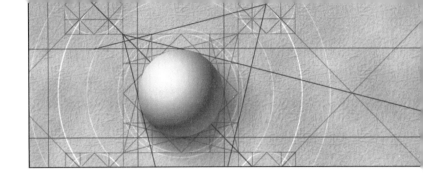

Working with Predefined Interfaces

One question we haven't really considered to this point is the effect of predefined interfaces on your managed component development. A predefined interface is one in which the interface is already defined and in use. For example, *IUnknown* is the predefined interface that every COM component supports.

We'll discuss the implications of predefined interfaces on development in this chapter. You'll learn why they're important and what you can do to create them in a managed component. This chapter will also show you some of the tools you have at your disposal for working with predefined interfaces. For example, we'll discuss the OLE/COM Object Viewer—an essential tool for discovering the intricacies of predefined interfaces.

The final sections of this chapter will show how to work with predefined interfaces in your components. You'll find that working with predefined interfaces, even those you have to discover by using documentation and other sources, is easy once you break the problem into manageable pieces.

COM Requires Specific Interfaces

An essential trait of every component and control you create is their support of specific interfaces. The interface is a contract between the client and the server that specifies the server will provide certain functionality. When the client implements the interface, it's accepting the contract and uses the functionality provided by the server. This part of the theory hasn't changed much since Microsoft first introduced COM and is unlikely to ever change.

Now, however, you're working in the managed environment—an environment that exists outside of the COM environment. We've seen throughout the book that this isolation can cause certain problems and requires you to perform certain tasks to ensure your code will work as anticipated. For example, in most cases, the common language runtime will marshal data between the two environments automatically, but at times you will have to perform this task yourself. Listing 8-3 (from Chapter 8) demonstrates how this works, as the code imports a Win32 API function and uses specific techniques to marshal data for this call. (You can find many other examples of this kind of activity throughout the book.)

The developer who writes applications that require services from a component has an advantage, in most cases, because the interfaces required to use a component or control from an application are well known and completely documented. However, what happens when you begin working with a container application? The Microsoft Management Console (MMC) is such an application. It provides no functionality on its own—the functionality resides within the MMC snap-ins (components created especially for MMC). The MMC snap-ins enable the user, network administrator, and developer to perform a myriad of tasks using essentially the same user interface for every task. Container applications such as MMC often reduce the learning curve required to use an application. Using a container application definitely reduces developer work because the developer doesn't have to worry about the user interface—only the interfaces between the component and the container are important.

To create a component for MMC, you have to define specific interfaces and that means you have to learn what MMC expects. When you insert an MMC snap-in into MMC, the container application looks for specific interfaces in that MMC snap-in and calls the functions they contain. You can't even display a component in MMC without defining certain interfaces. In sum, your component has to implement an interface that the .NET Framework might not know about to interoperate with this container application.

You need to consider special interfaces in all kinds of circumstances. For example, a component that provides access to text in a file might have to implement the *IDocument* interface. Whether it does or not depends on what the container application expects to access on the component.

> **Tip** You can find everything you need to know to implement specialized components for many Microsoft products if you know where to look. For example, the interfaces used to create an MMC snap-in appear in the MMC-Related COM Interfaces help topic at http://msdn.microsoft.com/library/en-us/mmc/mmc/mmc_related_com_interfaces.asp. You'll see that the list isn't very long. You'll find a list of the basic MMC snap-in types and the required interfaces (some interfaces are optional) at http://msdn.microsoft.com/library/en-us/mmc/mmc/snap_in_modes_and_required_interfaces.asp. The list of required interfaces tells you what you must implement to create even a simple MMC snap-in.

The interfaces you must implement aren't always clear initially. For example, an MMC snap-in must implement the *IComponent* interface. It might appear simple at first, but we're not talking about the *IComponent* interface that comes with the .NET Framework—you must implement the *IComponent* interface for the unmanaged environment. Listing 14-1 shows the definition for the unmanaged *IComponent* interface.

```
/// <summary>
/// This interface allows communication between MMC
/// and the snap-in at the view level.
/// </summary>
[ComImport,
 InterfaceType(ComInterfaceType.InterfaceIsIUnknown),
 Guid("43136EB2-D36C-11CF-ADBC-00AA00A80033")]
public interface IComponent
{
   void Initialize(
      [MarshalAs(UnmanagedType.Interface)]Object lpConsole);
   [PreserveSig()]
   RESULT_VAL Notify(IntPtr lpDataObject,
            MMC_NOTIFY_TYPE aevent,
            Int32 arg,
            Int32 param);
   void Destroy(Int32 cookie);
   void QueryDataObject(Int32 cookie,
                  DATA_OBJECT_TYPES type,
                  out IDataObject ppDataObject);
```

Listing 14-1 Unmanaged version of the *IComponent* interface

```
            [PreserveSig()]
            RESULT_VAL GetResultViewType(Int32 cookie,
                            out IntPtr ppViewType,
                            out Int32 pViewOptions);
            void GetDisplayInfo(ref RESULTDATAITEM ResultDataItem);
            [PreserveSig()]
            RESULT_VAL CompareObjects(IDataObject lpDataObjectA,
                            IDataObject lpDataObjectB);
         }
```

As you can see, this interface bears little resemblance to the .NET Framework version. A look at the .NET Framework documentation shows that the managed version of *IComponent* exposes only one property, *Site*, and one event, *Disposed()*. We'll discuss this code more in the "Re-creating COM Interfaces Using Managed Code" section of the chapter. For now, however, you need to realize that creating interfaces for container applications requires a certain amount of detective work in some cases.

You'll find one additional lesson in the code shown in Figure 14-1 that will be covered in this section of the chapter. Notice that the *CompareObjects()* method includes an additional interface (two variables that use the same interface) as input. The documentation doesn't list the interface as an essential MMC snap-in interface because Microsoft wrote the documentation with unmanaged component development in mind. The fact remains that you must implement the *IDataObject* interface within the MMC snap-in because the component will require the functionality the interface provides. This is an admittedly complex example, but the lesson it provides is important. The interface you implement because you can see it easily might have functions that rely on other interfaces you can't see during the initial research for the component. In summary, you might initially think that a component requires three or four interfaces and later in the project find that it requires a far greater number.

Using the OLE/COM Object Viewer

As previously mentioned, every component or control you create relies on interfaces of some sort. At the very least, a component or control must implement the *IUnknown* interface. An interface is a technique for bundling methods in a way that's independent of programming language. When a client needs access to an interface that it knows exists on the server, it queries that interface and accepts a pointer to it. The client uses the interface by calling the methods that it contains.

Most development languages today hide the gory details of interface interaction from the programmer. In most respects, the simplification of interface use is good because it boosts developer productivity and reduces the number of bugs in the resulting application. However, one problem with this approach is that many developers don't realize that interface access is also a process of manipulating pointers. You saw how important it was to know this when working through the Microsoft Visual C++ examples in this book, which showed that Visual C++ still requires thorough knowledge of interface operations.

Whether or not you know how an interface works, the concept of the interface is still important. You need to know which interfaces a component provides to interact with that component. Microsoft Visual Studio provides a handy utility, named OLE/COM Object Viewer, which you can use to view these interfaces in more detail. (Some releases of Visual Studio shortened the name to OLE View). We'll use this utility several times in this chapter, so you might want to install it if you haven't done so already.

> **Note** As your copy of Visual Studio gets older, so do the tools that came with it. In many cases, you'll want to obtain updates for those tools as needed to ensure the tool provides everything needed—this is especially true of the OLE/COM Object Viewer because Microsoft updates this tool regularly. You can obtain this update from the main COM Web site at the URL *http://www.microsoft.com/com/resources/downloads.asp*. This section of the chapter uses the latest version of the OLE/COM Object Viewer at the time of writing (version 2.10.059). Some screen shots in this book might look slightly different from the ones you'll see when using an older version of the product. Because the latest version of the OLE/COM Object Viewer fixes several important problems with previous versions of the product, you'll want to download and install the latest version of the product as quickly as possible.

A Quick Overview of Interfaces

It's important to understand how the OLE/COM Object Viewer can help you during the development process. Suppose you want to find out about the interfaces provided by the MyMath component that we've discussed several times in this book. The OLE/COM Object Viewer could help you find out about those interfaces and the associated entries in the registry. Even if you're familiar with the registry entries for an unmanaged component, it pays to look at the managed component entries because they're different.

> **Note** The version of the MyMath component used in this section is the one found in the Chapter11\MyMath\bin\Debug folder of the book's companion content. If you use one of the other versions, the interfaces will vary from those shown in this section. You also need to unregister previous versions of the component that you might have installed so that you don't confuse it with the target component.

Some developers wonder how this information will actually help reduce development time or provide some other performance gain. Knowing how the entries differ can help you locate problems later in your applications. You could use this information to debug problems with the way that a component (or other COM object, such as a document server) registers itself. Obviously, this information also comes in handy to develop a better view of how the component is put together. As previously mentioned, you need to know what the component can provide before you can use it in an application.

For the .NET developer, the OLE/COM Object Viewer also provides a window into existing components. For example, we discussed the *IComponent* interface used in the typical MMC snap-in. Your workstation includes a number of MMC snap-ins you can use as templates. Analysis of these templates would help you understand that the MMC snap-in requires the *IComponent* interface. Research into this interface would demonstrate that you need to build it for the .NET environment.

> **Caution** Strange things can happen if you create an instance of an application or component in the OLE/COM Object Viewer and then don't release it. For example, your computer might freeze unexpectedly. Every time you view the interfaces supported by an application or component, you have to create an instance to do it. You can tell whether there's an instance of an object by looking at the application name. The OLE/COM Object Viewer displays any open objects in boldface type. To release the instance of the object you created, right-click on the object name (such as XYZ Single Document), and then choose Release Instance from the context menu. Fortunately, the OLE/COM Object Viewer is good about closing instances of objects before you leave them, but you might need to take the aforementioned steps during a viewing session if your machine begins to run out of memory. Remember that every instance you create also uses some memory.

Viewing the .NET Category

Open the OLE/COM Object Viewer. (You can use the option on the Tools menu of the Visual Studio .NET IDE to perform this task.) You'll see a set of folders that encompass the various types of objects. It will look similar to the one shown in Figure 14-1. Notice that these statically defined classes are rather broad. There's a very good chance that a component or other type of COM server could appear within more than one folder, depending on which interfaces it implements.

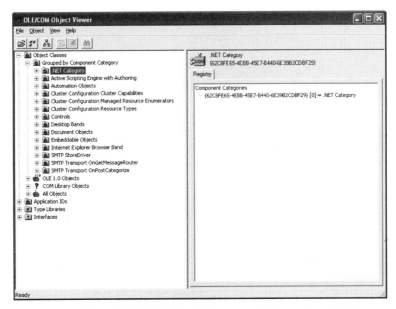

Figure 14-1 The OLE/COM Object Viewer sorts the various COM servers into easily understood categories.

Notice that the OLE/COM Object Viewer includes a special .NET Category entry. Open this folder, and look through the list to find the *MyMath.MathFunctions* class. Open the class, and you'll see a list of interfaces like the one shown in Figure 14-2. This is the first time you've actually seen all the interfaces the *MyMath.MathFunctions* class supports.

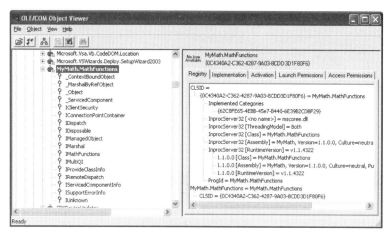

Figure 14-2 The *MyMath.MathFunctions* class contains a number of interfaces you might not have seen before.

Compare the list of interfaces shown in Figure 14-2 to the one in Figure 14-3. The Component Services console shows only the interfaces COM+ thinks you'll find interesting. It hides interfaces such as *IUnknown* because there's no reason to display them as part of a COM+ application. However, there's good reason to know that the interfaces exist. For example, notice in Figure 14-2 that the *MyMath.MathFunctions* class supports the *ISupportErrorInfo* interface. When you look up this interface in the documentation, you'll learn that all automation objects must support it. In addition, this interface enables propagation of error information as needed to the component—this is the source of error information received from an unmanaged source.

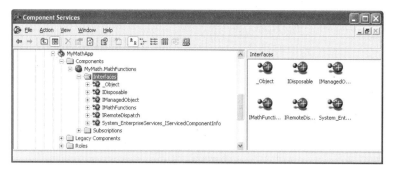

Figure 14-3 Component services generally shows only the interfaces that COM+ thinks you'll need to know about.

Look at the *IMathFunctions* interface in Figure 14-2. The entries in the right pane tell you about the registry entries for this interface. For example, you'll find out that the registry indicates the component has a threading model of *Both*. In addition, you'll see the descriptive text provided for this interface and the location of the type library that holds it.

With the *IMathFunctions* interface selected in the OLE/COM Object Viewer, click the View button. You'll see a short description of the *IMathFunctions* interface. Click View Type Library, and you'll see a description of the *IMathFunctions* interface like the one shown in Figure 14-4.

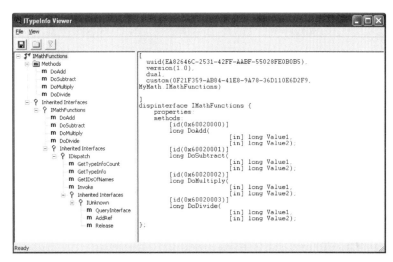

Figure 14-4 Viewing the type library information tells you a lot about a component.

As you can see, this view lays out all the information you might want to know about this interface. This information becomes important as you decipher the intricacies of a component that you want to model. Notice that the information you receive includes variable type and even variable name information.

Whenever you finish using a component, remember to release it. You can do this by right-clicking the *MyMath.MathFunctions* class entry and choosing Release Instance from the context menu. The interface listing will close, and the OLE/COM Object Viewer will remove the highlight from the entry. (The OLE/COM Object View will list in boldface type all classes that you instantiate.)

Viewing an Unmanaged Control

The previous section helped you see some intricacies of a managed component type. In this section, we look at an unmanaged control. Viewing an unmanaged control will provide additional insight into the use of the OLE/COM Object Viewer. Open the OLE/COM Object Viewer if you haven't done so already.

Let's look at a control. Open the Controls folder, and then open the Microsoft Forms 2.0 CommandButton control (or another control if you don't have this component registered on your machine). You'll see the list of interfaces shown in Figure 14-5.

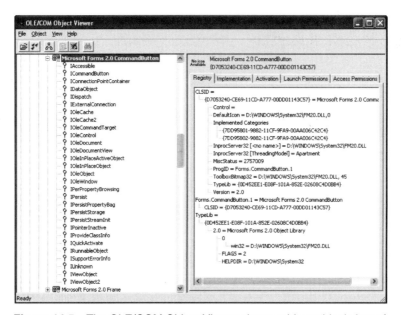

Figure 14-5 The OLE/COM Object Viewer shows a hierarchical view of objects, starting with the object type, proceeding to the name, and then showing the interfaces the object supports.

The interfaces tell you a lot about the support that the control provides. For example, notice that the control includes the *IAccessible* interface to enable accessible devices to learn more about the control. Like the managed component we discussed earlier, the component entry contains a wealth of information. In this example, the information includes the following:

- Registry details
- Implementation details (such as the location of files and threading model)

- Activation details (such as the remote activation site when required)
- Launch permissions (such as who can run the application)
- Access permissions (such as who can look at the component's settings)

All these settings have default values based on what the developer specified during the development process. Viewing these details can help you use the control as a template for developing controls of your own. Comparing the unmanaged control list of interfaces and the settings of features in those interfaces to the same information in a managed control you create can help reduce the chance of interoperability problems.

Performing Interface Analysis

At some point, you'll want to perform some type of analysis on the control so that you can duplicate its interface set (not necessarily the functionality) in your own control. Getting this information means spending time in interface analysis.

Begin by highlighting the *IUnknown* interface. You'll see a display similar to the one shown in Figure 14-6. If you look in the right pane, you'll see that this interface has three methods. Of course, those three methods are *QueryInterface()*, *AddRef()*, and *Release()*. In addition, you can find the class ID of the proxy stub for this interface. Because *IUnknown* is a standard interface, you can be certain it will always contain all three methods—this is just part of the interface's standard package.

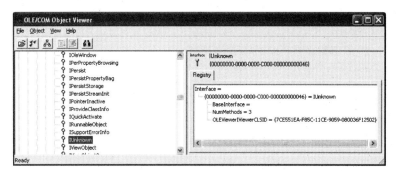

Figure 14-6 Selecting a specific interface will allow you to see the registry entries for that interface, along with details such as the number of methods it supports.

In many cases, you can use the information you'll find in OLE/COM Object Viewer to learn more about the way interfaces work together. For example, look at the *IViewObject2* interface shown in Figure 14-7.

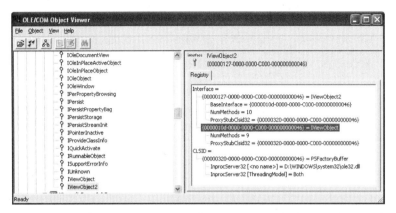

Figure 14-7 Sometimes one interface is actually built out of several interfaces—inheritance will play a role in how you view components.

Notice that this interface depends on the *IViewObject* interface. (See the highlighted entry in the right pane.) Therefore, while the *IViewObject2* interface has only 10 unique methods, it can actually provide access to 19 methods by adding the capabilities of the *IViewObject* interface. Notice also that this interface includes a CLSID (class ID) entry. The CLSID entry tells Microsoft Windows where to find the file that contains the interface. Files such as OLE32.DLL contain many interfaces, each of which requires a separate entry in the registry. This is the method Windows uses for keeping all facts about an interface together in one place.

The OLE/COM Object Viewer can also help you find problems with the interface support in your components. For example, if you look at the contents of the Controls That Are Safely Scriptable folder, you'll find a list of controls that have the proper interfaces and registry entries. The combination of features determines the location of the control in this case. Controls that appear in the Controls folder also appear here, so it might be helpful to see what they have that the managed control you create doesn't provide. Realize that you're searching for clues—you can accept what the OLE/COM Object Viewer gives you as absolute fact. However, it's far from certain that this utility will put you on the right track. That's where careful observation and time spent in the documentation come into play.

Note The Controls That Are Safely Scriptable folder might not show up in some versions of Windows. You can still check the controls for the correct interfaces.

If you take time to perform the analysis, you'll find that controls that don't normally appear in the Controls That Are Safely Scriptable folder won't include support for the *IOleWindow* interface. Further research will tell you that the *IOleWindow* interface is used to obtain window handles for in-place activation and provide context-sensitive help. Because some scripting environments require components that provide in-place activation capability, a component that doesn't implement *IOleWindow* isn't safely scriptable.

However, adding the *IOleWindow* interface would merely make the component safe for scripting—it still wouldn't place the component in the scripting folder. Windows assumes nothing about a component that you don't tell it through registry settings or through the implementation of an interface. You need to perform additional research to learn how to place the component in the scripting folder. The component also has to be marked as scriptable before it will appear in the Controls That Are Safely Scriptable folder. This is something you'd take care of once you knew all the required interfaces were in place and had tested the component fully.

You can use two methods to mark the component as safe for scripting. You can implement the *IObjectSafety* interface or make changes in the registry that show the component is safe. We won't go into the implementation details here; the point is that you could at least get started making your component safe for scripting by using the OLE/COM Object Viewer.

Re-creating COM Interfaces Using Managed Code

Earlier in the chapter, you saw a re-created interface in Listing 14-1. This is the unmanaged form of the *IComponent* interface. Figure 14-8 (on the next page) shows how the interface appears without all the managed information added in Listing 14-1.

Looking at Figure 14-8 should tell you a few things about the code in Listing 14-1. First, the code uses the *[ComImport]* attribute to show that this interface is in a previously defined type library. You don't want the managed version of the interface to appear as an original (new) interface. Notice the *[Guid]* attribute has the same GUID as the unmanaged version shown in Figure 14-8. This is a requirement if you want other applications to react to the managed interface as if it were the unmanaged version. Finally, the *[InterfaceType]* attribute shows that the managed interface derives from *IUnknown*, just as the unmanaged version does.

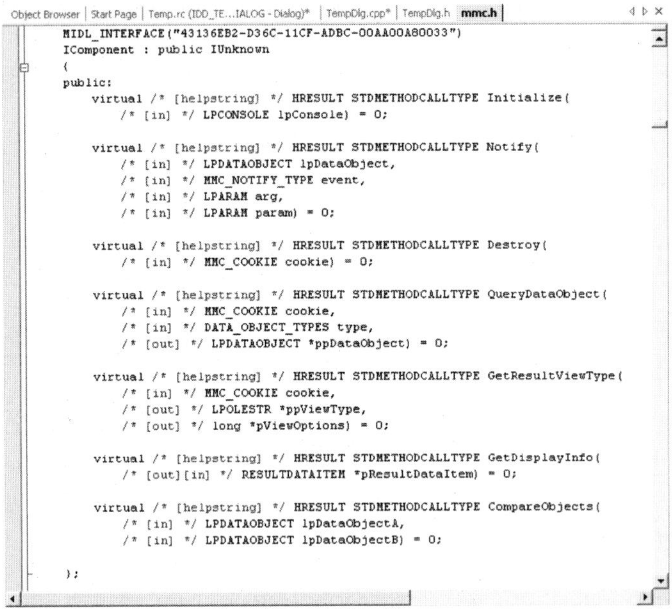
Object Browser | Start Page | Temp.rc (IDD_TE...IALOG - Dialog)* | TempDlg.cpp* | TempDlg.h | mmc.h
MIDL_INTERFACE("43136EB2-D36C-11CF-ADBC-00AA00A80033")
IComponent : public IUnknown
{
public:
virtual /* [helpstring] */ HRESULT STDMETHODCALLTYPE Initialize(
/* [in] */ LPCONSOLE lpConsole) = 0;
virtual /* [helpstring] */ HRESULT STDMETHODCALLTYPE Notify(
/* [in] */ LPDATAOBJECT lpDataObject,
/* [in] */ MMC_NOTIFY_TYPE event,
/* [in] */ LPARAM arg,
/* [in] */ LPARAM param) = 0;
virtual /* [helpstring] */ HRESULT STDMETHODCALLTYPE Destroy(
/* [in] */ MMC_COOKIE cookie) = 0;
virtual /* [helpstring] */ HRESULT STDMETHODCALLTYPE QueryDataObject(
/* [in] */ MMC_COOKIE cookie,
/* [in] */ DATA_OBJECT_TYPES type,
/* [out] */ LPDATAOBJECT *ppDataObject) = 0;
virtual /* [helpstring] */ HRESULT STDMETHODCALLTYPE GetResultViewType(
/* [in] */ MMC_COOKIE cookie,
/* [out] */ LPOLESTR *ppViewType,
/* [out] */ long *pViewOptions) = 0;
virtual /* [helpstring] */ HRESULT STDMETHODCALLTYPE GetDisplayInfo(
/* [out][in] */ RESULTDATAITEM *pResultDataItem) = 0;
virtual /* [helpstring] */ HRESULT STDMETHODCALLTYPE CompareObjects(
/* [in] */ LPDATAOBJECT lpDataObjectA,
/* [in] */ LPDATAOBJECT lpDataObjectB) = 0;
};

Figure 14-8 The unmanaged form of the *IComponent* interface

This particular interface has some interesting marshaling requirements you need to consider when you create interfaces of your own. Look at the method used to marshal *lpConsole*. In the unmanaged version, this variable holds a pointer to the *IConsole* interface. This interface provides access to the MMC console. The MMC snap-in doesn't implement this interface, so storing it in an object makes sense at the outset of the initialization process. However, the component still has to marshal the object as an *UnmanagedType.Interface*.

The next declaration method is preceded by the *[PreserveSig()]* attribute. If you look at the unmanaged versions of the *Notify()* and *Initialize()* methods, you'll see that they both return *HRESULT* values. In reality, however, only the *Notify()* method actually returns an *HRESULT*. The common language runtime normally performs a transformation as it creates output for the unmanaged environment. When you return a value from a function, the value actually appears as an *[out, retval]* entry in the function argument list. Using the *[PreserveSig()]* attribute suppresses this behavior so that the returned value appears as an *HRESULT* instead of the *[out, retval]* entry. The only time you should use this technique is when the code must return an *HRESULT*, and not a value, to the caller.

The *Notify()* method has another interesting difference from the *Initialize()* method. The *lpDataObject* argument is a pointer to an *IDataObject* interface. In both cases, the caller passes the interface to the method, so there's no discernable difference in the unmanaged declaration for the interface. The difference, in this case, is in the implementation. The *Initialize()* method uses the object passed by the caller to query interfaces the console supports. The *Notify()* method, on the other hand, has to determine what type of information the interface will provide, and then it uses the *Marshal.GetObjectForIUnknown()* method to convert the *IntPtr* to a local object using the technique shown here:

```
(IDataObject)Marshal.GetObjectForIUnknown(lpDataObject)
```

In short, the use of an argument determines the interface's declaration in the managed interface as much as the original data type in the unmanaged version of the interface. In some cases, this means you'll have to redefine the managed version of the interface as your component develops.

Both the managed and unmanaged versions of the *Notify()* method contain an *MMC_NOTIFY_TYPE* enumeration. In many cases, you can simply copy the enumeration from the Visual C++ header and convert it to a managed equivalent. However, you must ensure that the managed version values match the unmanaged form precisely, as shown in Listing 14-2.

```
/// <summary>
/// This enumeration contains a list of user action notifications
/// that a snap-in can receive.
/// </summary>
public enum MMC_NOTIFY_TYPE
{
    MMCN_ACTIVATE           = 0x8001,
    MMCN_ADD_IMAGES         = 0x8002,
    MMCN_BTN_CLICK          = 0x8003,
    MMCN_CLICK              = 0x8004,
    MMCN_COLUMN_CLICK       = 0x8005,
    MMCN_CONTEXTMENU        = 0x8006,
    MMCN_CUTORMOVE          = 0x8007,
    MMCN_DBLCLICK           = 0x8008,
    MMCN_DELETE             = 0x8009,
    MMCN_DESELECT_ALL       = 0x800A,
    MMCN_EXPAND             = 0x800B,
    MMCN_HELP               = 0x800C,
    MMCN_MENU_BTNCLICK      = 0x800D,
    MMCN_MINIMIZED          = 0x800E,
    MMCN_PASTE              = 0x800F,
    MMCN_PROPERTY_CHANGE    = 0x8010,
    MMCN_QUERY_PASTE        = 0x8011,
```

Listing 14-2 The managed form of the MMC_NOTIFY_TYPE enumeration

```
    MMCN_REFRESH              = 0x8012,
    MMCN_REMOVE_CHILDREN      = 0x8013,
    MMCN_RENAME               = 0x8014,
    MMCN_SELECT               = 0x8015,
    MMCN_SHOW                 = 0x8016,
    MMCN_VIEW_CHANGE          = 0x8017,
    MMCN_SNAPINHELP           = 0x8018,
    MMCN_CONTEXTHELP          = 0x8019,
    MMCN_INITOCX              = 0x801A,
    MMCN_FILTER_CHANGE        = 0x801B,
    MMCN_FILTERBTN_CLICK      = 0x801C,
    MMCN_RESTORE_VIEW         = 0x801D,
    MMCN_PRINT                = 0x801E,
    MMCN_PRELOAD              = 0x801F,
    MMCN_LISTPAD              = 0x8020,
    MMCN_EXPANDSYNC           = 0x8021,
    MMCN_COLUMNS_CHANGED      = 0x8022,
    MMCN_CANPASTE_OUTOFPROC   = 0x8023
}
```

As you can see, each enumerated member has a value associated with it. Using this technique reduces the probability that an individual member will have the wrong value, even if it appears in a different order than the original unmanaged version.

Some data conversions are relatively easy once you figure out what the value is going to do in your component. For example, the unmanaged version of the *Notify()* method contains two *LPARAM* values. These values easily convert to *Int32* values. Make sure you use caution when converting the values. In some cases, you have to use a UInt32 value to make the parameter work as anticipated. Otherwise, a value will appear negative when it's actually just large.

Look at the definition for the *GetResultViewType()* method. This method has two *out* values. In contrast, the *GetDisplayInfo()* method uses a *ref* value. As a rule of thumb, if the unmanaged code contains just an *[out]* attribute, you need to use the *out* keyword in the managed description. On the other hand, if the unmanaged code has both an *[in]* and an *[out]* attribute, use the *ref* keyword in the managed code. Obviously, this rule isn't cast in concrete, but it does work most of the time. If you run into problems with the interaction between a managed component and the container in which it resides, try using the other keyword (*out* in place of *ref* or *ref* in place of *out*).

At this point, you've seen how the OLE/COM Object Viewer can help you determine which interfaces you must implement and how careful analysis of the C header files can provide clues about interface implementation. Remember that you need to test every interface thoroughly and be ready to make changes as needed. Some decisions you must make to create the interface are less than straightforward because they depend on implementation details within the component or data expectations from the caller.

Creating a Component with Specialized Interfaces Example

Let's look at a simple implementation example. It's possible to create controls that are completely safe for scripting using Microsoft Visual Studio .NET. The only problem is that the managed version lacks the *IObjectSafety* interface that marks it as safe to use. Figure 14-9 shows what the unmanaged form of this interface looks like.

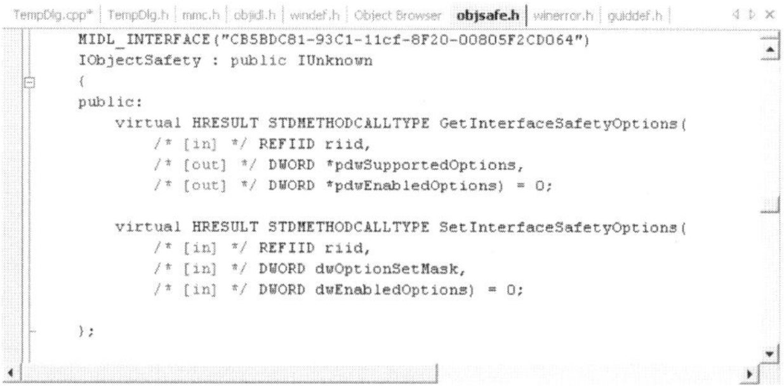
TempDlg.cpp* TempDlg.h mmc.h objidl.h windef.h Object Browser objsafe.h winerror.h guiddef.h
MIDL_INTERFACE("CB5BDC81-93C1-11cf-8F20-00805F2CD064")
IObjectSafety : public IUnknown
{
public:
virtual HRESULT STDMETHODCALLTYPE GetInterfaceSafetyOptions(
/* [in] */ REFIID riid,
/* [out] */ DWORD *pdwSupportedOptions,
/* [out] */ DWORD *pdwEnabledOptions) = 0;
virtual HRESULT STDMETHODCALLTYPE SetInterfaceSafetyOptions(
/* [in] */ REFIID riid,
/* [in] */ DWORD dwOptionSetMask,
/* [in] */ DWORD dwEnabledOptions) = 0;
};

Figure 14-9 You'll use the *IObjectSafety* interface to mark components and controls as safe for scripting.

> **Note** You can find the code for this example in the Chapter14\ScriptableControl folder of the book's companion content. You can download the sample content from the book's Web page at the URL *http://www.microsoft.com/mspress/books/6426.asp*.

For the purposes of this example, just the interface is important. The fact that this interface contains only two methods and most of the variables are relatively simple makes it an easy interface to begin with. Listing 14-3 shows the implementation of this interface in managed code.

```
[ComImport,
 InterfaceType(ComInterfaceType.InterfaceIsIUnknown),
 Guid("CB5BDC81-93C1-11cf-8F20-00805F2CD064")]
public interface IObjectSafety
{
   [PreserveSig()]
   UInt32 GetInterfaceSafetyOptions(
       ref Guid riid,
       out Int32 pdwSupportedOptions,
       out Int32 pdwEnabledOptions);

   [PreserveSig()]
   UInt32 SetInterfaceSafetyOptions(
       ref Guid riid,
       Int32 dwOptionSetMask,
       Int32 dwEnabledOptions);
}
```

Listing 14-3   The converted form of the *IObjectSafety* interface

The heading for this information is much the same as the *IComponent* interface we discussed earlier, so this example uses the same attributes as before. Notice that the *[Guid]* attribute contains the correct GUID for this interface, as shown in Figure 14-9.

Reading the documentation tells you that the methods in this interface both return values. Consequently, you must use *[PreserveSig()]* for both methods. The possible return values for this example include

```
public const UInt32 S_OK           = 0x00000000;
public const UInt32 E_FAIL         = 0x00000001;
public const UInt32 E_NOINTERFACE  = 0x80004002;
```

The *E_NOINTERFACE* return value isn't a failure as you might suppose. It simply indicates to the caller that the component or control hasn't implemented this method. Many callers will interpret this value as a failure, but some will also perform a default action based on the lack of support provided by the component or control. It's important to use the correct return value. Use *E_FAIL* only if the call actually failed.

One tricky piece of information required by this example is the *riid*. You need to track this value back to its origins to find that it's actually a pointer to an interface identifier (IID), which is nothing more than a GUID for the purposes of this example. The example could have used a number of other types for this input, including an *IntPtr*. The *Guid* type should work in most situations.

The final arguments are simply Int32 values. However, they have special meaning in this case because the caller interprets each bit position. You could create a flag enumeration for these two entries, but it isn't necessary. The bit positions needed to signify that the control is safe for scripting are contained in the two constants shown here:

```
public const Int32 INTERFACESAFE_FOR_UNTRUSTED_CALLER = 0x00000001;
public const Int32 INTERFACESAFE_FOR_UNTRUSTED_DATA   = 0x00000002;
```

It's time for the decisive moment—does the interface work? The sample control, ScriptableControl.MyButton, is extremely simple. The only purpose it serves is to demonstrate the *IObjectSafety* interface. Viewing this control in the OLE/COM Object Viewer will show you that it does indeed possess the *IObjectSafety* interface, as shown in Figure 14-10.

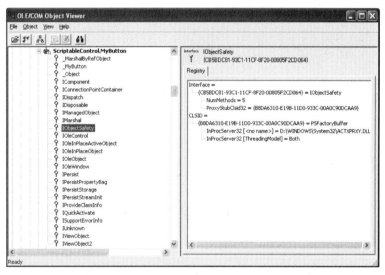

Figure 14-10 The sample control implements and exposes the *IObjectSafety* interface, which makes it possible to use the control in a scripting scenario.

Summary

This chapter has helped you learn about predefined interfaces. You've learned why the interfaces are important, discovered which interfaces you need to implement, and learned how to implement the interfaces in code. These are the three essential steps in learning to create components for particular needs such as container applications.

Now that you have some essential knowledge about using predefined interfaces, it's time to create some of your own. Begin by spending time looking at the various interfaces in the OLE/COM Object Viewer. Research the interfaces within the documentation for Visual Studio .NET. Finally, try to implement a component for a container or other application that accepts new components.

Congratulations, you've made it to the end of the book! We hope this isn't the end of your learning experience. All the tips and techniques we've presented will help you create better applications with Visual Studio .NET—applications that are interoperable with your existing components and applications.

Index

A

access checks, 44, 308
access requirements, 29, 33, 41
accessibility, 385
Account class, 151
Active Template Library (ATL). *See* ATL
ActiveX containers, 143
ActiveX controls. *See also* ATL Server
   adding, 100
   Aximp.exe utility, 101
   component access, 20–21, 24–25
   future of, 3
   identifying in registry, 144
   overview, 99–100
   referencing, 21
   Windows Forms, 4, 7, 100–102, 143–148
   wrapping, 6
Add An Assembly To The Assembly Cache link, 48
Add() method, 367
adding
   applications to Component Services, 35
   assemblies, 48
   COM+ components, 34, 38–40
   computers, 32
   queues to applications, 169
   role-based security, 41–45
AddRef method, 9, 140, 481
addresses, 452, 455–456
AddrOfPinnedObject object, 455
administrative tasks, 30
aggregatable attribute, 217, 221–224
aggregates attribute, 217, 221–224
aggregation, 221–224
AL.exe, 71
Alias declaration, 412
all-names operation mode, 306
Alloc method, 453
allocated memory, 10–11
allocating resources, COM+, 29
AllocHGlobal method, 446, 449
ANSI CString, 258
ANSI strings, 93, 438
Ansi values, 411, 425
apartments, 15–16
AppCollection object, 366
application development. *See* COM in .NET applications; COM+ in .NET applications
application dumps, 380–381
application hierarchies, COM+, 34

application identity, 37, 157
application level controls. COM+, 33
application level security, 43
application names, 36
application proxies, 45–46
application queues, 319
application roots, 405–407
application security, COM+, 33
application types, 179–181
ApplicationAccessControl attribute, 308
application-defined HRESULTs, 13
ApplicationName attribute, 308
arguments
   handler functions, 269, 274
   methods, 87
   return values, 60
   type library conversions, 65–66
   type library creation, 118
arithmetic operators, 427
arrays
   ATL
      classes, 234–238
      overview, 234
      SAFEARRAYs, 239–242
   attributed programming, 215
   converting, 81–83
   marshaling, 447–452
   pinning, 426
   sharing data, 426
   stack allocation, 427
ASP files, 261
ASP scripts, 381–382, 386, 393–396
ASP.NET, 394, 396
assemblies. *See also* Global Assembly Cache
   adding, 48
   configuring, 48–49
   directory, 68
   dynamic registration, 349
   exporting, 125–126
   identifying, 9
   installing, 72
   interop
      component referencing, 60
      generating, 55
      overview, 54
      TlbImp.exe, 57–61
      TypeLibConverter class, 61–67
      Visual Studio .NET, 56

491

assemblies, *continued*
  locations, 8, 67
  names, 125, 139
  object capability information, 9
  primary interop, 54, 73
  private keys and, 72
  properties, 68
  registering, 114
  removing, 72
  signing, 58, 71–72, 119
  strong names, 70–71
  versions, 67, 121, 126, 142
  viewing, 48–49
  visibility, 14, 112
Assembly Cache snap-in, 48
Assembly Linker, 71, 73
Assembly Registration tool, 73
AssemblyBuilder, 67
AssemblyInfo source files, 142
AssemblyVersion attribute, 143
asynchronous applications
  MSMQ
    client applications, 335–342
    listener/player, 327–335
    overview, 316–320
    recorder/player, 320–327
  overview, 315–316
async_uuid attribute, 212
ATL (Active Template Library). *See also* ATL Server; attributed programming
  breaking existing code, 258
  changes in, 233
  data handling
    classes, 234–238
    collections, 242
    overview, 234
    SAFEARRAYs, 239–242
  described, 189
  error handling, 224
  event handling, 225–230
  module classes, 209, 234
  operator& implementation, 257
  regular expression classes, 256–257
  security classes, 252–254
  shared classes, 243–250
  string conversion classes, 250–251
ATL DLL, 258
ATL Server
  architecture, 259–266
  described, 233
  overview, 259
  SRF files, 261–266

Web applications
  attributes, 266–268
  DLLs, 260–261, 272
  handler methods, 269–270, 274
  overview, 266
  parsing functions, 270, 275–277
  project setup, 271–274
  sample applications, 270–277
Web services
  C++, 283–286
  creating, 281–283
  implementing, 279–281
  overview, 277
  SOAP, 278–279
ATL Server library, 259
ATL70.dll, 258
AtlsHttpError function, 275–277
atoi function, 275–277
attribute parameters, 193, 201
attribute providers, 192, 199
attributed programming. *See also* attributed programming walkthroughs
  aggregation, 221–224
  arrays, 215
  C++ code, 193–194
  coclasses, 216–219
  described, 189
  error handling, 224
  event handling, 225–230
  interfaces, 211–216
  linker options, 231
  methods, 214–215
  modules, 207–211
  parameters, 214–215
  return types, 214–215
attributed programming walkthroughs
  IDL and, 199
  inserted code, 195–196
  methods, 200–203
  objects, 196–200
  overview, 194–195
  properties, 200–203
  testing, 203
  text editor process, 204–207
attributes, 192
  aggregates, 221–224
  arrays, 215
  C++ code, 193–194
  coclass, 216–219
  custom, 141, 194, 210–211
  emitidl, 220
  error handling, 224
  event handling, 225–230
  importing, 74

interface definitions, 211–216
methods, 214–215
module, 207–211
.NET interoperability and, 141
.NET types exposed to COM, 108–114
overview, 190–191
RegSvcs utility and, 295
stand-alone, 219–221
Web applications, 266–268
authorized user options, 307
Auto prefix, 109
Auto value, 409, 413
AutoDispatch attribute, 107, 110
automated subscriptions, 368
automatic component updates, 171
automatic memory management, 401
automatically generated IIDs, 128
Automation marshaler, 112
AutomationProxy attribute, 112
Aximp.exe, 101

B

backward compatibility. *See* integrating COM in .NET; integrating COM+ in .NET
base classes, 158
BaseType parameter, 247–248
batch files, 35
BeginDoAdd() method, 380
binary data transfer technology, 172
bindable attribute, 214
binding policies, 48
blit, 16
blittable types, 16, 93, 447, 453
Body property, 327, 335
bound information, 239–242
browsers, 393–396
BSTRs, 15, 77, 435, 438
_bstr_t object, 307
built-in system marshaler, 112
button components, 355

C

C memory management, 403
C Runtime Library, 247–248
C++ programming. *See also* ATL; attributed programming
assembly names, 139
COM and, 5
component registration, 123–125
delayed assembly signing, 73
destructors, 409
IntPtrs, 77–78
libraries, 233

memory, 11, 403
pinning, 455
Platform Invoke, 421–422, 428–432
Runtime Callable Wrappers, 56
signed assemblies, 71
versioning, 142
Web applications
attributes, 266–268
handler methods, 269–270
overview, 266
sample applications, 270–277
Web services
consuming, 283–286
creating, 281–283
implementing, 279–281
overview, 277
SOAP, 278–279
C# programming
component registration, 120–122
destructors, 409
enumeration conversions, 138
inheritance hierarchy, 129–131
IntPtrs, 77
Platform Invoke, 417–420, 422–427
property conversions, 134–136
Runtime Callable Wrappers, 56
signed assemblies, 71
type library conversions, 62
value type conversions, 137
versioning, 142
Windows Forms controls, 145–148
caching SRF files, 262
CAdapt class, 257
call wait times, 326
callback interfaces, 95
callbacks, 456, 461–466
calling exported member functions, 430
calling methods, 86
CAltRegExp class, 256–257
carriage returns, 389
CatalogObject object, 367, 371
catalogs, 345–347, 363, 371
CATCID_Control, 144
CAtlArray class, 237–238
CAtlREMatchContext object, 257
CComBSTR class, 257
CComPtr class, 257
CComSafeArray class, 239–242
CComSafeArrayBound class, 239–242
CCWs (COM Callable Wrappers). *See* COM Callable Wrappers
CElementTraits class, 237
chain references, application root, 406

channels, 49
character encoding, 411, 438
CharSet parameter, 415, 425, 438, 441, 445
class IDs (CLSIDs), 482
class interfaces, 106–111
Class View window, 285
classes. *See also* ATL; attributed programming
   changing, 140
   COM+ catalog and, 346
   exporting, 127–128
   visibility, 112
classid attribute, 148
ClassInterface attribute, 107–111, 292
ClassInterfaceType enumeration, 108
CLB (component load balancing), 163, 170, 290, 315
client applications
   COM+, 296–298, 306–308, 311–312
   MSMQ, 335–342
client-side scripts, 382–384, 394
CLR (common language runtime). *See* common language runtime
CLSIDs (class IDs), 480
clusters, 290
coclass attribute, 191, 207, 216–219
coclasses
   attributed programming, 196, 216–219
   ClassInterface attribute, 110–111
   importing, 83–85
   inheritance and, 127
   type information, 13
code. *See also* integrating COM in .NET; integrating COM+ in .NET; integrating .NET in COM; integrating .NET in COM+
   execution policies, 50
   pointers, 77–79
   unsafe, 79–81
Code Behind, 394
Code Groups folder, 50
codebases, assembly, 48
codepage tag, 262
COM aggregation, 221–224
COM arrays, 81–83
COM attributes, 192. *See also* attributed programming walkthroughs
   aggregation, 221–224
   C++ code, 193–194
   coclasses, 216–219
   error handling, 224
   event handling, 225–230
   interfaces, 211–216
   linker options, 231
   modules, 207–211
   vs. .NET attributes, 74
   overview, 190–191
   stand-alone, 219–221
COM Callable Wrappers (CCWs). *See also* exporting
   attributes, 108–114
   COM client code, 120–125
   described, 54
   generating, 108
   interfaces, 105–108
   objects, 104
   overview, 103
   registry entries, 119–120
   signed assemblies, 119
   type library creation, 114–119
   visibility, 14
COM client code, .NET components in, 120–125
COM coclasses, 13, 83–85, 196, 216–219
COM components. *See also* integrating COM in .NET
   ActiveX controls, 99–102
   assemblies, 53–55
   data handling, 15–18
   design considerations, 91–94
   examples, 22–24
   future of, 3–5
   identifying, 8
   locations, 7–8, 20–21
   .NET appearing as, 6
   .NET integration, 5–7, 19–25, 53
   registry and, 7
   type information, 13
   visibility, 14
   wrapping, 6
COM connection points, 95
COM delegation, 221–224
COM entity conversions
   arrays, 81–83
   attributes, 74
   coclasses, 83–85
   constants, 90
   data types, 75–83
   enumerations, 90
   interfaces, 85–88
   libraries, 74–75
   methods, 87
   modules, 91
   properties, 87
   structures, 88
   typedefs, 90
   unions, 89
COM enumerations, 138
COM event handling, 19, 94–99, 141, 148–152
COM identities, 104
COM IEnum interfaces, 242
COM improvements, 3

COM in .NET applications. *See also* converting; Runtime Callable Wrappers
  component integration
    accessing, 19–25
    ActiveX controls, 99–102
    COM interop, 53–55
    design considerations, 91–94
    event handling, 94–99
    overview, 53
  differences
    component identification, 8
    component locations, 7–8
    data handling, 15–18
    error handling, 13
    event handling, 19
    garbage collection, 10–13
    object-oriented principles, 10
    objects, 9
    type information, 13
    visibility, 14–15
  future of, 3–5
  overview, 5–7
COM interface IDs, 128
COM interfaces
  changing, 140
  converting, 85–88
  managed environments and, 471–474
  .NET interfaces implemented as, 6
  re-creating with managed code, 483–487
  Web services, 279
COM interop
  described, 5
  interop assemblies, 54
  MarshalAs attribute, 435–437
  marshaling arrays, 451–452
  marshaling data, 15
COM objects, 6, 9–10
COM progIDs, 112
COM runtime, 175
COM security, 4
COM strings, 438
COM structs, 18
COM type libraries
  arrays, 81–83
  attributes, 74
  coclasses, 83–85
  constants, 90
  converting, 74–75
  data types, 75–83
  enumerations, 90
  interfaces, 85–88
  interop assemblies, 54
  modules, 91

  primary interop assemblies, 55
  referencing, 60
  structures, 88
  TlbImp.exe, 57–61
  typedefs, 90
  TypeLibConverter class, 61–67
  unions, 89
COM+, 28, 166–169, 378–380
COM+ 1.0 Admin Type Library, 346, 361
COM+ Application Install Wizard, 36–37
COM+ application types, 179–181
COM+ applications. *See also* COM+ examples; COM+ in .NET applications; Web-based applications
  accessibility, 385
  background information, 163
  COM vs. COM+, 156
  connections, 173–178
  constructor strings, 309–310, 312
  creating, 34–40
  data flow optimization, 178
  DCOM, 172–178
  disconnected, 28, 166–169
  distributed architecture, 163
  dumps, 380–381
  dynamic registration, 349
  error handling, 182
  exporting, 45–46
  interoperability, 156–162
  messaging, 166–169
  moving, 32
  security, 41–45, 183–184
  SOAP, 374–380
COM+ Applications folders, 32
COM+ background information, 163
COM+ catalogs, 345–347, 363, 371
COM+ client access requirements, 29, 41
COM+ collections, 347
COM+ components. *See also* COM+ examples
  accessing, 157
  application types, 179–181
  company structure and, 42
  Component class, 158–160
  configuring, 44
  data flow optimization, 178
  DCOM, 172–178
  described, 44
  dynamic registration, 349
  error handling, 182
  installing, 34, 38–40
  interoperability, 156–162
  proxy applications, 45–46
  Object class, 158
  recognition, 158

COM+ components, *continued*
  registering, 34, 38, 293–295
  samples, 34
  security, 29, 33, 41–45
  ServicedComponent class, 158, 160–162
COM+ event handling, 19, 170
COM+ Event System Service, 348
COM+ examples
  Component class
    clients, 306–308
    deriving from, 300–305
    overview, 300
    setup, 305
  GUIDs, 289–290
  overview, 289
  ServicedComponent class
    clients, 311–312
    deriving from, 309–310
    overview, 308–309
    setup, 310
  simple component
    clients, 296–298
    creating, 291–292
    exporting, 295–296
    overview, 290–291
    registering, 293–295
    testing, 298–300
COM+ improvements, 29
COM+ in .NET applications. *See also* Component Services snap-in
  benefits of, 28–29
  improvements, 29
  .NET Framework Configuration snap-in, 47–50
  overview, 27
  problems, 29–30
COM+ management, 30
COM+ problems, 29
COM+ publish/subscribe model, 30
COM+ security, 28, 41–45, 170, 183–184
COM+ services, 169–171
COM+ transaction management, 164–165
combo boxes, 307
ComImport attribute, 118, 483
ComInterface attribute, 85
com_interface_entry attribute, 217
ComInterfaceType enumeration, 128
comment tag, 262
common language runtime
  future of, 5
  garbage collection, 10–13
  GUIDs and, 290
  heaps, 15
  IDispatch interface methods, 113
  lifetimes, 9, 104

  managed code and, 402
  security policies, 50
compacting heaps, 404, 406
CompareObjects() method, 474
comparing interfaces, 481
CompCollection object, 367
compensating resource manager, 171
compiler options, attributed code, 231
completed transactions, 28
Component class, 158–160, 300–308
component load balancing (CLB), 163, 170, 290, 315
Component Services
  COM+ catalog, 346
  subscriptions, 360, 368
  transaction management, 165
Component Services console
  application testing, 299
  interface information, 478
  overview, 30
Component Services snap-in
  application development, 34–37
  component installation, 38–40
  exporting, 45–46
  operating systems and, 32
  overview, 30
  samples, 34
  security, 41–45
  user interface, 30–34
component subscribers, 355–360
components. *See also* COM components; COM+ components; .NET components
  ActiveX controls, 99–102
  counterfeit, 72
  GUIDs, 289–290
  interface research, 475–476
  non-PIA, 73
  scripting, 482, 487
  Web applications, 381–382, 386, 390–393
Components folders, 33
Computer Management console, 168
computer names, 300
COMPUTER_NAME_FORMAT enumeration, 303–304, 307
computers, viewing, 31–32
ComRegisterFunction attribute, 114
ComSourceInterfaces attribute, 141, 149
ComUnregisterFunction attribute, 114
ComVisible attribute, 14, 112, 118, 127
conditional processing, 265
configured assemblies, 49
Configured Assemblies snap-in, 48
conformant arrays, 83
conformant varying arrays, 83
Connect To Another Computer option, 31

connection points, 95, 225
connections
    COM+, 29
    Component Services snap-in, 32
    DCOM, 173–178
    message queues, 322–323
    MSMQ, 316, 336
    Web applications, 382, 393
consoles
    Component Services, 30
    described, 27
    .NET Framework Configuration, 47–50
constants, importing, 90
Construct() method, 310
ConstructionEnabled attribute, 310
constructors
    calls, 193
    COM vs. .NET, 10
    default, 139
    strings, 309–310, 312
    subscriber applications, 362
_ConstructorValue variable, 310
container applications, 472–474
Container class, 12
content appearance, 389
context menus, Component Services, 31
context-sensitive help, 483
control attribute, 217
Control subkey, 144
controls. *See also* ActiveX controls; Windows Forms controls
    Safely Scriptable folder, 482
    unmanaged, 480–481
ConvertAssemblyToTypeLib method, 116–119
converting
    arrays, 81–83
    assemblies, 125–126
    classes, 127–128
    coclasses, 83–85
    constants, 90
    data types, 75–83, 136–137
    enumerations, 90, 138
    exceptions, 132–133
    handler arguments, 269, 274
    HRESULTs, 132–133
    interfaces, 85–88, 106, 128–136
    methods, 87, 132–134
    modules, 91
    namespaces, 126
    pointers, 77–79
    properties, 87, 134–136
    strings, 250–251
    structures, 88

type libraries, 74–75
typedefs, 90
unions, 89
value types, 137
ConvertTypeLibToAssembly method, 61–67
cookies, 385
copying applications to disk, 380–381
copying assemblies, 48
counterfeit components, 72
cpp_quote attribute, 219
CPU registers, 405
CreateFile function, 417–420
CreateObject() method, 396
CreateStdDispatch API, 113
CRequestHandlerT class, 266–268
cross-apartment marshaling, 15
cross-language data communication, 4
CSimpleArray class, 235–237
CSimpleArrayEqualHelper class, 235
CSimpleStringT class, 244–246
CString class, 244, 258
CStringA class, 258
CStringT class, 246–250
CStringW class, 258
C-style arrays, 82–83
culture information, 70
current server status, 170
custom
    attribute providers, 192
    attributes, 141, 194
    exception classes, 142
    indexes, 388
    interfaces, 106–108
    memory management, 245, 247
    MSMQ formats, 325
    parsing functions, 275–277
    proxies, 112
custom attribute, 75, 138, 210–212, 217, 219

D

data encapsulation, 336–337
data flow optimization, 178
data handling. *See also* disconnected applications
    ATL, 234–242
    COM vs. .NET, 15–18
    COM+, 164–165
    converting, 486
    DCOM, 172–178
    design considerations, 92
    Web applications, 390–393
data integrity, 164, 319
data marshaling, 15–18, 82
data pointers, 77–79

data types
    converting, 75–83
    exporting, 136–137
    Platform Invoke, 403, 416–417, 428
databases
    COM+, 28, 345–347
    management system, 386
    network locations, 309
    Web applications, 386–389, 393–396
DBMS (database management system), 386
DCE-RPC network protocol, 176, 177
DCOM (Distributed Component Object Model)
    additional information, 172
    COM+, 29–30
    connections, 173–178
    data flow optimization, 178
    overview, 172–173
    protocols, 176–177
    replacement for, 4
DCOM Config folder, 173
DCOMCnfg.exe, 173
dead letter queues, 319
debugging
    registration commands, 35
    scripts, 382–384
    Web applications, 380–381
Declare statement, 411
default
    attribute, 217, 219
    Component Services applications, 32
    constructors, 10, 121, 139
    desktops, 462
    destructors, 10, 127
    GUIDs, 111
    handlers, 273
    interfaces, 219
    progIDs, 111
definition compatibility, 92
delayed assembly signing, 72
Delegate keyword, 463
delegates, 95, 463–467
delegation, 221–224
delete command, 11
deleting assemblies, 48
dependent MSMQ clients, 317
Depends utility, 304
desktop applications vs. Web applications, 374
destructors
    COM vs. .NET, 10
    garbage collection, 11–12, 409
dialog-based subscribers
    overview, 360–363
    permanent, 363–369
    transient, 369–372

digital signatures, 9, 70
disconnected applications. *See also* Web-based
        applications
    COM+, 28, 166–169
    MSMQ
        client applications, 335–342
        listener/player, 327–335
        overview, 316–320
        recorder/player, 320–327
    overview, 315–316
dispatch IDs, 107, 109, 215
dispatch interfaces, 106–108, 110, 113, 215
dispIds, 107, 109, 215
dispinterface attribute, 212
dispinterfaces, 106–108, 110, 113, 215
displaying international Web applications, 384
displaying MSMQ messages, 324–325
Dispose method, 407–409
Disposed() event, 474
distributed applications. *See also* subscriptions
    COM, 4
    COM+, 28–29, 163
    transaction management, 164–165
distributed architecture, 163
Distributed Component Object Model (DCOM). *See*
        DCOM
Distributed Transaction Coordinator (DTC), 165
Distributed Transaction Coordinator folders, 32
DllImport attribute, 304, 412, 415, 438, 458
DLLs. *See also* Platform Invoke
    ISAPI, 260
    loading dynamically, 458–460, 470
    Web applications, 260–261, 272
DoAdd() method, 380
document style, 280
Drop List, 307
DTC (Distributed Transaction Coordinator), 165
dual attribute, 212
dual interfaces, 92, 108, 113, 128
duplicate dispatch IDs, 215
dynamic content, 261, 265
dynamic registration, 349
dynamic server status, 170
dynamically allocated memory, 10–11
dynamically loading DLLs, 458–460

E

Edit Code Group Properties link, 50
E_FAIL return value, 488
email error reporting, 182
emitidl attribute, 205, 220
empty COM+ applications, 34
Enabled property, 367, 371
encodings, XML Web services, 4

Enforce Access Checks For This Application option, 44
E_NOINTERFACE return value, 488
enterprise applications, COM+, 163
Enterprise level security, 50
EnterpriseServices namespace, 160–162, 308
entity conversions
    arrays, 81–83
    assemblies, 125–126
    attributes, 74
    classes, 127–128
    coclasses, 83–85
    constants, 90
    data types, 75–83, 136–137
    enumerations, 90, 138
    interfaces, 85–88, 128–136
    libraries, 74–75
    methods, 87, 132–134
    modules, 91
    namespaces, 126
    properties, 87, 134–136
    structures, 88
    typedefs, 90
    unions, 89
    value types, 137
entry point ordinals, 414
EntryPoint parameter, 414, 430
enumerations
    converting, 90
    exporting, 138
    IEnum interface, 242
    RegKind, 65
EnumWindowStations function, 462, 465
equality classes, 235–237
equality operators, 79
errors
    attributed programming, 224
    COM, 13
    COM+, 31, 182
    design considerations, 93
    MSMQ, 330
    .NET exceptions, 13
    Platform Invoke, 415
    publish/subscribe system, 350
    Web applications, 380–384, 386
event handling. *See also* subscriptions
    attributed programming, 225–230
    callbacks and, 461–466
    COM, 94–99
    COM vs. .NET, 19
    COM+, 170
    .NET, 118, 141, 148–152
event logs, 30, 182, 330, 335–336, 341

event objects
    component subscribers, 356
    creating, 350
    designing, 350–352
    installing, 352–353
event prototypes, 351
event sinks, 95, 118, 225
event sources, 225
Event Viewer snap-in, 30
EventCLSID property, 367
EventLog object, 330
event_receiver attribute, 217, 228
event_source attribute, 217, 225
event-source interfaces, 141, 149–151
Everything entry, 50
ExactSpelling parameter, 415
exceptions
    converting, 132–133
    custom classes, 142
    vs. HRESULTs, 93
    .NET, 13
explicit conversions, 258
explicit memory layouts, 89, 442–443
explicit source interfaces, 149–151
explicitly marking nonvisible types, 14
explicitly releasing resources, 92
export attribute, 212
exported member functions, 430
exporting
    assemblies, 125–126
    classes, 127–128
    COM+ applications, 45–46, 295–296
    data types, 136–137
    enumerations, 138
    interfaces, 128–136
    methods, 132–134
    namespaces, 126
    properties, 134–136
    value types, 18, 137
exposing .NET types to COM. *See* integrating .NET in COM
extern functions, 420
extracting public keys, 73

F

failed transactions, 28
FieldOffset attribute, 89, 442
files, attribute-inserted code, 192, 195
filtering
    callbacks and, 461–466
    message information, 326
finalization, 407–409, 454
Finalize method, 407–409
finalizer queues, 408, 454

finalizers, 11
finalizing objects, 10–13
FireBroadcastMsg() method, 351, 355–356
firewalls
  COM, 4
  COM+, 29, 172
firing events, 353
fixed GUIDs, 143
fixed keyword, 425–427
fixed-length arrays, 82
flagging memory blocks, 407
for loops, 367
foreach statement, 242, 367
FormatMessage function, 417–420, 460
formatting MSMQ messages, 318, 325
FormFlags method, 268
FreeHGlobal method, 446
freeing allocated memory, 11
fully dynamic DLL loading, 460
fully qualified names, 8
function call errors, 305
function calls, 304
function declarations, 304
function pointers, 461, 463
/Fx compiler option, 192, 195

G

GAC (Global Assembly Cache). *See* Global Assembly Cache
Gacutil.exe, 69, 72, 122
garbage collection
  delegates and, 467–469
  described, 402
  finalization, 10–13, 407–409
  generations, 404
  large object heaps, 405
  overview, 404
  pointers, 79, 457
  premature, 467
  preventing, 467
  resurrection, 454
  roots, 405–407
  wrong times, 468
__gc pointer, 429
GCHandle class, 453, 455
gcroot class, 456–458
generations, 404
generic pointers, 77
get method, 134, 136
GetAllNames() method, 305
GetCollection() method, 366
GetComputerNameEx() function, 300, 304
GetConstructorString() method, 310

GetCurSel() method, 307
GetDisplayInfo() method, 486
GetIdsOfNames method, 140
GetLastError API, 415
GetLastError() function, 304
GetLastWin32Error function, 304, 420, 460
GetResultViewType() method, 486
GetSingleName() method, 304–305
GetTitle() method, 396
GetTopic() method, 396
GetTypeInfo method, 140
GetTypeInfoCount method, 140
GetValue() method, 393
global
  catalogs, 347
  constants, 91
  language support, 384
  methods, 91
  object pointers, 405
  security functions, 253
Global Assembly Cache (GAC)
  assembly installations, 72
  assembly management, 48
  delayed signing, 72
  described, 8
  dynamic registration, 349
  file additions, 69
  location, 68
  .NET components from COM, 122
  overview, 67–69
  signed assemblies, 71
  strong names, 70–71
Globally Unique IDs (GUIDs). *See* GUIDs
GUI method, 293, 310
Guid attribute, 85, 111, 128, 158, 289–290, 483
GUIDs (Globally Unique IDs)
  COM interface IDs, 128
  component identification, 8
  component location, 7
  control identification, 144
  importance of, 289–290
  interface information, 483, 488
  overriding, 111
  subscribers, 356, 367
  version numbers and, 142

H

handler classes, 263, 280
handler functions, 456
handler methods, 269–270, 274
handler tag, 262–263, 265
HandleRef types, 468–469
handles, 453, 468, 483

headers, 204, 285, 431
heaps, 15, 104, 404–406
HelpAccess interface pointer, 396
helpcontext attribute, 212, 217
help-desk application scenario
   accessibility, 385
   browser support, 393–396
   component communication, 386
   component interactions, 381–382
   data access, 390–393
   databases, 386–389
   dumps, 380–381
   human-language support, 384
   overview, 373
   scripting error handling, 382–384
   SOAP, 374–380
   testing, 396–397
helpfile attribute, 212, 217
helpstring attribute, 207, 212, 214, 217
helpstringcontext attribute, 212, 217
hidden attribute, 212, 214, 217
hidden interfaces, 478
hiding component visibility, 112
hierarchies
   COM+ applications, 34
   exceptions, 13
   inheritance, 129–131, 479
   visibility, 14
__hook keyword, 230
hosting Windows Forms, 143–148
HRESULTs, 13, 93, 132–133, 142, 182, 415
HTML pages, 148, 277
HTML tags, 389, 396
HTTP, 278
human-language support, 384

I

IAccessible interface, 480
IAltMemMgr interface, 245
IAsyncResult variable, 380
IAtlStringMgr interface, 245–246
ICatalogCollection object, 346, 363, 366
ICatalogObject object, 347
ICheckString interface, 310
IComponent interface, 160, 473, 476, 483
IComputerName interface, 303
icons, Component Services, 31–32
id attribute, 214
IDataObject interface, 474, 484
IDE, component access with, 19–25
identifying
   assemblies, 9
   components, 8
   controls, 144

identity options, 37
IDispatch interface, 106, 113, 140
IDispatch method, 85
IDispatchImpl attribute, 113
IDisposable interface, 160, 162, 300, 305, 408
IDL (Interface Definition Language). *See also* attributed
     programming
   described, 13
   generating, 231
   suppressing generation, 231
   type conversions, 75–77, 136–137
   value types and, 137
/idlout compiler option, 23
idl_quote attribute, 219
IEnum interfaces, 242
IErrorInfo, 93
/ignoreidl compiler option, 231
IIDs (interface IDs), 128, 488
IJW (It Just Works mechanism), 431–432
IL (Microsoft Intermediate Language), 10
IL Disassembler, 88
ILDasm.exe, 88
Image Dump Directory values, 381
IManagedObject interface, 162
Implemented Categories subkey, 144
implements attribute, 217
implements_category attribute, 217
implicit conversions, 258
import attribute, 219
importer. *See* type library importer
importidl attribute, 219
importing
   ActiveX controls, 100
   arrays, 81–83
   attributes, 74
   coclasses, 83–85
   constants, 90
   data types, 75–83
   enumerations, 90
   interfaces, 85–88
   methods, 87
   modules, 91
   properties, 87
   structures, 88
   type libraries, 74–75
   typedefs, 90
   unions, 89
importlib attribute, 219
IMyInterface interface, 106
in attribute, 132, 214, 447, 486
In parameter, 132, 447
include tag, 262, 264
independent MSMQ clients, 317
indexes, Web application, 388

inequality operators, 79
inheritance
   class exportation and, 127
   exceptions, 13
   hierarchy, 129–131, 481
   visibility, 14
inherited roles, 45
Initialize method, 484
initializing objects, 10
in-memory interop assemblies, 61
in-memory type libraries, 61
in-place activation, 483
inserted code, viewing, 192, 195
instances
   lifetime management, 9
   releasing, 476
instantiating components, 84
Int32 values, 486, 488
integrating COM in .NET. *See also* converting; Runtime Callable Wrappers
   COM interop, 53–55
   component integration
      accessing, 19–25
      ActiveX controls, 99–102
      design considerations, 91–94
      event handling, 94–99
      overview, 53
   differences
      component identification, 8
      component locations, 7–8
      data handling, 15–18
      error handling, 13
      event handling, 19
      garbage collection, 10–13
      object-oriented principles, 10
      objects, 9
      type information, 13
      visibility, 14–15
   future of, 3–5
   overview, 5–7
integrating COM+ in .NET. *See also* Component Services snap-in
   benefits of, 28–29
   improvements, 29
   .NET Framework Configuration snap-in, 47–50
   overview, 27
   problems, 29–30
integrating .NET in COM. *See also* COM Callable Wrappers; exporting
   attributes, 108–114, 141
   from COM client code, 120–125
   default constructors, 139
   design considerations, 139–143
   event handling, 141, 148–152

HRESULTs, 142
interfaces, 105–108, 140
naming problems, 139–140
objects, 104
registry entries, 119–120
static methods, 139
type libraries, 114–119
version numbers, 142
Windows Forms controls, 143–148
integrating .NET in COM+. *See also* COM+ examples
   application types, 179–181
   COM vs. COM+, 156
   COM+ background information, 163
   COM+ services, 169–171
   connections, 173–178
   data flow optimization, 178
   DCOM, 172–178
   distributed architecture, 163
   error handling, 182
   interoperability, 156–162
   messaging, 166–169
   overview, 155
   security, 183–184
   transactions, 164–165
Interactive User option, 37
interceptors, 29
Interface Definition Language (IDL). *See* IDL
interface IDs (IIDs), 128, 488
__interface keyword, 198, 206, 211
interface pointers, 94, 104
InterfaceID property, 367
interfaces. *See also* COM interfaces; .NET interfaces
   analyzing, 481–483
   attributed programming, 211–216
   CCW implemented, 105–108
   changes to, 107
   changing, 140
   class, 106–108
   comparing, 481
   converting, 85–88, 106
   custom, 106–108
   described, 474
   design considerations, 92
   dispatch, 215
   explicit source, 149–151
   exporting, 128–136
   multiple implemented, 84
   re-creating with managed code, 483–487
   researching, 475–476
   type produced, 128
   verifying, 482
   viewing, 477–479
   visibility, 112
InterfaceType attribute, 111, 118, 128, 292, 330, 483

internal types, 14
InternalDispose method, 409
international considerations, 384
Internet
   COM+ and, 29, 169
   DCOM and, 172
Internet Explorer, 143, 145–148
interop assemblies. *See also* Runtime Callable Wrappers
   ActiveX controls, 101
   component referencing, 60
   delayed signing, 72
   generating
      overview, 55
      TlbImp.exe, 57–61
      TypeLibConverter class, 61–67
      Visual Studio .NET, 56
   Global Assembly Cache, 67–73
   library conversions, 74
   namespaces, 59
   overview, 54
   signing, 71
   strong names, 70–71
interop marshaling, 16
interoperability. *See* integrating COM in .NET; integrating COM+ in .NET; Platform Invoke; unmanaged code
IntPtrs, 77–81, 420, 439
invalid progIDs, 112
Invoke method, 140
IObjectSafety interface, 483, 487
IOleWindow interface, 483
IProvideClassInfo, 94
IRemoteDispatch interface, 162
ISAPI extensions, 260, 272
ISAPI filters, 261
ISecurityCallContext interface, 183–184
IString interface, 121, 123
ISupportErrorInfo interface, 93, 478
It Just Works (IJW) mechanism, 431–432
iteration classes, 238
IUnknown interface, 104, 106, 140, 474, 481
IUnknown method, 85
IViewObject interface, 482
IViewObject2 interface, 482

J
Journal Messages folder, 322
journal queues, 319

K
KeepAlive method, 467–468
key pairs, 71, 73
keywords, COM+ catalog, 347

L
label information, message, 324, 327, 335
Label property, 327, 335
large object heaps, 405
late-bound clients, 107, 110, 141, 215
LayoutKind enumeration, 440
LCIDs (locale identifiers), 125
leaked memory, 403
left pane, Component Services snap-in, 31
legacy applications, 171
legacy code, 401
Legacy Components folders, 33
LIBIDs (library IDs), 125
libraries. *See also* type libraries
   applications, 36, 44, 180
   block, 208
   C++, 233
library_block attribute, 212
licensed attribute, 217
lifetime object management, 4, 6, 9, 104
link libraries, 431
linker options, 231
listener/player applications
   component creation, 328–331
   overview, 327
   rules, 331–334
   testing, 334–335
   triggers, 331–334
listeners
   COM+, 28
   message, 318, 327–335
listing assemblies
   configured, 49
   GAC, 48
   affecting .NET security, 50
listing permissions, 50
LittleString class, 120–122
load balancing, 163, 170, 290, 315
loading DLLs dynamically, 458–460, 470
LoadLibrary function, 459
LoadTypeLib, 66
LoadTypeLibEx, 65
local attribute, 212, 214
local catalogs, 347
local computer names, 300
local connections, 32
local queues, 168, 316
locale identifiers (LCIDs), 125
locale information, assemblies, 48
locale tag, 262
locating
   components, 7–8, 20–21
   controls, 482
   DLLs, 458–460

logging events, 30, 182, 330, 335–336, 341
login desktops, 462
LPARAMs, 466, 486
LPArray parameter, 451
lpDataObject argument, 484
LPSTRs, 77, 435, 438
LPTSTRs, 438, 466
LPWSTRs, 77, 438

M

Machine level security, 50
machine names, 300
mailboxes. *See* message queues
managed arrays
   marshaling, 447–452
   pinning, 426
managed C++
   delayed assembly signing, 73
   destructors, 409
   garbage collection, 11
   IntPtrs, 77, 78
   managed and unmanaged, 456–458
   pinning, 455
   Platform Invoke, 421–422, 428–432
   Runtime Callable Wrappers, 56
   signed assemblies, 71
   versioning, 142
managed clients, 341
managed code. *See also* marshaling; Platform Invoke;
    predefined interfaces
   COM integration, 5
   interfaces, re-creating, 483–487
   overview, 402
   unmanaged code interaction, 403–404, 456–458
   Visual C++, 428–432
   Visual C#, 422–427
managed components, 169
managed heaps, 15, 104, 404–406
managed memory, 16
managed pointers to unmanaged code, 452–458
managed strings, 437–440
managed structures, 440–447
ManagedType destructor, 12
managed/unmanaged transitions, 94
mandatory attribute parameters, 193
mangled names, 430
manual memory management, 403
manual object lifetime management, 4
manual subscriptions, 368
manually redefining COM interfaces, 92
manually writing COM event code, 227–228
mapping exceptions and HRESULTs, 132–133, 142
mapping COM arrays to .NET, 81–83

Marshal class, 18, 77
MarshalAs attribute, 420, 435–437, 449
Marshal.GetLastWin32Error() method, 304
marshaling
   arrays
      COM interop, 451–452
      Platform Invoke, 447–450
      structures, 449–450
   data, 15–18, 82, 112
   data types, 75–77, 136–137, 403, 428
   interface requirements, 484
   name mapping, 415
   overriding defaults, 435–437
   performance considerations, 469–470
   strings, 437–440
   structures, 17–18, 440–447
master interop assemblies, 55
Match function, 256–257
MathFunctions class, 378
Maximum Number Of Dump Images setting, 381
member visibility, 14, 112
memory
   allocator classes, 245
   array data, 82
   garbage collection, 404–409
   instance releasing, 476
   leaks, 403
   managed code, 402
   manager classes, 245–246
   managing, 403
   pinning, 425, 429, 455
   pointers, 78
   reclaiming, 10–11
   stack allocation, 427
   structure layout, 89
   unmanaged code, 402
merge inserted code option, 192, 195
message listeners, 318, 327–335
Message object, 324
message players
   described, 318
   listener/player, 327–335
   recorder/player, 320–327
message processing, COM+, 28, 166–169
message queues
   accessing, 322–323
   adding, 169
   application, 319
   client applications, 337–340
   client types, 317
   COM+, 28
   creating, 320–322
   displaying, 324–325

overview, 166–169
retrieving from, 325–327
rules, 331–334
sending to, 323–324
setup options, 317
system, 319
testing, 324–325
transactions, 319
triggers, 331–334
types, 319
Message Queuing (MSMQ). *See* MSMQ
Message Queuing folder, 168
Message Queuing snap-in, 320
message recorders, 318, 320–327
message-based applications, COM+, 28
MessageQueue object, 323, 326
MessageQueueException exception, 327
metadata. *See also* .NET entity conversions
  attributed programming, 190, 210
  COM types, 53
  component location, 8
  object capabilities, 9
  type information, 14
MethodName property, 367
methods
  attributed programming, 214–215
  calling, 86
  COM+ security, 29, 33, 41
  described, 33
  design considerations, 92
  exporting, 132–134
  handler, 269–270, 274
  importing, 87
  names, 140
  overloaded, 133, 139
  static, 139
  viewing information, 481
MFC (Microsoft Foundation Classes), 233, 243
Microsoft C++ libraries, 233
Microsoft distributed architecture, 163
Microsoft Distributed Component Object Model (DCOM). *See* DCOM
Microsoft Intermediate Language (IL). *See* IL
Microsoft Message Queuing (MSMQ). *See* MSMQ
Microsoft SQL Server. *See* SQL Server
Microsoft Transaction Server. *See* Transaction Server
MIDL compiler, 13
/midl compiler option, 231
MiscStatus subkey, 144
MMC snap-ins (Microsoft Management Console snap-ins)
  COM+ services, 171
  Component Services
    application development, 34–37
    component installation, 38–40
    exporting, 45–46
    overview, 30
    security, 41–45
    user interface, 30–34
  described, 27
  interfaces and, 472
  Microsoft Transaction Server, 164
  .NET Framework Configuration, 47–50
MMC_NOTIFY_TYPE enumeration, 485
module attribute, 195, 205, 207–211, 219
modules, importing, 91
moving COM+ applications, 32
.mrg files, 195
MSIL (Microsoft Intermediate Language), 10
MSMQ (Message Queuing)
  client applications
    data encapsulation, 336–337
    managed clients, 341
    overview, 335–336
    queue design, 337–339
    queue setup, 339–340
    testing, 341–342
  client types, 317
  COM+, 28
  event handling, 349
  formats, 318, 325
  listener/player
    component creation, 328–331
    overview, 327
    rules, 331–334
    testing, 334–335
    triggers, 331–334
  overview, 166–169, 316–320
  performance costs, 317
  recorder/player
    overview, 320
    queue access, 322–323
    queue setup, 320–322
    retrieving messages, 325–327
    sending messages, 323–324
    testing messages, 324–325
MTAs (multi-threaded apartments), 15
MTAThreadAttribute, 15
MTS (Microsoft Transaction Server), 164–165
multicast events, 170
multiple interfaces implemented, 84
multiple languages, 384
multi-threaded apartments (MTAs), 15
MyCallback() method, 380
MyMath sample component, 34

N

name type information, 300, 303, 307
named parameters, 193
names
    applications, 36, 308
    assemblies, 74, 125, 139
    computers, 300
    conflicts, 73
    enumerations, 138
    GAC subdirectories, 68
    hiding C++ conventions, 281
    interface IDs and, 128
    invalid progIDs, 112
    libraries, 75
    mangled, 430
    marshaler name mapping, 415
    methods, 133, 139–140
    multiple interfaces, 85
    namespaces, 59
    .NET interoperability and, 139–140
    string conversion classes, 251
    strong names, 70–71, 125
namespaces
    COM+ example, 292
    EnterpriseServices, 308
    naming, 59
    prefixes, 126
    subscribers, 356
native code. *See* managed code
natural boundaries, 441
navigating Component Services console, 30–34
navigating .NET Framework Configuration console, 47–50
nested structures, 443–447
.NET arrays, 81–83
.NET assemblies, 114, 125–126
.NET attributes, 74, 108–114, 141
.NET Category folder, 477–479
.NET classes, 83, 127–128
.NET code. *See* managed code
.NET components. *See also* COM Callable Wrappers; subscriptions
    COM appearance, 6
    from COM client code, 120–125
    COM component implementation, 10
    COM objects implemented as, 6
    data handling, 15–18
    design considerations, 139–143
    identifying, 8
    locations, 8
    marshaling, 112
    namespaces, 126
    naming problems, 139–140
    registered, 38
    registry entries, 119–120
    type library creation, 114–119
    value types, 137
    visibility, 112
    Windows Forms controls, 143–148
.NET data types, 136–137, 416–417
.NET entity conversions
    assemblies, 125–126
    classes, 127–128
    data types, 136–137
    enumerations, 138
    interfaces, 128–136
    methods, 132–134
    namespaces, 126
    properties, 134–136
    value types, 137
.NET enumerations, 90, 138
.NET event handling, 19, 94–99, 141, 148–152
.NET exceptions. *See* exceptions
.NET Framework Configuration console, 47–50
.NET Framework Services Installation Utility, 293–295, 310
.NET in COM applications. *See also* COM Callable Wrappers; converting; exporting
    attributes, 108–114, 141
    from COM client code, 120–125
    component integration
        accessing, 19–25
        ActiveX controls, 99–102
        COM interop, 53–55
        design considerations, 91–94
        event handling, 94–99
        overview, 53
    design considerations, 139–143
    differences
        component identification, 8
        component locations, 7–8
        data handling, 15–18
        error handling, 13
        event handling, 19
        garbage collection, 10–13
        object-oriented principles, 10
        objects, 9
        type information, 13
        visibility, 14–15
    future of, 3–5
    naming problems, 139–140
    objects, 104
    overview, 5–7
    registry entries, 119–120
    type libraries, 114–119
    version numbers, 142
    Windows Forms controls, 143–148

.NET in COM+ applications. *See also* COM+ examples
   application types, 179–181
   COM vs. COM+, 156
   COM+ background information, 163
   COM+ services, 169–171
   connections, 173–178
   data flow optimization, 178
   DCOM, 172–178
   distributed architecture, 163
   error handling, 182
   interoperability, 156–162
   messaging, 166–169
   overview, 155
   security, 183–184
   transactions, 164–165
.NET interfaces
   changing, 140
   COM interfaces implemented as, 6
   converting to, 83, 85–88
   exporting, 128–136
   standard COM interfaces and, 105–111
   type produced, 128
.NET interop marshaler, 15
.NET interoperability, 5, 156–162
.NET methods, 132–134
.NET objects, 9, 104
.NET parameters, 132
.NET properties, 88, 134–136
.NET Remoting, 4
.NET security, 50
.NET type conversions, 75–77, 136–137
.NET value types, 17, 137
.NET wrapper classes, 6
network communication, 172
network protocols, 172–178
network traffic, 178
New option, 34
no_injected_text attribute, 219
nonblittable types, 16, 93, 447
nonbrowsable attribute, 214
nonconstructors, 10
noncreatable attribute, 127, 217
nondeterministic finalization, 10–13
nonextensible attribute, 212
non-PIA components, 73
non-real time communication. *See* COM+
non-UI components, 20
nonvisible members, 14
normal handles, 453
Notepad, attributed programming, 204–207
notifications, COM event, 95
Notify() method, 484
null references, 118

O

object attribute, 212
Object class, 158
Object Remote Procedure Call (ORPC), 176
ObjectDisposedException exception, 409
objects. *See also* attributed programming
   capabilities, 9
   COM integration, 6
   finalization, 10–13
   finalizers, 407–409, 454
   identity, 104
   lifetime management, 4, 6, 9, 104
   pinning, 425, 429, 455
   reference counts, 6
   roots, 406
odl attribute, 212
OLE Miscellaneous Status Bits, 144
Ole32.dll, 175, 177
oleautomation attribute, 212
OLE/COM Object Viewer
   error resolution, 350
   instance releasing, 476
   interface analysis, 481–483
   interface research, 475–476
   .NET Category folder, 477–479
   opening, 477
   overview, 474–475
   unmanaged controls, 480–481
OLEMISC, 144
one-dimensional arrays, 242, 451
opaque handles, 453
operating systems
   COM and, 3–5
   Component Services content, 32
operator& implementation, 257
operator= implementation, 235
optional attribute parameters, 193
optional parameters, 92
ORPC (Object Remote Procedure Call), 176
OSF DCE-RPC specification, 172
out attribute, 132, 214, 447, 486
out keyword, 486
Out parameters, 132
Outgoing Queues folder, 168, 320, 342
out-of-process servers, 179
overloaded methods, 85, 133, 139
overloaded operators, 79
overriding
   attribute providers, 199
   default conversions, 435–437
   GUIDs, 111
   IIDs, 128
   interfaces, 106
   progIDs, 111

P

Pack parameter, 441–442
packing, 441
parameters
   application roots, 405
   attributed programming, 193, 201, 207, 214–215
   DllImport attribute, 413
   parsing functions, 270, 275–277
   replacement tags, 269
   Web service implementation, 280
Parse function, 257
parse_func parameter, 270
ParseSquareData function, 275–276
parsing COM+ catalogs, 363, 371
parsing functions, 270, 275–277
partial pattern matches, 257
partially signed assemblies, 72
PassArrayRef function, 448
passing arrays
   COM, 451
   references, 448, 450
   values, 447, 449
passing managed pointers to unmanaged code, 452–458
Path property, 323, 330
path to DLLs at run time, 458–460
pattern matching, 256–257
permanent catalog changes, 347
permanent subscriptions
   creating, 363–368
   overview, 349
   subscriber applications, 360
   testing, 368–369
Permission Sets folder, 50
permissions, setting, 50
PIAs (primary interop assemblies)
   installing, 73
   locations, 73
   namespaces, 59
   overview, 54
   referencing components, 60
__pin keyword, 429, 455
pinned handles, 453
pinning, 425, 429, 455
Platform Invoke. *See also* marshaling
   described, 5
   DLLs, 458–460
   It Just Works mechanism, 431–432
   managed C++, 421–422, 428–432
   mangled names, 430
   overview, 410
   performance considerations, 469–470
   pointers, 452
   type conversions, 416–417, 428
   unsafe keyword, 424
   Visual Basic .NET, 410–415
   Visual C#, 417–420, 422–427
players, message
   described, 28, 318
   listener/player, 327–335
   recorder/player, 320–327
pnElements parameter, 448
Point instances, 443
pointer_default attribute, 212
pointers
   application roots, 405
   callbacks and, 461–466
   converting, 77–79
   function, 461
   interface usage, 474
   managed code interoperability, 429
   passing to unmanaged code, 452–458
   rules, 104
   smart, 457
   unmanaged code interoperability, 401–404, 420, 422
Policy Assemblies folder, 50
Populate() method, 347, 366
populating collections, 366
positional parameters, 193
pragma attribute, 219
pre-built applications, 36
predefined interfaces
   analyzing, 481–483
   COM, 471–474, 483–487
   comparisons, 481
   examples, 487–489
   overview, 471
   researching, 475–476
   unmanaged controls, 480–481
   verifying, 482
   viewing, 477–479
prefixes, namespace, 126
preinstalled applications, 181
Prelink method, 470
PrelinkAll method, 470
preloading DLLs, 470
premature garbage collection, 467
PreserveSig attribute, 132, 484, 488
PreserveSig parameter, 415
preventing garbage collection, 467
primary interop assemblies (PIAs)
   component referencing, 60
   installing, 73
   locations, 73
   namespaces, 59
   overview, 54

PrimaryInteropAssembly attribute, 55, 73
priority information, message, 324, 326–327, 335
Priority property, 326–327, 335
private assemblies, 8, 67, 70
private keys, 71–72
private members, 141
private queues, 320
Private Queues folder, 168, 320
ProcessMessage() method, 330
product registration numbers, 309
progid attribute, 111, 207, 217
progIDs, 7, 111
properties
  COM+ settings, 33
  exporting, 134–136
  importing, 87
propget attribute, 87, 134–136, 214
propput attribute, 87, 134–136, 214
propputref attribute, 87, 134–136, 214
protected members, 141
protected types, 14
protocol stacks, 176
protocols
  DCOM, 172–178
  HTTP, 278
  SOAP, 278–279, 283
prototypes, event, 351
proxy applications
  COM+, 45–46, 156, 295–296
  DCOM connections, 175, 178
  overview, 180
proxy/stub DLLs, 112
ptr attribute, 214
public
  default constructors, 10
  fields, 136
  key tokens, 48
  keys, 70–73, 125, 142
  members, 14, 141
  queues, 320
  types, 14
Public Queues folder, 168, 320, 324
publishers, 350–355
publish/subscribe model
  COM+ catalogs, 345–347
  component subscribers, 355–360
  described, 171
  errors, 350
  event objects, 350–353, 356
  overview, 347–349
  publishers, 353–355
  vs. request/reply, 345
  subscriptions, 347–349
  testing, 360

Q
QueryInterface method, 9, 140, 481
Queue Messages folder, 322
queue status, COM+, 28
queued applications. *See* MSMQ
Queued Components, 166–169, 171
queues. *See* message queues

R
ragged arrays, 452
RateChangeHandler object, 149
RCWs (Runtime Callable Wrappers)
  delayed signing, 72
  described, 6, 54
  generating
    overview, 55
    primary interop assemblies, 73
    TlbImp.exe, 57–61
    TypeLibConverter class, 61–67
    Visual Studio .NET, 56
  GAC, 67–73
  installing, 72
  signed assemblies, 71
  strong names, 70–71
Read() method, 393
Reader variable, 393
Receive() method, 326
reclaiming memory, 10–11
recorder/player applications
  overview, 320
  queue access, 322–323
  queue setup, 320–322
  retrieving messages, 325–327
  sending messages, 323–324
  testing, 324–325
recorders, message, 28, 318, 320–327
re-creating interfaces with managed code, 483–487
Rectangle structures, 443
ref keyword, 444, 448, 486
reference chains, 406
reference counts, 6, 104, 407, 452
reference object parameters, 405
reference types, 17
referencing
  ActiveX controls, 21
  arrays, 448, 450
  COM components, 20
  type libraries, 60
reflection, 9, 113, 139, 141
reflection emit, 460
Refresh command, 324
RegAsm.exe, 34, 73, 115–116, 119, 122
Register For COM Interop option, 119
RegisterAssembly method, 119

registering assemblies, 114
registering components
    COM+, 34, 38, 290–295, 349
    components, 119–122
    MSMQ, 331
registration numbers, 309
registration_script attribute, 217
RegistrationServices class, 119
registry
    attributes and, 191
    component information, 7, 34, 119–122
    export process and, 114
    GUIDs and, 289–290
    interface research, 475–476, 479, 481
    primary interop assemblies, 73
    Windows Forms controls, 144–145
RegKind, 65
REGKIND_DEFAULT, 66
REGKIND_NONE, 66
REGKIND_REGISTER, 66
RegSvcs.exe, 293–295, 310
RegSvr32 utility, 34
regular expression classes, 256–257
Release method, 9, 92, 104, 140, 481
releasing instances, 476
reliability, 28
remote. *See also* disconnected applications; Web-based applications
    applications, 360
    components, 173
    connections, 32
    object creation, 175
    queues, 28, 168
    users, 28
Remoting Services, 49, 169
Remove() method, 368
removing assemblies, 72
removing registry entries, 114
reordering methods, 140
replacement tags
    defining, 265–266
    handler, 263–264
    include, 264
    overview, 261–262
    parameters, 269
    predefined, 262
    subhandler, 263–264
ReportEvent method, 66, 118
repository, component code, 7
request handlers, 261, 263
request_handler attribute, 266–268
request/reply model, 345
requires_category attribute, 217

researching interfaces, 475–476
ResolveRef method, 66, 118
resource allocation, 29
resource management, 167
resource pooling, 164
resource releasing, 9, 92
restricted attribute, 212, 217
results pane, Component Services snap-in, 31
resurrection, 454
retrieving messages from queue, 325–327
return types, attributed programming, 214–215
retval attribute, 214
right pane, Component Services snap-in, 31
riids, 488
role-based security
    adding, 41–45
    assigning, 44
    described, 29
    inherited roles, 45
    options, 33
roles, 41, 44–45
Roles folders, 33
Roles Inherited By Select Items list box, 45
roots, 405–407
rpc style, 280
rules, MSMQ, 331–334
runtime. *See* common language runtime
Runtime Callable Wrappers (RCWs)
    delayed signing, 72
    described, 6, 54
    generating
        overview, 55
        primary interop assemblies, 73
        TlbImp.exe, 57–61
        TypeLibConverter class, 61–67
        Visual Studio .NET, 56
    GAC, 67–73
    installing, 72
    signed assemblies, 71
    strong names, 70–71
Runtime Security Policy snap-in, 50

S

SAFEARRAYBOUND structure, 239–240
SAFEARRAYs, 15, 81–82, 93, 239–242, 451
same-apartment marshaling, 15
SaveChanges() method, 347
saving application dumps, 380–381
SayHello method, 458
scalability, 163
SCM (Service Control Manager), 175, 177
scope pane, Component Services snap-in, 31
screen-save desktops, 462

Script Debugger option, 383
scripts
    components safe for, 482, 487
    debugging, 383
    server-side, 382–384, 394
    Web applications, 381–384, 386, 393–396
sealed classes, 91
search criteria, 393
Section 508 requirements, 385
security. *See also* role-based security
    ATL classes, 252–254
    COM, 4
    COM+, 28, 41–45, 164, 170, 183–184, 299
    DCOM, 173, 175
    GAC, 67
    Platform Invoke and, 469
    providers, 175
    runtime policies, 50
    SOAP communication, 279
    XML Web services, 4
SecurityCallContext class, 183–184
self-contained components. *See* ActiveX controls;
        Windows Forms controls
Send() method, 324
sending messages to queue, 323–324
SendMsg object, 371
sequential member layouts, 89
serializable classes, 141
serialization, 165
server applications, 179
server components, 163
Server Explorer, 168, 322–323
server queues, 316
Server Response Files (SRF files). *See* SRF files
server-side programming. *See* ATL
server-side scripts, 382–384, 394
Service Control Manager (SCM), 175, 177
ServicedComponent class, 158, 160–162, 293, 308–312
set method, 134, 136
set property, 121
SetLastError API, 415, 420
SetLastError() function, 304
SetLastError parameter, 420
SetName method, 458
SetWindowText() method, 307
shared assemblies, 8–9, 67, 70
shared classes
    CSimpleStringT, 244–246
    CStringT, 246–250
    listed, 243
short*, 448
shortcuts, Component Services console, 30
signing assemblies, 58, 71, 119

simple component example
    clients, 296–298
    creating, 291–292
    exporting, 295–296
    overview, 290–291
    registering, 293–295
    testing, 298–300
Simple Object Access Protocol (SOAP), 4, 278–279, 283,
        374–380
Sin function, 463
Sin method, 464
single-dimensional arrays, 242
single-name operation mode, 306
single-threaded apartments, 15
Site property, 474
Size parameter, 441
SizeConst parameter, 451
size_is attribute, 451
SizeOf function, 449
SizeParamIndex parameter, 451
smart pointers, 457
snap-ins. *See also* MMC snap-ins
    Assembly Cache, 48
    Configured Assemblies, 48
    described, 27
    Remoting Services, 49
    Runtime Security Policy, 50
    View List Of Configured Assemblies in the
        Configured Assemblies, 49
sn.exe, 71, 122
SOAP (Simple Object Access Protocol), 4, 278–279, 283,
        374–380
SOAP Quick Test applications, 378–380
soap_handler attribute, 280–281
soap_method attribute, 281
SoapSuds utility, 376
software evolution, 3
S_OK, 132
source attribute, 217
SQL Server, 386
SQL Server Enterprise Manager, 387
SqlDataReader object, 393
SRF files (Server Response Files)
    conditional processing, 265
    handler tags, 263–264
    included files, 264
    overview, 261–262
    replacement tags, 265–266
    subhandler tags, 263–264
    syntax, 262
    URLs, 261–262
    Web application DLLs, 261
stack memory allocation, 427

stack trace information, 13
stackalloc keyword, 427
stand-alone attributes, 219–221
Standard Template Library classes, 242
STAs (single-threaded apartments), 15
STAThreadAttribute, 15
static content, 261, 262
static functions, 420
static methods, 139
static object pointers, 405
stencil processor code, 262
stencils. *See* SRF files
string attribute, 214
String object, 439–440
StringBuilder object, 304–305, 307, 439–440
strings
    constructor, 309–310, 312
    conversion classes, 250–251
    data, 15
    IntPtrs, 79
    marshaling, 437–440
    memory management, 245–250
    Platform Invoke and, 420, 425
    regular expression matching, 256–257
StringTraits parameter, 247–248
Strong Name tool, 71, 122
strong names, 8, 48, 70–71, 125
strongly rooted objects, 407
StructLayout attribute, 89, 137, 440–443
structs, 18
structures. *See also* SAFEARRAYs
    importing, 88
    marshaling, 17–18, 440–447
    unmanaged code interoperability, 404
StructureToPtr method, 446
stubs, 176–177
SubCollection object, 367
subhandler tag, 262–264, 265
SubscriberInterface property, 371
subscribers
    component
        designing, 355–357
        installing, 357–360
        overview, 355
        testing, 360
    dialog-based
        overview, 360–363
        permanent, 363–369
        transient, 369–372
    event objects and, 350
subscriptions. *See also* permanent subscriptions;
        transient subscriptions
    COM+ catalogs, 345–347
    errors, 350
    event objects, 350–353, 356
    overview, 347–349
    publishers, 353–355
    vs. request/reply model, 345
suffixes, method name, 133, 140
Sum function, 426
support_error_info attribute, 217, 224
suppressing IDL generation, 231
SuppressUnmanagedCodeSecurity attribute, 469
synchronize attribute, 214
synchronous applications, 378–380
system queues, 319
System Queues folder, 168, 320
system services, 5
System_EnterpriseServices_IServicedComponentInfo
    interface, 162
system-defined HRESULTs, 13
system-dependent strings, 438

T

tables, Web application scenario, 388
tag_name attribute, 268
tagging classes, 141
Tan method, 464
tasks, Component Services snap-in, 30
TempMQ object, 330
temporary queues, 168
temporary subscriptions
    creating, 369–371
    overview, 349
    subscriber applications, 360
    testing, 372
testing
    COM+ applications, 298–300, 307
    listener/player applications, 334–335
    MSMQ client applications, 341–342
    publish/subscribe system, 360
    recorder/player applications, 324–325
    scripts, 382
    subscriptions, 368–369, 372
    Web applications, 274, 396–397
test-signing assemblies, 73
text appearance, 389
text displayed on screen, 307
text editor, attributed programming, 204–207
third-party applications, 36
this pointer, 430
ThisCall convention, 431
thread safe, 15
threading attribute, 199, 207, 217
timeouts, 210
TimeSpan values, 326

timing garbage collections, 468
Title variable, 394
TlbExp.exe, 115–116, 134, 136–137
TlbImp.exe. *See* type library importer
/tlbout compiler option, 231
tool versions, 475
Topic variable, 394
traditional ActiveX controls, 21
traits classes, 237
Transaction Server, 164–165
transactions
   COM+, 28, 164–165
   described, 28, 164
   MSMQ, 319
/transform[col]dispret option, 60
transient subscriptions
   creating, 369–371
   overview, 349
   subscriber applications, 360
   testing, 372
TransientSubscriptions collection, 371
transport mechanisms, XML Web services, 4
TrigDelegate object, 463
triggers, 331–334
Triggers folder, 322
trigonometric functions, 463
try...catch block, 327
two-dimensional arrays, 242, 451
type conversions, 416–417, 428
type information, 13, 94
type libraries. *See also* entity conversions
   arrays, 81–83
   assemblies, 54–55, 125
   attributes, 74, 191
   coclasses, 83–85
   COM+ catalog and, 346, 361
   constants, 90
   converting, 74–75
   creating, 114–119
   data types, 75–83
   described, 13
   design considerations, 94
   dispatch IDs, 107
   enumerations, 90
   identifying, 125
   interfaces, 85–88
   modules, 91
   non-PIA components, 73
   referencing, 60
   structures, 17, 88
   typedefs, 90
   TypeLibConverter class, 61–67, 116–119
   unions, 89

viewing information, 479
visibility, 112
type library exporter, 115–116, 134, 136–137
type library importer. *See also* Runtime Callable
     Wrappers
   COM source events, 95
   constants, 90
   multiple interfaces, implemented, 84
   overview, 57–61
   pointers, 77
typedefs, 90
TypeLib subkey, 144
TypeLibConverter class, 61–67, 116–119
TypeLibFuncAttribute, 74
TypeLibImporterFlags, enumeration, 67
TypeLibTypeAttribute, 74
TypeLibVarAttribute, 74

U
UI components, 20, 21
unbound events, 170
__unhook keyword, 230
unicast events, 170
Unicode CString, 258
Unicode strings, 93, 438
Unicode values, 411
unions, 89, 442
Universal marshaler, 112
unmanaged arrays, 447–452
unmanaged code. *See also* marshaling; Platform Invoke
   COM integration, 6
   COM vs. .NET, 120–125
   garbage collection
      finalization, 407–409
      generations, 404
      large object heaps, 405
      overview, 404
      roots, 405–407
   interacting with, 401, 403–404
   managed code interaction, 456–458
   managed pointers to, 452–458
   memory management, 402–403
   overview, 402
   Visual C#, 422–427
unmanaged components, COM+ catalog, 345–347
unmanaged controls, 480–481
unmanaged heaps, 15, 104
unmanaged IComponent interface, 483
unmanaged memory, 16
unmanaged strings, 437–440
unmanaged structures, 440–447
UnmanagedType destructor, 12
UnmanagedType enumeration, 435–437

unpinning objects, 426
UnregisterAssembly method, 119
unregistering components, 119, 290, 350
unsafe code, 79–81, 423
unsafe context, 423
unsafe keyword, 423–425, 427
unused memory, 10, 403
upgrading tools, 475
user access
   Component Services content, 32
   roles. *See* role-based security
user interface, Component Services, 30–34
User level security, 50
user options, 307
user-configured displays, 384
user-defined replacement tags, 263
uuid attribute, 207, 212, 217

V

ValidateAndExchange method, 273
validating catalog changes, 347
Value() method, 347
value types, 15, 17, 137
variables, application root, 405
varying arrays, 82
verifiable subscriptions, 363
verifying interfaces, 482
version attribute, 207, 217
Version subkey, 144
versions
   assemblies, 48, 67, 121, 126
   GUIDs, 142, 290
View List Of Assemblies In The Assemblies Cache link, 48
View List Of Configured Assemblies in the Configured Assemblies snap-in, 49
View Remoting Services Properties link, 49
viewing
   assemblies, 48, 49
   attribute-inserted code, 192, 195
   COM+ components, 157
   computers, 31–32
   interfaces, 477–479
   roles, 44
   unmanaged controls, 480–481
vi_progid attribute, 207, 217
virtual memory, 404
VirtualAlloc function, 404
visible subscriptions, 363
Visual Basic
   assembly names, 139
   event handling, 151–152
   type conversions, 75–77, 136–137
   versioning, 142
Visual Basic .NET
   component registration, 120
   IntPtrs, 77
   Platform Invoke, 410–415
   RCWs, 56
   signed assemblies, 71
Visual C memory management, 403
Visual C++. *See also* ATL; attributed programming
   assembly names, 139
   component registration, 123–125
   destructors, 409
   libraries, 233
   memory management, 403
   Platform Invoke, 421–422, 428–432
   Web applications
      attributes, 266–268
      handler methods, 269–270
      overview, 266
      sample applications, 270–277
   Web services
      consuming, 283–286
      creating, 281–283
      implementing, 279–281
      overview, 277
      SOAP, 278–279
Visual C#
   component registration, 120–122
   destructors, 409
   enumeration conversions, 138
   inheritance hierarchy, 129–131
   IntPtrs, 77
   Platform Invoke, 417–420, 422–427
   property conversions, 134–136
   RCWs, 56
   signed assemblies, 71
   type library conversions, 62
   unsafe code, 79–81
   value type conversions, 137
   versioning, 142
   Windows Forms controls, 145–148
Visual Studio .NET. *See also* attributed programming; Web services
   assembly names, 140
   COM integration, 5, 19–25
   delayed assembly signing, 73
   message queues, 168, 322
   RCWs, 56
   signed assemblies, 71
   versioning, 142
void* pointers, 77–79, 92

W

weak handles, 454
weak object references, 407
Web services
  ATL Server
    client access, 278–279
    examples, 281–283
    implementing, 279–281
    overview, 277
    SOAP, 278–279
  C++, 283–286
  COM, 4
  COM+, 28, 169
  DCOM and, 172
Web Services Description Language (WSDL), 279–280, 284, 376
Web-based applications
  accessibility, 385
  ATL Server
    attributes, 266–268
    DLLs, 260–261, 272
    handler methods, 269–270, 274
    overview, 266
    parsing functions, 270, 275–277
    project setup, 271–274
    sample applications, 270–277
  browser support, 393–396
  component communication, 386
  component interactions, 381–382
  data access, 390–393
  databases, 386–389
  vs. desktop applications, 374
  dumps, 380–381
  error handling, 382–384
  human-language support, 384
  overview, 373–374
  scripts, 381–384
  SOAP, 374–380
  testing, 396–397
  vs. Web services, 277
while loop, 265
window handles, 483
window stations, 462
window text, 307
Windows
  code. *See* unmanaged code
  COM and, 3–5
  Component Services content, 32
  data types, 416–417
  security, 41, 44, 252
Windows Explorer, 68
Windows Forms controls
  ActiveX controls and, 7, 99–102, 143–148
  component access, 19–25
  described, 4
Windows Forms form, 143
wire protocols, 176
wrappers. *See also* COM Callable Wrappers; Runtime Callable Wrappers
  classes, 6, 456
  COM+ services, 169–171
Write() method, 396
WriteEntry() method, 331
writing
  ATL COM components. *See* attributed programming
  attribute providers, 192
  COM event code manually, 227–228
  custom attributes, 194
WSDL (Web Services Description Language), 279, 280, 284, 376

X

XML, 278–279, 325
XML Web services. *See* Web services
XmlMessageFormatter object, 326

Z

zero reference counts, 9

Julian Templeman

Julian Templeman first touched fingers to keypunch in 1972 and has since programmed everything from 8-bit microcomputers to Cray supercomputers. He currently runs a consultancy and training company in London, specializing in Microsoft .NET, COM, C++, and Java. Julian has written several programming books, including titles on Microsoft Visual C#, Visual Basic .NET, and ATL.

John Paul Mueller

John Mueller is a freelance author and technical editor. He has writing in his blood, having produced 57 books and over 200 articles to date. The topics range from networking to artificial intelligence and from database management to heads-down programming. Some of his current books include several C# developer guides, a small business and home office networking guide, a book on SOAP, and several Windows XP user guides. His technical editing skills have helped over 31 authors refine the content of their manuscripts. John has provided technical editing services to *Databased Advisor* and contributed articles to a number of magazines. He is currently the editor of the .NET electronic newsletter for Pinnacle Publishing.

Air Compressor

An air compressor, also known as an air pump, is a machine that decreases the volume and increases the pressure of a quantity of air by mechanical means. Air thus compressed possesses great potential energy because when the external pressure is removed, the air expands rapidly. The controlled expansive force of compressed air is used in many ways and provides the motive force for air motors and tools, including pneumatic hammers, air drills, sandblasting machines, and paint sprayers.

At Microsoft Press, we use tools to illustrate our books for software developers and IT professionals. Tools very simply and powerfully symbolize human inventiveness. They're a metaphor for people extending their capabilities, precision, and reach. From simple calipers and pliers to digital micrometers and lasers, these stylized illustrations give each book a visual identity, and a personality to the series. With tools and knowledge, there's no limit to creativity and innovation. Our tagline says it all: the tools you need to put technology to work.

The manuscript for this book was prepared and galleyed using Microsoft Word. Pages were composed by Microsoft Press using Adobe FrameMaker+SGML for Windows, with text in Garamond and display type in Helvetica Condensed. Composed pages were delivered to the printer as electronic prepress files.

Cover Designer: Methodologie, Inc.
Interior Graphic Designer: James D. Kramer
Principal Compositor: Gina Cassill
Interior Artist: Michael Kloepfer
Copy Editor: Roger LeBlanc
Proofreader: nSight, Inc.
Indexer: Julie Hatley